The Collected Courses of the Academy of European Law
Series Editors: Professor Gráinne de Búrca,
Fordham Law School, New York;
Professor Bruno de Witte, and
Professor Francesco Francioni,
European University Institute,
Florence
Assistant Editor: Barbara Ciomei, *European University*
Institute, Florence

VOLUME XV/3
Political Rights under Stress in 21st Century Europe

The Collected Courses of the Academy of European Law
Edited by Professor Gráinne de Búrca,
Professor Bruno de Witte, and Professor Francesco Francioni
Assistant Editor: Barbara Ciomei

This series brings together the Collected Courses of the
Academy of European Law in Florence. The Academy's mission is to
produce scholarly analyses which are at the cutting edge of the two
fields in which it works: European Union law and human rights law.
A 'general course' is given each year in each field, by a
distinguished scholar and/or practitioner, who either examines the
field as a whole through a particular thematic, conceptual, or
philosophical lens, or who looks at a particular theme in the context
of the overall body of law in the field. The Academy also publishes
each year a volume of collected essays with a specific theme in each
of the two fields.

Political Rights under Stress in 21st Century Europe

Edited by
WOJCIECH SADURSKI

Academy of European Law
European University Institute

OXFORD
UNIVERSITY PRESS

OXFORD
UNIVERSITY PRESS

Great Clarendon Street, Oxford OX2 6DP

Oxford University Press is a department of the University of Oxford.
It furthers the University's objective of excellence in research, scholarship,
and education by publishing worldwide in

Oxford New York

Auckland Cape Town Dar es Salaam Hong Kong Karachi
Kuala Lumpur Madrid Melbourne Mexico City Nairobi
New Delhi Shanghai Taipei Toronto

With offices in

Argentina Austria Brazil Chile Czech Republic France Greece
Guatemala Hungary Italy Japan Poland Portugal Singapore
South Korea Switzerland Thailand Turkey Ukraine Vietnam

Oxford is a registered trade mark of Oxford University Press
in the UK and in certain other countries

Published in the United States
by Oxford University Press Inc., New York

© The various contributors, 2006

The moral rights of the authors have been asserted
Database right Oxford University Press (maker)

Crown copyright material is reproduced under Class Licence
Number C01P0000148 with the permission of OPSI
and the Queen's Printer for Scotland

First published 2006

British Library Cataloguing in Publication Data
Data available

Library of Congress Cataloging in Publication Data
Political rights under stress in 21st century Europe/edited by Wojciech Sadurski.
    p. cm.
Includes bibliographical references and index.
ISBN-13: 978–0–19–929602–6 ((hardback): alk. paper)
ISBN-13: 978–0–19–929603–3 ((pbk.): alk. paper) 1. Political Rights—Europe.
2. Civil rights—Europe. 3. Minorities—Civil rights—Europe. 4. Political rights—
European Union countries. I. Sadurski, Wojciech, 1950–
KJC5132.P65 2006
323.5094—dc22   2006029626

Typeset by Newgen Imaging Systems (P) Ltd., Chennai, India
Printed in Great Britain
on acid-free paper by
Biddles Ltd, King's Lynn, Norfolk

ISBN 0–19–929602–2   978–0–19–929602–6
ISBN 0–19–929603–0–(Pbk.)   978–0–19–929603–3 (Pbk.)

1 3 5 7 9 10 8 6 4 2

Contents

Notes on Contributors

Eva Brems studied Law at the universities of Namur (candidat en droit, 1989), Leuven (licenciaat rechtsgeleerdheid, 1992), Bologna (exchange student, 1991), and Harvard (LL.M., 1995). She obtained a Ph.D. in Law from the University of Leuven (1999), with a dissertation on 'Human Rights: Universality and Diversity' (The Hague/Boston/London: Martinus Nijhoff, 2001). Before joining Ghent University, she was a researcher at the University of Leuven (1992–94 and 1995–99) and a lecturer at the University of Maastricht (1999–2000). In Ghent, she is a Professor of Human Rights Law and non-Western law. Her research in the human rights field covers most areas of human rights law (Belgian law, European law, international law, and comparative law). She is the author of numerous publications in this field in Belgian and international journals and books, and a member of the editorial board of several law journals. She is the chair of the Flemish section of Amnesty International and an activist in several human rights organizations.

Damian Chalmers is Professor of European Union Law. Prior to coming to the London School of Economics and Political Science, he worked as a research officer for the British Institute of International and Comparative Law, and as a lecturer at the University of Liverpool. He has also been Professor at the College of Europe, has held visiting appointments at Copenhagen, Lund, Helsinki and Fudan (PRC), and was Jean Monnet Fellow at the European University Institute 2003–04. He is currently co-editor of the *European Law Review*. His most recent publications include: *European Union Law* (with C. Hadjiemmanuil, G. Monti, and A. Tomkins, Cambridge: Cambridge University Press, 2006); 'The Reconstitution of Europe's Public Spheres' (2003) 9 *European Law Journal* 127; 'Reconciling European Risks and Traditional Ways of Life' (2003) 66 *Modern Law Review* 532; 'Judicial Authority and the Constitutional Treaty' (2005) 4 *I.CON* 428; and 'Risk, Anxiety and the European Mediation of the Politics of Life' (2005) 30 *European Law Review* 649.

Victor Ferreres Comella is Professor of Constitutional Law at Pompeu Fabra University (Barcelona) and at the Spanish Escuela Judicial. He obtained his JSD at Yale Law School, with a thesis on 'Judicial Review and Democracy' (1996). His most important work has focused on the constitutional review of legislation and fundamental rights. He has written two books in Spanish: *Justicia constitucional y democracia* (Madrid: Centro de Estudios Constitucionales, 1997), and *El principio de taxatividad en material penal y el valor normativo de la jurisprudencia* (Madrid: Civitas, 2002). He is currently working on the role of Constitutional Courts in Europe. His most recent articles in this field include 'The European Model of

Constitutional Review of Legislation: Toward Decentralization?' (2004) 2(3) *I. CON. International Journal of Constitutional Law* 461, and 'The Consequences of Centralizing Constitutional Review in a Special Court: Some Thoughts on Judicial Activism' (2004) 83 *Texas Law Review* 1705. He has taught at the Law Schools of Universidad de Puerto Rico, University of Texas, and New York University. He is one of the Article Editors of *I.CON, International Journal of Constitutional Law.*

Jiří Přibáň, Professor of Law, Cardiff University, and Visiting Professor of Legal Philosophy and Sociology, Charles University, Prague; is author of *Dissidents of Law* (Aldershot: Ashgate, 2002); *Systems of Justice in Transition* (Aldershot: Ashgate, 2003), edited with P. Roberts and J. Young; *Law's New Boundaries* (Aldershot: Ashgate, 2001), edited with D. Nelken; *The Rule of Law in Central Europe* (Aldershot: Ashgate, 1999) edited with J. Young; and other books in English and Czech. Areas of research include social theory and law, jurisprudence, theory of constitutionalism, and human rights.

Michel Rosenfeld is the Justice Sydney L. Robins Professor of Human Rights at the Benjamin N. Cardozo School of Law in New York City. He has lectured extensively on American constitutional law, comparative constitutional law, and legal philosophy throughout the world. He has written extensively on these subjects, and many of his writings have been translated into several languages. His books include: *Affirmative Action and Justice: A Philosophical and Constitutional Inquiry* (New Haven, CT: Yale University Press, 1991); *Just Interpretations: Law Between Ethics and Politics* (Berkeley, CA: University of California Press, 1998); *Comparative Constitutionalism: Cases and Materials* (St Paul, MN: Thomson West, 2003) (co-author); and *The Identity of the Constitutional Subject* (New York: Routledge, forthcoming). He is also the Editor-in-Chief of the *International Journal of Constitutional Law* (*I.CON*) published by Oxford University Press.

Wojciech Sadurski is Professor at the Department of Law, European University Institute, Florence, since 1999, and at the University of Sydney where he holds the Personal Chair in Legal Philosophy. He also taught, as visiting professor, at a number of universities in the United States, Asia, and Europe. He has written extensively on the philosophy of law, political philosophy, and constitutional theory; his main English-language books include *Giving Desert its Due: Social Justice and Legal Theory* (Dordrecht: Reidel, 1980); *Moral Pluralism and Legal Neutrality* (Dordrecht: Kluwer, 1985); *Freedom of Speech and its Limits* (1999); and *Rights before Courts: A Study of Constitutional Courts in Postcommunist States of Central and Eastern Europe* (Dordrecht: Springer, 2005). His recent articles include 'Law's Legitimacy and "Democracy-Plus"' (2006) 26(2) *Oxford Journal of Legal Studies* 377.

Gwendolyn Sasse is Senior Lecturer in Comparative European Politics at the European Institute and the Department of Government at the London School of

Economics and Political Science. Her research concentrates on post-communist transitions, ethnic conflict, and conflict-prevention, and the EU's eastward enlargement; conditionality, minority rights, and migration. Among her publications are 'Migrants and Minorities in Europe' (2005) 43:4 *Journal of Common Market Studies*, 655 (co-edited with Eiko Thielemann); *Europeanization and Regionalization in the EU's Enlargement to Central and Eastern Europe: The Myth of Conditionality* (Houndsmill: Palgrave, 2004) (with James Hughes and Claire Gordon); and *Ethnicity and Territory in the Former Soviet Union: Regions in Conflict* (London: Frank Cass, 2001) (co-edited with James Hughes).

Introduction

Wojciech Sadurski

All rights are political. They are political by virtue of their pedigree: they emerge and are generated through an interaction among individuals against the background of power and authority in the society. They are political in their content: they deal with the claims, interests, and values which people espouse and press upon each other in a political community, constituted always by the relations of power and against a coercively sustained distribution of scarce resources. And they are political in their implementation and enforcement: they are being interpreted, construed, applied, and enforced in the context of institutions which are intrinsic to politics. In these, and many other, senses, rights are political through and through, and the concept of 'political rights' is a tautology.

But of course in this volume, as in the contemporary literature on human rights in general, 'political rights' are understood in a narrower and more precise way. The concept is intended to carve out a sub-category of those human rights which are connected to a political process: the rights that are instrumental, and perhaps indispensable, to the participation of citizens in the exercise of political power in their society. And, since we are talking about the design of a political system in which citizens are included as rights bearers, rather than as mere 'stake-holders', as subjects who simply endure the consequences of political decisions, or as those whom wise political authorities should 'consult' about decisions applying to them—since, in other words, we are talking about an institutional design in which citizens are considered as co-authors of the decisions which apply to them, the natural home for political rights is a democratic political system.[1]

This is self-evident, but everything else is contested and inherently controversial. There is no one canonical conception of democracy and different conceptions will yield different views about the optimal model of political

---

[1] But note the observation of the commentators on the International Covenant of Civil and Political Rights (ICCPR) that the right to political participation (Article 25) included in this covenant addresses rights whose purposes, basic meanings, and even validity are formally disputed, and that even non-democratic states declare their conformity with this Article: 'states that reject the core practices of political democracy may justify different forms of political organization ranging from hereditary leadership to a theocracy', Henry Steiner and Philip Alston, *International Human Rights in Context: Law, Politics, Morals* (Oxford: Oxford University Press, 2000), at 145. The malleability of Article 25, and its susceptibility to different interpretations that stretch its meaning well beyond the classical democratic pattern, is indirectly confirmed by the fact that state parties (arguably, many of them less than perfectly democratic) have entered very few reservations to this provision, see K. J. Partsch, 'Freedom of Conscience and Expression, and Political Freedoms', in L. Henkin (ed.) *The International Bill of Rights: The Covenant on Civil and Political Rights* (New York: Columbia University Press, 1981), ch. 9, at 209–45.

rights. The implications for the shape of political rights are different if we opt
for a purely majoritarian-procedural theory of democracy, or a constitutional
conception with strong substantive rights limiting the scope of majority
decision, or a deliberative democratic conception that attempts to overcome the
procedural-constitutional distinction and identifies the main criterion of
democracy as lying in deliberation among citizens with the aim of justifying
their collective decisions to one another.[2] But even if one puts the different
substantive conceptions of democracy to one side, there is no agreement about
which rights (however substantially shaped) are sufficiently related to *a*
democratic process in order for those rights to be deemed political.

Some rights are 'political' in an obvious and banal way: the right to vote in
elections, the right to stand for election, or the right to set up and belong to
political parties. But beyond this rather thin minimum, agreement ends. And in
seeking to identify a plausible category of the 'political' within a broader genus of
human rights, we are not helped by the taxonomies discernible in various
international and national human rights documents. UN and regional human
rights instruments, as well as national constitutions and bills of rights, typically
enumerate civil and political rights within a single, internally undifferentiated
category. There has never been any major debate concerning the demarcation of
these two sub-categories, in contrast to the heated debates and controversies
surrounding the distinction between 'civil and political', on the one hand, and
socio-economic rights, on the other. (The contingent and uncertain boundary
between 'civil' and 'political' rights is raised at the beginning of Gwendolyn
Sasse's chapter in this book.) The main international instrument on civil and
political rights, the International Covenant on Civil and Political Rights
(ICCPR), lists only one, individual political right (or, rather, set of rights): the
right, political *par excellence*, to take part in the conduct of public affairs, to vote
and be elected at genuine periodic elections, and to have access to public service
(Article 25), and one collective right: that of peoples to self-determination
(Article 1). But these rights are not placed in a separate category of 'political', and
the ICCPR lists a number of other rights, some clearly removed from the political
process (the right to life, Article 6; the right of those deprived of liberty to be
treated with humanity, Article 10; various rights comprising the entitlement to
fair criminal trial, Articles 14 and 15); and also rights that, under some interpretations at least, are closely connected to political processes (freedom of
expression, Article 19, and freedom of assembly, Article 21).[3] This lack of

---

[2] For this trichotomy of procedural, constitutional, and deliberative democracy, see A. Gutman
and D. Thompson, *Democracy and Disagreement* (Cambridge, MA: Harvard University Press,
1996), at 26–51.

[3] In addition to Article 25 the following five provisions of ICCPR are found by a prominent
international lawyer to be related to 'a citizen's participatory rights': the right to hold opinions
(Article 19), to peaceful assembly (Article 21), to freedom of association (Article 22), to freedom
from discrimination (Article 24), and to equality before the law (Article 26): G. H. Fox, 'The Right
to Political Participation In International Law' (1992) 17 *Yale J Int'l Law* 539–607, at 553, n. 58.

demarcation between 'political' and 'civil' is tracked by important regional human rights instruments: the American Convention on Human Rights, Chapter II, entitled 'Civil and Political Rights', basically echoes the ICCPR provisions with, for instance, the right of political participation (Article 23) an almost *verbatim* repetition of ICCPR's Article 25. In contrast, the African Charter on Human and Peoples' Rights does not draw any distinction between different categories of Charter rights (its Article 13(1) includes, in rather pale formulation, the right to political participation[4]). Similarly, the European Convention for the Protection of Human Rights and Fundamental Freedoms does not list, in the body of the Convention itself, any right to political participation, but imposes, in Protocol No. 1, a duty on states parties to hold free elections at reasonable intervals by secret ballot.[5]

But surely the right to political participation (understood as participation in regular, free, fair, and genuine elections, and the right to stand for election) does not exhaust the scope of political rights: the election (parliamentary or presidential, local, or national, etc.) is neither the first, nor the last step in the trajectory of democratic self-government. So, even assuming that we know the boundaries of the right of political participation (which cannot, in fact, be taken for granted),[6] we need to go well beyond these in order to ascertain the set of rights which are indispensable to meaningful political freedom. But exactly how far must we go?

Take the right to free speech. Undoubtedly, much speech in society concerns public matters which can be dubbed 'political', and in this sense a right to (relatively) unrestrained political speech is necessarily political, but surely this does not exhaust the content of speech which we would like to be protected, as within the scope of the relevant 'right'. A temptation to disaggregate the right to free speech, so considering only speech on political matters as 'political' should be resisted: a declaration that a right to free speech is political insofar as the

---

[4] Unlike the ICCPR, the American Convention and the First Protocol to the European Convention on Human Rights, Article 13 of the African Convention fails to stipulate that an electoral choice must reflect the free expression of the electors' will or the opinion of the people (thus implying, at least to some observers, the permissibility of one-party systems, see Fox, ibid, at 568). It also lacks provisions on discrimination, universal suffrage, and secret ballots, and stipulates that the right need only be 'in accordance with the provisions of the law', suggesting no more extensive obligations are imposed on states than those already established under their respective national laws.

[5] Though note that through dynamic interpretation, the ECHR/Commission has established a subjective right to bring complaints, see *Mathieu-Mohin and Clerfayt v Belgium*, Appl. No. 9267/81 (2 March 1987), 10 EHRR 1. For further discussion, see Manfred Nowak, 'Civil and Political Rights', in J. Symonides (ed.) *Human Rights: Concept and Standards* (Dartmouth: Ashgate, 2000), ch. 3, at 69–107, and Fox, ibid, at 562–63.

[6] Note the remark by Henry J. Steiner that norms defining political participation are 'vague, or when explicit, bear sharply disputed meanings. Within the framework of human rights law, the right expresses less a vital concept meant to universalize certain practices than a bundle of concepts sometimes complementary but sometimes antagonistic', H. J. Steiner, 'Political Participation as a Human Right' (1988) 1 *Harvard Human Rights Yearbook* 77–134, at 77.

speech intended by a speaker is political contains an obvious circularity. So perhaps a better way of discerning the political aspects of rights such as that to free speech is by inquiring into the justifications, or rationales, provided for the entrenchment of and respect given to these rights. As is well known, the right to free speech (including to false, offensive, or insulting speech of the sort discussed by Victor Ferreres Comella in this volume) has been given different justifications, not all of them connecting sufficiently with the political sphere to qualify the right, so defended, as political. If one sees a right to free speech as fundamentally aimed at the protection of the speaker's sense of human dignity, self-worth and self-fulfilment, there is no need of seeing this right as 'political', any more than the right to physical integrity or personal reputation is political. Or if one cherishes the right to free speech on the basis of the better capacity of unrestrained human communication to reach the truth of the matter, then such an epistemically defended right is no more political than the right to academic freedom or unrestrained scholarly pursuit. To be sure, these rights *are* political, but only in the broadest sense of the 'political', identified right at the beginning of this Introduction.[7]

If, however, one discerns the main value of free speech in its ability to make a democratic system of political self-government meaningful, and the main casualty of violations of free speech is seen as the undermining of the pre-conditions for democratic choice, then freedom of speech is inherently 'political', in the strictest and narrowest sense. The argument is quite straightforward: democracy requires that all citizens be free to receive all information potentially affecting their choices in processes of collective decision-making, in particular, the voting process. This rationale was most famously propounded by American scholar Alexander Meiklejohn, who insisted that the range of free speech justified on this basis is not excessively narrow (as many of his critics suggested) because 'there are many forms of thought and expression . . . from which the voter derives the knowledge, intelligence, sensitivity to human values: the capacity for sane and objective judgment which, so far as possible, a ballot should express'.[8] This idea was adopted by the US Supreme Court as authoritative doctrine. Subsequently, it has also been widely adopted in Europe. In a landmark decision of the European Court of Human Rights (ECHR), quoted at the beginning of Ferreres Comella's chapter, the Strasbourg Court declared that 'freedom of political debate is at the very core of the concept of a democratic society'.[9]

However, this standard political rationale for freedom of speech does not necessarily capture the entire range of speech which we intuitively wish to be

---

[7] For more on the political and non-political dimensions of free speech rights, see the chapter by Michel Rosenfeld in this volume.

[8] Al. Meiklejohn, 'The First Amendment Is an Absolute' (1961) *Supreme Court Review* 245–66, at 256.

[9] *Lingens v Austria*, Judgment of 8 July 1986, quoted in the chapter by Victor Ferreres Comella in this volume, at 84.

protected by a robust right to free speech (incidentally, its scope of protection may also be *wider* than many would think sensible). As observed by Michel Rosenfeld in the opening chapter of this volume, this just goes to show that 'the same rights may be political or non-political'.[10] And it is no answer to this point to suggest that we do not need to choose between different rationales for one and the same right because a right may perform different functions, and thus rest comfortably upon a number of different justifications. This is no doubt true, but it does not follow that we can disconnect the substance (or sphere of coverage) of a particular right from the rationale provided for entrenching it against day-to-day changes in the political views of the majority in a democratic polity. Each different rationale will yield a different understanding of the proper contours of the right: we may regard a particular right as valuable due to its role in protecting human self-realization (in which case we will argue that the right should be subject to those restrictions with which all other means of self-fulfilment must comply), or because it is a condition of truth-seeking (in which case we need not protect speech that does not even purport to describe external reality), or because it is a condition of democratic self-government (in which case speech addressing purely private matters will not qualify for rights-based protection). These (and many other) candidate rationales for a right to unrestrained speech lead to differing, and sometimes mutually conflicting, conclusions about its scope.

A similar argument can be made with regard to a number of other 'rights' which, depending on the sort of argument provided, may or may not strike us as 'political'. Consider freedom of religion. One possible way of defending this right is by arguing about the role of the free exercise of religion in the life of the individual. Another argument takes a slightly different tack: it suggests the importance of values which underwrite the separation of a religious sphere of life (and institutional churches) from the institutions of state. It would seem that these two different arguments will yield a right to freedom of religion in each case with slightly different contours. If we emphasize the value of the free exercise of religious beliefs, we will consequently support some governmental accommodation of religion (in order to ensure that the free exercise of religion is unburdened from neutral requirements that might disproportionately impact on certain believers; exemptions from military service, or from work on certain days, are good examples). In turn, if we emphasize a strict separation between secular and religious spheres, we will naturally be sceptical about such accommodations, and discern in them questionable privileges based on religious convictions, perhaps even the indirect 'establishment' of a favoured religion by the state, violating the rights of non-believers. Now it is clear that the second, but not the first, strategy of arguing about freedom of religion can be characterized as 'political': it is based directly on ideas about the distinction between the religious and the political in the public sphere of democratic society.

[10] Rosenfeld, in this volume, at 4.

All this shows that, as in the case of all other rights, discourse about political rights is fundamentally concerned with the foundations, arguments, and justifications provided for the elevation of certain values to the exalted rank of 'rights'. In this sense, political rights share all the peculiarities and ambiguities ascertained in relation to rights discourse more generally. Two classical distinctions, further reflected in the discussions contained in this volume, are worth noting. One is between so-called negative and positive rights. This distinction, famous as much for its endorsement, as for its rejection in the literature on rights, applies to political rights in more than one way. First, we can talk about 'negative' as opposed to 'positive' dimensions of rights, in the sense that the former call for abstention of the state and other individuals from interference in the right-holder's action (and in the case of political rights, non-interference in the actions of political communication, party membership, act of voting, etc. is crucial for the operation of democratic mechanisms). The latter, by contrast, call for specific actions to be undertaken by the state to provide a legal and material infrastructure for making political rights meaningful. Second, as Damien Chalmers notes in his chapter, we can talk about the right to political participation but also about a right to abstain from politics: in this sense, the positive/negative distinction is related to the nature of individual preferences, desires, and aspirations vis-à-vis political life. Whether the latter, 'negative' rights of being left alone by the political structure are equal in significance to the right to positive involvement, again, crucially depends on precisely what justifying moral-political conception stands behind a given version of democracy. In this respect, Rosenfeld's discussion of three grand theories providing different philosophical bases to constitutional democracy, liberalism, republicanism, and communitarianism, is instructive.

The second central distinction, applicable as much to rights discourse in general as to political rights specifically, is that between individual and group rights. Political rights confer certain benefits and privileges upon individuals. This much is clear. But in what sense can we talk about group political rights? Can nations, national minorities, regions, etc. have rights, as much as individuals can? This question emerges with particular force in considering political rights of minorities—a topic taken up by Gwendolyn Sasse's chapter, with regard to post-communist Central and Eastern Europe. At first glance, it might appear that minority rights are necessarily group rights, an attitude confirmed by some of the legal wordings used to describe political rights of minorities, analysed by Sasse, such as the Hungarian law guaranteeing rights of political representation and collective participation in public life to national and ethnic minorities, via the institutions of local and national self-government.[11] This, however, is not

---

[11] See Sasse, in this volume, at 254–57. In addition, the Hungarian constitution proclaims that 'national and ethnic minorities will be assured collective participation in public affairs' and that 'The laws of the Republic of Hungary shall ensure representation for the national and ethnic minorities living within [the] country,' Article 68(2) and (3). Note also that this group character of

necessarily the case: one should distinguish between group rights *sensu stricto*, where the proper claimant and beneficiary of a right is a group as a whole (and where, presumably, the right is exercised in accordance with the decisions of some recognized leaders and representatives of the group) and, on the other hand, rights that are conferred upon *individuals* by virtue of their belonging to an ethnic, national, or other minority. Group-specific rights may be individual in the sense that a claim-holder is an individual, even though the basis of her claim is that she belongs to a group. Whether the distinction is significant in practice is another matter. The point can be made that individuals are best able to exercise their minority-based rights when they act in concert with other members of the same minority: 'we may insist that a certain right . . . is due to individuals but the enjoyment of that right is nonetheless unthinkable without others'.[12] But this is a practical and contingent matter; and need not always be the case. As one commentator has observed, 'for some aspects of minority/indigenous protection— such as standing to bring complaints before international bodies—it may be important to determine whether a right is collectively or individually held'.[13] Some rights, by their very nature, better lend themselves to a collectivist articulation than to an individualist one, or vice versa. Generally speaking, one may venture the proposition that, if a right more closely resembles an *exemption from* a general duty (such as conscientious objection) than a *claim to* the provision of certain services, it is perfectly imaginable and practicable to assert that right individually and regardless of others, even if its basis is membership of a certain group. In that case, there is no need to collapse an individual group-based right into a group right in the strict sense.

As a general proposition, therefore, these two understandings of rights are quite distinct from each other. In the case of a group right *sensu stricto* there must be an officially recognizable (and recognized) collective body that speaks on behalf of the group. This raises the obvious problem of whether that body has the legitimate authority to represent all of its members. The process of decision-making as to the exercise of a right is then taken away from the individuals concerned—who may actually reject the group's authority to represent them—and centralized in one group-representative body. In the case of individually-worded group rights (where the individuals are entitled to claim,

political rights has been given even more explicit support by the 1993 Act on the Rights of Ethnic and National Minorities, discussed extensively by Sasse, which proclaims in its introduction that 'minority rights cannot be fully guaranteed within the bounds of individual civil rights; thus, they are also to be formulated as rights of particular groups in society', quoted in S. Deets, 'Reconsidering East European Minority Policy: Liberal Theory and European Norms' (2002) 16 *East European Politics & Societies* 30–53, at 49.

[12] Dimitrina Petrova, 'Racial Discrimination and the Rights of Minority Cultures', in S. Fredman (ed.) *Discrimination and Human Rights: The Case of Racism* (Oxford: Oxford University Press, 2001), at 66.

[13] M. J. Aukerman, 'Definitions and Justifications: Minority and Indigenous Rights in a Central/East European Context' (2000) 22 *Human Rights Quarterly* 1011–50, at 1032.

for example, access to education in their own language) the problem of representation disappears. However, as a practical matter, it is inconceivable that
such a right can be satisfied without a critical mass of people to claim it.

*

The issue of political rights is universal but each historical moment imparts
upon the discussion of those rights its own special concerns. This volume has
been written at a time when two phenomena give it a particular slant, and when
political rights have acquired a special urgency, colour, and relevance. The
chapters in this volume reflect these characteristics and the distinctive context in
which the discussion of political rights has been conducted in recent years.

The first phenomenon informing the contributions is the rise of political
terrorism, and political responses to the new place that terrorism now occupies
in the life of democratic societies. As popular cliché has it, 'After 9/11, the world
is different.' In one way this is manifestly false: terrorism and politically
motivated violence have endured for decades. On the other hand, it is
undoubtedly true that since the attacks in the US on 11 September 2001, the
bombings in Madrid on 11 March 2004 and in London on 7 July 2005, the
gravity of the danger of terrorism and arising from possible (and sometimes
real) responses to it is qualitatively different.

Difficulties lie in the very characterization of the period we inhabit. Rosenfeld
suggests a concept of 'times of stress', lying somewhere on a spectrum between
ordinary times and times of crisis, and differing from times of crisis in terms of
the severity, intensity, and duration of threats involved. Chalmers, focusing on
governmental responses rather that their causes, talks about 'government under
stress', in contrast to emergency government, drawing distinctions in terms of
the general rather than extraordinary reorientation of the government, of greater
consolidation and integration of the government under stress, and in terms of
the former's rationale, of the preservation of the *status quo*, rather than the
latter's assumption of the restoration of the *status quo ante*. These approaches
are complementary, approaching the same phenomenon from two different
perspectives.

So what is this 'war on terror': how does it compare to established character-
izations of special periods (emergency, war, martial law, etc.) in which the government has a right (perhaps a duty) to suspend our normal expectations about the
scope of various rights (including political rights)? Is it comparable to a state of
emergency? After all, it is an established part of the international law of human
rights and of national constitutional systems that in times of emergency certain
political (and other) rights may be suspended. The ICCPR recognizes that '[i]n
time of public emergency which threatens the life of the nation . . . the state Parties . . . may take measures derogating from their obligations under the present
Covenant to the extent strictly required by the exigencies of the situation. . . .'
(Article 4.1); Article 25 is not among those provisions explicitly listed (in
Article 4.2) as not capable of derogation. That is why it is important to be clear (as

both Rosenfeld and Chalmers underline) about how the circumstances sur-rounding terrorism and the 'war on terror' are *not* the same as a time of emergency.

Rosenfeld emphasizes that we should be very careful about drawing, from the risk of terrorism, hasty conclusions about permissible restrictions on political rights: it is not the case, he says, that political rights in times of stress may plausibly be interpreted as lying halfway between political rights in ordinary times and in times of crisis. On the contrary, he argues, 'when the unity of the polity begins to crack but it is in no imminent danger of collapse, it would seem better to reinforce rather than weaken political rights'.[14] One is reminded, in this context, of John Rawls' warning against any quick inferences from the existence of an emergency to the need to suspend political rights. And yet, Rawls argued, '[a] number of historical cases illustrate that free democratic political institutions have operated effectively to take the necessary measures in serious emergencies without restricting free political speech; and in some cases where such restrictions have been imposed they were unnecessary and made no contribution whatever to meeting the emergency'.[15]

This is an important point: in their responses to terrorist attacks many governments have been prepared to ignore or violate many important indi-vidual rights and liberties. Not all of these rights can be characterized as 'political' *stricto sensu*: the most egregious cases are the actions of the Bush administration in expanding surveillance of private individuals and the col-lection of data about them, detaining many hundreds of prisoners indefinitely and in secret, establishing special military tribunals where traditional safeguards to protect the innocent from wrongful conviction are not available, etc. The European Union has taken several steps aimed at combating terrorism, including a framework decision taken by the European Council on combating terrorism[16] which has caused some concern among non-governmental organi-zations, particularly with respect to possible chilling effects upon the normal exercise of democratic rights of legitimate public protest. After the 2005 London bombings, and although it had already enacted anti-terrorism legisla-tion in December 2001,[17] the Blair government devised new proposals aimed at 'extremists', not only targeting 'foreign preachers' who 'glorify terrorism' (an arguably vague offence, whose potential injustice is exacerbated by the conferral on the Home Secretary of the power to decide which kinds of terrorist acts it will be illegal to 'glorify') but also threatening naturalized citizens with deportation—and thus creating the spectre of two classes of citizens with dif-ferent free-expression rights. All this has led an influential weekly magazine, not known for radical views, to issue the extraordinary comment that: 'The prime minister's proposals would serve the terrorists' ends by undermining the

---

[14] Rosenfeld, in this volume, at 44.
[15] J. Rawls, *Political Liberalism* (New York: Columbia University Press, 1993), at 354.
[16] Council Framework Decision of 13 June 2002 on combating terrorism, 2002/475/JHA.
[17] Anti-terrorism, Crime and Security Act 2001 of 14 December 2001.

civilisation they attack. Free speech is not a privilege, to be revoked if it is misused, but a pillar of democracy.'[18] Even more worrying, perhaps, is the significant support that both US and European governments enjoy in these actions in their own societies, often based on the belief that they constitute justifiable and proportionate responses to the terrorist threat, as a 'lesser evil', along the lines of the following argument: 'Defending a right of an individual . . . to freedom of association in times of safety protects the liberty of all. But protecting the same individual in a time of emergency may do harm to all. A terrorist emergency is precisely a case where allowing individual liberty—to plan, to plot, to evade detection—may threaten a vital majority interest.'[19]

It is important not to confuse issues surrounding political responses to terrorism (and their impact on political rights) with restrictions on democracy and on political rights imposed in the defence of democracy itself against those propounding anti-democratic ideas and who are likely to engage in actions intended to destroy democratic order. This latter engage the issue of so-called militant democracy (sometimes misleadingly referred to as a substantive conception of democracy[20]), a democracy that restricts the political rights of non-democratic actors. One specific, and probably crucial, dimension in which the militant-democracy approach may adversely affect political rights is described in detail by Eva Brems in this volume, namely, the question of closures and other restrictions upon parties deemed anti-democratic. The dilemma implicated by a militant-democracy principle is obvious: isn't the medicine so strong that it will kill the patient? Or, if the remedy is not applied, will the patient still survive? In reality, the dilemma presents itself to us in a more complex way as there is no canonical definition of what a 'democratic' party is, and 'our' standards (i.e. the standards of those who would argue for the closure of non-democratic parties) may be self-serving, biased or based on a too narrow conception of democracy. The real danger is that, as one commentator recently noted, 'an excessively narrow definition of the scope [of] political action to the exclusion of a number of different anti-democratic parties endangers political pluralism and . . . creates . . . a kind of petrified oligarchy instead of a modern, pluralist democracy'.[21] While there is no room here for further discussion of this dilemma, at minimum it can be said that a clear distinction must be maintained between the question of internal, democracy-driven restrictions upon democracy, and restrictions on the exercise of democratic political rights occasioned

---

[18] 'Dealing with traitors' (editorial), *The Economist*, 13 August 2005, 12–13, at 13.

[19] M. Ignatieff, *The Lesser Evil: Political Ethics in an Age of Terror* (Princeton, NJ: Princeton University Press, 2003), at 3–4.

[20] A strongly liberal conception (which tolerates the rights of non-democratic actors to operate) is no less substantive, and no more 'procedural' than 'militant' democracy. It just ranks differently various values promoted by a democratic system, and is based on a different diagnosis about the capacity of non-democratic actors to destroy the democratic system as a whole.

[21] P. Harvey, 'Militant Democracy and the European Convention on Human Rights' (2004) 29 *ELRev* 407–20, at 409, footnote omitted.

by concerns about political terrorism. As a reading of Brems' chapter suggests, terrorism-related reasons hardly ever figure in the most effective and persuasive arguments for militant-democracy type measures.

As stated, this volume is coloured by two sets of phenomena informing the consideration of political rights in recent years. The first concerns responses to political terrorism and violence. The second, much happier phenomenon is the transition of a very large number of hitherto authoritarian states to a more democratic system.[22] In addition to democratic transitions in Africa (most notably in South Africa), South-East Asia (Thailand, South Korea, Taiwan, Indonesia, etc.), and in South America, democratization was very prominently brought about by the collapse of Communism in Central and Eastern Europe and the emergence of over twenty new democracies in this region. Has the design of political rights in these states simply emulated Western European and US models? Or have indigenous variants of the contours and shapes of those rights been formulated? The chapter by Jiří Přibáň and Wojciech Sadurski looks at the political-rights landscape in Central and Eastern Europe generally, while Gwendolyn Sasse explores in detail one particularly vexed category of political rights for this region: political rights of national and ethnic minorities. The lessons are not in every possible respect entirely edifying. But then neither is respect for, and interpretation of, political rights in the more consolidated democracies of Western Europe and elsewhere fully satisfactory. Ultimately, one lesson that can be drawn is that even if everyone is 'for' political rights, their meaning and scope are continuously contested, challenged, and questioned. We hope that the chapters included in this book will provide some new evidence of the trajectories that these contestations and challenges in Europe, and in the wider world, are following.

---

[22] According to Freedom House—which produces annual surveys in which each country in the world is given a rating of 1 to 7 on two scales, respect for political rights and respect for civil liberties—while in 1974 the number of countries characterized as 'free' was 42 and as not free 63, for 2005 these numbers were, respectively, 89 and 49: see http://www.freedomhouse.org/template. cfm?page = 130&year = 2005.

1

A Pluralist Theory of Political Rights in Times of Stress

Michel Rosenfeld

1.1 INTRODUCTION

It is hardly clear which rights should qualify as political, much less which political rights should be deemed indispensable in times of stress. In a narrow sense, political rights are distinct from civil rights and from social and economic rights. Of the 53 Articles of the UN's International Covenant on Civil and Political Rights, only two deal strictly speaking with political rights. Article 25 grants citizens an individual right to political participation that boils down to the right to vote and the right to be eligible for elective office. Article 1, in turn, provides a collective right entitling peoples to self-determination, that is to 'freely determine their political status and freely pursue their economic, social and cultural development'. The collective right seems as broad as the individual right seems narrow, but if one places the latter in its proper context it only remains meaningful so long as it is inextricably linked to a significant bundle of other rights. Indeed, voting and eligibility for public office are valuable above all as means to participate in, direct, or lead the public affairs of one's polity. Furthermore, to do so meaningfully and effectively, one must be informed, able to assemble with others, organize interest groups and political parties, possess sufficient resources to make one's voice heard, etc. In short, in the broad sense, political rights encompass a wide array of rights ordinarily categorized as civil rights, such as freedom of expression, association, assembly, equality, privacy, and dignity. Furthermore, if political rights are understood not only as rights of participation, but as rights of *effective* participation, then their realization may depend on vindication of some social and economic rights. Indeed, only an educated electorate that is adequately housed and fed can fully and effectively exercise its right to participate in its polity's process of self-determination.

Times of stress, on the other hand, are neither ordinary times nor times of crisis. In the context of a crisis, be it military, economic, social, or natural, the head of government may be entitled to proclaim exceptional powers and to suspend constitutional rights, including political rights. In an acute crisis, the polity is singularly focused on survival and all other political concerns and objectives recede into the background.[1] In contrast, in ordinary times, the polity can readily absorb the full impact of the give and take of everyday politics, and political rights as well as other constitutional rights ought to be protected to their fullest possible extent.

Times of stress differ from those of crisis primarily in terms of the severity, intensity, and duration of the respective threats involved. The line between the two may be difficult to draw, but a less severe, less intense, and more durable threat is likely to give rise to times of stress whereas a severe, intense, con-centrated threat, of relatively shorter duration, is likely to provoke a crisis. For example, a foreign military invasion or a widespread domestic insurrection is likely to provoke a crisis. On the other hand, the aftermath of the terrorist attacks such as those against New York City on 11 September 2001, Madrid on 11 March 2004, or London on 7 July 2005, which may involve threats, per-ceived threats, launching a 'war on terror' fought mainly in far away countries, arrest and detention of potential terrorists, but no further terrorist attacks on the three countries involved as of the time of this writing, has produced times of stress rather than times of crisis.[2]

Should political rights in times of stress fall somewhere between political rights in times of crisis and those in ordinary times? Should political rights in times of stress be the same as those prevalent in ordinary times, but be protected to a lesser extent than the latter? Should there be any special political rights for times of stress?

Cogent answers to these questions depend on an adequate handle on the nature and function of political rights in contemporary constitutional democracies. Given the dichotomy between political rights in the narrow sense and in the broad sense, and given the multiplicity of conceptions of, and the diversity and com-plexity of configurations of, contemporary constitutional democracies, however, a full analysis of all the relevant issues remains beyond the scope of the present undertaking. To render the task more manageable, therefore, I will approach political rights from a singular perspective and limit the analysis to a single conception (among many plausible ones) of contemporary constitutional democracy. Eschewing the distinction between political rights in the narrow or

---

[1] The grant and duration of exceptional emergency powers are problematic, not in relation to their proper use as means to combat threats to the life of the polity, but in relation to the potential for abuse in the invocation or prolongation of such powers. See B. Ackerman, 'The Emergency Constitution' (2004) 113 *Yale LJ* 1029, at 1040.

[2] It is important, for example, to distinguish the long-term aftermath from the immediate impact and short-term consequences of the 11 September attacks. Indeed, the day of the attacks which resulted in around 3,000 deaths, and subsequent days in which the American nation had to cope with the shock of the sudden and unexpected attacks and with the prospect of the imminence of further such attacks can be fairly characterized as a time of crisis. The long period of disquiet that followed those first few weeks, however, is better described as one of stress than of crisis.

broad sense, I consider those rights—or those aspects or applications of those rights—as political rights that are indispensable for citizens either to run their polity or to benefit from (and/or not be unduly hurt by) the way in which their polity is run. The conception of contemporary constitutional democracy that I adopt, on the other hand, is one that is oriented to preserving and fostering pluralism through a constitutional framework that aims at a proper balance between majoritarian and countermajoritarian institutions.

What links the approach to political rights and the conception of constitutional democracy advanced here is that they are both dynamic and functional. Their paramount task is to cope with the evolving and shifting tensions between identity and difference—or unity and diversity—that confronts all pluralistic polities, that is polities in which the citizenry embraces diverse and often competing or conflicting conceptions of the good.[3] In other words, pluralistic polities—and all contemporary constitutional democracies are pluralistic in the sense understood here—must constantly strive to cope with conflicts between the need to maintain or promote sufficient unity, on the one hand, and the need to accommodate broad enough diversity to allow for optimal coexistence among adherents of different and often divergent conceptions of the good, on the other. In this context, political rights are those that relate to the conduct of the affairs of the polity as mediated by a constitutional system that allows for harmonization of key elements of unity and of diversity through a dynamic interplay between majoritarian and countermajoritarian processes and institutions.

To allow for a systematic examination of the nature, role, and place, of political rights within a pluralistic conception of constitutional democracy, I will proceed as follows. Part 2 will articulate the broad outlines of the conceptual framework within which the inquiry into political rights will be carried out. It will focus on the theoretical underpinnings of the pluralist conception of constitutional democracy by stressing the distinction between pluralism-in-fact and pluralism-as-norm; explore the proper role of the political in a pluralist polity in which the citizenry both divides and coheres along the cleavage between self and other; place constitutional democracy within a pluralist perspective; assess the relevance of the distinction between negative and positive political rights within that perspective; and attempt a more systematic differentiation between ordinary conditions, times of stress, and times of crisis within the confines of the pluralist vision. Part 3 will focus on the three principal approaches to constitutional democracy, namely the liberal, republican, and communitarian approach, each of which justifying a different configuration of, and role for, political rights. Each of these approaches and the political rights it fosters, will be compared to the others and critically assessed from a pluralist standpoint. Part 4 will explore the nature, function, and derivation of political

---

[3] See M. Rosenfeld, *Just Interpretations: Law between Ethics and Politics* (Berkeley, CA: University of California Press), at 201–2 (describing such polities as being 'pluralistic-in-fact' as distinguished from espousing pluralism as a normative goal or aspiration).

rights in a pluralist democracy. Emphasis will be placed both on how constitutional democracy itself may imply political rights that are not explicitly constitutionally protected and on the political dimension of protected constitutional rights that are not political in the narrow sense. Finally, Part 5 will concentrate on political rights in times of stress through the examination of issues arising out of the war on terror, the limits of tolerance, militant democracy, and the prospects of peaceful and constitutionally sanctioned secession.

1.2 A PLURALIST CONCEPTUAL FRAMEWORK FOR POLITICAL RIGHTS

In Aristotle's famous dictum, man (today we would say the human being) is a political animal.[4] Human beings are thus supposed to be immersed in the affairs of their polis and to pursue their well-being and realization of the good through wise and virtuous stewardship of their city-state. In a democracy, moreover, it is all the citizens, rather than one or a few of them that are called upon to determine the political course of their city-state. In other words, in a democracy, citizens must rule for themselves, and in modern parlance, they must possess the rights necessary to permit self-rule without undue impediments or constraints.

What political rights are necessary for successful self-rule depends on whether there is a commonly shared conception of the good or whether citizens within the polity are divided over what constitutes the good. As already noted, all contemporary constitutional democracies are pluralistic, meaning that individuals and groups within them disagree over *the* good. In pluralistic polities, therefore, politics and political rights are concerned not only with implementation of the common good but also with handling conflicts among proponents of competing conceptions of the good. Accordingly, pluralistic polities must determine what good ought to be pursued in the interests of the citizenry as a whole.

1.2.1 Politics and Contests over the Good

If in politics both means and ends are constantly subject to challenges as being parasitic on contested conceptions of the good, it is hard to imagine how any bundle of political rights might be universally acceptable as being fair. Rawls attempted to overcome this difficulty by drawing on the Kantian divide between issues of justice and of the right, on the one hand, and issues of the good, on the other. According to Rawls, his criterion of justice as fairness legitimates a series of basic rights, including political rights, that remain neutral as between different contested conceptions of the good.[5] It is dubious, however, that in a polity confronting vigorous clashes between various religious and secular world-views,

---

[4] Aristotle, *Politics* I.2.1253a (E. Barker trans.) (Oxford: Clarendon Press, 1946).
[5] J. Rawls, *A Theory of Justice* (Cambridge, MA: Harvard University Press, 1971), at 11–17.

any conception of comprehensive justice and the rights it entails would ultimately prove neutral. For example, extensive freedom of expression and of inquiry may well end up privileging secular conceptions of the good over at least some of the competing religious ones.

Mindful of this problem, Rawls retreated from his claim of neutrality for comprehensive justice to embrace a much more confined political justice which may 'gain the support of an overlapping consensus of reasonable religious, philosophical and moral doctrines in a society regulated by it'.[6] At least three important consequences follow from Rawls' shift to political justice. First, to the extent that political rights derive from political rather than comprehensive justice, much of what is important to those who espouse comprehensive moral, religious, or ideological views must remain outside the realm of politics. Accordingly, political rights must both determine what belongs legitimately to the realm of politics and what though outside or beyond politics must nevertheless be afforded political, or more precisely, political rights protection. Second, the notion of 'overlapping consensus' implies that proponents of different comprehensive conceptions of the good may agree to the same thing for different reasons. It seems inherently contingent, however, whether there is an overlapping consensus and whether it is broad enough to allow for a workable political community. For example, in a polity divided between militant secularists and religious fundamentalists, the overlapping consensus may be non-existent or merely confined to a common preference for peaceful coexistence over civil war. Finally, the fact that only proponents of 'reasonable' comprehensive views are allowed to contribute to shaping political justice means that many citizens may remain alienated from the operative conception of political justice and corresponding political rights to which they would in no way have granted their consent.

By restricting participation in the elaboration of political justice to those who agree to 'reasonable' world-views, Rawls insures the emergence of a sufficiently broad domain of overlapping consensus to allow for a workable array of political rights. He does this, however, at a very high cost. Indeed, on the one hand, what is 'reasonable' may be contested, but even if it is not, proponents of non-reasonable world-views are excluded. From their standpoint, therefore, the political rights that emerge from an overlapping consensus are the equivalent to rights tied to a competing conception of the good that one thoroughly rejects. On the other hand, the linking of the 'reasonable' conceptions to the 'overlapping consensus', makes the process circular if not entirely superfluous. In other words, the consensus depends on the reasonableness of the conceptions of the good that are taken into account, and that does not differ, except in scope, from the kind of operation involved in the derivation of political rights from the dictates of comprehensive justice.

---

[6] J. Rawls, *Political Liberalism* (New York: Columbia University, 1993), at 10.

Consistent with the preceding observations, in polities that are significantly divided over clashing conceptions of the good, justice all the way down cannot be bracketed away from the good. Thus, not only comprehensive justice, but also political, legal, and constitutional justice cannot escape favouring or promoting some conceptions of the good at the expense of others. To remedy that, it is necessary to move away from the Rawlsian dichotomy between justice and the good. And that precisely is what the pluralist approach attempts to do.

1.2.2 Comprehensive Pluralism and the Competition between Conceptions of the Good

As a systematic approach, pluralism, or what I refer to as 'comprehensive pluralism',[7] holds that in societies that are pluralistic-in-fact, the good consists in promoting pluralism as the norm.[8] In a nutshell, comprehensive pluralism maintains that in a polity that is pluralist-in-fact, it is good to protect and promote as many competing conceptions of the good as possible, and that justice is inextricably connected to pursuit of the pluralist good. From the pluralist standpoint, no religion is inherently superior to, or 'truer' than, any other, and no ideology, culture, or life-style is *prima facie* better than any other.[9] Moreover, pluralist justice is concerned with eradicating institutional entrenchment and advantages of certain conceptions of the good at the expense of others and with opening up as much space as possible to encompass equitably as many of the existing conceptions of the good within the polity as practically feasible without compromising the normative aims of pluralism.

Before pursuing the pluralist approach to political rights any further, it is necessary to deal with two anticipated objections. The first is that comprehensive pluralism's conception of justice sketched above does not ultimately differ in substance from Rawls', and in particular from his conception of political justice. The second is that comprehensive pluralism is yet another conception of the good among many and that to privilege it with respect to political justice is as arbitrary as choosing one religious or secular conception over others. More generally, at a more abstract level, these two objections represent two sides of the same overall critique: either comprehensive pluralism is but one more monistic theory or it collapses into relativism.[10]

---

[7] See M. Rosenfeld, *Just Interpretations*, above, n. 3, at 200–1.

[8] See ibid, at 200. The discussion that follows is based on the more extensive one provided in the book.

[9] Cf. W. Kymlicka, *Multicultural Citizenship: A Liberal Theory of Minority Rights* (Oxford: Oxford University Press, 1995), at 18–19 (distinguishing between ethno-cultural differences and 'life-style' differences such as those associated with feminist or gay perspectives).

[10] 'Monism' is 'roughly defined as the view that there is a single conception of the good that is correct and that all value preferences are to be judged in terms of that conception'. In contrast, 'relativism' is 'the view that all value preferences are ultimately purely subjective and so contextually bound to the conception of the good from which they emerge that it would be meaningless to gauge

Rawls' liberalism (as all liberalism) is monistic in that it embraces an individualistic perspective that privileges individual liberty and equality over collective values and objectives. Consistent with this, Rawls' conception of justice, whether political or comprehensive, cannot achieve neutrality with respect to the good as it is necessarily privileges liberal values and outlooks over illiberal ones. Furthermore, whereas Rawlsian liberalism embraces pluralism and tolerance, it is confined to limited pluralism—i.e., those values and outlooks that are not incompatible with liberal individualism.[11] In contrast, comprehensive pluralism is pluralistic all the way, and thus does not privilege individualist perspectives over collective ones or vice versa. But, if that is so, does not comprehensive pluralism ultimately collapse into mere relativism? For if it does, then it is self-contradictory. Indeed, if all conceptions of the good are merely subjective, and if there can be no justice independent from the good, then pluralism is no more justified than anti-pluralism, nor is tolerance more legitimate than intolerance.

Comprehensive pluralism can only escape from the trap of monism and relativism if it is understood dynamically as operating dialectically. Moreover, this understanding is crucial for purposes of articulating the pluralist conception of political justice and political rights, including those that ought to prevail in times of stress.

In the broadest terms, the dynamic that animates comprehensive pluralism consists in the unfolding of two concurrent processes that can be conceptualized as two successive moments within a single logic. The first logical moment comprises the equalization through leveling of all existing conceptions of the good within the polity. This first moment is the negative one. At any given time in the institutions and life of a polity, certain conceptions of the good predominate over others. For example, a polity's constitution may privilege secular outlooks over religious ones, or the polity's institutional life may favour certain religions and harm the interests of others. Accordingly, the first negative moment consists in a systematic eradication of all entrenchment or project of entrenchment of any existing conception of the good.[12] Taken to its logical conclusion, moreover, this negative process would expel all conceptions of the good from the polity, thus completely undermining the very basis for pluralism. In other words, complete equality among all conceptions of the good can only be achieved through total suppression of each. For this reason, for the logic of pluralism to make sense, its negative moment must be supplemented by a positive one.

---

them from the standpoint of any other perspective'. M. Rosenfeld, *Just Interpretations*, above, n. 3, at 206.

[11] This amounts to another way of stating that Rawlsian justice is only compatible with 'reasonable' comprehensive views.

[12] The justification for this negative moment depends on the presupposition that there is no conception of the good, the entrenchment of which would be compatible with the equal entrenchment of all other conceptions of the good.

The positive moment requires launching a process of reintegration for all conceptions of the good levelled during the negative moment. This process of reintegration must be according to the precepts of comprehensive pluralism: the polity must accommodate as many existing conceptions of the good as possible for admission consistent with equal admission and equal opportunity for each to flourish. Accordingly, not all conceptions can be readmitted, and even those that are, cannot be readmitted on their own terms. For example, a conception of the good, such as that of a crusading religion bent on converting by force or killing the infidel may have to be excluded altogether.[13] Other conceptions, such as certain religious ones may be readmitted, but on condition of reigning in certain of their precepts, such as the duty to engage in certain overly intrusive forms of proselytism.

From the standpoint of comprehensive pluralism, every actual institutional arrangement is subject to critical assessment in terms of the dialectic framed by the tension between the two moments identified above. In actual polities, at no time are all conceptions of the good equally leveled, and at all times proponents of certain conceptions are likely to have plausible arguments for better and fuller inclusion of their viewpoint within the life of the polity. Consistent with this, comprehensive pluralism can be viewed as fighting at once on two fronts: on the one hand, it seeks to eradicate privilege among conceptions of the good; on the other, it seeks greater inclusion of, consistent with mutual coexistence among, existing competing conceptions.

If these two fronts are considered separately, then comprehensive pluralism would seem to collapse into relativism with respect to the first and into monism with respect to the second. Indeed, in its leveling mode, comprehensive pluralism treats all conceptions of the good as equivalent regardless of their actual normative content. On the other hand, in its positive moment, comprehensive pluralism deals with claims to recognition by previously leveled conceptions of the good exclusively in terms of its own normative criteria.[14]

Understood dialectically, however, comprehensive pluralism is only relativistic in its struggle against privilege and hegemony among conceptions of the good; and it is only monistic in its endeavour to be both fair and as inclusive as possible with respect to granting space within the polity to competing conceptions of the good. Ultimately, comprehensive pluralism depends for its survival on the availability of conceptions of the good that differ from its own views. Liberalism, in contrast, does not depend on illiberal world-views for its vindication, though it can afford limited tolerance towards the latter.

---

[13] Whether such a religion may in any way be readmitted would depend on whether any of its beliefs, customs, and practices could be effectively segregated from its crusading aims. If yes, then only its crusading aspects would have to be suppressed; if not, then the religion altogether would have to be suppressed.

[14] In this sense, though its criteria differ from those of liberalism, comprehensive pluralism's inclusiveness seems monistic, much like liberal tolerance is.

Comprehensive pluralism is a conception of the good, but it differs from all others in being both open toward, and dependent on, other conceptions of the good. Within the perspective of comprehensive pluralism, moreover, pluralist norms play a regulative role geared to implementation of the dialectical logic of equalization and accommodation of competing conceptions of the good. In their regulative capacity, pluralist norms constitute second-order norms as opposed to the norms espoused by other conceptions of the good, which can be characterized as first-order norms. Furthermore, as regulative, pluralism's second-order norms are hierarchically superior to first-order norms. Accordingly, when implementation of the dictates of a first-order norm would thwart the *regulative* mission of second-order norms, the former would have to yield to the latter. In other words, first-order norms must only yield when they hinder the regulative function of second-order norms. For example, tolerance is a second-order norm, but its regulative operation does not require excluding or significantly restricting all intolerant perspectives. Thus, an intolerant religion practiced by a self-contained group that has little contact with outsiders, but is at peace with them, would be unlikely to thwart the polity's institutional implementation of appropriate norms of tolerance. In contrast, an intolerant religion that proselytizes aggressively and seeks to impose its precepts on everyone within the polity would clearly interfere with the smooth implementation of pluralist tolerance.

1.2.3 Constitutional Framework and Pluralist Politics

From the standpoint of the institutional structure of the pluralist polity, pluralism's second-order norms determine the constitutional framework, provide a substantive normative criterion for assessing or designing a working constitutional order, and circumscribe the normative space for constitutional politics. In terms of actual constitutional essentials, pluralist constitutionalism shares much in common with its liberal counterpart: they both require limitation and division of powers, adherence to the rule of law, and protection of fundamental rights.[15] The differences between the two, some of which will be addressed in greater detail below, are most apparent when focusing on details or limits. For example, as already mentioned, pluralist tolerance is different from liberal tolerance, and hence the scope of pluralist freedom of expression rights is likely to differ from that of its liberal counterpart. Similarity, the mutual relationship between individual and group rights is bound to differ as pluralism does not share liberalism's bias toward individualism.

In the pluralist context, constitutional politics relates to the operation of second-order norms on the polity's institutional design and its deployment.

---

[15] See M. Rosenfeld, 'Modern Constitutionalism as Interplay between Identity and Diversity' in M. Rosenfeld (ed.) *Constitutionalism, Identity, Difference and Legitimacy: Theoretical* Perspectives (Durham, NC: Duke University Press, 1994), at 3.

This boils down to two principal tasks: 1) constitutional design through application of the relevant second-order norms to the particular circumstances of the polity involved; and 2) determining which subjects ought to be entrusted to the realm of constitutional politics, and which to the realm of ordinary politics.[16] Concerning the first of these two tasks, pluralism's second-order norms do not dictate all constitutional particulars. For example, whether a constitution ought to establish a federal or a unitary republic depends on the actual make up of the polity in question and on the actual spread of conceptions of the good represented within it. For example, in a polity made up of different religious, linguistic, or ethnic groups, each living within its own discrete geographic area, identity-based federalism may optimize equalization and mutual accommodation of existing conceptions of the good.[17] Sometimes it may be obvious which constitutional institutions would be optimal for all conceptions of the good concerned, and sometimes it may not be. Particularly in the latter cases, it is important that proponents of competing conceptions of the good be politically empowered to participate in constitution-making and in the constitution-amending processes necessary to accommodate, consistent with the relevant second-order norms, changes in the balance of powers among existing conceptions of the good.

Concerning the second of the above-mentioned tasks, on the other hand, which subject should be entrusted to constitutional politics and protection, and which to ordinary majoritarian politics, cannot in many cases be determined from a mere consideration of the dictates of pluralism's second-order norms. Such determinations may depend on the range of conceptions of the good represented within the polity or on choices among a range of plausible interpretations of the implications of the relevant second-order norms. For example, whether linguistic rights should be inscribed in the constitution or left to parliamentary majorities is not self-evident from a pluralist standpoint. The answer may depend on the circumstances. For example, the linguistic claims of Korean immigrants in the

---

[16] The distinction between constitutional and ordinary politics is one drawn by Bruce Ackerman to distinguish between politics motivated by the good of the polity as a whole and politics motivated by narrow self-interests. See B. Ackerman, *We The People: Foundations* (Cambridge, MA: Harvard University Press, 1991), at 12–13, 261–62, 265. In contrast to Ackerman, I use this distinction to underscore the difference between what the second-order norms of comprehensive pluralism require be inscribed in the institutional design of the polity or protected from majoritarian politics and what ought to be left to infra-constitutional political competition subjected to majoritarian decision-making processes. In other words, in my conception, it is the dictates of the second-order norms, not the perceptions and intentions of political actors, that inform the distinction between constitutional and ordinary politics.

[17] 'Identity-based federalism' is designed to allow for significant autonomy and self-rule for a group with a strong common identity that differs sharply from that of the polity as a whole. In contrast, 'distributive federalism' refers to vertical divisions of power designed to empower regional and local majorities for certain purposes relating to the distribution of societal benefits or burdens though the regional or local groups involved have no identity issues with the polity as a whole. See N. Dorsen, *et al.*, *Comparative Constitutionalism: Cases and Material* (Minneapolis, MN: West Group, 2003), at 351.

United States seem less compelling than those of the French-speaking population in Quebec or the Flemish-speaking population in Belgium.[18] What ought to be included and what excluded from the realm of the constitution is itself a matter of constitutional politics framed by the constraints of the second-order norms of pluralism. Consistent with this, the polity must guarantee political rights of participation in the constitutional politics pursued to settle on which subjects to constitutionalize and which to leave to parliamentary politics.

1.2.4 Political Rights and the Struggle between Self and Other

Comprehensive pluralism calls for political rights relating to constitutional politics and to ordinary politics. Before dwelling any further on whether or how they differ and on what they may actually consist of, however, it is necessary briefly to examine how the realm of political relationships (both constitutional and ordinary) is circumscribed from the standpoint of comprehensive pluralism. In the context of competition among a plurality of distinct conceptions of the good, proponents of the same conception can regard their common beliefs, practices, customs, and objectives as those of a coherent *self* competing against those who do not share these and who with varying degrees of vehemence actually oppose them. The latter, in turn, constitute the *other* that stands against the self identified above. Viewed thus, moreover, political relations are the external relations between a self and another that share a common historical trajectory within a particular geographic space.[19]

Self and other are understood here in a fluid, relational sense. For example, Catholics and Protestants in Northern Ireland relate as self and other; so do French-speaking Quebecois and anglophone Canadians; Democrats and Republicans, in the United States; and ethnic Hungarians and the rest of the population in Romania. Not only do these examples refer to splits along different divides (respectively religious, linguistic, ideological, and ethnic) but also the individuals and groups involved can belong at once to different political selves and others and the boundaries between self and other can shift so that former others can become members of the same collective self and vice versa. Thus, for example, individuals who belong respectively to the Democratic and Republican Party in the United States are bound to relate as self to other in a presidential election, but they group themselves as a single self in relation to the kind of Islamic fundamentalism that stood behind the attacks of 11 September 2001. For her part, a Catholic Swiss citizen from a French-speaking canton

[18] Korean speakers enjoy no special linguistic rights under the United States Constitution, whereas both English-speaking and French-speaking Canadians have linguistic rights enshrined in their constitution. See Constitution Act of Canada, 1982, ss. 16–23.
[19] Legal relations are also external relations among selves and others, and as such constitute a subset of political relationships. For a discussion of the similarities and differences between legal and political relations, see M. Rosenfeld, *Just Interpretations*, above, n. 3, at 76–78.

belongs to many intersecting selves confronting an equal number of intersecting others. Our citizen as part of a collective self may be opposed to different others in the context of her country's politics. Thus, she may be a Catholic as opposed to Protestants, a French speaker as opposed to German, Italian, and Romanch speakers, a French-speaking Catholic as opposed to French-speaking Protestants, a citizen of her own canton as opposed to other cantons, a Swiss citizen as opposed to citizens of the European Union, and a feminist as opposed to anti-feminists within her own country. These multiple selves and others overlap, and one's political opponents in one setting may be part of one's collective self in another. Thus, French- and German-speaking feminists may unite in the struggle for women's equality but divide over cultural and linguistic policy.

Relationships of self as against other can also occur within a single group. Take, for example, the case of Catholic gays. Whereas the Catholic Church rejects homosexuality, it purports to exclude the lifestyle involved, but not the person engaged in it. According to Catholicism, the homosexual is a sinner, but so are all humans and the Church is compassionate, and makes room for eventual repentance and redemption of all sinners. Does that make a Catholic gay an insider or an outsider? It may depend on the degree of alienation experienced by the gay person or group involved. At least some gay Catholics have sought to remain within their religious community and to influence it to becoming more accepting of their lifestyle. Accordingly, some gay Catholics have argued that the Church should accept homosexual sex though it does not lead to procreation just as it recognized the validity of marriage and sex among sterile heterosexual couples.[20] More generally, self and other and different conceptions of the good need not be impermeable to one another. Issues such as that of women or gay priests in religions where the priesthood traditionally has been the exclusive preserve of heterosexual men, have been divisive, and have in certain cases cast the feminists or gays involved as others within their own religious community. In other cases, however, the religion involved has adjusted and accepted women or gays as priests. In the latter cases, certain conceptions of the good have evolved, blending with, or incorporating, aspects of other such conceptions.

In spite of the complexity and fluidity of the relationships between self and other, and between conceptions of the good, pluralist political rights can be boiled down to the following. These rights are meant to regulate the external relationships between self and other (or more precisely, others, for though at some level all that is not self is other, in political terms, different others may pose different threats or challenges, e.g., a particular religion may face different threats from other religions than from secular ideologies) in such a way as to equalize and

---

[20] S. Macedo, *Homosexuality and the Conservative Mind* (1995) 84 *Geo LJ* 261, at 275; P. J. Weithman, 'Natural Law, Morality and Sexual Complementarity', in D. M. Estlund and M. C. Nussbaum (eds.) *Sex, Preference, and Family* (Oxford: Oxford University Press, 1997), at 227, 238; R. West, 'Symposium: Fidelity in Constitutional Theory: Fidelity as Integrity: Integrity and Universality: A Comment on Ronald Dworkin's Freedom's Law' (1997) 65 *Fordham L Rev* 1313, at 1328.

accommodate as much as possible the position of self and other within the polity consistent with adherence to the second-order norms of comprehensive pluralism. Because in any complex and diverse society there are many overlapping and shifting selves and others, the political order and political rights must allow for a proper balance between unity and diversity. A polity cannot survive as such within the context of constitutional democracy unless all its constituents can identify at some level as belonging to a single political self. In some sense, all those who belong to the polity must combine into a self that stands against all those who do not belong to it and who, for this purpose, constitute the other. The bond of identity involved at the polity-wide level may be profound and deeply lasting, as in the case of a culturally, ethnically, and religiously homogeneous group that has shared the same geographic space over a long period of history. Or, the bond in question may be relatively shallow and fragile, as in the case of a number of disparate groups with different traditions coming together to organize into a single polity for purely external reasons, such as to better be able to defend themselves against a common enemy, or to better compete in global markets.

All individuals and groups within the polity must invest something of themselves into the polity-wide self in order to forge a common identity. At the same time, all those within the polity must protect against allowing the common polity-wide self to unduly threaten or eradicate their more particular identity as a self among others within the polity. Catholic, Protestant, Muslim, Jewish, Hindu, etc. Americans must reach across religious boundaries to constitute a single political community of citizens of the United States, but each of them will want to do so in a way that does not undermine the life of her religious community within the polity. To best achieve this may require the grant of both positive and negative political rights: positive rights to participate at the constitutional and infra-constitutional level in the politics of the polity as a whole; and, negative rights to shield at least certain aspects of communal (whether religious or not) life and individual life from inter-group politics.

Positive and negative rights are understood here also in relational terms. For example, a religious group may have a negative right against the state requiring that the latter refrain from intervening in that group's internal affairs. At the same time, that group could have a positive right to both organize its institutional life and to impose its norms on its members. Moreover, the arena for the combined negative and positive rights involved here could be a governmental one—if the religious group were large enough and gathered in a geographically contiguous area, it could become a federated unit within a federal polity—or a non-governmental one—in case such group could function as an NGO.[21]

---

[21] In the case of the NGO, the negative and positive rights involved are arguably non-political. A right to be left alone by government and free to organize a religious community may appear to be a civil rather than a political right. Functionally, however, there seems little difference between self-organization and self-government as a federated entity or as a powerful NGO with virtually complete control over its internal affairs. In both cases, the rights involved are quite different from paradigmatic civil rights, such as the right to own private property.

Finally, a dissident member of a self-governing governmental or non-governmental group would have a negative right vis-à-vis that group, which may
amount to a right of exit.[22] Moreover, such a dissident would also have a
positive right of participation in relation to the formation of a new group or to
active adhesion to another existing group.

From the standpoint of the dialectic between self and other that animates the
politics of the pluralist polity, there is an important distinction between policies that
impact on the very identity of self or other and policies that apportion benefits and
burdens among the two. In other words, there are policies that threaten the very
survival or integrity of a conception of the good, and others that merely somewhat
advance or hinder the implementation of its societal project without affecting it at its
core. Upon close inspection, it becomes apparent that there is no bright line
between identity-related policies and benefit-burden-related ones. For example, a
complete deprivation of all material resources from an organized religion would
threaten its very identity. Indeed, whereas such deprivation would not directly aim
at that religion's dogma, beliefs, or world-view, it would make it impossible for the
religion in question to carry out basic education and group-worship functions that
may be essential to its survival. Consistent with this, whether a benefit deprivation
also results in an identity-related deprivation is a matter of degree.

In most cases, however, the distinction is workable. For example, a law that
prohibited male circumcision would clearly seem identity-threatening for the
Jewish and Muslim communities within the polity, as circumcision constitutes
an essential link in the covenant between God and Abraham. On the other
hand, the deprivation involved in the *City of Boerne* case decided by the US
Supreme Court,[23] in no way seems identity-threatening. In that case, a landmark preservation law that prevented Catholic religious authorities from
expanding a church building to accommodate a growing community of the
faithful was upheld. While the law inconvenienced Catholic group worship in
the local area, such a burden is hardly identity-threatening.

Ideally, identity-related politics should be relegated to the constitutional
level, and benefit-burden-related politics to the infra-constitutional one. From
a practical standpoint, two difficult issues arise: 1) the already-mentioned
problem of benefit-burden-related politics that significantly threaten self-
identity; and 2) identity conflicts between self and other, such as those
policies those are identity-reinforcing for self are identity-threatening for other
and vice versa. In such a case, conflicts must be resolved according to the
dictates of pluralism's second-order norms (at the constitutional level) and in
relation to a comparison of the respective hierarchy of values within each self

---

[22] A religious group may impose obligations on its individual members only so long as the latter
are free to leave the group and thus escape its communal obligations, if they so choose. From the
standpoint of a pluralist polity, the dissident's conception of the good is prima facie as worthy
of respect as that of the group in which the dissident has been a member.
[23] *City of Boerne v Flores*, 521 US 507 (1997).

and other. In other words, if the competing identity-related claims of self and other are equally legitimate under the relevant second-order norms, then they should be compared in terms of the hierarchy of norms of each, and be resolved in proportion to the relative identity-threat to each. Thus, if the threat to self is clearly greater than that to other then self should be favoured over other, but if the threat to other is greater, then other should be favoured over self. Institutional mechanisms of resolution for such identity-related conflicts among competing conceptions of the good must be available within the political sphere. But whether these should operate at the constitutional or infra-constitutional level, and what political rights would better serve their purposes, are matters that depend on the particular circumstances involved.[24] Because of this, these issues will not be discussed further here. They will be mentioned when appropriate in the course of the following discussion.

1.2.5 Pluralism and the Distinction between Ordinary Times, Times of Crisis, and Times of Stress

The distinction between ordinary times, times of crisis, and times of stress briefly sketched at the outset can be further elaborated consistent with the pluralist conception of politics as the ongoing confrontation between self and other. In ordinary times, conflicts between self and other do not threaten the unity of the polity and find resolution, or at least confinement, within the existing constitutional, institutional, and political framework. Thus, in spite of the fact that a number of struggles relating to identity and to the apportionment of benefits and burdens throughout the polity split the citizenry into a multiplicity of selves pitted against numerous others, the common self that binds all citizens to the unity of the polity remains glued together and shows no danger of unravelling. For such overall common identity to remain secure, no significant group must feel so alienated or excluded from the political life of the polity as to seriously consider abandoning adhesion to the self that binds together the citizenry as a whole. For all groups concerned firmly to adhere to the indivisibility of the polity, the conception of the good of each must be sufficiently integrated and accommodated within the polity that they can generally accept the resolution of identity and benefit/burden conflicts within the existing constitutional and political order as capable of meeting the requisite minimum degree of justice and fairness. In ordinary times, neither self nor other are fully satisfied with their fate and are likely to struggle continuously to ameliorate their respective position. Neither of them, however, is likely to become so

---

[24] On the theoretical plane, conflicts among equally legitimate claims launched respectively from the standpoint of competing conceptions of the good can be resolved through the implementation of 'justice as reversible reciprocity' which allows for comparing the intensity of the respective claims and for resolution in terms of their respective centrality. For a discussion of this criterion of justice, see M. Rosenfeld, *Affirmative Action and Justice: A Philosophical and Constitutional Inquiry* (New Haven, CT: Yale University Press, 1991), at 249–50.

dissatisfied with his or her status or with the existing institutional framework for processing conflicts as to want to withdraw from the polity.

Times of crisis, in contrast, occur when the common identity or the very life of the polity are in imminent peril. The cause of the peril may be external, as in the case of a foreign war, or internal, as in the case of civil war or violent secession. In times of crisis, the conception of the good of self or other is so little integrated or accommodated within the polity that all possible institutional resolutions of the conflict between self and other will strike one or both of them as deeply unsatisfactory and unjust.

As already pointed out, times of stress stand halfway between ordinary times and times of crisis. In times of stress, there is less extensive and less successful accommodation and integration of significantly represented conceptions of the good. Self and other are less likely than in ordinary times to consider an institutional process of conflict resolution to be just or fair. The identity or unity of the common self that is supposed to bind together the citizenry is not disintegrating, but it is destabilized and under various pressures. Whereas violent secession creates a crisis, a push for peaceful secession is likely to put the polity under stress. Whereas the threat to overthrow a democratically elected government seems bound to result in a crisis, the increasing popularity of a non-democratic party within a democracy is likely to cause stress. Whereas a conventional war may cause a crisis, terrorism and the war on terror seems more likely to create stress. Indeed, unlike a military invasion, terrorist acts are likely to be sporadic and widespread causing more psychological than physical harm. Having terrorists hidden within the polity's population would undoubtedly be unnerving and can easily lead to reactions and overreactions, undue suppression of fundamental rights, or exacerbation of ethnic or racial prejudice such that certain selves and the conceptions of the good they endorse may become increasingly unhinged. At some point erosion of accommodation of certain conceptions of the good may place increasing strain on the working unity of the polity's citizenry.

Further inquiry into the effect of conditions of stress on political rights will be postponed till Part 5 below, in order to focus on the role of political rights in contemporary constitutional democracies.

1.3 LIBERAL, REPUBLICAN, AND COMMUNITARIAN APPROACHES TO CONSTITUTIONAL DEMOCRACY AND POLITICAL RIGHTS

Liberalism, republicanism, and communitarianism are complex comprehensive conceptions, and there are many variants within each of them.[25] It is therefore

[25] For example, John Stuart Mill, Frederick Hayek, John Rawls, Robert Nozick, Joseph Raz, and Ronald Dworkin are all liberals, but their respective views range from libertarianism to welfare-egalitarianism. Compare, e.g., J. Rawls, *A Theory of Justice*, above, n. 5, with R. Nozick, *Anarchy, State and Utopia* (New York: Basic Books, 1974).

well beyond the scope of the present undertaking to do justice to their respective views regarding constitutional democracy or political rights, but that is not what is called for here. Instead, I shall approach these comprehensive conceptions from a heuristic standpoint for purposes of sketching out their contrasting approaches to constitutional democracy and politics. These contrasting approaches are rooted in the respective overriding values of each of these comprehensive conceptions, and, as we shall see, bear significant relevance to a pluralistic approach to constitutional democracy and politics. Indeed, though comprehensive pluralism rejects the overriding nature of the paramount values of liberalism, republicanism, and communitarianism, it does have room for them, with some limitations and modifications, within its own dialectical framework.

1.3.1 Liberalism's, Republicanism's, and Communitarianism's Overriding Values and Pluralism

As already noted, liberalism is individualistic as it primes the individual over the group. Its overriding values are individual liberty and equality and its principal aim to optimize the chances of reaching a proper equilibrium between individual autonomy and individual welfare.[26] For libertarians, such equilibrium may be best achieved through extensive liberty and private property rights together with formal equality rights. For welfare-egalitarian liberals, on the other hand, sub-stantive equality and positive welfare rights may be necessary even if they limit negative liberty and property rights. Beyond these differences, however, at a higher level of abstraction, liberalism is pluralistic-in-fact and its ultimate goal is to promote the best possible conditions for individual self-realization. Liberalism is pluralistic-in-fact, in that different individuals are bound to have different conceptions of the good or of their self-interest and hence, to use Rawls' expression, are bound to pursue different 'life plans'.[27] Consistent with that, moreover, the principal objective of the liberal polity is to promote the most extensive possible equal opportunity for individual *self-realization*.

For republicanism, in contrast, the overriding value is *self-government*. Leaving aside, for the moment, whether republicanism is compatible with pluralism-in-fact, for our purposes the principal difference between the latter and liberalism relates to a shift in the locus of the conflict between self and other. For liberalism, the conflict is between individual selves and individual others with clashing self-interests and life-plans. The liberal polity, in turn, is supposed to provide appropriate rules and conditions consistent with respect for individual liberty and equality that make for fair competition between self and

---

[26] See M. Rosenfeld, *Just Interpretations*, above, n. 3, at 216. The following discussion draws upon the more extensive treatment of the relation between comprehensive pluralism and liberalism, republicanism and communitariansism, in ibid, at 213–34.

[27] See J. Rawls, *A Theory of Justice*, above, n. 5, at 407–16.

other in their respective and in most cases antagonistic quest for self-realization. Republicanism, on the other hand, requires subordination of individual self-realization to deliberative self-government. This emerges clearly in the context of Rousseau's republicanism, in terms of the distinction he draws between the private individual (*bourgeois*) and the public citizen (*citoyen*).[28] For Rousseau, each person is both part of the governed and of the governors, a private individual with particular desires and notions of self-interest and a public citizen obligated to join with fellow citizens to govern the polity according to the dictates of the 'general will'.[29] Within this vision, the conflict between self and other is not a conflict *among* individuals, but rather a conflict *within* each individual. The conflict between self and other is that between the *bourgeois* and the public citizen within each of us, between the private person's self-interested particular will and the public citizen's obligation to govern herself and help govern over others by imposing the polity's general will above the clash of particular wills. Whereas the notion of the 'general will' advanced by Rousseau remains mysterious—he characterizes it as the sum of differences between all the individual wills or as the 'agreement of all interests' that 'is produced by opposition to that of each'[30]—it is clear that self-government must achieve priority over self-realization. Thus, the political self within each of us must prevail over our private self (which for purposes of self-government must be cast as the other or as one other among many others if we take account of the fact that all public citizens are also private persons). In short, civic virtue must prevail over self-interest.

For communitarianism, community is paramount and *communal solidarity* the overriding value. For communitarians, moreover, the self is the community and the other is that which lies outside the relevant community. The communities in question may vary in their composition, origin, ideology, etc. They may be national, ethnic, or religious communities or primarily socio-political ones, such as communes or kibbutzim. Once again, I leave aside for the moment whether communitarianism is compatible with pluralism. What is essential, is that for communitarianism the other is always 'outside'. Most obviously, the 'others' are other communities. However, to the extent that an individual within a particular community departs from communal values and objectives, he or she becomes, at least in part, an 'other' vis-à-vis his or her own communal self. In other words, the dissident individual places herself, 'outside' her community. Unlike a deficiency in civic virtue in the context of republicanism, which involves some failure to curb or dominate one's *own* self-interest or particular will, dissent from one's community is more like betrayal, as it involves a breach of communal solidarity (and hence implies some kind of loyalty to some 'outside' rival community).

[28] *See* J. J. Rousseau, *The Social Contract* (Riverside, NJ: Haffner Press, 1947) (ed. C. Frankel), at 14–16. [29] Ibid.
[30] Ibid, n. 2, at 26.

It is now time briefly to address whether and to what extent, liberalism, republicanism, and communitarianism may be compatible with pluralism. As already noted, liberalism is pluralistic-in-fact. From a normative standpoint, moreover, liberalism is *individualistically* pluralist. This means that liberalism tolerates and even encourages a plurality of views, projects, beliefs, commitments, and interests among individuals. It does not, however, recognize or promote group-based pluralism. Thus, for example, religious freedom for the individual is crucial within liberalism, but not the collective life or project of any particular religion.[31] In other words, in liberalism, groups have no organic collective identity of their own; they become reduced to associations or mere aggregates of individuals. Consistent with this, therefore, from the standpoint of comprehensive pluralism, liberalism is partially pluralistic. Accordingly, liberal constitutional democracy and liberal political rights seem bound to have some relevance in relation to identifying political rights consistent with comprehensive pluralism.

It is by no means as clear that republicanism or communitarianism are compatible with pluralism. Some have even argued that they are not.[32] Moreover, one can easily imagine that republican self-government is incompatible with the pursuit of a plurality of interests,[33] and that communitarianism requires homogeneity and organic unity.

Nevertheless, neither republicanism nor communitarianism are necessarily incompatible with some degree of pluralism. For republicanism, the question is whether the general will can incorporate, albeit by transforming them, a plurality of particular interests, or, whether, by its very nature, it must stand against all particularity. It is difficult to answer this question with respect to Rousseau given the opacity of his conception of the general will. If the general will is regarded as a universal will that stands against all particularity, then republicanism would be incompatible with pluralism, and self-government would exclude self-realization.[34] Going beyond Rousseau, however, it seems quite plausible to conceive the general will as meant to incorporate as much as possible what is sought by particular wills consistent with maintaining

---

[31] It may be that by a combination of individual freedom of religion rights and freedom of association rights, the collective aims of a particular religion may obtain full protection within a liberal framework. Nevertheless, that protection would be purely contingent and parasitic on the vindication of the individual rights involved.

[32] See, e.g., C. Sunstein, *The Partial Constitution* (Cambridge, MA: Harvard University Press, 1993), at 20 (arguing that classical republicanism postulates that civic virtue can only flourish in small, homogeneous communities); and M. Sandel, *Liberalism and the Limits of Justice* (Cambridge: Cambridge University Press, 1982), at 151 (contrasting the unity of community in a constitutive sense to the plurality associated with Rawlsian liberalism).

[33] See C. Sunstein, *The Partial Constitution*, above, n. 32, at 26–27, 38–39 for a statement on this position.

[34] Consistent with this kind of interpretation it has been suggested that Rousseau was a precursor to totalitarianism. See R. Masters, *The Political Philosophy of Rousseau* (Princeton, NJ: Princeton University Press, 1968), at 315.

neutrality among particular wills and with maintaining the good of the polity as a whole as paramount. In other words, there is no logical impediment against there being an overlap between the general will and at least part of what is aimed for by some, if not all, particular wills. Consistent with this, republicanism can be compatible with at least some form of limited pluralism.[35] Moreover, republicanism would thus be relevant for comprehensive pluralism. Indeed, the work of the general will would seem to bear some analogy to that of pluralism's second-order norms. Even in that case, however, republicanism and comprehensive pluralism would remain fundamentally different. Unlike for republicanism, for comprehensive pluralism civic virtue and self-government may be positive values, but they would never become overriding ones.

At first, communitarianism and communal solidarity seem completely incompatible with pluralism. Whether the glue is ethnic, religious, or ideological, the relevant community is the self and the rest of the world is not only 'other', but completely 'outside'. Other communities are thus alien if not downright the enemy.[36] In this conception, pluralism looms as inherently antagonistic to the overriding values of communal solidarity and group loyalty.

Upon closer inspection, however, even if comunitarianism and pluralism remain incompatible from a metaphysical standpoint, they need not be mutually exclusive from a political standpoint. Even if one thinks in purely communal terms, one can distinguish between *intra*-communal and *inter*-communal relationships. Assuming, for the moment that intra-communal relations completely preclude pluralism, it does not follow that inter-communal ones must likewise do so. For example, in a polity made up of several distinct ethnic groups, it is quite plausible for each of them to embrace inter-communal pluralism. Thus, each of these groups may become allied with all the others to promote group rights against individual rights, and ethnic-based group autonomy and self-government against universal, polity-wide majoritarianism. Furthermore, in contemporary polities that are pluralistic-in-fact, communal based pluralism may extend beyond the realm of constitutional design into that of everyday politics. For example, religions may join hands to combat the forces of secularism within their polity. In that case, religious leaders are likely to forge bonds of limited solidarity among themselves for purposes of their joint struggle while each of them would remain loyal to his or her own religious tradition. Also, to the extent that the different religions involved are antagonistic to one another, the religious leaders involved may at once share limited solidarity against secularism while remaining adversaries on issues of religious dogma and doctrine.

---

[35] See F. Michelman, 'Law's Republic' (1988) 97 *Yale LJ* 1493 (elaborating a deliberative republican approach that incorporates pluralism-in-fact).
[36] Cf. C. Schmitt, *The Concept of the Political* (Chicago, IL: University of Chicago Press, 1996) (G. Schwab trans.), at 54 (conceiving politics as the struggle between 'friends' and enemies); D. Luban, 'A Theory of Crimes Against Humanity' (2004) 29 *Yale J Int'l L* 85, at 122.

As noted above, in many contemporary pluralistic polities, communities are unlikely to remain impervious to outside views or influences. As the struggle within certain religions to open the clergy to women demonstrates, it is often difficult neatly to separate intra-communal from inter-communal relationships *within* the same community. As separate communities interact and become open to incorporating certain outside influences, communitarianism becomes adapted to coexistence with some degree of pluralism. Accordingly, some kinds of contemporary communitariansim are relevant to pluralism though the latter rejects the paramouncy of communal solidarity.

1.3.2 Comparing Liberal, Republican, and Communitarian Political Rights

Actual contemporary constitutional democracies and the political rights they promote are likely to contain liberal, republican, and communitarian elements that coexist side by side.[37] It is useful, however, to distinguish between a liberal, republican, and communitarian paradigm for constitutional democracy and political rights. Not only do these contrasting paradigms provide helpful heuristic tools that facilitate critical appraisal. But also, because each of these paradigms is in its own way partially open to pluralism, a comparison between them can pave the way for the elaboration of an alternative paradigm consistent with the normative dictates of comprehensive pluralism.

Under the liberal paradigm, constitutional democracy and political rights should be devised so as to maximize equal opportunity for individual self-realization; under the republican paradigm, so as to enable the citizens of the polity to resolve its problems and conflicts through self-government and the spread of civic virtue; and, under the communitarian paradigm, so as to reinforce the community or communities involved by promoting and privileging the bonds of communal solidarity.

In the liberal vision, constitutional democracy and political rights are primarily necessary to protect the individual from undue interference with his or her pursuit of self-realization. Within this perspective, political rights would be subordinated to civil rights and constitutionally constrained government kept to a minimum.[38] In a liberal paradise, everyone would be adequately

---

[37] See, e.g., the Spanish or Canadian Constitution, which protect core liberal rights, such as freedom of expression and individual equality; self-government (and hence arguably republican) rights through federalism or devolution of powers to 'autonomous regions'; and, communitarian rights, such as those granted to Anglophones and Francophones or to indigenous groups under the Canadian Constitution, or those that flow from the increased powers of autonomous regions, such as Catalonia, in Spain. Spanish Constitution, Part VIII, Chapter 3, Self-Governing Communities, ss. 143–58; Constitutional Amendment, 1999 (Quebec), Amendment to Constitution Act, 1867 (excludes Quebec from the section relating to the organization of schools in the province (s. 93), thus granting Quebec the sole power to determine the system of education used there).

[38] Cf. R. Nozick, *Anarchy, State and Utopia*, above, n. 24, at 26–27, for an argument that the most extensive government that can be justified is the minimal 'night-watchman' state limited to

equipped to pursue self-realization, no one would interfere with his neighbour, and government and political rights would be largely superfluous. However, because down on earth there are always actual and potential threats to the unimpeded pursuit of individual self-realization, the state is a necessary presence and politics inevitable.

In the liberal vision, neither the state nor politics becomes a vehicle for individual self-realization. The state and politics must be used to prevent or remove impediments to the pursuit of individual self-realization, which pursuit itself remains *outside* of politics. Accordingly, the liberal state and liberal politics are supposed to assume an essentially negative role: they must insure that the individual be (sufficiently) left alone to be able meaningfully to devote his or her self to the pursuit of self-realization.

What is actually required for the individual to be free of undue impediments in her quest for self-realization depends on which conception of liberalism is at stake. For libertarians, individuals are largely self-sufficient, provided the state protects their fundamental negative rights. This requires a minimal Nozickean state that does not intervene in the economic sphere other than to prevent or punish interference with the free market. In this scenario, moreover, there is very little use for politics, and distinct political rights would be confined to the right to vote, to allow the citizenry to replace those in charge of government who do not carry out satisfactorily the minimal state's night-watchman's duties. Consistent with the Lockean metaphor, the state's governors should be viewed as trustees of the citizens,[39] and the latter should be able to replace those who must act on their behalf to secure the space for individual self-realization whenever a majority of the citizenry feels that their 'trustees' have let them down.[40]

At the other end of the spectrum, for welfare-egalitarian liberals, the state apparatus must be massive as it is entrusted with an extensive distributive function. The welfare state must insure that each individual within the polity is guaranteed a level of material well-being that will enable her meaningfully to pursue individual self-realization. Because in a complex contemporary

---

affording protection against foreign enemies, providing police protection against physical violence and interference with private property and supplying the institutional support necessary for the enforcement of private contracts.

[39] See J. Locke, *Two Treatises of Government: Second Treatise* (New York: Mentor Books, 1960), § 135 (P. Laslett ed.), at 375–76.

[40] The space for government policy choices is highly confined within the libertarian vision, since extensive protection of negative rights combined with prohibition against interference with free markets leave very little to the discretion of governors or of their constituencies. Ideally, there would be no need for voting or voting rights, as the performance of those in charge in government would be amenable to universally accepted criteria of rational determination. In practice, however, there are no universally accepted criteria for evaluating performance in office under evolving conditions. Accordingly, majority rule is introduced as the best available default mechanism, and the political rights it requires—namely, voting, since the other relevant rights, such as freedom of expression and of assembly are already guaranteed civil rights—must be afforded institutional protection.

economy, the private sector cannot alone provide sufficient material welfare to all, the government must administer public goods so as to fulfill the basic needs of all.

Whereas the liberal-welfare state is a maximal rather than a minimal state, the former no more than the latter is supposed to be a *political* state. Neither of these states is meant to have a direct role in the pursuit of individual self-realization, but instead, is supposed to guarantee the requisite preconditions to equality of opportunity in such pursuit. The night-watchman state does so by fulfilling a police function; the welfare state by *administering* as efficiently as possible the distribution of material resources necessary to grant all individuals the requite minimum of welfare consistent with an equal opportunity to pursue self-realization.[41] Neither the night-watchman state not the welfare state is thus political[42] and they hence both call for minimal political rights. As already mentioned, the minimal state promotes negative rights and confines the legitimate role of political rights to control over attempts to unduly increase or abuse governmental power. For its part, the liberal-egalitarian welfare state concentrates on welfare entitlements and largely restricts legitimate political rights to maintaining accountability with respect to efficiency and corruption issues relating to the vast state administrative apparatus.[43]

In contrast to the narrow space left to politics by liberalism, in the republican vision all intersubjective dealings—and if one accounts for the Rousseauean struggle between self and other within each individual, all subjective dealings as well—fall within a nearly all-encompassing realm of politics. Paradoxically, if all or nearly all is politics, or within the realm of the political (understood as involving the responsibility to set and to manage the course of the polity), then there may be little left for constitutionalism or political *rights*. In a most extreme Rousseauean universe, with primary emphasis on his dictum that society must 'force' all its members to be free,[44] and in which civic virtue is interpreted as requiring complete surrender to a general will that stands completely against all

---

[41] Cf. J. Habermas, 'Paradigms of Law' in M. Rosenfeld and A. Arato (eds.) *Habermas on Law and Democracy: Critical Exchange* (Berkeley, CA: University of California Press, 1998), at 13–25 (distinguishing between a 'bourgeois-formal' and a 'social-welfare' paradigm of law, the first concerned primarily with negative rights, the second with the administration of welfare which reduces the citizen to being a 'client' of the state). In neither of these paradigms can one detect any significant input traceable to politics.

[42] This does not mean, of course, that critiques of either or both of these are not political. Calls for the overhaul of the minimal state on the grounds that it exacerbates disparities in wealth or of the welfare state on the grounds that it fosters passive dependence, for example, are quite obviously political in nature.

[43] Arguably, this latter political function can be exercised through the right to vote for political officials accountable for the proper functioning of the state's administrative apparatus. It is quite plausible, however, to maintain that the integrity of the administrative state is better protected by an impartial judiciary than by elected politicians. In the latter case, the scope for legitimate political rights would be even more modest.

[44] J.-J. Rousseau, *The Social Contract* (1762) (London: Penguin Books, 1968) (Maurice Cronston trans.), at 63–64.

private interests, all intersubjective dealings would be within the realm of the political as defined above, but civic virtue and all norms related to the political would be *moral* norms, not political ones.

Moral norms regulate internal relationships as opposed to legal and political norms which, as we have seen, operate with respect to external relationships.[45] Accordingly, if civic virtue demands the political involvement of all, and requires that each person surrender private needs and interests to the general will, then there is no room for political rights, only for political duties. Moreover, in this scenario virtually no role is left for politics in the conduct of the affairs of the polity: they must be settled according the all-encompassing morals of civic virtue which operates primarily through self-denial (of the bourgeois 'other' within the public citizen's 'self'). Finally, consistent with this, there is little room for either constitutional politics or ordinary politics as the realm of external relations would be completely subordinated to that of internal ones. In other words, there would be no room for politics, only for legal-political reinforcement of the all-encompassing moral norms embodied in civic virtue.

In a more moderate conception of republicanism open to some degree of pluralism, however, democracy and political rights can play a prominent role. If the general will is understood as capable of incorporating objectives that are in part compatible with a plurality of extant private interests, and if the exercise of civic virtue is viewed as involving comparable measures of morals and politics— i.e., an internal obligation to promote self-rule for the common good combined with an external obligation to negotiate with all other citizens so as to shape the actual definition and pursuit of the public good encompassed within the general will in ways that can accommodate as many different private preferences as possible—then self-government involves political choice as well as moral imperative. Indeed, the need for negotiation and accommodation in the course of the process of endowing the general will with a concrete substantive content calls for both constitutional and ordinary politics. In this conception, although self-realization is subordinated to self-government, the former is not altogether excluded by the latter. Accordingly, to the extent that it is possible to draw on different conceptions of self-realization to shape the course of self-government,

---

[45] For a more extended discussion on this distinction, see M. Rosenfeld, *Just Interpretations*, above, n. 3, at 69–75. This distinction is meant to be understood as a relational one and not as one designed to settle substantive content-based issues. The same norm, 'thou shalt not kill', for example, may be both a moral and a legal–political one. It is a moral one inasmuch as it is an 'internal' prohibition arising from the relationship between God and humans, or out of the basic precepts of secular humanistic morality. On the other hand, it is an 'external' prohibition subject to legal sanction to the extent that it is prescribed pursuant to a law enacted by a democratically elected parliament. Some norms are purely 'internal', such as 'thou shalt never lie to a friend' with no external consequences in case of transgression. Conversely, other norms are inherently external, such as 'thou shalt drive on the right side of the road', i.e. there is nothing inherently moral or immoral about driving on the right or left side of the road, though it may be derivatively immoral to do so if it is against the law and if it thus unduly endangers the life and safety of others.

the institutional framework guaranteed by constitutional democracy and the protection of political rights can be regarded as playing an indispensable role within this alternative, more moderate republican vision.

Moderate republicanism open to some degree of pluralism requires strong constitutional protection of democratic politics as well as broad-ranging political rights and duties. Constitutional protection should extend not only to voting, but also to political party formation, organization, and management, as deployment of a multiplicity of political parties becomes imperative for purposes of a well functioning, politically grounded self-government drawing on a plurality of views. Moreover, given the priority that republicanism grants to self-government over self-realization, a moderately republican constitution would have to insist on maintenance of a vigorous, unimpeded democratic process. Finally, with respect to the individual citizen, moderate republican constitutionalism should combine protection of extensive political participation rights with imposition of an obligation to participate in self-government through a legally enforceable duty to vote in periodic elections, for example.[46]

Communitarianism shares with liberalism the pursuit of self-realization, though in the case of communitarianism it is collective self-realization rather than individual. Furthermore, communitarianism shares with republicanism the need for self-government, though for communitarians that need is but a means to better secure communal integrity and solidarity. Thus, how much self-government, and of what kind, depends on many factors, such as whether the community involved is a minority within a multi-ethnic polity or whether it encompasses the totality of the polity by itself. Finally, what kind of constitutional democracy or political rights are called for under a communitarian vision depends on whether a communally monistic or a communally pluralistic collectivity is involved.

In a communally monistic collectivity, such as a homogeneous ethnocentric nation-state, there may not be a strong need for a vigorous constitutional democracy or for extensive political rights.[47] In a communally pluralistic polity, however, constitutional democracy and political rights, in particular collective ones, are crucial to the maintenance of communal integrity. Where various groups are concentrated in different geographic locations, constitutionally protected identity-based federalism may provide the best means to intra-communal self-determination and harmonious inter-communal coexistence. Where different communities

---

[46] Some contemporary democracies make voting mandatory and the failure to vote subject to legal sanction, such as the levy of a fine. See e.g., Argentina, Australia, Austria, Belgium, Bolivia, Brazil, Dominican Republic, Egypt, Greece, Guatemala, Honduras, Liechtenstein, Luxembourg, Panama, Philippines, Switzerland (some cantons only), Singapore, Uruguay, and Venezuela.

[47] This observation is consistent with C Schmitt's conception of an anti-pluralist ethnocentric constitutionalism, the purpose of which was the advancement of the German ethnos and culture and its protection against all 'external' enemies, including those within Germany's borders. In Schmitt's view, the collective self-realization of the German ethnos might as well be entrusted to a dictator imbued with the German spirit. See C. Schmitt, *The Crisis of Parliamentary Democracy* (1923) (Cambridge, MA: MIT Press, 1985) (E. Kennedy trans.).

are not neatly separated geographically, on the other hand, other means can be used to bolster intra-communal unity and solidarity. For example, as exemplified by the *millet* system used in the Ottoman Empire, in a religiously pluralistic polity, each religious community can be granted powers of legislation and administration over communal affairs and over the personal affairs (e.g., marriage, divorce) of individual members of that community. Moreover, depending on whether a particular community constitutes a majority or a minority within the polity, the nature of the most important collective rights may vary. For a majority community, political rights of self-determination and self-government would seem paramount; for a minority community, in contrast, collective civil rights would seem most urgent, such as, for example, a collective freedom of religion right which would prevent legislative majorities within the polity from interfering with the intra-communal affairs of the religious minority involved.

In one respect, communitatianism is like liberalism and both are unlike republicanism. For republicans, self-government and hence politics—or at least the political—encompass all human endeavours. In contrast, as already mentioned, for liberals, much of individual self-realization is besides or beyond politics. To a significant extent, for communitarians self-realization in the form of the achievement of intra-communal solidarity is, strictly speaking, outside of politics. Thus, fulfilment of the communal life prescribed by a minority religion may well depend on the protection of the religious community involved from certain encroachments by majoritarian politics.

Though both liberal individuals and communally oriented groups need protection from external political forces, communally solidaristic groups seemingly more than liberal individuals also require political power to manage their intra-communal life. Thus, within the communitarian vision, communal units must combine freedom *from* external politics and freedom to conduct internal politics to guide intra-communal life and promote communal solidarity. In other words, communal units must all be protected from external domination and granted power over internal affairs, including the power to stifle individual dissent within the community to the extent that it poses a threat to communal solidarity.

There seems to be a paradox in that protection against external threats posed by more powerful groups or political majorities requires negative rights that are much like liberal rights, whereas the powers required to deal with internal intra-communal threats will inevitably include some that are bound to be highly illiberal. Moreover, beyond the seeming incongruity of demanding liberal rights for oneself while at the same time insisting on illiberal powers over others, there is a further and potentially even more serious contradiction. Viewing the polity as a whole from a communitarian standpoint, communal solidarity should operate at the level of the nation-state as the relevant unit, not at that of ethnic or religious minorities within it. Accordingly, polity-wide relationships would be intra-communal, and all claims by minority groups perceived as threats to solidarity within the nation-state treated as dangerous intra-communal dissent properly subject to suppression. On the other hand, from the standpoint of a minority group involved, relations with the polity as a whole would be clearly inter-communal, and as such would call for negative rights that would allow the minority to defend its collective identity and to promote what it deems to be its legitimate intra-communal solidarity.

There are two complementary ways to minimize this problem: one formal and the other substantive. On the formal level, this problem can be addressed by inserting in the polity's constitution which groups are entitled to communal autonomy, what rights such autonomy entails, and how conflicts among such communal entities or among the latter and the polity as a whole ought to be resolved. Once these questions are constitutionally settled, friction and conflict may be significantly reduced. On the other hand, by constitutionally enshrining certain forms of group autonomy and groups rights, the polity does not necessarily solve the problem once and for all, but rather shifts the locus of conflicts from the realm of ordinary politics to that of constitutional politics. Such a shift may nonetheless be advantageous as constitutional arrangements may be regarded as more authoritative and weighty and they may be more difficult to change provided amendment criteria are sufficiently onerous. Furthermore, the shift in question is likely to require reinforcement of rights to participate in constitutional politics, including rights of exit, such as rights of secession in case inter-communal consensus breaks down.

On the substantive level, the tension between the pursuit of inter-communal tolerance and that of intra-communal intolerance can be dramatically reduced by embracing communal-based pluralism. Consistent with such pluralism, the polity would comprise a multiplicity of overlapping and intersecting communal groups that would remain fairly open to mutual influence. This, in turn, would make for inter-communal as well as intra-communal solidarity, and would allow dissidents within a group either to foster intra-communal changes or to voluntarily leave their own groups and pursue other group affiliations. Moreover, within this vision of communal pluralism, communal solidarity would still remain paramount, but multiple group affiliations requiring varying degrees of communal solidarity would improve the chances of striking a balance between intra-communal and inter-communal commitments. Finally, whereas this kind of pluralistic communitarianism would still require protection of collective rights, including collective self-government rights, it would greatly reduce the need for illiberal treatment of dissidents within one's group.

1.4 PLURALISM AND THE DERIVATION OF POLITICAL RIGHTS

As indicated in the course of the preceding discussion, liberalism, republicanism, and communitarianism are all compatible with varying degrees of limited pluralism. They hence afford a glimpse into what a pluralist regime of political rights might include. To obtain a fuller and more accurate account of the complement of political rights required by comprehensive pluralism, however, it is necessary to shift perspectives. In Part 1.3, I examined perspectives within which pluralism occupied a subordinate position; in what follows, I return to the issues raised in Part 1.3 from the perspective of comprehensive pluralism which posits pluralism as paramount. As we shall see, within a pluralist perspective, there is room for limited liberalism, republicanism, and communitarianism, as all three play a subordinate though indispensable role in the elaboration of pluralist politics and political rights. Furthermore, within a pluralist perspective, the determination of political rights is less categorical than relational and hence context-dependent.

1.4.1 Pluralism and Limited Liberalism, Republicanism and Communitarianism

Comprehensive pluralism encompasses limited liberalism, republicanism, and communitarianism in as much as it recognizes that individual self-realization, self-government, and communal solidarity and communal self-determination have a legitimate place within a pluralist polity.[48] Moreover, liberalism, republicanism, and communitarianism play both a mutually antagonistic and a complementary role when viewed from the dialectical standpoint of comprehensive pluralism. Indeed, the struggle between self and other within a pluralistic perspective is neither a purely individualistic one nor an exclusively communal one, particularly if communities are conceived as homogeneous, self-enclosed, organic units. Self-realization may be *within* or *through* one's community, or even outside of the latter. Whether the self be the individual within a community or a subgroup within a larger group, there is likely to be a conflict between self-realization and group-wide solidarity. Whereas liberalism privileges the individual over the group and communitarianism conversely primes the group over the individual, pluralism favours neither. Instead, pluralism seeks to overcome conflicts involving individual versus group, subgroup versus group, and one group versus another, by subjecting the antagonistic first-order norms competing for vindication to the edicts emanating from second-order norms. Furthermore, within a pluralistic perspective, liberalism and communitarianism are complementary as well as antagonistic inasmuch as the vices of an overly individualistic political order can be mitigated by greater communal emphasis and vice versa.

For its part, republican self-government is not justified for its own sake within a pluralist perspective, but rather for purposes of establishing a political course that maximizes inclusion of competing conceptions of the good

---

[48] This draws upon, and expands on, my discussion of these issues in M. Rosenfeld, *Just Interpretations*, above, n. 3, at 216–24.

consistent with the dictates of second-order norms. This means that every member of the polity—be it an individual or a communal member—must to some degree refrain from the pursuit of self-realization to join with others to manage mutual tensions and to foster mutual accommodation. Unlike republican self-government in its Rousseauean incarnation, pluralist self-government doesn't require suppressing all interests for the common good. It only requires working together to implement mutual restraints that will allow for the proliferation of a plurality of modes of self-realization. Accordingly, whereas pluralist self-government is in tension with individual and communal self-realization, it complements these in the sense that it does not allow either to become dominant or one-sided. Conversely, polity-wide pluralist self-government is not supposed to impose a single society-wide common good, but rather to set the stage for coexistence among a plurality of competing conceptions of good. And consistent with this, both the pursuit of individual self-realization and of communal solidarity serve to confine the realm of self-government and to place many societal endeavours beyond its reach.

A well ordered pluralist polity requires sustaining a dynamic tension between liberal, republican, and communitarian tendencies to produce an equilibrium for the purposes of accommodating as broad a spectrum of diverse conceptions of the good as possible consistent with adherence to pluralist norms. Approximation of the requisite equilibrium depends on the deployment of an array of political rights, both negative and positive, of certain rights of freedom *from* politics, and on the imposition of certain duties of political participation. Moreover, the nature and scope of the rights and duties in question are predominantly relational and contextual. These rights and duties are relational in the sense that they are the rights of a particular self against a particular other in relation to an identifiable intersubjective domain. For example, an aboriginal minority may have a right to freedom from subjection to the politics of the non-aboriginal majority within the polity in relation to intra-aboriginal affairs and in relation to regulation of aboriginal lands. On the other hand, aboriginal individuals may have different rights and duties vis-à-vis one another with respect to their intersubjective dealings within the same domain. Also consistent with these sets of relations, from the standpoint of the particular polity involved as a whole, intra-aboriginal affairs are beyond politics, whereas these same affairs are most likely political when considered from within the aboriginal community.[49]

Pluralist political rights are contextual inasmuch as the optimal inclusion of diverse conceptions of the good depends on the nature of the conceptions involved and on the particular circumstances at stake. For example, in a polity comprising several ethnic groups, each living within its own distinct geographic

---

[49] In theory at least, it would be possible for intra-aboriginal dealings not to be political, i.e. not to involve external relationships, but only moral. This would be the case if all involved acted pursuant to internalized moral or religious imperatives rather than on the basis of political objectives.

location, federalism and the political rights it entails may be clearly called for. In contrast, if these same ethnic groups were not split along geographical lines, federalism would most likely be of little use in dealing with inter-ethnic group affairs. Moreover, where federalism is not a viable option, the optimal form of political organization and the particular array of political rights which it would require would depend on the actual contending conceptions of the good and on the degree of antagonism among their respective proponents. For example, where ethnic differences are sharp and intense, it might be preferable to discourage ethnic-based political parties, and to shape political rights in ways that minimize rather than exacerbate ethnic tensions. On the other hand, where ethnic tensions are not that intense, but where the interests of certain ethnic minorities tend to get lost in the shuffle, some degree of ethnic-based political representation may well further the aims of pluralism.

1.4.2 Relational and Contextual Pluralist Political Rights in Action: The Example of Free Speech

The relational and contextual nature of legitimate political rights within a pluralist perspective not only entails that particular political rights may be appropriate in some contexts but not in others, but also that depending on the particular context involved, the same rights may be political or non-political. A good example of such a right is the right to free speech, which will be examined below. Indeed, a functioning democracy is inconceivable in the absence of free speech rights, yet not all conceptions or uses of free speech are in any meaningful sense political.

Certain rights, like the right to vote, are always political and from the standpoint of pluralism are indispensable in all contexts. In the presence of pluralism-in-fact, there are bound to be conflicts between proponents of different first-order objectives that cannot be resolved by appeal to second-order norms. At least in some of these cases, reliance on democratic majorities provides the best alternative and call for enforcement of the right to vote.

Other rights, such as the right to privacy with respect to a person's intimate relations are inherently not political though the determination of whether or not to afford them, or to what extent to recognize them, is political. In other words, persons do not usually use their right to choose with whom to engage in an intimate relationship for political purposes. Accordingly, in almost all conceivable circumstances, the right to privacy with respect to intimate associations is a civil right not a political one.

Free speech rights, in contrast, are sometimes political rights, and at other times non political or only incidentally political. Clearly, democracy cannot function without political will-formation or without open and wide-ranging discussion of political alternatives. On the other hand, freedom of artistic expression or freedom to communicate one's feelings may, but need not, be political, and often is not.[50] For example, an abstract painting may neither be intended by the artist who created it nor understood by the viewing public as conveying a political message.[51] Consistent with this, moreover, freedom to exhibit abstract art need not be protected speech inasmuch as freedom of speech is construed as a political right. Or, more precisely, abstract art need not be protected under a positive political right, but it may have to be protected by a negative political right—i.e., be protected from intrusions coming from politics at large in order to be free to engage in the politics of art—or as a civil right.

Not only is freedom of speech in a democracy bound to be in part a political right, but also, in certain circumstances, political rights may imply at least a limited free speech right even where such right is afforded no protection as a civil right. This latter case is well illustrated by the Australian High Court's decision in *Australian Capital Television v The Commonwealth of Australia*.[52] Australian law prohibited broadcasting paid political advertisements and otherwise restricted political discussion on the airwaves as elections were nearing. The High Court upheld a challenge against this law notwithstanding that Australia lacks a bill of rights, on the grounds that freedom to propagate and discuss political views prior to an election can be derived from the Australian Constitution's guarantee of a system of representative government. In other words, without freedom to exchange political views, there cannot be genuine representative government and hence a right to free speech is an inextricable part of a more broadly encompassing right to democratic self-government.

More generally, political rights cannot be captured by formal definitions or categorical classifications. Whether a right is political depends on its relation to politics and to the political. Moreover, within the perspective of comprehensive pluralism, all external relationship are directly or indirectly political.[53] Accordingly, a proper carving out of political rights requires submission of first-order pursuits to the constraints imposed by second-order norms supplemented

[50] See M. Rosenfeld, 'The Philosophy of Free Speech in the United States,' in Peter Hänni (ed.) *Mensch und Staat* (Friboury: University of Fribourg Press, 2003), at 437 (distinguishing four distinct justifications for free speech: 1) free speech contributes to discovery of the truth; 2) it is a necessary condition of democracy; 3) free self-expression is indispensable for purposes of achieving individual autonomy; and 4) free speech promotes human dignity. Only justification 2) is distinctly political, and the respective domains carved out by each of these justifications vary in scope, with some being more expansive than others though there is a significant amount of overlap among them.

[51] This does not mean that abstract art lacks political significance, or more broadly, that any bright line can be drawn between political and non-political expression.

[52] (1992) 177 CLR 106.

[53] Legal relationships are also external and yet are distinct from political ones. Legal rights and duties are distinguishable from their political counterparts, but there is a strong connection between law and politics, as law can be characterized as frozen or suspended politics. For further discussion, see M. Rosenfeld, *Just Interpretations*, above, n. 3, at 74–83. In a democracy, laws are the product of parliamentary politics, and are subject to subsequent amendment or repeal through further parliamentary politics. Notwithstanding these strong connections, legal rights and duties remain distinct from their political counterparts even if the former depends for their existence on the latter.

by mutual accommodation of competing objectives equally compatible with second-order norms—through democratic politics, including majoritarian decision-making—with a view to maximizing inclusiveness of diverse conceptions of the good. In short, comprehensive pluralism provides a framework for establishing and assessing legitimate political rights, with the actual rights thus identified varying to some degree depending on the particular circumstances involved.

1.5 PLURALIST POLITICAL RIGHTS IN TIMES OF STRESS

As noted in 1.2.5 above, in ordinary times self and other (or more precisely selves and others) disagree and compete with one another, but they reach sufficient accommodation to prevent erosion or fragmentation of the overarching binding self that envelops the polity as a whole. Consistent with that, in ordinary times, citizens can enjoy the full panoply of civil and political rights derived from pluralism's second-order norms, and applied to the actual plurality of competing agendas issued from different conceptions of the good and related to different political perspectives.[54] In contrast, in times of crisis, the overarching polity-wide self is threatened with destruction, either from within or from without, and consequently all other objectives may have to be suspended to provide undivided attention to the fight for survival. In an acute crisis, civil and political rights may have to be temporarily suspended. What is more, even from the standpoint of comprehensive pluralism, the pursuit of pluralism may itself have to be provisionally abandoned till the crisis is overcome. This may sound paradoxical, but remains consistent with the logic of pluralism. Indeed, averting destruction of the space reserved for interaction among a plurality of perspectives must take priority over any actual attempt to foster accommodation within that space.

Times of stress cover the broad spectrum between ordinary times and times of emergency, that is between times where the unity of the polity seems entirely secure and times of struggle devoted to repelling mortal threats posed by an internal or external enemy. Accordingly, it would seem that political rights in times of stress should fall somewhere between the full protection called in ordinary times and the full suspension that may be warranted in an acute crisis.

Upon closer examination, however, it does not necessarily follow that because times of stress are sandwiched between ordinary times and those of crisis that political rights in conditions of stress should be more restricted than those in

---

[54] Different political agendas may be tied to different conceptions of the good, e.g. promoting religion in public schools tied to religious ideologies versus campaigning for secular public education tied to humanistic non-religious perspectives. Different political agendas, however, may also be linked to the same conception of the good when self and other disagree over the best means to the same end. For example, two liberals may differ over whether welfare entitlements promote or stifle individual pursuit of self-realization.

ordinary times. On the contrary, arguably when the unity of the polity begins to crack but is in no imminent danger of collapse, it would seem better to reinforce rather than weaken political rights. Indeed, when self and other begin to evolve from adversaries committed to cannons of civility and rules of fair play toward downright enemies, pluralist democracy and the political rights that sustain it would seem to need reinforcement not constriction.[55]

Whatever the logic behind political rights in times of stress, the shift from ordinary times to times of stress generates its own dialectic which defies the dictates of any straightforward logic. For example, conditions of stress seem to call for militant democracy—that is, a democracy that leaves no room for anti-democratic political parties. Militant democracy, in turn, shrinks the scope of political rights by refusing to extend them to those who seek to use democratic means toward non-democratic ends. By the same token, however, militant democracy affords greater rights—or similar rights bearing greater weight—to all political operatives who pursue democratic ends, by eliminating or severely handicapping some of their fiercest competitors. On balance, does militant democracy increase political rights? Decrease them? Or, change their nature?

To get a better handle on the dialectic at work in shifts from ordinary times to those of stress and from the latter to times of crisis, it is useful to focus on the following exemplary subjects frequently linked to conditions of stress: hate speech and militant democracy; the war on terror; and pacted secession.

1.5.1 Hate Speech and Militant Democracy

Hate speech—e.g., expressing highly offensive, insulting, and demeaning views regarding certain racial, ethnic or religious groups—certainly runs counter to the spirit of pluralism's second-order norms. And, so do anti-democratic political parties bent on using the democratic process to destroy democracy. It does not follow, however, that hate speech and anti-democratic political parties must be banned from the political arena because they contravene pluralist morals. As in the case of crusading religions discussed above,[56] inconsistency with second-order norms is not grounds for suspension. Only interference with the *implementation* of second-order norms is.[57] Consistent with this there may be, from the standpoint of comprehensive pluralism, normative or strategic reasons for tolerating anti-democratic parties or hate speech. For example, an anti-democratic party may provide the means for adherents of a particular religion to

---

[55] See C. Mouffe, 'The Limits of Liberal Pluralism: Towards an Agonistic Multipolar World Order' in A. Sajo (ed.) *Militant Democracy* (Amsterdam: Eleven International Publishing, 2004), at 69, 70 (distinguishing 'agonism' or relation among adversaries from 'antagonism' or relation among enemies and arguing that the goal of democratic politics should be to transform antagonism into agonism).   [56] See above, at 1.2.2.

[57] Otherwise pluralism itself would disintegrate, as acceptable first-order norms would have to be collapsible into second-order norms. Pluralism ultimately depends on maintaining a dialectical tension between first- and second-order norms.

pursue their conceptions of the good, which, as long as it did not trample on similar pursuits by proponents of other conceptions, would remain in conformity with pluralist morals. Tolerance of hate speech, on the other hand, may be arguably warranted from a strategic standpoint inasmuch as suppression of such speech might eventually strengthen rather than weaken its proponents.[58]

There are many plausible arguments for and against toleration of hate speech or anti-democratic political parties, but the only relevant ones, for present purposes, are those that revolve around the distinction between ordinary times and times of stress. Banning hate speech and insisting on militant democracy seem much more justified in times of stress than in ordinary ones. This is perhaps best illustrated by the different ways in which the United States and Germany treat Neo-Nazi speech. As made manifest by the *Skokie* cases,[59] the United States can afford to tolerate Neo-Nazi propaganda because of its minimal effect on its intended audience or on the affairs of the polity. In contrast, in Germany because of the Nazi past and of the fear that the Nazi monster may one day be reawakened, Neo-Nazi hate speech does loom as a potential threat to the unity and integrity of the polity.[60]

More generally, the distinction between ordinary times and times of stress may account for different responses to what Karl Popper has termed the 'paradox of tolerance'.[61] According to this paradox, tolerance of the intolerant may pave the way for the latter to come into power and eventually put an end to tolerance. Popper argues that, accordingly, to preserve tolerance one must be intolerant of the intolerant. Based on the distinction between ordinary times and those of stress, however, it is plausible to argue that from a strategic standpoint it is preferable to tolerate the intolerant so long as the fabric of the pluralist polity is not threatened.[62] Indeed, in the context of the American

---

[58] This rationale has played a prominent role in the United States' broad tolerance for hate speech. In the United States, hate speech is constitutionally protected so long as it does not incite to violence, whereas in most of the rest of the world, hate speech that incites to racial, ethnic, or religious hatred can be constitutionally banned. See M. Rosenfeld, 'Hate Speech in Constitutional Jurisprudence: A Comparative Analysis' (2003) 24 *Cardozo L Rev* 1523.

[59] *Collin v Smith*, 447 F Supp 676 (ND Ill.), aff'd, 578 F2d 1197 (7th Cir), cert. denied, 439 US 916 (1978); *Village of Skokie v National Socialist Party*, 69 Ill 2d 605, 373 NE 2d 21 (1978).

[60] E. Stein, 'History Against Free Speech: The New German Law Against the "Auschwitz" and Other "Lies"' (1986) 85 *Mich L Rev* 277, at 279–80; Note, David E. Weiss, "'Striking a Difficult Balance: Combatting the Threat of Neo-Nazism in Germany While Preserving Individual Liberties'" (1994) 27, *Vanderbilt Journal of Transnational Law* 899–939 (suggesting that Article 194(2) of the Penal Code could be used to combat neo-Nazi hate speech and propaganda); 'New German law restricting cyberspace', *New York Times* 5 July 1997, summary republished by EduCom, 6 July 1997.

[61] See K. Popper, *The Open Society and Its Enemies* (5th edn) (Princeton, NJ: Princeton University Press, 1966), n. 4, at 265–66.

[62] There are of course other arguments in favour of tolerance of the intolerant. For example, consistent with a Millian belief in the eventual triumph of reason through uninhibited public discourse, refutation of the arguments of the intolerant is much more likely to be successful than attempts at suppression. See J. S. Mill, *On Liberty*, ch. 2, 1, at 19–32, in *The Philosophy of John Stuart Mill* (Indianapolis, IN: Hackett, 1961) (M. Cohen, ed.), at 205, 223–37. For present purposes, however, these other arguments need not be addressed.

Skokie cases, for example, the legal struggle over whether or not to permit a march by a small group of Neo-Nazis had a much greater impact than the march itself, which eventually took place with barely any notice.[63] Under these circumstances, suppression of the march would have had greater negative consequences for the American polity than did the isolated utterance of Nazi propaganda largely ignored by the American public.

In times of stress, however, tolerance of the intolerant may pave the way to times of crisis. For example, had Nazi ideology been ruthlessly suppressed during the 1920s and 1930s, perhaps the Nazis would not have come to power democratically only to destroy tolerance and democracy. In post-World War II Germany, it is the memory of the Nazi nightmare and the fear of its possible return that create conditions of stress with respect to Nazi propaganda and Neo-Nazi political activity.[64]

Intolerance of the intolerant undoubtedly shrinks the scope of tolerance, and when intolerant political speech is involved, the result is a reduction of the scope of political rights. On the other hand, as the jurisprudence under the German Basic law exemplifies, intolerance of the intolerant may also bolster other rights, including rights with a distinct political dimension.[65] Thus, one reason offered by the German Constitutional Court in justification of its finding intolerance of pro-Nazi expression to be constitutional was that such intolerance was necessary to uphold the dignity of the post-war Jewish population in Germany.[66] Because of their historical experience, tolerance of Neo-Nazi views in post-war Germany would cause the Jewish community to feel excluded from the communal and political life of the contemporary German polity.[67]

In short, unlike in the United States, in Germany Neo-Nazi propaganda created conditions of stress by threatening to drive out German Jews from the overarching self that binds the German polity together. To counter this threat, the German Constitutional Court prescribed a reduction in the scope of political speech to reinforce dignity rights indispensable to a sense of belonging to the polity and to meaningful and effective political participation within it.

There are obvious analogies between curbing hate speech and embracing militant democracy.[68] In an ordinary democracy, all political parties that abide by the rules of the game are allowed to compete for power whatever their ideology. In contrast, in a militant democracy, political parties that pursue

[63] M. Rosenfeld, *Hate Speech in Constitutional Jurisprudence*, above, n. 58, at 1538.

[64] As this example indicates, conditions of stress may be confined to particular areas of a polity's life or they may be pervasive throughout all areas within the polity.

[65] E. J. Eberle, 'Public Discourse in Contemporary Germany' (1997) 47 *Case W Res* 797, at 824 n. 115, 833–41.   [66] Ibid, at 893 (citing Auschwitz Lie, 90 BVerfGE 241 (1994)).
[67] Ibid.

[68] See, K. Roach, 'Anti-Terrorism and Militant Democracy', in Andras Sajo (ed.) *Militant Democracy*, above, n. 55, at 171, 183.

anti-democratic ends through democratic means can be constitutionally ban-ned.[69] Furthermore, it is also evident that adherence to militant democracy is likely to be more compelling in times of stress than in ordinary times.

There are also, however, significant disanalogies between the two cases. Pure hate speech—i.e., insulting and demeaning expression against a particular group—possesses no genuine social value, and can hence be altogether banned consistent with comprehensive pluralism. If such hate speech is not banned in ordinary times, it is only for purely strategic (political) reasons. In contrast, the anti-democratic agenda of a political party may encompass norms and values entitled to all least partial protection under the dictates of comprehensive pluralism. In addition, upon closer examination, militant democracy taken to its logical extreme seems to rest on an internal contradiction. Ideally, in a democracy, all political views and agendas should be vetted and discussed and eventually submitted to the operative democratic decision-making processes in force within the polity. Moreover, within this ideal scheme, each political party should project a particular agenda distinct from all the other agendas issuing from the competing conceptions of the good vying for vindication within the polity. For each political party to remain true to its unique agenda, however, it would be necessary for it to curb internal heterodoxy or dissent. In other words, to foster optimal inter-party competition and thus best contribute to the ideal of democracy by giving each political position its own voice, political parties may have to be internally non-democratic or even internally autocratic.

Aiming thus for representation for all political views implicitly or explicitly embraced within the polity requires militancy with respect to process—or *process-based militant democracy*. In contrast, what is customarily referred to as 'militant democracy', which calls for suppression of political parties with anti-democratic agendas, involves militancy regarding outcomes—or *outcome-based militant democracy*. In either case, militant democracy requires reliance on anti-democratic devices. Moreover, if one posits that there is bound to be an eventually unavoidable link between democratic means and ends and between anti-demo-cratic means and ends, then process-based and outcome-based militant democracy seem to be at loggerheads.

Both representation of all views, which calls for process-based militancy, and exclusion of anti-democratic political parties, which calls for outcome-based

---

[69] Eberle, 'Public Discourse in Contemporary Germany', above, n. 65, at 825, n. 119 (quoting *Klass Case*, 30 BVerfGE 1, at 19–20 (1970), translated in D. P. Kommers, *The Constitutional Jurisprudence of the Federal Republic of Germany* (Durham, NC: Duke University Press, 1989), at 230 (citation omitted):

> Constitutional provisions must not be interpreted in isolation but rather in a manner consistent with the Basic Law's fundamental principles and its system of values . . . In the context of this case it is especially significant that the Constitution . . . has decided in favor of 'militant democracy' that does not submit to abuse of basic rights or an attack on the liberal order of the state. Enemies of the Constitution must not be allowed to endanger, impair, or destroy the existence of the state while claiming protection of rights granted by the Basic Law.

militancy, seem much more compelling in times of stress than in ordinary times. Indeed, in times of stress, various viewpoints are, or seem, threatened with exclusion, and the unity of the polity is sufficiently frayed to make possible an eventual takeover by anti-democratic forces. No such pressures are present in ordinary times, which allows for greater fluidity in the articulation of political positions and for greater tolerance of political parties with anti-democratic objectives. Accordingly, in ordinary times, neither process-based nor outcome-based militancy loom as necessary or desirable.

In times of stress, perceived threats to the unity of the polity are not only likely to be associated with anti-democratic political parties, but also with illiberal ones. Illiberal parties need not be anti-democratic. For example, a religious fundamentalist party that has the support of a majority of the elect-orate of a polity can remain essentially democratic both internally and externally, and yet systematically spread illiberalism. Even from the standpoint of militant democracy, however, illiberal is not synonymous with anti-demo-cratic, and hence prohibition of illiberal parties in times of stress would not be justified as suppression of anti-democratic ones would be. Even if suppression of the latter is justified in times of stress, suppression of illiberal parties poses vexing problems that go to the heart of pluralism and democracy. This is well illustrated by the case of *Refah Partisi v Turkey*.[70] In a divided decision, the European Court of Human Rights held that the dissolution of the Islamic Party, Refah, the largest party in Turkey's parliament, ordered by the Turkish Constitutional Court was not contrary to the European Convention on Human Rights. The Turkish Court had acted because it found Refah to be a 'center of activities' contrary to the principle of secularism enshrined in the Turkish Constitution. Although Refah's means and ends were both democratic in nature, the European Court's majority found that Refah's advocacy of women wearing headscarves in public places and adherence to the Koran would, if successful, lead to an impermissible surrender of the people's democratic rights to religious authorities who even if backed by large majorities, would imple-ment illiberal policies discriminatory on the basis of sex and of religion. For the European Court's dissenting judges, however, dissolution for mere advocacy of peaceful and legal changes—through constitutional amendment, if necessary—by a political party that is democratic with respect to means and ends and that declares its adherence to the requirement of secularism imposed by the Turkish Constitution, is an unwarranted, overly drastic and disproportionate result.

From the standpoint of pluralism, unlike from that of liberalism, illiberal ideals need not be automatically excluded from the arena of democratic politics. Furthermore, from the standpoint of conditions of stress, if retreat from radical secularism were genuinely likely eventually to culminate in the dissolution of the Turkish polity, then the suppression of Refah would be justified. It could

---

[70] (2002) 35 ECHR 3.

even be defended on grounds of militant democracy, but it would result in less democracy and less pluralism.[71]

On the other hand, if discord over secularism created conditions of stress in contemporary Turkey, but moving away from radical secularism would not risk the break up of the polity, but merely a realignment that may or may not live up to the prescriptions of the European Convention on Human Rights, then suppression of Refah would not be justified. In that case the risk of greater stress would not justify significantly curbing democracy and pluralism in the absence of actual erosion of the rights protected by the Convention.

What the preceding discussion on the *Refah* case illustrates is that conditions of stress do not necessarily call for militant democracy or an increase or decrease in democratic rights or in the reach of pluralism. Instead, the right solution requires a proper readjustment and balancing of competing rights and objectives depending on the particular circumstances involved, and on how far or near existing conditions of stress happen to be from conditions of crisis.

1.5.2 The War on Terror

If the issues surrounding militant democracy invite comparisons between conditions of stress and ordinary conditions, the issues raised by the war on terror require focus on the comparison between conditions of stress and states of crisis. Terrorism, as noted above, can provoke a state of crisis, such as seemed to be the case in the immediate aftermath of the attacks of 11 September in the United States. In the long run, however, as also already emphasized, the war on terror, whether it be that against Al Quaeda, or those against ETA in Spain or, the IRA in Northern Ireland, is more likely to produce times of stress than to sustain a state of crisis.

At first sight, the war on terror seems much more likely to affect civil rights, the rights of criminal defendants, and those of detainees held without charges for long indefinite periods of time than political rights. Upon closer consideration, however, the war on terror is likely to have some effect on certain political rights, such as, for example, the right freely to associate in pursuit of a common political project. Indeed, the war on terror may, at least prima facie, justify infiltration of certain political groups and thus adversely affect their ability to compete effectively in the political arena. Moreover, to the extent that a political party is suspected of acting in concert with, or of pursuing the agenda of, terrorists, such as was the case with the Batasuna party linked to ETA in Spain,[72] the war on terror may give rise to genuine

---

[71] It could still be consistent with comprehensive pluralism, depending on how close the conditions of stress happened to be in relation to conditions of crisis.

[72] See V. Ferreres Comella, 'The New Regulations of Political Parties in Spain, and the Decision to Outlaw Batasuna', in A. Sajo. (ed.) *Militant Democracy*, above, at 133.

militant democracy concerns comparable to those raised by political parties that use democratic means to achieve anti-democratic ends.

The most significant nexus between the war on terror and the political, however, concerns the boundary between a state of crisis and conditions of stress. The more the war on terror is like a veritable war, the more emergency powers may be justified with the consequent diminution of civil and political rights. On the other hand, the more the war on terror approximates combating and prosecuting crimes, the greater is the justification for those institutions that are customarily deployed in times of stress rather than for those appropriate for a state of crisis.[73]

So long as the war on terror unfolds under conditions of stress, two kinds of constraints that may be suspended in states of emergency remain in force: rights-based constraints and democracy-based constraints. For example, it may be justified in times of crisis, but not in times of stress, to suspend habeas corpus rights.[74] Furthermore, whereas ordinary parliamentary democratic politics may be suspended during a state of emergency,[75] no such suspension could be justified in times of stress.

The war on terror does not justify suspension of fundamental rights, but it does allow for recalibration of the scope of such rights to account for greater concerns regarding the polity's security and well-being. This can be accomplished through the judicial deployment of ordinary balancing approaches and proportionality analysis.[76] In the context of the war on terror, the weight of the fundamental rights at stake would remain the same as that ascribed to them in ordinary times. The weight accorded to security concerns and to protection of the polity's identity, however, would be greater in the war on terror than during ordinary times. Thus, in the *Hamdi* case that arose out of the United States war against Al Quaeda and the Taliban in Afghanistan, the greater weight given to the state's security interests in the midst of the war on terror resulted in significantly less extensive procedural rights for a detainee claiming that he was mistakenly arrested as an enemy combatant in Afghanistan than for an ordinary domestic criminal suspect, including one believed to be a serial killer. Even if the presumed enemy combatant poses no greater threat to life than the suspected serial killer, granting the former somewhat lesser procedural rights than

---

[73] Ordinary crime does not trigger conditions of stress so long as it does not threaten to drive a wedge in the polity's collective self. Even intermittent terrorist activity, in contrast, seems likely to render that collective self more vulnerable.

[74] See, e.g., US Const. Art. I, § 9, cl. 2, allowing for such suspension.

[75] See e.g., French Const. Art. 16 giving, president a virtually complete power monopoly during a state of emergency.

[76] See, e.g., *Hamdi v Rumsfeld*, 124 S Ct 2633 (2004) (US Supreme Court plurality opinion used a balancing test to determine the validity of the continued detention without charges of a war on terror prisoner); *Beit Sourik Village*, HCJ 2056/04 (SCT. of Israel, 2004) (Israel Supreme Court use of proportionality analysis to determine the legality of the separation wall designed to protect Israeli civilians from would-be Palestinian suicide bombers).

the latter may well be justified under a judicial balancing approach. Ordinary criminals, and even serial killers do not appear to pose polity-wide threats, or to strike against the very collective identity of the citizenry. Arguably, the threat that would-be terrorists pose against the felt unity and cohesiveness of the polity may alone justify according greater weight to the polity's security interests and hence legitimate some constriction of fundamental rights.

Terrorists, such as those who struck New York on 11 September 2001, Madrid on 11 March 2004, or London on 7 July 2005, or else ETA or the IRA, are not likely to pose a danger of destroying a polity the way a foreign war or a full-fledged civil war might. Nevertheless, terrorism, by its very unexpected and seemingly senseless and random nature, creates fears and anxieties that affect a polity's self-confidence and self-image. These changes in turn, are likely to bring about conditions of stress. Under such conditions, moreover, and in connection with waging the war on terror, collective security and identity reinforcement may justify curtailing the scope of certain rights both civil and political. And with respect to political rights, whereas the war on terror may call for suppression of certain political parties, such as Batistuna as discussed above,[77] just as does adherence to militant democracy, the respective reasons involved are different. In the case of militant democracy, the principal fear is that democracy could be compromised; in that of the war on terror, that security will be threatened and the collective self-image of the polity destabilized.[78]

In short, to the extent that the war on terror unfolds, under conditions of stress, it does not require abolition of political rights or creation of new ones. What is called for, is proportionate readjustment that is likely to lead to some shrinking of the scope of certain civil and political rights. Which rights, and how much shrinking, will depend on the particular circumstances involved.

1.5.3 Pacted Secession

Attempts at unilateral secession, such as those that led to civil war in the United States in the 1860s, invariably create conditions of crisis. Efforts to achieve a pacted secession, in contrast, are likely to arise under, and/or produce, conditions of stress, but may well avoid falling into conditions of crisis. This may seem at first paradoxical or even contradictory, given that the distinction

---

[77] See above, at note 72.

[78] This latter point is vividly illustrated by the *Batistuna* case. In relation to the self-image of post-Franco Spain, where the identity of the polity depends on a delicate balance between a sense of national unity and accommodation of the diversity represented by autonomous regions such as Cataluña and the Basque region, Basque terrorism and separatism seem to pose a much greater identity-based threat than a security one. Indeed, such terrorism risks to upset the delicate balance between unity and diversity, thus raising the possibility of repressive unity such as that imposed by Franco, or that of a civil war between those that would yearn for a return to authoritarian rule to preserve Spain's unity, those who would preserve the status quo, and those who would seek the secession of certain autonomous regions.

between conditions of stress and of crisis has been cast throughout the present analysis in terms of the difference between more remote and more immediate or more imminent threats to the unity and coherence of the polity. Under further analysis, and from the perspective of comprehensive pluralism, however, no real contradiction is involved as the unity or coherence of any particular polity is not an ultimate good. Instead, a working polity that does not actually face any plausible threat of dissolution possesses a viable framework that allows for a sufficient degree of integration among the various selves and others that share the same political space. More specifically, the framework in question must provide for a well balanced array of nodes of identification and differentiation—e.g., through federalism, political party democracy, minority rights—to allow all the selves and others involved to engage in dynamic and peaceful interaction while cohering together through identification with the common overall self that binds the polity together without unduly sacrificing adherence to more particular or local selves. For example, one should be able to be German without abandoning being Bavarian or be at once Italian and also Florentine.

Existing nation-states do not necessarily provide the best suited framework for the achievement of the optimal balance between identification and differentiation within a viable political space. Sometimes, such optimal equilibrium may require integration of other selves within a larger political space, such as that provided by a transnational polity. For example, it is quite plausible that differences between Flemish-speaking and French-speaking Belgians might better be addressed within the larger framework of the European Union than within the narrower bounds of the Belgian polity. On the other hand, at other times, such optimal equilibrium is unlikely to be achieved without disentangling selves and others that are in such constant confrontation as threatens the unity and well-being of their common nation-state. For example, approximating the requisite balance between identification and differentiation was arguably better achieved by splitting the former Czechoslovak nation-state into the Czech Republic and the Republic of Slovakia.

Dissolution and reconstitution of polities to achieve better integration of identification and differentiation is thus not *per se* contrary to the edicts of comprehensive pluralism. *Involuntary* dissolution (from the standpoint of all or of some groups within the polity) is certain to provoke a crisis if it seems imminent, and conditions of stress if it seems plausible but more remote. On the other hand, a successfully concluded secession pact should produce neither crisis nor stress. Finally, the *prospect* of a pacted secession would most likely take place under conditions of stress inasmuch as it would indicate a willingness to negotiate a peaceful pacted secession coupled with uncertainty about the outcome of such negotiations which, if they were to fail, could eventually culminate in a unilateral secession or civil war.

The prospect of pacted secession was considered by the Canadian Supreme Court in *Reference re Secession of Quebec.*[79] The key question before the Court was whether Quebec was legally entitled to secede unilaterally from Canada. The Court answered in the negative, but added that if a clear majority in Quebec wanted to secede, the remaining provinces had an obligation to negotiate with Quebec in good faith in order to determine whether an agreement could be reached on a pacted secession. The Court specified that considerations of democracy and federalism, among others, required that negotiations regarding secession be as serious and solemn as deliberations concerning adoption of a proposed constitutional amendment. Ultimately, these negotiations would be political in nature.

The Court indicated that the outcome of the political process of negotiation at stake was uncertain, and refused to speculate over what ought to follow should negotiations toward pacted secession fail. In terms of politics, negotiations with a view to pacted secession ought to be constitutional politics. Moreover, given the tension created within the Canadian polity by Quebec's separatist movement, these negotiations would seem bound to take place under conditions of stress.

As constitutional politics intended to redesign relationships between self and other within and across polities, a pacted secession, such as that contemplated by the Canadian Supreme Court, deals with subject-related conflicts rather than with those regarding mere benefit or burden allocations. Accordingly, consistent with comprehensive pluralism, such pacted secession should draw directly on the second-order norms that define the pluralist ethos. In short, inasmuch as they arise in conditions of stress, pacted secessions require both enhanced consideration of the other by the self and intensification of the role of self-government. In other words, pacted secession under stress requires greater valorization and protection of the identity rights of self and other and an increased self-restraint to preserve self-government from accrued temptations to govern for self-realization to the exclusion of the other who seeks secession or from whom secession is sought.

In the last analysis, all three cases examined above, those of hate speech and militant democracy, of the war on terror, and of pacted secession, indicate that there is a common task under various conditions of stress. That task is to strengthen or prevent further weakening of the bonds between the multiple selves and others that in spite of the various layers of differentiation that separate them continue to cohere as a unified whole within the bounds of relevant polity. What precisely needs to be done in any particular case depends on the circumstances. In some cases, it requires strengthening certain rights, or strengthening some and weakening others. In other cases, it may require constricting the scope of certain rights to readjust proportionately the interplay between identity and difference. In yet other cases, it requires great self-restraint and self-control to prevent

---

[79] (1998) 2 SCR 217.

outright exclusion of an other that has seemingly become too distant. In any event, conditions of stress do not call for any wholesale rejection or reinvention of the political rights suited for ordinary times. In most cases, conditions of stress merely require refinement and readjustment.

1.6 CONCLUSION

Within the ambit of comprehensive pluralism, politics and political rights are meant to stir external dealings between self and other so as to strive to a maximum possible degree of overall unity combined with accommodation of the most extensive possible diversity. In ordinary times, political rights must encourage vigorous self-government, foster or protect communal solidarity and carve out a space for individual and collective self-realization. In times of crisis, the threat to unity is so grave that the polity may have to suspend its pursuit of diversity and temporarily cease recognition or enforcement of political rights. In the course of a genuine struggle for survival, what unifies or can unify the polity as a whole must trump what does, or could further, divide it.

What is required in times of stress is less obvious because the prime objective at such times may either be a return to ordinary times or avoidance at all cost to deteriorate inexorably towards times of crisis, or both. To the extent that the focus is on return to ordinary times, the emphasis should be on reinforcement of political rights, or of the most important ones even if that can only be done at the expense of others. Thus, if democracy is threatened, recourse to militant democracy, which intensifies commitment to democracy but somewhat restricts its scope, may be the best weapon to ward off such threat. On the other hand, if the task is to prevent at all costs falling into conditions of crisis, the primary concern should be to defuse clashes between self and other. And that may require increasing or decreasing the scope of political rights or adjusting their weight. Thus, in the war on terror, limiting certain civil and political rights may inoculate against eventually having to suspend them altogether in the face of a crisis. Furthermore, in the case of pacted secession, the goal is to narrow the range of differences within a polity, by reassigning increasingly incompatible differences to different polities.

In the end, pluralism does not furnish a list of political rights for each of the three different times discussed throughout. Instead, it provides a logic and a dialectic that allow for a determination of the particular political rights that are best suited for given circumstances. In this context, the political rights suited for times of stress are not that different than those suited for other times. Nevertheless, in times of stress, the same rights are likely to be more or less extensive and more or less intense, depending on whether the most urgent need is to strengthen bonds between self and other or defuse conflict between them.

2

Political Rights and Political Reason in European Union Law in Times of Stress

Damian Chalmers

2.1 INTRODUCTION

Political rights are best seen as a form of reason grounding the justification for politics in popular authorship. Formally, they are set out in the International Covenant of Civil and Political Rights 1996 (ICCPR) and comprise the legal entitlements granted to collective subjects (e.g. peoples or nations) to found a polity and to individual members (e.g. citizens) to participate in and be free from the politics of that polity. The meaning of these entitlements depends, however, upon some notion of the political which enables political acts to be identified and situated, and some idea of what it means for the subjects of these rights to be the bearers of these rights, most notably why they have been granted rights and the norms that are to guide the exercise of these rights. Political rights are not therefore assumed to be securely established in regimes that are either chaotic and violent or oppressive. In this regard, the ICCPR forms part of the liberal Statist tradition, which has an idea of the political as a stable, indivisible political community with sufficient symbolic presence to justify the presence of a machinery of government acting in its name and for that government to ask its subjects to die in that name and a political process which will comprise author-itative decision-making, the ranking of policy options, the regulation of dissent, the development of political visions and the mobilization of support for political decisions.[1] This tradition also assumes certain qualities of its subjects.[2] They are assumed to have the resources to make capable judgments; to know the best route to their own self-realization; and recognize equivalent qualities in other subjects.[3]

---

[1] M. Freeden, 'What Should the "Political" in Political Theory Explore?' (2005) 13 *Journal of Political Philosophy* 113 at 115.

[2] J. Habermas, 'Conceptions of Modernity: A Look Back at Two Traditions', in J. Habermas, *The Postnational Constellation* (Oxford: Polity, 2001), at 130, 133.

[3] C. Taylor, 'The Politics of Recognition', in A. Gutmann (ed.) *Multiculturalism: Examining the Politics of Recognition* (Princeton, NJ: Princeton University Press, 1994).

The traditional idea of political rights rests upon a particular conception of the Body Politic and Practical Reason, which is typically measured in terms of both the praxis and commitments of states.

The European Union represents a paradox for political rights. Whilst it apes some of the trappings of states and contains many of the political rights set out in the ICCPR, it does not set itself up as the government of the European Union acting on behalf of the European people, allocating values and providing a complete set of citizenship rights for this people. It recognizes the importance of popular authorship but there is no commitment to realize this ideal for itself. Alongside this, the European Union commits itself to a new form of politics, a politics 'beyond the nation state' generated by the perception that there is a political deficit which nation-states acting alone or traditional international arrangements cannot address. The consequence is a bifurcated form of political reason in EU law. On the one hand, one finds weak reflections of the traditional political reason and political rights found in states. Alongside this, another form of political reason has emerged: that of the government of the European Union market society. This is located in the institutions which regulate market activities within the European Union and is associated with three political principles. Political porousness requires regulatory institutions to take account of traditionally under-represented interests. Regulatory authorship requires regulatory acts not to be taken in the name of the public good, but increasingly on behalf of various stakeholders. Public–private accountability involves increasing numbers of public acts being carried out by private institutions, but these being held accountable in quasi-political manners to public actors.

If this esoterism of the European Union poses interesting questions about political rights, the circumstances under which many of these are currently exercised adds a further twist. As Rosenfeld's piece in this volume argues, we are living increasingly in an age of 'government under stress'. Government under stress is not crisis government, where political rights are suspended. It acknowledges the importance and presence of political rights, but rather calls for a re-examination of the place, functions, and justifications for political rights in this new age of anxiety and fear. If political rights are a manifestation of the dominant forms of political reason of a polity, government under stress is nothing less, therefore, than a recasting of the political reason of the polity. This existential moment in the case of the Union is complicated by the presence of these two forms of political rights. The emergence of government under stress has, it will be argued, led to a strengthening of that political reason in EU law concerned with government of the market society. This has become the dominant form of political reason, but there has been a recasting of its central principles. Alongside the principles of porousness, regulatory authorship, and public–private accountability, three counter-principles have emerged. These are respectively those of the politics of suspicion, the political community of victimhood, and a public–private notion of police. These do not act so much to negate the earlier principles but merely to counteract and qualify them. Political reason becomes thickened so that, for example, Union law is increasingly porous to a limited set of values and interests but suspicious and antipathetic to the rest. Such a world is a world of unstable and anomalous distinctions in which there is little sense of overall coherence. But, if anything, that is the one redeeming feature of government under stress. It recognizes that it is acting in a fearful and distorted manner. It is within this self-awareness, it will be concluded, that the possibilities of emancipation lie.

2.2 THE TWO TRADITIONS OF POLITICAL RIGHTS IN EUROPEAN UNION LAW

There is an element of European Union law which purports to emulate the idea of political authorship found in states. It has emerged through the externalization of domestic norms of democratic governance as a response to the perceived crisis in confidence in the Union.[4] This element is not concerned with establishing a single United States of Europe in which the Union competencies and capacities comes to replace national ones. It operates at a more epistemological level in which the Union tries to emulate national modes of justification so that the types of political rights found in nation-states are framed at a Union level and the performance of all institutional actors acting within the framework of Union law—be they Union, national, regional, or local—is measured against how political rights are exercised in liberal nation-states.[5] This is the world in which different collectivities—be they towns, regions, nations, or transnational government—all congregate within some EU delimited frame, and, provided all citizens enjoy analogous rights against any of these acts, everything is hunky-dory.[6]

The other form of political reason, participation in the government of the European Union market society, has been prompted by two dynamics: those of supranationalism and the growth of the European regulatory state. Supranationalism is concerned with the primacy of the nation-state. It is impossible to conceive of politics without it. Yet it is also concerned with its insufficiency, both at a functional level to deal effectively with problems confronting it and at

[4] M. Pollack, *The Engines of European Integration: Delegation, Agency and Agenda-Setting in the EU* (Oxford: Oxford University Press, 2003), ch. 4; B. Rittberger, *Building Europe's Parliament: Democratic Representation Beyond the Nation-State* (Oxford: Oxford University Press, 2005), at 27–34.

[5] On elements of 'stateness' in EU law see J. Shaw and A. Wiener, 'The Paradox of the "European Polity"', in M. Green Cowles and M. Smith (eds.) *The State of the European Union: Volume 5: Risks, Reform, Resistance, and Revival* (Oxford: Oxford University Press, 2000), at 64, 75–84.

[6] E.g. I. Pernice, 'Multilevel Constitutionalism in the European Union' (2002) 27 *ELRev* 511; R. Howse and K. Nicolaidis, 'Introduction: The Federal Vision, Levels of Governance and Legitimacy', in K. Nicolaidis and R. Howse (eds.) *The Federal Vision: Legitimacy and Levels of Governance in the United States and the European Union* (Oxford: Oxford University Press, 2001).

a representative level to take external interests into account. To be sure, regulation preceded the establishment of the European Union. However, the European Union is synonymous with the detachment of regulatory policy from the rest of the state. Regulatory agencies were to be independent and were to regulate a 'market beyond the State' with this market being understood as much as a set of autonomous institutions with their own needs and expectations as a set of transactions.[7] If supranationalism is concerned with extending the vision of government, the growth of the regulatory state concerns with giving that government not merely an independent physical presence through the establishment of independent market regulators, both at a national and pan-Union level, but also an independent political presence. Insofar as the Union presents itself as a political actor, it requires these to justify themselves not in exclusively regulatory terms but also politically through notions of representation, accountability, participation, and contestation.

2.2.1 The Political Rights of Union Statehood

The legal manifestations of this form of political reason are most present in the Union debates on citizenship and governance. EU citizenship concerns itself, *inter alia*, with the grant of political right to Union citizens that would allow them to make the same type of claims against the Union polity as against their own states. They are thus granted the right to vote and stand for election in municipal and European Parliament elections, the right to impartial treatment by the Community administration; the right to access to documents held by the Community institutions; and the right to petition the European Parliament and the European Ombudsman for acts of maladministration done by the Community Institutions.[8] The Commission White Paper on Governance emerged out of a crisis of confidence in Commission administration. It seeks to legitimize not just Commission government, but also the administration of Union law and finances by national governments in just the same way that national governments might seek to justify their own administrations. Openness, transparency, inclusiveness, effectiveness, and coherence were to render the benefits of Union government clear to its citizens and give them a sense of ownership over the process. The follow-up to the Commission White Paper on Governance has thus sought to increase rights of participation and transparency,[9] rationalize and simplify

[7] C. Joerges, 'The Market Without the State? The "Economic Constitution" of the European Community and the Rebirth of Regulatory Politics', *European Integration online Papers*, 1997, Vol. 1, No. 19. The view of the Union as a mixed polity, a composite body representing different regulatory and territorial interests, is not dissimilar. G. Majone, *Dilemmas of European Integration* (Oxford: Oxford University Press, 2005), at 46–49.   [8] Articles 19, 21, and 255 EC.
[9] EC Commission, *General principles and minimum standards for consultation of interested parties by the Commission* COM (2002) 704; Regulation EC 1049/2001 regarding public access to European Parliament, Council and Commission Documents, [2001] OJ L145/43.

Union law,[10] and justify and target Union law more effectively through systems of prior impact assessment.[11]

If notions of representation, participation, and accountability exist in Union law, they are not shaped by a strong autonomous pan-Union conception of the Body Politic or Practical Reason. The Union has no general human rights competence through which it can enjoy a hegemony over the allocation of political values.[12] The European Parliament, the central representative body, is not a legislature with exclusive responsibility for making the law and appointing the executive.[13] It has only the power to veto about 50 per cent of primary legislation and veto the appointment of half the executive, namely the Commission, and this exists only with regard to the EC pillar.[14] There are no pan-European parties or a political press to inform the European public sphere.[15] There exists only an attenuated right to participate in or to hold the administration to account in EU law, as whilst various rights can be asserted against EU Institutions, these form only a small part of the administrative apparatus of the Union, with the bulk of the administration of EU law being done by national governments, who are largely free from these constraints.[16] By contrast, the central powers associated with collective self-authorship are firmly retained at the national level, ring-fenced away from EU law. The right to vote in national elections is reserved to a state's own nationals, as is the right to hold office. Determination of nationality is a matter for the state alone to decide and European Union law is not to affect the rights and responsibilities of national citizens.[17]

As democratic politics is an optional activity for citizens, these features structure the praxis of representation, accountability, and transparency at a Union level so that these are fundamentally different from their national counterparts.[18] In the case of representation, election turn outs for the European Parliament are low, notwithstanding there being a requirement to vote in some Member States, with the average turn out for the 2004 elections being 45 per cent, with there being just a 16.96 per cent turn out in Slovakia

[10] EC Commission, *Implementing the Community Lisbon programme: A strategy for the simplification of the regulatory environment*, COM (2005) 535.

[11] EC Commission, *Impact Assessment Guidelines* SEC (2005) 791, 1–15.

[12] *Opinion 2/94 On Accession to the ECHR* [1996] ECR I-1759.

[13] On these features of parliaments see P. Norton, *Legislatures* (Oxford: Oxford University Press, 1990), 179.

[14] On legislative statistics on this see S. Hix, *The Political System of the European Union* (2nd edn) (Basingstoke: Palgrave, 2000), 77.

[15] On elements of a European public sphere see E. Eriksen, 'An Emerging European Public Sphere' (2005) 8 *European Journal of Social Theory* 341.

[16] Member States can request Community Institutions not to disclose documents originating from it. These cannot go behind its request. Case T-76/02 *Messina v Commission*, Judgment of 17 September 2003.   [17] Article 17(1) EC.

[18] On this more broadly see W. Thaa, ' "Lean Citizenship": The Fading Away of the Political in Transnational Democracy' (2001) 7 *EJIR* 503; P. Mair, 'Popular Democracy and the European Union Polity' *Eurogov Working Paper 5/03*.

and a 20.87 per cent turn out in Poland.[19] Broader studies of turn out in
Europe suggest that this will be the case where electorates do not think the body
will take decisions significantly affecting their lives or they perceive an absence
of political competition and choice.[20] Both elements are true in the case of the
European Parliament. It does not have significant involvement in redistributive
or fiscal matters—fields that voters consider matter most strongly to them. Nor
do European Parliament elections have significant immediate effects on the
direction of Union policy, as it is but one part of the legislative jigsaw. A similar
pattern is similar when one looks at other norms. If one looks at the use of the
Transparency Regulation, the central instrument of open government in the
Union, over 40 per cent of applications were made by companies, law firms,
and NGOs, and over a quarter from persons resident in Brussels. The central
items of interest were competition, customs duties, internal market, and the
environment.[21] In short, the central beneficiaries of greater 'openness' were
insiders, usually based in Brussels, concerned with market regulation. Requests
by individuals wishing just to inform themselves about and participate in the
law-making process were almost non-existent. A similar self-reinforcing process
takes place with participation. Whilst the Commission indicates that, in
principle, anybody can submit observations, to make its consultations practicable it defines target groups whose views it thinks are particularly important.
These are defined by the nature of the policy, their interest in the policy, and
whether they are responsible for implementing the policy.[22] In short, consultation is predicated to a large extent upon participation in a pre-existing policy
community, which is inevitably forged by the nature of the Brussels processes.

2.2.2 Participation in the Government of the European Market Society

The second form of political reason is centred around three principles. The first is
the principle of political porousness. The initial elements for this are to be found in
the doctrine of mutual recognition developed in *Cassis de Dijon*.[23] At an ephemeral
level, the doctrine requires the interests of foreign traders to be taken into account
by domestic processes. In this case, the Germans had failed to consider that the

[19] http://www.elections2004.eu.int/ep-election/sites/en/results1306/turnout_ep/turnout_table.html
Turnout for the Polish elections in October 2005 was, by contrast, about 41 per cent. A similar
pattern was present in the United Kingdom. Turnout for the European Parliament elections in 2004
was 38 per cent, whilst for the 2005 General Election it was 61.4 per cent.
[20] C. Jeffery, 'Sloth-Turnout a Problem in UK Politics?' in I. Stewart and R. Vaitilingam (eds.)
Seven Deadly Sins: A New Look at Society Through an Old Lens (London: ESRC, 2005).
[21] EC Commission, *On the application in 2004 of Regulation (EC) No. 1049/2001 of the European Parliament and of the Council regarding public access to European Parliament, Council and
Commission documents*, COM (2005) 348.
[22] EC Commission, *Towards a reinforced culture of consultation and dialogue—General principles
and minimum standards for consultation of interested parties by the Commission*, COM (2002) 704,
19–20. [23] Case 120/78 *Rewe v Bundesmonopolverwaltung für Branntwein* [1979] ECR 649.

content of French spirits may have been properly regulated beforehand in France. It is, however, a broader doctrine which requires market regulators to consider traditionally under-represented interests or values. Under the mandatory requirements doctrine, therefore, authorities are permitted to ignore the arguments of foreign traders, if they can show that there are marginalized interests, which should prevail (e.g. protection of the environment or public health, socio-cultural traditions). At a practical level, therefore, this doctrine does not just bind importing state authorities, but all authorities across the Union. For traders and exporting authorities know that if they are going to sell their goods unfettered in other Member States, they have to take account of the public, consumer protection interests, etc. in the regulation in the home State.[24] Mutual recognition is, therefore, above all, a commitment to pluralism and to plural interests and values being represented before market regulators. It is thus, in many ways, better to see it as part of a principle of porousness which requires regulators to reconsider the limits of the political community of which they form a part. Porousness requires them, therefore, to reconsider the limits of the national market not just by considering the position of foreign traders, but also the role of diffuse interests, such as consumer and public health protection. It also extends beyond the formal notion of mutual recognition to incorporate acts such as Directive 2000/43/EC prohibiting discrimination on grounds of race or ethnic origin,[25] Directive 2000/78/EC establishing a general framework for equal treatment in employment and occupation,[26] and the legislation promoting equal treatment between men and women.[27] Combined, this legislation requires market actors and regulators to recognize, respect, and value a wide range of identities by prohibiting discrimination on the grounds of sex, race, ethnicity, religion or belief, age, disability, or sexual orientation. This valorization and recognition generates a new politics of understanding as it affects the self-understanding of all who participate in this process, both of those doing the recognizing and those being recognized. Heterosexual men have to relativize and relocate their sexual identity in recognizing homosexual identities. Men have to reconsider the division of labour between them and women in applying the norms of equal treatment between the sexes. Hegemonic groups have to re-examine their own cultural histories in explaining why certain racial or ethnic groups have come to be structurally disadvantaged.

[24] EC Commission, *Second Biannual Report on the Application of Mutual Recognition*, COM (2002) 419, 20.   [25] [2000] OJ L180/22.
[26] [2000] OJ L303/16.
[27] Directive 75/117/EEC relating to the principle of equal pay for men and women [1975] OJ L45/19; Directive 76/207/EEC on the principle of equal treatment between men and women [1976] OJ L39/40; Directive 79/7/EEC on equal treatment between men and women in social security [1979] OJ L6/24; Directive 86/378/EC on equal treatment in occupational social security schemes [1986] OJ L225/40 as amended by [1997] OJ L46/20; Directive 86/616/EEC on equal treatment between men and women engaged in a self-employed activity [1986] OJ L359/56; Directive 96/34/EC on parental leave [1996] OJ L145/4 as amended by [1998] OJ L10/24; Directive 2004/113/EC implementing the principle of equal treatment between men and women in the access to and supply of goods and services [2004] OJ L373/37.

The second principle is the recasting of acts of the regulatory state as acts of collective self-authorship. This development emerged in the field of environmental law where decisions over major hazard risks, environmental impact assessment, and integrated pollution prevention and control all involved the establishment of public hearings where stakeholders would be consulted and could express their views.[28] These processes of prior consultation and participation have now extended to decision-making involving food safety, consumer protection, competition law, and electronic communications.[29] In all cases, there is a commitment to, on the one hand, independent decision-making by regulatory authorities, but these are no longer permitted to see the exercise as simply a 'market perfecting' one where the technical norms needed to protect public goods are applied with the least cost to market actors. Instead, there is a commitment that these fora become sites of political contestation where interested parties can debate and political decision-making takes place. To be sure, it is still the regulatory authority who takes the decision but the basis of the decision has changed. The decision is now half about public good and half about political community, which is why the central arenas in recent years for the interplay between science and lay views on risk or between the instrumental rationality of the market place and the inter-subjective reason of the lifeworld are those governed by EC law.

Thirdly, there is the political holding to account of private law-making. The Community is not the first political settlement to allow private bodies to set enforceable norms and realize public tasks.[30] Because of the limits of its resources, it is a body which is, however, heavily dependent on these. One can point to the New Approach to Harmonisation for the setting of product standards recognized throughout the Union;[31] the use of the social dialogues between management and labour to set and implement labour law for the Union;[32] the use of environmental agreements to set standards in the field of ecological protection;[33] the use of the standards of professional associations to fight corruption;[34] and the proposed

---

[28] On this see J. Holder and J. Scott, 'Law and New Environmental Governance in the EU', in G. de Búrca and J. Scott (eds.) *Law and New Approaches to Governance in the EU and US* (Oxford: Hart Publishing, 2006).

[29] Directive 2002/21/EC on a common regulatory framework for electronic communications [2002] OJ L108/33, Article 6.

[30] On its growth in the United States, for example, see J. Freeman, 'The Private Role in Public Governance' (2000) 75 *NYU Law Review* 543; H. Schepel, *The Constitution of Private Governance* (Oxford: Hart Publishing, 2005), ch. 5.

[31] Directive 97/23/EC on the approximation of laws concerning pressure equipment [1997] OJ L181/1.

[32] EC Commission, *Partnership for change in an enlarged Europe—Enhancing the contribution of European social dialogue*, COM (2004) 557, especially Annex 1.

[33] E.g. on carbon dioxide emissions from passenger cars, Decision 1753/2000/EC [2000] OJ L202/1.

[34] The Charter of the European Professional Associations in support of the fight against organized crime set out the offence of private corruption, 1998. http://europa.eu.int/comm/justice_home/news/forum_crimen/documents/charte_en.htm.

extension of systems of self-regulation and co-regulation to broadcasting.[35] The proportion and heterogeneity of tasks delegated to private actors is probably unmatched. Equally significant is that in all cases private actors are not given a free hand but are held accountable for their norm setting to Community Institutions. One thus finds that the most popular policy tool is not self-regulation but co-regulation where the Commission set targets for private parties to meet and duties of accountability with the threat of legislative intervention if the parties do not comply.[36] In the field of the single market, a system of delegation and holding to account is put in place where standards recognized under the New Approach will only be recognized once they have been vetted by the Council.[37] The Commission and the Council have imposed requirements of due process, efficiency, transparency, and pluralism on the standardization bodies. With regard to collective agreements, one finds parallel demands that these be representative before they will be recognized in EU law. In like manner, environmental agreements will not be recognized unless they have concrete objectives and are transparent and representative.[38]

These principles are not invoked in the classic arenas of legislative and administrative politics, but the newer, more fluid ones of regulatory politics described variously by the Commission as a 'common area of free movement'[39] or 'European public order'.[40] Albeit inchoate, the author prefers the term 'market society'. This term gives the idea of the market as, in the first place, an institutional presence, a set of institutions and relations that enable transactions to take place and public goods to be adequately protected. The term also conveys the idea that this is not some crude neoclassical market community, but that the market is a social enterprise based around social ties, which includes not just classic market institutions but also the welfare and policing institutions underpinning the market and seek to address its excesses.[41] The market society would thus incorporate governance regimes regulating market transactions and the deployment of property rights; agencies classically responsible for 'law and order'; and agencies of the welfare state such as those responsible for heath care, social security, education, and public services.

---

[35] EC Commission, *Proposal for a Directive amending Directive 89/552/EC*, COM (2005) 646.
[36] *Inter-Institutional Agreement on Better Law-Making*, paras 20–21 [2003] OJ C321/1.
[37] Directive 2001/95/EC, on general product safety [2002] OJ L11/4, Article 3(2).
[38] EC Commission, *Environmental Agreements at Community Level—Within the Framework of the Action Plan on the Simplification and Improvement of the Regulatory Environment*, COM (2002) 412.
[39] EC Commission, *Towards Integrated Management of the External Borders of the Member States of the European Union*, COM (2002) 233, Annex 1.
[40] EC Commission, *Towards an Area of Freedom, Security and Justice*, COM (98) 459, 9; European Convention, *Final Report of Working Group X 'Freedom, Security and Justice'* CONV 426/02.
[41] On markets as a stable set of social relations between producers that simultaneously implicate public and private actors, see N. Fligstein, 'Markets as Politics: A Politico-Cultural Approach to the Problem of Economic Institutions' (1996) 61 *American Sociological Review* 656.

2.3 THE TRAJECTORIES OF EUROPEAN UNION
POLITICAL REASON IN A PERIOD OF STRESS

Government under stress has come to be associated with the responses and tensions that have emerged since 11 September, yet the bifurcated and attenuated nature of political reason in EU law results in its being particularly vulnerable to a wide range of forms of stress. Possible pandemics from avian flu or SARS; systemic risk in financial markets; the possibility of catastrophic risk from GM crops or global warming; the ineluctable and pervasive growth of organized crime—all these are seen as generating exceptional responses from EU law. Government under stress is a far more pervasive notion, therefore, than simply a series of concrete measures in response to the attacks of 11 September 2001 and subsequent terrorist attacks. The response of the European Union to these attacks should therefore be seen as symptomatic of a more general politics of nervousness being incorporated into and shaping EU law. The history of the war on terror is nevertheless illuminating because it sets out more explicitly and more saliently how political reason within EU law have responded to the idea of 'government under stress'. It suggests, in particular that the latter has been subject to three trajectories.

First, European Union government under stress, unlike emergency government, is posited as a general rather than exceptional reorientation of government. Whilst the traditional justification for emergency government is that its emergency nature prevents contagion of the wider body politic[42] and is thus assumed to be limited in time and confined to discrete fields, government under stress is used to redeploy norms, priorities, and justifications for action in all EU policy areas. The initial Action Plan on the Fight Against Terrorism, passed on 21 September 2001, provided for the adoption of 79 measures, of which only 13 were 'foreign affairs' measures. It was to involve a 'coordinated and interdisciplinary approach embracing all Union policies', so that, in addition to specific legislation on terrorism, new measures were to be adopted in the fields of policing, money laundering, investigation, surveillance, and border controls.[43] A similar pattern took place following the bombings in Madrid on 11 March 2004. The European Council on 25–26 March 2004 announced a new long-term strategy on counter-terrorism involving a further 57 measures, which led to further measures in criminal law, surveillance, the law of evidence and criminal procedure, and border and document control.[44] The unbounded nature of these

---

[42] J. Ferejohn and P. Pasquino, 'The Law of the Exception: A Typology of Emergency Powers' (2004) 2 *ICON* 210, at 233–35.

[43] The latest version of this Roadmap is Council of the European Union, *European Union Plan of Action on Combating Terrorism*, Council Doc. 10010/3/04, 11 June 2004.

[44] Declaration of the European Council on Combating Terrorism, 25 March 2004. http://ue.eu.int/showPage.ASP?id = 406&lang = en.

developments, with many not directed explicitly at countering terrorism,[45] inevitably resulted in the discourse having an uneven effect. It is invoked only where there is a perception of a threat to security, and its force will depend upon the nature and scale of the perceived threat, which can vary over time.

The second trajectory is that of greater integration, administrative consolidation, and centralization. The effect of 11 September was to break political log-jams and transform proposals in the field of policing that had previously been considered too 'federalist' into tools of necessary and effective protection that were included in the Action Plan of 21 September.[46] The 21 September European Council, therefore, stated that the fight against terror was to include a renewed commitment to complete as soon as possible the programme, set out by the 1999 Tampere European Council, of an 'area of freedom, security and justice'.[47] Existing path-dependencies were to be accelerated with the Union's contribution to protecting security being to realize policies to which it had already committed. It was given a more autonomous role in the government of security within Europe following the Madrid bombings. The European Council stated that, from that date, Member States would act jointly against terrorist attacks with an attack directed against any one Member State deemed to be an attack on all of them.[48] To this end, autonomous Union counter-terrorism structures were to be put in place with the establishment of a Counter-Terrorism Coordinator who was to oversee all Union policies and monitor cooperation between Member States.[49]

The consequence was a ripple effect. The Union's specific role in counter-terrorism is enhanced and strengthened and is now set out in the European Union Counter-Terrorism Strategy of 30 November 2005.[50] Its tenet is that the Union can 'add value' to the fight in four ways. It can strengthen national capabilities to fight terrorism through disseminating knowledge and sharing best practice. It can facilitate European cooperation through the sharing of information and the establishment of mechanisms to facilitate police and judicial cooperation. It can develop collective capabilities through enabling collective policy responses. It can, finally, promote cooperation with non-EU states.

The 'war on terror' has, however, also been central to the shaping of the Area of Freedom Security and Justice (AFSJ). This was most apparent at the review

---

[45] The Non-Governmental Organisation Statewatch numbered these new measures at 57, of which it claimed 27 had little to do with counter-terrorism: http://www.statewatch.org/news/2004/mar/swscoreboard.pdf.

[46] J. Occhipinti, *The Politics of European Police Cooperation: Towards a European FBI?* (Boulder, CO: Lynne Rieder, 2003), at 153.

[47] Conclusions of the Presidency of the European Council of 15 and 16 October 1999. At the Extraordinary European Council of 21 September 2001, the Justice and Home Affairs Council was instructed, as a response, to implement as quickly as possible the entire package of measures agreed at Tampere: http://ue.eu.int/en/Info/eurocouncil/index.htm.

[48] Declaration of the European Council on Combating Terrorism, above, n. 44, Section 2.

[49] The Coordinator is Guy De Vries.

[50] EU Council, *The European Union Counter-Terrorism Strategy*, Council Doc. 14469/4/05.

of the AFSJ in 2004 at The Hague. The AFSJ now involves the management of an array of policies and instruments:

> The objective of the Hague programme is to improve the common capability of the Union and its Member States to guarantee fundamental rights, minimum procedural safeguards and access to justice, to provide protection in accordance with the Geneva Convention on Refugees and other international treaties to persons in need, to regulate migration flows and to control the external borders of the Union, to fight organised cross-border crime and repress the threat of terrorism, to realise the potential of Europol and Eurojust, to carry further the mutual recognition of judicial decisions and certificates both in civil and in criminal matters, and to eliminate legal and judicial obstacles in litigation in civil and family matters with cross-border implications.

The systematization and integration of all these measures within a common agenda has been done through making them part of a common security field with terrorist attacks as its central totem.

> The security of the European Union and its Member States has acquired a new urgency, especially in the light of the terrorist attacks in the United States on 11 September 2001 and in Madrid on 11 March 2004. The citizens of Europe rightly expect the European Union, while guaranteeing respect for fundamental freedoms and rights, to take a more effective, joint approach to cross-border problems such as illegal migration, trafficking in and smuggling of human beings, terrorism and organised crime, as well as the prevention thereof.[51]

Security is a selective good as not everything can be protected. It has its own hierarchy of values as to what and who is worth protecting. As early as 1998 a Commission document stated that the purpose of the AFSJ was to secure:

> ...the freedom to live in a law-abiding environment in the knowledge that public authorities are using everything in their individual and collective power (nationally, at the level of the Union and beyond) to combat and contain those who seek to deny or abuse that.[52]

It was set out more explicitly in 2002 where the Commission describes a 'common area of free movement' as securing a:

> level of protection enjoyed in the area of free movement by natural persons and bodies corporate, goods and properties of all kinds, capital, the provision of services and all lawful commercial transactions, as well as attacks on their interests or threats caused by failure to comply with EC or national regulations; crime, terrorism, trafficking...[53]

In other words, the concern is to secure the operations of the European Union market society. This involves not merely protecting it from perceived

[51] EU Council, *The Hague Programme: strengthening freedom, security and justice in the European Union*, Council Doc. 16054/04.
[52] EC Commission, *Towards an Area of Freedom, Security and Justice*, COM (98) 459, 5.
[53] EC Commission, *Towards Integrated Management of the External Borders of the Member States of the European Union*, COM (2002) 233, Annex 1.

external threats, but also ensuring that it does not implode or degrade internally. In this regard, the concern with developing European Union criminal law is particularly illuminating, as criminal law is as much about securing the good behaviour of market actors as about protecting them from third parties.

The third trajectory is that government under stress does not seek a restoration, but a preservation of the status quo. Unlike emergency government, its rationale does not lie in us having fallen into bad times with a wish to return to the good times. Instead, it is based on the rationale that the current good life is particularly vulnerable to external threats. It is about a politics of guardianship, therefore, which seeks to identify, sacralize, and preserve certain existing practices on the grounds that they are central to our way of life and exercise of our freedoms. The Hague programme therefore stated:

> . . . the common project of strengthening the area of freedom, security and justice is vital to securing safe communities, mutual trust and the rule of law throughout the Union. Freedom, justice, control at the external borders, internal security and the prevention of terrorism should henceforth be considered indivisible within the Union as a whole. An optimal level of protection of the area of freedom, security and justice requires multidisciplinary and concerted action both at EU level and at national level between the competent law enforcement authorities, especially police, customs and border guards.

In this the connection drawn between security and freedom is so tight that each is increasingly measured by its relationship to the other with it being difficult to dissociate the two. A secure environment is seen as an a priori condition for the exercise of freedoms, whilst the choice of security measures is informed by the types of institution to be protected. This manifests itself a number of ways. Subjects' capabilities and capacity for self-determination are measured not only in terms of their ability to run their own lives, but also to protect and secure the lives of others. As we shall see in fields as diverse as aviation, the internet, and financial services, subjects are also increasingly required to police the activities over which they have control not on the grounds of protection of some state interest, but to secure the good functioning of the activities they are carrying out.

2.4 THE EUROPEAN UNION RESPONSE TO 9/11 AND PROTECTION OF THE MARKET SOCIETY

The effects of the trajectories described in the preceding section recalibrate the relationship between the two types of political reason present in EU law. It leads to an atrophying of the Statist tradition of political rights whilst leading to an expansion of that found in the government of the European market society.

2.4.1 The Shrinking of the Statist Tradition of Political Rights in Union Law

Whilst security measures have never been characterized by strong notions of popular participation and authorship, the weak notions of popular account-ability and representation have been undermined by a disembedding of administrative and judicial networks from their national political contexts and associated arenas of participatory and parliamentary politics which has been accompanied by the development of new vectors of accountability under which administrative and judicial actors are increasingly answerable to each other as part of some self-referential network rather than to their citizenry. This has happened both specifically within the counter-terrorism strategy and more generally to protect security and combat crime within the AFSJ.

The central work on the counter-terrorism strategy is carried out by COR-EPER, which is to be informed by the Commission and the Counter-Terrorism Coordinator, and the Joint Situation Centre, an intelligence-analyzing unit set up in 2004 within the Council. The latter carries out risk assessments, whilst the former, on the basis of these assessments, sets out an overall strategy. This is then presented to the Council, Parliament, and Commission who agree it as part of a 'High Level Political Dialogue'. Political oversight is provided by the European Council who discusses it once per Presidency. Although there is some space provided for the European Parliament, it is more an *ex post* control, as the strategy has largely already been formulated.[54]

Within AFSJ a similar ouster has taken place, most evident in two show-piece measures of law-enforcement developed following the 9/11 attacks, the European Arrest Warrant and Eurojust. The European Arrest Warrant pro-vides that extradition should be possible for any criminal offence considered significant by the requesting state[55] and that a final decision upon the sur-render and extradition of a suspect must be taken by the executing state within sixty days from the day of arrest.[56] Although the executing Member State may insist that the constituent elements of the offence constitute an offence within its territory,[57] this restriction does not apply to thirty-two more serious offences where these are punishable by three years or more where double criminality has been abolished. A state must surrender a suspect to any other Member State which has issued a warrant, irrespective of whether the alleged matter would be an offence in its territory.[58] This violates the central tenets of the political authorship, which hold that it is the possibility of participation,

---

[54] It was telling, therefore, that the 2005 strategy was published as a Council document.
[55] Framework Decision 2002/584/JHA on the European arrest warrant and the surrender procedures between Member States [2002] OJ L190/1. The Framework Decision allows surrender for any offence punishable by more than one year or where sentence has been passed of more than four months' imprisonment. Ibid, Article 2(1).   [56] Ibid, Article 17(3).
[57] Ibid, Article 2(4).   [58] Ibid, Article 2(2).

directly or indirectly through representatives, in law formation that provides the only justification for law encroaching upon a citizen's autonomy, as through the possibility of participation he or she is able to contribute to the law's creation. It violates it, moreover, in two ways. It allows individuals to be extradited and incarcerated for acts over whose content, they as foreigners, could have no possibility of input. Both the Polish and Cypriot Constitutional Courts have therefore held the Arrest Warrant to violate their constitutions on this basis, as both constitutions explicitly prohibit the extraditing of one of its own citizens.[59] A further two states, Portugal and Slovenia, have, furthermore, had to amend their constitutions on this basis.[60] By allowing citizens to be incarcerated for acts which are not even recognizable as an offence in their home state, it prevents even a counterfactual logic applying, namely that if the act had taken the place at home they would have implicitly consented to being punished for it. The British House of Lords, therefore, expressed indignation that British citizens may have to be extradited for abortion or euthanasia on the grounds that these are classified as grievous bodily harm and murder in some Member States.[61] For this reason, Italian legislation has provided that an Italian citizen cannot be extradited for an offence if he or she did not know it to be an offence when he or she committed the act.[62]

A similar logic is present with Eurojust.[63] A college of prosecutors with responsibilities for serious transnational organized crime, Eurojust's duties include instigating investigations by national authorities; supporting investigations by national authorities; improving cooperation in investigations between national authorities; and coordinating investigations between national authorities.[64] Although it cannot force national authorities to carry out an investigation, invariably they have followed its requests, with 381 cases passing through Eurojust in 2004.[65] This has led to Eurojust becoming the central hub for organizing the prosecution of transnational organized crime within the Union. It renders law enforcement authorities increasingly responsible to other law enforcement bodies rather than to their own populations, which are increasingly viewed as no more than a group to be policed. This accountability stretches beyond individual investigations, moreover, to the overall orientation of policing within a state. For a commitment to assist with Eurojust investigations,

[59] Judgment of the Polish Constitutional Tribunal P 1/05 Concerning the European Arrest Warrant, Judgment of 27 April 2005.
[60] EC Commission, *The European Arrest Warrant and the Surrender Procedures between Member States*, COM (2006) 8, 2.
[61] House of Lords, *European Arrest Warrant—Recent Developments* (30th Report, European Union Committee, Session 2005–2006, SO, London), paras 11–12.
[62] EC Commission, above, n. 60, 3.
[63] Decision 2002/187/JHA setting up Eurojust with a view to reinforcing the fight against serious crime [2002] OJ L63/1. For a more extensive analysis see C. van den Wyngaert, 'Eurojust and the European Public Prosecutor in the *Corpus Juris* Model: Water and Fire', in N. Walker (ed.) *Europe's Area of Freedom, Security and Justice* (Oxford: Oxford University Press, 2004).
[64] Ibid, Article 4.   [65] Eurojust, *Annual Report 2004* (The Hague, 2005), 22.

particularly for the smaller states, represents a commitment to allocate resources to that mode of law enforcement rather than to other problems closer to home, which may be of more concern to the local population.

2.4.2 The Growth and Growth of the Union Market Society

By contrast, the Union's war on terror reinforced and extended the other form of political reason, that of government of the Union's market society. This is seen most symbolically in the creation of the terrorist offence in Union law in Decision 2002/475/JHA.[66] This does not criminalize something that was previously lawful, but resurrects the idea of the political crime. The criminal effects of flying a plane into a building are not merely its impact upon its direct victims but also its more general destabilizing effects on the polity. A requirement of all terrorist offences is the presence of an intention on the part of the perpetrator to damage those political structures which are seen as the central identifiers of the polity.

The central identifiers for terrorist offences in Union law were crucially not simply administrative structures. An offence was to be terrorist in nature where it 'seriously damage(s) a country or an international organisation' and has the aim of:

—seriously intimidating a population, or
—unduly compelling a Government or international organisation to perform or abstain from performing any act, or
—seriously destabilising or destroying the fundamental political, constitutional, economic or social structures of a country or an international organisation.[67]

Unlike in the United States, the Decision does not create a series of pre-textual offences which give the administration greater powers in respect of those suspected of engaging in terrorist activities or being involved in ancillary activities. Indeed, there is a commitment not to 'reduce or restrict fundamental rights or liberties'.[68] Instead, the Decision only commits Member States to criminalize these offences qua terrorist offences,[69] to prosecute and to impose effective and dissuasive penalities against both legal[70] and natural persons[71] involved in their commission.

The innovative feature of the Decision lies in the institutions recognized by it as integral to the European Union Body Politic. Unlike international instruments

[66] Decision 2002/475/JHA on combating terrorism [2002] OJ L164/3.
[67] Ibid, Article 1. It is an offence to direct a terrorist group or to participate in its activities by supplying information, material resources, or funding, with knowledge that these will contribute to the criminal activities of the group. Ibid, Article 2.   [68] Ibid, Preamble, 10th Recital.
[69] Ibid, Articles 1, 3, and 4.
[70] Ibid, Article 7. This establishes a legal liability for organizations if any act is carried out by a representative or person authorized to take decisions or exercise control within the organization, or an act occurs as a result of a failure of supervision by these.   [71] Ibid, Article 5.

or national measures, the Decision considers an act to be terrorist if it aims to destabilize or destroy the 'fundamental . . . economic or social structures of a country or an international organisation'. Concern about the breadth of the Decision led the Council, therefore, to seek to place boundaries on it by stating in a Declaration attached to the Decision that actions of trade unions or anti-globalization protesters would not be categorized as terrorist under the Decision. The Commission noted, however, that it could still be applied to acts of 'urban violence'.[72] It would seem to incorporate, therefore, attacks by animal liberation protestors on laboratories or blockades of oil refineries by lorry drivers who consider the latter to be engaging in excessive pricing. This orientation is, moreover, not merely symbolic. If one looks at the central actions taken in the war on terror, they have been to protect the European Union market society.

The centre-piece was a wide-ranging resettlement on the combatting of crime. This included not just the establishment of the European Arrest Warrant and Eurojust, but a more far-reaching commitment to the principle of mutual recognition, with the proposed European Evidence Warrant, which allows evidence taken in one jurisdiction to be recognized in another, being the clearest example.[73] Alongside this, a whole host of agreements have been signed with non-EU States on cooperation in investigations, information-sharing, and extradition,[74] and a more prominent role granted for Europol in the analysis and sharing of data on transorganized crime.[75] None of these measures are targeted at terrorism, *per se*, but instead focus more broadly at that transnational crime which undermines faith in market institutions within the Union.

The second type of measure taken has been in the field of migration. The central ones have been Frontex, the Agency on External Frontiers, and a series of measures requiring biometric identification. Frontex is to strengthen controls and surveillance at the EU's external border through risk assessment and training. It is above all concerned with general border policing and limiting the overall porousness of the EU's external borders rather than the migration of

[72] European Report, 'Justice and Home Affairs: MEPs split over Commission Antiterrorism Package,' 10 September 2001, quoted in Occhipinti, *The Politics of European Police Cooperation*, above, n. 46, at 153.

[73] EC Commission, *Proposal for a Framework Decision on the European Evidence Warrant for obtaining objects, documents and data for use in proceedings in criminal matters*, COM (2003) 688.

[74] It is now standard for EU agreements with third states to have provisions for cooperation combating terrorism. In the first year following the attacks, for example, the EU concluded some agreements with all its accession states, the United States, Canada, Algeria, Lebanon, India, Russia, and Israel. For a list of the agreements signed with the United States see: http://ue.eu.int/cms3_fo/showPage.asp?id = 635&lang = EN&mode = g.

[75] Member States are required to provide Europol with all relevant criminal intelligence relating to terrorism as soon as this is available, and to that end it has established a Counter-Terrorism Task Force within it. Provision has also been made for it to enter information-sharing agreements with third-state police authorities, Council Decision Authorizing the Director of Europol to enter into negotiations on agreements with third countries and non-EU bodies [2000] OJ C106/1 as amended by [2002] OJ C150/1.

radical borders.[76] It is there, in other words, to enable the Union to manage migration: to let into its territory only those that it wishes and, thereby, to secure a stable population of migrants that can be governed and over which stable calculations can be made. Biometrics are also used to secure entry to the Union, but in a different way, as they are only required of certain individuals. They are demanded, on the one hand, to identify those most integrated into the EU market society, EU citizens,[77] and long-term residents, who are required to have them in their documents. The other category required to hold them are visa holders.[78] Visas, once again, are central to migration management. They are used as a form of pre-border screening to channel nationals most likely to be economic migrants or asylum seekers through consulates in their home state. They are also central to the management of quotas as they enable not only pre-selection but also pre-identification of those migrants who will belong to certain migrant categories such as workers or students.

This feeling that these measures are taken not so much to protect territorial integrity or protect the Union from dangerous political radicals is reinforced by migration processes being merged more generally into policing networks. In particular, information technology is to be used to create a large interactive network between all national authorities, which contains details of visa decisions, persons with criminal convictions, irregular migrants, and deportees or those refused entry. The information is to be made available by the establishment of a Visa Information System, on which all visa decisions are to be contained,[79] and by the upgrading of the Schengen Information System (SIS) containing details on illegal migrants and those with criminal convictions.[80] These systems are to be made available to both policing and immigration authorities.[81] Crucial to this is PROSECUR, a procedure which will establish direct and interactive links between the person checking persons and goods at a frontier and other customs, immigration, and policing authorities, with frontier operators able to inform other agencies, in real time, of the observance of a particular threat or offence, with the latter in turn providing the former with detailed information to enable them to carry out further surveillance or

---

[76] Regulation 2007/2004 establishing a European Agency for the Management of Operational Cooperation at the External Borders of the Member States of the European Union [2004] OJ L349/1.

[77] Regulation 2133/2004 on biometric features in EU passports [2004] OJ L369/5.

[78] EC Commission, *Proposals for Regulations amending Regulation 1683/95 laying down a uniform format for visas and Regulation 1030/2002 laying down a uniform format for residence permits for third-country nationals*, COM (2003) 558.

[79] Decision 2004/512/EC establishing the Visa Information System [2004] OJ L213/5.

[80] EC Commission, *Proposal for a Council Decision on the establishment, operation and use of the second generation Schengen information system (SIS II)*, COM (2005) 230; EC Commission, *Proposal for a Regulation on the establishment, operation and use of the second generation Schengen information system(SIS II)*, COM (2005) 236.

[81] Regulation 871/2004/EC concerning the introduction of some new functions for the Schengen Information System, including in the fight against terrorism [2004] OJ L162/29.

checks.[82] The culmination of these measures is not just that external frontiers can be used to exclude individuals from entry, but that they become far more pro-active policing posts, points through which individuals must pass through and through which it is easy to police and detain them.

The final set of measures taken to protect the market society was taken in the fields of financial services and electronic communications. These fields are seen as the central vessels of globalization. As flows of information and capital that move seamlessly beyond the state, they are both seen as threatening to the nation-state and as particularly vulnerable to sabotage or corruption. To this end, measures were brought in to police and protect the internet and financial system. The measures extended beyond this, however, to result in these becoming active policers of civil society. In the case of the financial system, this has been done through money laundering legislation. Directive 2001/97 EC applies the legislation not merely to the activities of credit institutions, but investment firms, auditors, lawyers, estate agents, casinos, notaries, and dealers in high-value goods.[83] All are required to demand provision of identification for any transaction when entering into business relation with a person or where they are involved with a transaction of more than €15,000.[84] They are also under obligations to report any suspicious transaction to the authorities and to keep records of that transaction. In the case of electronic communications, national authorities can require service providers to retain data for reasons of state security, prosecution of criminal offences, or unauthorized use of electronic communications.[85] The type of data to be held and the length of duration are currently under discussion, but the Commission proposes that data be held for one year. Whilst the data to be held would not include the contents of a communication, it would include the identity of the source and destination, the time, duration, device, and location of a communication.[86]

2.5 THE NEW POLITICS OF THE EUROPEAN UNION MARKET SOCIETY

So far it has been argued that the European Union developed a new form of political reason to accommodate a series of demands that were not met by national political rights. This political reason was that of the government of the

[82] EC Commission, *Towards integrated management of the external borders of the Member States of the European Union*, COM (2002) 233, 15–16; EC Commission, *On Enhancing Ship and Port Facility Security*, COM (2003) 229, 13; EC Commission, *The role of customs in the integrated management of external borders*, COM (2003) 452, 12.

[83] Directive 2001/97/EC amending Directive 91/308/EEC on prevention of the use of the financial system for the purpose of money laundering [2001] OJ L344/76, Article 2.

[84] Ibid, Article 3(1) and (2). It is €1,000 in the case of casinos, ibid, Article 3(5).

[85] Directive 2002/58/EC on the processing of personal data and protection of privacy in the electronic communications sector [2002] OJ L201/37, Article 15(1).

[86] EC Commission, Proposal on the retention of data processed in connection with the provision of public electronic communication services and amending Directive 2002/58/EC, COM (2005) 438.

European Union market society. This political reason was governed by three principles of porousness, regulatory authorship, and mutual public–private accountability. The emergence of a European Union 'government under stress' reinforced this form of political reason at the expense of other forms of political reason, but it also reorientated it. Alongside the earlier political principles of the market society, three counter-principles became more salient, those of suspicion, public–private police, and collective victimhood.

2.5.1 The European Union and the Politics of Suspicion

In a world of government under stress, as the nature and source of threats becomes impossible to identify sufficiently precisely until it is too late, a distinction emerges between an ordered safe way of life and a disordered and threatening state of nature.[87] This leads to a concern with borders as markers between the two. Whilst territoriality remains a powerful marker, concern has shifted beyond protection of territory to protection of the structures central to the market society. In this regard, porousness is particularly problematic, as it indicates that the structure cannot be isolated from the environment and the external threat.

The central means of combating this has been the development of new processes of identification, which make the verification of identity compulsory for participation in the European Union market society. Whilst identification at territorial frontiers is still seen as important, it is becoming less axiomatic with identification becoming a prerequisite for many activities within the territory of the Union. With regard to the external frontiers of the Union, we have seen how biometric identifiers are not being used so much to stop entry to the territory, as many foreigners do not require them in their passports. They are used rather as identifiers of an individual's status within the Union market society. Participants in the market society—Union citizens, long-term residents, and those with the right to work or to be self-employed—are required to have them in their passports, as are those who are considered likely to pose a burden on the labour market or welfare institutions of the market society, namely those nationals who require a visa to enter the Union.[88] A similar pattern is present with regard to the internal frontiers of the Union. Directive 2004/58/EC,[89] the Directive on the right of citizens and their families to move and reside within the Union, provides that citizens have the right to enter and reside within another state's territory for three months upon mere presentation of a passport or an ID card.[90] Yet frontiers do not exhaust their duties to possess identity documents, but are merely one point where it may be necessary. Member States

---

[87] This type of distinction was first noted by Thomas Hobbes. For a discussion see C. Robin, *Fear: The History of a Political Idea* (Oxford: Oxford University Press, 2004), ch. 1.
[88] See 77–78.   [89] [2004] OJ L229/35.   [90] Ibid, Article 5(1).

can require citizens of the Union to carry proof of their identity provided similar requirements exist for their own nationals.[91]

Proof of identity thus becomes central to a number of core activities within the Union. It is pivotal to access to finance. The opening of accounts with credit institutions and the carrying out of transactions worth €15,000 or more all require proof of identification.[92] It is also present in all dealings with professional associations. The Charter of European Professional Associations in support of the fight against Organized Crime, signed in 1999, under the auspices of the Commission,[93] by the European professional associations for lawyers, notaries, accountants and auditors, and tax experts commits professionals, *inter alia*, to verify client identity and withdraw from any case if there is a risk of assisting in criminal activities. A similar pattern is present on the internet. Directive 2002/58/EC requires service providers to identify and hold onto data for reasons of security. It also makes them responsible for the integrity of personal communications. To that end, they must secure data against accidental or unlawful destruction or loss, alteration, unauthorized disclosure, or access.[94] They are thus simultaneously responsible for both the integrity of the electronic communications and for their policing.

Formal identification may not be enough, however, to eliminate a threat. A politics of suspicion has, correspondingly, emerged alongside these processes of identification. A central example are the Wolfsberg principles. A Code of Conduct combating money-laundering agreed in 2000 between the banks that hold 60 per cent of the world's private banking, this is the central regime for policing and combating money-laundering.[95] Based on the 'Know Your Customer' and 'Due Diligence' principles, it structures and formalizes, in a detailed way, the bank–client relationship.[96] Banks are required to ask for extensive documentation about the identity of the client and the purpose of the account before opening an account. Certain categories of client are marked as requiring additional due diligence. Once the accounts are opened, they are to be monitored continually for suspicious or unusual activities, and clients' files are to be regularly updated.

The response to 11 September was to entrench and strengthen these trajectories. The Group issued a statement on the Suppression of Financing of Terrorism in which it committed itself to participate in the fight against terrorism.[97] It consequently extended the Know Your Customer Principle through increased information exchange between jurisdictions and with government agencies, and through the establishment and consultation of lists of

---

[91] Ibid, Article 26.   [92] See 73.

[93] http://europa.eu.int/comm/justice_home/news/forum_crimen/documents/charte_en.htm.

[94] Above, n. 85, Article 4(1).

[95] On their development see M. Peith and G. Aiolfi, 'The Private Sector Becomes Active: The Wolfsberg Process.' http://www.wolfsberg-principles.com/pdf/wolfsbergprocess.pdf.

[96] The current revision is contained at: http://www.wolfsberg-principles.com/privat-banking.html.   [97] To be found at: http://www.wolfsberg-principles.com/financing-terrorism.html.

non-desirable persons.[98] Processes of exclusion are therefore to be generalized and formalized. Rejection by one bank is likely to lead to rejection by others. There is also an extension of the Due Diligence Principle in which the Group commits itself to having restricted business with new 'High-Risk' sectors. For remittance businesses, exchange houses, casas de cambio, bureaux de change, and money transfer agents the Group commits itself to deal only with those 'subject to appropriate regulation'.[99]

2.5.2 The Politics of Public–Private Police

The position of private parties as purveyors of public goods also changes. Previously, the state endowed these bodies with law-making powers precisely because they had capacities not possessed by it. The relationship was not one of principal-agent where they were carrying out its broader desires. Instead, as it was assumed rather that they were able to identify and protect a public good in ways not available to the administration, the relationship was more one of good faith and ensuring that they made their best efforts to secure these goods. The relationship was a fiduciary one, therefore, based on *ex post* controls. With government under stress, these arrangements acquired public order responsibilities. They are not only responsible for securing a public good, but also public order more generally. They are also seen as less comfortably self-regulating. A feature of government under stress is a general nervousness where there is less confidence in individual arrangements to operate in a stable manner and these arrangements are seen as more vulnerable to external threats. The consequence is that, on the one hand, these arrangements acquire policing functions with their being required to monitor and verify the activities that take place within their aegis. Simultaneously, the state has to police them, checking not merely that they discharge their policing duties, but that they do not engage in illegal activities themselves. A world of policing emerges similar to that set out by Poulantzas thirty years ago in which there is:

> a lifting of the traditional boundaries between the normal and the abnormal (ie supposedly 'anti-social' elements); thus, control is shifted from the criminal act to the crime-inducing situation, from the pathological case to the pathogenic surroundings, in such a way that each citizen becomes, as it were, an a priori suspect or potential criminal. But this is doubled in a supporting mechanism of police control over the population: each citizen becomes in turn a watcher or potential policeman through an endless series of reports.[100]

The system of public–private policing has, however, a couple of twists to the order he describes. One also finds, therefore, a return to the seventeenth-century idea of *Polizeiwissenschaft*. In an atmosphere of so much mistrust, the only way to police a society is to record and register all transactions and activities. Yet this

---

[98] Ibid, Statement 4.   [99] Ibid, Statement 5.
[100] N. Poulantzas, *State, Power, Socialism* (London: Verso, 2000), at 186–87.

recording and registration is not done by the administration, but is to be done by private parties, who are then to make available to the authorities their records. The duties of internet service providers to hold onto data from electronic communications have already been described.[101] A parallel regime exists for financial transactions. All institutions covered by the money-laundering legislation are subject either to a pre-existing system of prior authorization or registration with the authorities. An extensive, recurring relationship therefore exists between every institution and the administration, which, in the United Kingdom, for example, requires the former to hold onto records of all financial transactions for five years and have these available for the authorities.[102] Alongside these developments, it is worth mentioning those in the transport sector where all carriers are required to hold and communicate data, in particular, the nationality, date of birth, and documentation, on all passengers entering the Union to the authorities.[103]

Sporadic, selective interventions by the state are also associated with these politics. The relationship between the administration and these bodies is a highly fluid one. They are, after all, both guardians of public order and objects of suspicion. The conditions under which public authorities can intervene are thus left extremely vague. In the case of money-laundering, institutions are required to report any suspicious transaction to the authorities.[104] The circumstances under which national authorities could access data from internet service providers were initially left undefined.[105] Similarly, the conditions under which private bodies hold this information and their duties with regard to this information are often unclear. In Austria, for example, the Constitutional Court has ruled that the requirement for telecommunications service providers to install phone tapping equipment at their own cost was unconstitutional as it imposed too extensive liabilities on them.[106] Similarly, in the United Kingdom, the Court of Appeal has held that carriers, liability regimes, which impose fines on firms for bringing individuals into the country without appropriate documentation were illegal in that, insofar as they did not allow the possibility of mitigation, they unduly infringed the latter's property rights and imposed criminal liabilities on them

---

[101] See 85–86.

[102] The Directive is typically vague on this issue, requiring institutions to furnish all necessary information to the authorities. Above, n. 83, Article 6(1)(b). The United Kingdom regime is set out in Money Laundering Regulations 2003, SI 2003/3075, Regulation 6(3).

[103] Directive 2004/82/EC, on the obligation of carriers to communicate passenger data [2004] OJ L261/24.

[104] Ibid, Article 6(1). There is a derogation where information is obtained in the context of professionals representing a party in judicial proceedings or instructing them how to avoid judicial proceedings, ibid, Article 6(2).

[105] There is a Commission proposal that data be retained for one year. EC Commission, *Proposal for a Directive on the retention of data processed in connection with the provision of public electronic communication services and amending Directive 2002/58/EC*, COM (2005) 438, Article 7.

[106] *T-Mobile and Others v Bundesminister für Verkehr, Innovation und Technologie*, Judgment of 27 February 2003: http://www.epic.org/privacy/intl/austrian_ct_dec_022703.html.

without due process.[107] The modalities of cooperation, furthermore, are formalized nowhere, so there is no duty to record cooperation or to follow procedures. It is not therefore unheard of for regulatory authorities to have agents working within credit institutions or internet service providers. The consequence is a hybridized form of policing where it is often difficult to identify where public policing begins and private policing ends.[108]

The politics of policing finally changes the internal dynamics of the private arrangements. In addition to formalizing the terms under which banks accept, terminate, and supervise accounts, the principles also systematize and centralize power within the bank. Provision is made for approval from senior management before accounts requiring due diligence are opened. The establishment of control procedures for the monitoring of accounts involves compliance and internal audit units as well as senior management. There is also provision for the establishment of all records for five years and the establishment of a central anti-money-laundering unit. The bank–client relationship is, however, simultaneously always a commercial and a public order one. The principles of Due Diligence and Know Your Customer might help reduce money-laundering, but they also provide a justification for banks to filter away certain types of customer or transaction, which represent too great a commercial risk. Whole sectors, types of business activity, and economic jurisdictions can be refused finance on the ground that they are typically exposed to money-laundering. As such, they have to pay a risk premium if they are to have access to the bank's resources. Equally, establishment of internal control procedures is necessary to prevent rogue bankers engaging in money-laundering, but it also acts as a useful management tool for controlling units of the bank, supervising individuals and centralizing judgments of questions of financial risk. A survey of compliance officers in the United Kingdom found that the biggest obstacles to curbing money-laundering were insufficient control of local offices, poor record-keeping, and poor staff training. Ninety-one per cent believed that organizational self-knowledge—knowing how your business worked and its strong and weak links—were the most central determinant of effective performance.[109] In particular, one of the greatest risks was that local branches of organizations tended to waive procedures for customers they thought they knew well.[110] Increasingly, therefore, there is investment in anti-money-laundering technology, which monitors transactions against statistical norms.[111] The precise

---

[107] *International Transport Roth v Secretary of State for the Home Department* [2002] EuLR 74.
[108] This is the tale of the brilliant M. Taussig, *Law in a Lawless Land* (Chicago, IL: University of Chicago Press, 2003).
[109] D. Brouwnlow, 'In a Spin over Money Laundering' (February 2004) *Financial World* 24–55.
[110] Ibid, Figure 7.
[111] Estimates in the United States suggest, for example, that $700 million will be invested by the brokerage industry alone in this technology between 2003 and 2006. 'Brokers will spend big on anti-money-laundering' *Wall Street Journal* 1 May 2003.

purpose of this technology is to disembed and depersonify relationships by removing the 'human' element, which is seen as involving both unpredictable judgment and increased exposure to risk and, to that end, securing greater control over individual operators' activities.

A similar pattern prevails with customers. The Group commits itself to the continuation and development of procedures for monitoring 'unusual or suspicious' transactions.[112] Most wide-ranging is the extension of a risk-based rather than a rule-based approach to bank–client relations. The 'due diligence' test introduced by the Wolfsberg principles requires a bank to assess in some detail the politico-economic risk of a customer before taking him or her on. Increasingly, this approach is also being applied to the execution of all transactions. The Group has adopted a series of principles on the Monitoring and Screening of Transactions, which call for each institution to develop its own risk criteria with regard to any transaction and real-time screening is to be introduced for particularly risky or sensitive types of transactions. This allows payment instructions to be screened (and therefore stopped) prior to execution.[113] Combined, these allow the bank to evaluate not just the state but the anticipated state of the relationship during the whole cycle of the relationship, as well as to evaluate and stop particularly risky types of transactions.

2.5.3 The Political Community of Victimhood

Vulnerability has been identified as arguably the central dynamic behind forms of human community. It unites humans in that they are aware of their vulnerability to the actions of others and are also able to empathize with the vulnerability of others. Government under stress intensifies these communitarian processes by emphasizing vulnerability to an omnipresent, incommensurable threat. Yet a particular form of vulnerability is emphasized. It is that of victimhood. At its most narrowly focused, this concern with victimhood is expressed in the statement in the EU Strategy on Counter-Terrorism that 'solidarity, assistance and compensation of the victims of terrorism and their families constitute an integral part of the response to terrorism at national and European level'.[114] More broadly, victimhood is a central mantra of the European Union area of freedom, security, and justice. There are thus a host of measures either offering a haven to victims or protecting them from further victimization. These include measures concerned with human

---

[112] Above, n. 97, Statement 6. The Group has also drawn up principles of additional due diligence on correspondent banking, a particularly risky form of banking as it involves a bank holding an account on behalf of another bank. It is therefore one remove away from the customer: http://www.wolfsberg-principles.com/corresp-banking.html.
[113] These are at: http://www.wolfsberg-principles.com/monitoring.html.
[114] Above, n. 44, para. 36.

trafficking;[115] refugees;[116] protection of victims in the criminal process;[117] and compensation for victims who suffered from violent crime in another Member State.[118]

Victimhood, in all cases, is presaged on both the recognition of particular human suffering and the presence of a particular egregious act which caused that suffering, be it terrorism, foreign persecution, racial hatred, or serious crime. Suffering or extreme disadvantage is not considered sufficient alone. Instead, the egregious act causing it must be seen as something external and antithetical to the European Union market society. Political community is thus not just premised on recognition of each others' vulnerability but also on the idea of members being subject to external aggression: be it the aggression by criminals, terrorists, traffickers, or genocidal regimes. Those adversely affected by the internal operations of the market society or measures taken to protect it are not considered victims and their suffering not recognised as there is no presence of external aggression. This is not simply a matter of insiders and outsiders, but amounts to a derecognition of 'outsiders'' humanity,[119] as recognition of suffering is a central element of the recognition of somebody's humanity. It is precisely where suffering and vulnerability are not recognized, therefore, that one finds most widespread violation of human rights.

This derecognition occurs where to do otherwise would undermine the government of European market society. It is done so most explicitly in the case of asylum seekers and irregular migrants whose lack of humanity stems from their being suspected of being illicit economic migrants or welfare tourists. In the Hague Programme, irregular migrants and asylum seekers—neither of which are criminal activities—are grouped alongside not petty misdemeanours but terrorism, organized crime, and human-trafficking as evils to be confronted.[120]

In the case of irregular migrants who ask no public provision other than the right of residence, it is found in the absolutism of the requirement of return. Current Commission proposals require states to remove and return migrants in breach of their conditions of residence and to ban them from re-entry for five years.[121] This requirement can only be waived if it violates the right to non-refoulment, the right to education, and the right to family unity.[122] There is no

---

[115] Directive 2004/81/EC on the residence permit issued to third-country nationals who are victims of trafficking in human beings or who have been the subject of an action to facilitate illegal immigration, who cooperate with the competent authorities [2004] OJ L 261/19.

[116] Directive 2005/85/EC on minimum standards on procedures in Member States for granting and withdrawing refugee status [2005] OJ L326/13.

[117] Framework Decision 2001/220/JHA on the standing of victims in criminal proceedings [2001] OJ L82/1.

[118] Directive 2004/80/EC relating to compensation to crime victims [2004] OJ L261/15.

[119] J. Butler, *Precarious Life: The Powers of Mourning and Violence* (London/New York: Verso, 2004), at 33–35.   [120] Above, n. 51, 3.

[121] EC Commission, *Proposal for a Directive on common standards and procedures in Member States for returning illegally staying third country nationals*, COM (2005) 391 final, Articles 6, 7, and 9.

[122] Ibid, Article 6(4).

requirement of proportionality in the link between the severity of the breach and the decision to remove. The list of grounds is extremely narrow. The irregular migrant has either to be an asylum seeker, subject to protection under family reunification grounds, or a child. Whilst there is some recognition of his or her humanity in this, as there is in the requirement that excessive force should not be used on him or her,[123] only the bare elements of a human life are acknowledged—the right to schooling, to a family, and to flee persecution. There is nothing there to suggest that he or she has a right to a decent life or even a right to live. A return to starvation, disease, or even high levels of violence would not be good grounds for stopping his or her removal.

However, the teeth of the European Union are bared most for asylum seekers. For these make active demands of the European Union market society. They ask not only for residence but for welfare benefits, such as housing, education, and social assistance, and, in some cases, economic opportunities, such as the right to work. This has to be prevented insofar as it threatens to dislocate local labour markets and welfare institutions or generate public order problems from locals unhappy at the arrival of the newcomers. This involves not merely denial of those socio-economic benefits regarded as central to provide a decent life, but an active system of policing and detention to make sure that the asylum seekers cannot get access to these benefits, even indirectly.[124]

One central theme is the identification and control of the asylum seeker. He or she is required to register as soon as reasonably practical with the authorities.[125] Member States may decide where the asylum seeker is to reside for reasons, *inter alia*, of swift processing and effective monitoring.[126] He or she can be required to report to the authorities as often as these deem fit.[127] With regard to the control of the asylum seeker Member States may limit his or her movement to certain parts of the territory.[128] Benefits can be withdrawn if he or she breaches any reporting conditions, lies about his or her financial resources or abandons his or her residence.[129] The other sanction available is detention, which can be used wherever the asylum seeker's presence threatens to create public order problems.[130] In all this, there is also a concern to protect the institutions of the market society—be they markets or welfare institutions. In principle, therefore, asylum seekers should pay for any benefits they receive if they have the resources.[131] Access to the labour market is to be denied for the first year of the process. After this asylum seekers are not to have free access to the labour market, but under conditions to be determined by the Member State.[132]

The consequence is a very limited vision of the humanity of the asylum seeker. There is no requirement of family reunion. Detention is possible, albeit

---

[123] Ibid, Article 10(1).
[124] Directive 2003/9/EC on the reception of asylum seekers. [2003] OJ L31/18.
[125] Ibid, Article 16(2).   [126] Ibid, Article 7(2).   [127] Ibid, Article 16(1)(b).
[128] Ibid, Article 7(1).   [129] Ibid, Article 16(1).   [130] Ibid, Article 7(3).
[131] Ibid, Article 13(4).   [132] Ibid, Article 11.

that the asylum seeker has done nothing wrong. Failure to report can leave him or her destitute.[133] In fact, the inalienable benefits are very limited. There is a right to due process where benefits are withdrawn;[134] a right to essential health care;[135] a right to travel for humanitarian reasons;[136] and a requirement to take account of the situation of individuals with special needs.[137] Beyond that, everything is subject to a managerialist approach which balances the behaviour and resources of the asylum seeker, on the one hand, against the demands of the European Union market society, on the other.

2.6 CONCLUSION

In his impressive work on the history of the political idea of fear, Corey Robin concludes that it has traditionally been developed as an instrument of rule by the powerful over the less powerful. It is used to justify that power by holding out the possibility of anarchy and nothingness without the presence of an institutional order. By confining the idea of political fear to that sphere, the other forms of repression and fear in a society—be it loss of employment, imprisonment, restrictions on movement, or denial of social benefits—are downplayed.[138] Fear's ordering effects in EU law have given this argument a particular twist. The relationship between these two types of fear, one political and the other non-political, is no longer being obscured. As the political order is taken increasingly to incorporate market institutions, so the justification for the deployment of these other instruments is more explicitly political. They are there, in part at least, not merely to secure the effective functioning of the market but to protect the institutional ordering of the market society.

It is here that EU law 'under stress' generates its own sense of critique. There is a sense that this is not right, that it is too ready an importation of the inequalities and inequities of socio-economic life into a political order, which, in principle at least, aspires to be composed of 'free and equals'. Government under stress may be pervasive, therefore, but it is not to be omnipresent. It acknowledges a political and legal arena 'without stress', where its justifications and dynamics do not apply. One finds the paradox, therefore, that the Constitutional Treaty, which was adopted after the attacks on Madrid, even evinced a commitment to extend participatory democracy, most notably providing for citizens, initiatives whereby the Commission was required to consider any proposal signed by not less than a million citizens from a significant number of the Member States.[139]

---

[133] The British House of Lords has declared the equivalent British provision to be a violation of Article 3 ECHR in that it subjects the asylum seeker to inhuman and degrading treatment. *R v Secretary of State for the Home Department, ex parte Adam* [2005] UKHL 66.
[134] Ibid, Article 16(4) and (5).   [135] Ibid, Article 15(1).   [136] Ibid, Article 6(5).
[137] Ibid, Articles 17 and 18(2).   [138] Robin, above, n. 87, especially 20–25.
[139] Article I-47 CT.

If the presence of a bipartite logic would be the best that one could hope for, a shrivelled and diminished 'free and equal' arrangement sitting alongside the ones developed 'under stress', then things would be desperate. It is an arrangement where observers are clutching at straws, pointing to what is left, rather than investing any hopes in the European Union legal system as a whole. A more fertile seam of hope comes from the unusual dynamics put in play by government under stress. Even within its own arena of operations, it sets in play an unstable set of counterparts: porousness versus suspicion; accountability versus policing; popular authorship versus victimhood. Each does not negate the other in that we still find principles of porousness, etc. in the Union market society. Even in a government under stress, for example, the mutual recognition principle and the equal opportunities legislation still operate to require regulators to look beyond their regulatory horizons and recognize a number of vulnerable interests, values, and identities. Yet, next to this porousness, institutions are simultaneously required to be mistrustful of other identities and values. This patchiness makes no sense, and is unstable and incoherent. Why are certain vulnerable identities blessed and others cursed? Whilst this dynamic will never go away and there will be an inevitable selectiveness to this process, it generates its own internal sense of injustice and 'destablization rights' which is recognized in the very term 'government under stress'. One senses that it is this element which has to be nurtured and developed so that these dynamics become productive so that there is a gradual recognition and 'rehumanization' of new vulnerable identities.

3

Freedom of Expression in Political Contexts: Some Reflections on the Case Law of the European Court of Human Rights

Victor Ferreres Comella

3.1 INTRODUCTION

In its case law concerning freedom of expression, the European Court of Human Rights (ECHR) has linked this right both to collective and to individual interests. It has held that freedom of expression (which is protected in Article 10 of the European Convention) is 'one of the basic conditions for the progress of democratic societies and for the development of each individual'.[1] When speech relates to political matters, however, the collective aspect needs to be emphasized. The proper functioning of the democratic process requires that citizens can offer and receive information about, and exchange opinions about, public issues. As the ECHR has said, 'freedom of political debate is at the very core of the concept of a democratic society which prevails throughout the Convention'.[2] The Court has taken into account, for example, the electoral context of the speech; the fact that the speaker was an elected representative of the people; or the fact that the criticism was directed against the government, especially if the speaker was a member of the opposition party.[3]

---

[1] *Handyside v The United Kingdom*, Judgment of 7 December 1976, para. 49, Series A No. 24.

[2] *Lingens v Austria*, Judgment of 8 July, 1986, para. 72, Series A No. 103.

[3] Thus, in *Bowman v The United Kingdom*, Judgment of 19 February 1998, *Reports of Judgments and Decisions* 1998-I, the ECHR said: 'Free elections and freedom of expression, particularly freedom of political debate, together form the bedrock of any democratic system . . . For this reason, it is particularly important in the period preceding an election that opinions and information of all kinds are permitted to circulate freely' (para. 42). And in *Castells v Spain*, Judgment of 23 April 1992, Series A No. 236, the ECHR said that, 'while freedom of expression is important for everybody, it is especially so for an elected representative of the people. He represents his electorate, draws attention to their preoccupations and defends their interests' (para. 42). And it stressed the relevance of voices that are critical of the government: 'the limits of permissible criticism are wider

This does not mean that the ECHR has espoused a restrictive conception of what issues are of 'public interest' for the purposes of free speech law. Quite the contrary: it considers issues to be of public interest even if they are not strictly speaking 'political'.[4] And it tries to link private controversies to more general public discussions.[5] What is true, however, is that the Court holds the view that speech that is expressed in a political context should be especially protected.

My purpose in this chapter is to examine the case law of the ECHR in order to illustrate and discuss some problems in the field of freedom of speech, particularly when the speech involved has a political dimension of some sort. The problems I will consider can be organized in three parts. The first part relates to the general question whether and to what extent false information should be protected. The second refers to the issue whether the law should treat opinions (especially value judgments) in a different manner than information, and why this should be so. The third topic is whether it is justified for the law to introduce exceptions to the general principle that all speakers should be subjected to the same legal restrictions. Two particular cases are considered in this regard: speech by members of Parliament, and speech by, and relating to, judges. This is not, of course, a complete list of the many issues that the ECHR has had to deal with in this area. But they are relevant, and they are quite fundamental.[6]

with regard to government than in relation to a private citizen or even a politician' (para. 46). Therefore, 'interferences with the freedom of expression of an opposition member of parliament . . . call for the closest scrutiny on the part of the Court' (para. 42).

[4] In *Thorgeir Thorgeirson v Iceland* (Judgment of 25 June 1992, Series A No. 239), the government of Iceland had argued that the case law of the ECHR 'showed that the wide limits of acceptable criticism in political discussion did not apply to the same extent in the discussion of other matters of public interest', and that 'the issues of public interest raised by the applicant's articles [which referred to instances of police brutality] could not be included in the category of political discussion, which denoted direct or indirect participation by citizens in the decision-making process in a democratic society' (para. 61). The ECHR rejected this general proposition. It held that 'there is no warrant in its case-law for distinguishing, in the manner suggested by the Government, between political discussion and discussion of other matters of public concern' (para. 64). So, for example, in *Fressoz and Roire v France*, Judgment of 21 January 1999, [GC] No. 29183/95, ECHR 1999-I, the Court held that it was a contribution to a public debate on a matter of public interest for a newspaper to inform about the salary increases of the managing director of Peugeot, in the context of an industrial dispute where workers were seeking a pay rise which the management were refusing (para. 50).

[5] So, for example, in the case of *Marônek v Slovakia* (Judgment of 19 April 2001, No. 32686/96, ECHR 2001-III), the applicant wrote an open letter addressed to the Prime Minister, complaining of the fact that a particular person and his wife (who was a public prosecutor) had refused to let him occupy a flat that he thought he was legally entitled to use. The letter was posted up at several tram and bus stops in Bratislava. The ECHR linked this private controversy to a general debate on public housing: ' . . . the Court notes that the purpose of the applicant's open letter was not exclusively to resolve his individual problem. In fact, at the end of his letter the applicant called upon other persons with a similar problem, with a view to taking joint action. He expressed the view, apparently in good faith, that the resolution of the problem was important for strengthening the rule of law in the newly born democracy. The letter thus undeniably raised issues capable of affecting the general interest, namely housing policy at a period when State-owned flats were about to be denationalised' (para. 56).

[6] For a good summary of the ECHR's case law on freedom of speech, see Mark Janis, R. Kay, and A. Bradley, *European Human Rights Law: Texts and Materials* (Oxford: Oxford University

3.2 FREEDOM OF SPEECH AND FALSE INFORMATION

Citizens need accurate information in order to construct their political opinions and contribute to the process of collective decision-making. Getting the facts right is no less important in politics than in other spheres of life. Actually, to the extent that fundamental interests are usually at stake in politics and the decisions to be made are so grave, it is even more important to ensure that citizens have the relevant information. The press, of course, plays a key role in this regard. It is the basic institution that serves the public's right to receive information about current affairs. The ECHR has acknowledged its special position.[7]

The problem, however, is how to balance two competing goals. On the one hand, we want information to have a certain quality: we want it to be true or, at least, to have been properly checked to guarantee its truth. On the other hand, we want to encourage the press to divulge the information it has obtained, if it has good reasons to believe that it is true. We want quantity. But there is a tension between the two goals. If we have legal rules that are very strict in the protection of truth, they may generate a 'chilling effect': they may discourage the press from making public a piece of information that it believes is true (and is actually true), for fear of the negative legal consequences it will face if the information cannot finally be proven to be true. If the legal rules are instead very lenient, there will be no chilling effect, and the flow of information is likely to increase, but its average quality will probably decline.

There is no easy answer to this dilemma. The ECHR has been sensitive to the idea that legal rules that have a chilling effect on freedom of speech are suspect.[8] But in spite of this sensitivity, it has imposed on the press a general requirement

Press, 2000), at 138–224; Monica Macovei, *Liberté d'expression. Un guide sur la mise en oeuvre de l'article 10 de la Convention européene des Droits de l'Homme* (Strasbourg: Council of Europe, 2003). A useful website to consult is the one run by the Media Division of the Directorate General of Human Rights of the Council of Europe, at: http://www.coe.int/media.

[7] *Sunday Times v The United Kingdom (No. 1)*, Judgment of 26 April 1979, para. 65, Series A No. 30; *Lingens v Austria*, Judgment of 8 July 1986, para. 41, Series A No. 103. In *Busuioc v Moldova*, Judgment of 21 December 2004, No. 61513/00, the ECHR is very explicit in giving more protection to the press than to ordinary individuals. It says: 'in contrast to the statements made by the applicant as a private individual in the case of *Janowski*, the impugned article in the present case was written by the applicant in his capacity as a journalist and gave rise to issues of freedom of the press' (para. 64). And it then adds: 'Acordingly, the approach employed by the Court in the *Janowski* case is not applicable in the present case. On the contrary, the Court considers that since the freedom of the press was at stake, the Moldovan authorities enjoyed a less extensive margin of appreciation when deciding whether there was a pressing social need to interfere with the applicant's freedom of expression' (para. 65).

[8] The ECHR has used the chilling effect argument in several contexts. For example, in *Goodwin v The United Kingdom* (Judgment of 27 March 1996, *Reports of Judgments and Decisions* 1996-II) a case concerning the legitimacy of a judicial order requiring a journalist to disclose the source of a piece of information, the Court spoke of the 'potentially chilling effect an order of source disclosure has on the exercise of' freedom of speech (para. 39).

of good faith, and has allowed states to place the burden of proof on the press in defamation cases. In this regard, the ECHR has developed a different doctrine from the one articulated by the United States Supreme Court.

3.2.1 The Good Faith Requirement

The US Supreme Court has granted limited protection to defamation. It has held that public officials and public figures may not recover damages for defamation unless they prove, with convincing clarity, that the defamatory statement was made with 'actual malice', that is, with knowledge that it was false or with reckless disregard of whether it was false or not.[9] The Court has also held that a private figure who sues a media defendant for defamation may not recover without some showing of fault, although not necessarily of actual malice. However, if a defamatory falsehood involves a matter of public concern, then even a private figure must show actual malice in order to recover presumed damages (i.e., not actual financial damages) or punitive damages.[10] There are thus three different legal regimes, depending on the character of the plaintiff, and the presence or absence of a matter of public interest.

The ECHR's doctrinal framework is different. It has constructed a unified legal regime, which it applies in a flexible way, depending on the circumstances of the case. The public or private character of the plaintiff, and the public importance of the issue the information relates to, are relevant factors to take into account, but they do not trigger the application of sharply different legal rules. The ECHR's position, moreover, differs from that of its American counterpart in three important aspects.

3.2.1.1 The Standard of Diligence

The first aspect refers to the standard of diligence. The ECHR imposes a 'requirement of good faith' on the press. It protects journalists' right to divulge information on issues of general interest 'provided that they are acting in good faith and on an accurate factual basis and provide reliable and precise information in accordance with the ethics of journalism'.[11] This test is close to the test of diligence that the US Supreme Court imposes on the press when the victim of the false statement is a private figure. It is stricter (on the press) than the mere absence of malice that the US Supreme Court has established in cases where the victim is a public figure.[12]

---

[9] *New York Times v Sullivan*, 376 US 254 (1964); *Curtis Publishing Co. v Butts*, 388 US 130 (1967). The Court extended the *Sullivan* rule to criminal libel in *Garrison v Louisiana*, 379 US 64 (1964).

[10] *Gertz v Robert Welch Inc.*, 418 US 323 (1974).

[11] *Fressoz and Roire v France*, Judgment of 21 January 1999, para. 54, [GC] No. 29183/95, ECHR 1999-I. See also *Schwabe v Austria*, Judgment of 28 August 1992, para. 34, Series A No. 242-B; *Prager and Oberschlick v Austria*, Judgment of 26 April 1995, para. 37, Series A No. 313; *Dalban v. Romania*, Judgment of 28 September 1999, para. 49, [GC], No. 28114/95, ECHR 1999-VI.

[12] In *Garrison v Louisiana*, 379 US 64, 79 (1964), the Supreme Court made clear that 'the test which [was] laid down in the *New York Times* is not keyed to ordinary care; defeasance of the privilege is conditioned, not on mere negligence, but on reckless disregard for the truth'.

The good faith requirement, however, can be applied more or less severely. The ECHR has held that account must be taken of the nature and the gravity of the allegations made by the speaker.[13] 'The more serious the allegation, the more solid the factual basis has to be.'[14] But, quite apart from the relevance of this factor, the ECHR appears to be stricter in some cases while more tolerant in others.

In *Bladet Tromso and Stensaas v Norway*, for example, the ECHR seemed to be considerably lenient towards the press.[15] It protected a newspaper that had published false statements concerning the professional behaviour of the crew of a seal-hunting vessel (the name of which, *The Harmoni*, was mentioned in the article). Whereas the national courts in Norway considered that the newspaper had been reckless, for it should have checked the veracity of its allegations regarding the illegal actions of the crew, the ECHR found that it was sufficient for the newspaper to have relied on an official report that was delivered to the government by an inspector, in spite of the fact that the newspaper knew that the government had decided not to publish the report immediately, in order to check the allegations of illegality that it contained (para. 71). The Court also noted that the newspaper had published the point of view of the seal hunters on the matter (para. 63). Three judges dissented, however, calling for a more demanding standard of diligence on the press (judges Palm, Fuhrmann, and Baka). The applicant in this case had not satisfied the proper test, they argued. The report by the inspector could not be relied upon, since the Ministry decided not to make it public precisely because it thought it might contain libellous comments concerning private individuals. And the newspaper did not ask the crew members for their version of the events before publishing the article; it carried a story concerning their reactions later on, after the publication by the newspaper of the entire report, when the damage had already occurred. According to the dissenting judges, 'the judgment sends the wrong signal to the press in Europe'. 'Few stories can be so important in a democratic society or deserving of protection under Article 10 of the Convention, that the basic ethics of journalism—which require, *inter alia*, journalists to check their facts before going to press with a story in circumstances such as the present—can be sacrificed for the commercial gratification of an immediate scoop.'

In other cases, the ECHR seems to apply a more demanding test. In *Pedersen and Baadsgaard v Denmark*,[16] for example, the Court found no violation in the conviction of two television journalists who had produced two television programmes where the allegation was made that the head of the police unit in charge of the investigation of a murder case had suppressed a vital piece of

---

[13] *Bladet Tromso and Stensaas v Norway*, Judgment of 20 May 1999, [GC] No. 21980/93, ECHR 1999-III.
[14] *Pedersen and Baadsgaard v Denmark*, Judgment of 17 December 2004, para. 78, [GC], No. 49017/99, ECHR 2004.
[15] Judgment of 20 May 1999, [GC], No. 21980/93, ECHR 1999-III.
[16] Judgment of 17 December 2004, [GC], No 49017/99, ECHR 2004.

evidence that was favourable to the accused, who was later convicted by the courts. The criminal case was then reopened, a new trial was granted, and the accused was finally acquitted. The police chief brought actions against the journalists for defamation, and the courts fined them and ordered them to pay damages. The ECHR held that, given the seriousness of their allegation against the police chief, the journalists should have relied upon a more solid factual basis than the one they had. It was not sufficient to have had access to a piece of evidence that cast doubt on the culpability of the person that was convicted, together with the fact that there had been important procedural flaws in the investigation. Something more was needed to support the allegation that the head of the police unit had deliberately suppressed a vital piece of evidence. The ECHR was deeply divided in this case, though. (It was a nine to eight decision of the Grand Chamber.) The dissenters thought that the majority had applied too strict a test. In their opinion, the factual basis was sufficient to allow the journalists to publish their statements against the chief superintendent of police.

3.2.1.2 The Burden of Proof

The second important difference between the ECHR and the US Supreme Court concerns the rules on the burden of proof. Most European countries require the defendant to prove the truth of the information or, at least, to prove that he had good reasons to believe that the information was true. The ECHR has held that this requirement does not violate Article 10 of the European Convention. This is in contrast to the American doctrine: in defamation cases, the US Supreme Court places on the plaintiff the burden of proof (both of the falsity of the statement and of the existence of malice or, where applicable, negligence, on the part of the press).[17]

That the position of the ECHR departs from the American doctrine is clearly illustrated in *McVicar v The United Kingdom*.[18] The applicant was a journalist who had written an article suggesting that the athlete Linford Christie used banned performance-enhancing drugs. Mr Christie commenced an action for defamation against the journalist. Under English law, the burden is on the defendant in a libel action to prove the truth of the defamatory statement on the balance of probabilities. Since the journalist did not prove the truth of the allegation he had made, he was ordered to pay the costs of the action and was made subject to an injunction restraining him from repeating the relevant statement (Mr Christie had not sought damages). When the journalist went to Strasbourg, he supported his free speech arguments with a citation from a passage from *New York Times v Sullivan* on the burden of proof, where the US Supreme Court said that if the burden is placed on the defendant, 'would-be critics of official conduct may be deterred from voicing their criticism, even

---

[17] *New York Times v Sullivan*, 376 US 254 (1964); *Philadelphia Newspapers, Inc. v Hepps*, 475 US 767 (1986).   [18] Judgment of 7 May 2002, No. 46311/99, ECHR 2002-III.

though it is believed to be true and even though it is in fact true, because of
doubt whether it can be proved in court or fear of the expense of having to do
so' (paras 27 and 65). The ECHR disagreed. It unanimously considered that,
given the seriousness of the allegations against Mr Christie, 'the requirement
that the applicant prove that the allegations made in the article were substantially true on the balance of probabilities constituted a justified restriction on his
freedom of expression' (para. 87). The ECHR faulted the journalist for being
'concerned with verifying the truth or reliability of the allegations to a high
standard only after the event, once the defamation proceedings had been
commenced against him' (para. 86).

The ECHR has accepted that the defendant has the burden of proof in other
decisions as well. In *Cumpana and Mazare v Romania*,[19] for example, the ECHR
found the journalists at fault for having failed to adduce evidence at any stage of
the defamation proceedings to 'substantiate their allegations or provide a sufficient factual basis for them'. Similarly, in *Lesnik v Slovakia*, it held that the
allegations of the applicant, concerning the unlawful conduct of a public prosecutor, were 'statements of fact which the domestic courts rightly requested the
applicant to support by relevant evidence'.[20] In *Busuioc v Moldova*, the ECHR did
not protect certain pieces of information divulged by the journalist, since he had
not verified their accuracy before publication.[21] In some cases the ECHR has
found a breach of Article 10 because the defendant was not allowed to offer
evidence to prove the truth of his allegations, or the courts refused to examine it.
But this presupposes, of course, that it is not wrong for the domestic law to impose
on the defendant the burden of proof.[22]

---

[19] *Cumpana and Mazare v Romania*, Judgment of 17 December 2004, para. 104, [GC], No.
33348/96, ECHR 2004.

[20] *Lesnik v Slovakia*, Judgment of 11 March 2003, para. 57, No. 35640/97, ECHR 2003-IV.

[21] *Busuioc v Moldova*, Judgment of 21 December 2004, paras 70 and 78, No. 61513/00.

[22] Thus, in *Castells v Spain*, Judgment of 23 April 1992, Series A No. 236, the ECHR found
that Spain had violated Article 10 for not having allowed the defendant to prove the veracity of his
statements. Similarly, in *Dalban v Romania*, Judgment of 28 September 1999, para. 50, [GC], No.
28114/95, ECHR 1999-VI, the Court found a breach of Article 10 when the courts had not
examined the evidence that the defendant, a journalist, had put forward in order to prove his
allegations concerning the fraudulent activities of a public officer (for the courts had concluded that
the fact that the public prosecutor's office had decided on two occasions that the public officer had
no criminal case to answer was sufficient to prove the falsity of the allegations made by the journalist
in his article). The same kind of violation was found in *Jerusalem v Austria*, Judgment of 27
February 2001, para. 45, No. 26958/95, ECHR 2001-II; in *Colombani and Others v France*,
Judgment of 25 June 2002, para. 66, No. 51279/99, ECHR 2002-V; and in *Busuioc v
Moldova*, Judgment of 21 December 2004, para. 88, No. 61513/00. The Court went further in *De
Haes and Gijsels v Belgium*, Judgment of 24 February 1997, *Reports of Judgments and Decisions*
1997-I. The applicants (an editor and a journalist) had published several articles criticizing the
judges who had decided a child custody case. In the defamation proceedings, they said they were
prepared to prove the truth of their allegations, and asked the court to require the Crown counsel to
produce certain expert witness reports that had been examined in the custody case and that had been
cited by the applicants in their articles. The domestic court rejected the petition. A unanimous
ECHR found a violation of Article 6. It said that it did not share the domestic court's opinion that
'the request for production of documents demonstrated the lack of care with which Mr De Haes

It must be noted, however, that the ECHR is not completely clear what the burden of proof refers to in this context. Is the press expected to prove the truth of the information, or only that it properly checked its truth? In other words, is the defendant protected under the European Convention if he is not able to prove the truth of his allegation, but does prove that he acted in a diligent manner? Most cases suggest that the answer is yes. The ECHR seems to consider that good faith is a sufficient defence. In *McVicar v The United Kingdom*, for example, the English courts had found for the claimant in the defamation action because the journalist had not proven that the information was substantially true. The ECHR, however, before reaching its conclusion that there had been no violation of freedom of speech in this case, emphasized the recklessness with which the journalist had acted when he decided to publish a piece of information he had made no serious efforts to verify. Other cases, such as the ones mentioned above, support this understanding as well. In *Steel and Morris v The United Kingdom*,[23] however, the ECHR interpreted the *McVicar* judgment to have held 'that it was not in principle incompatible with Article 10 to place on the defendant in libel proceedings the onus of proving to the civil standard *the truth of defamatory statements*' (para. 93, emphasis added). This suggests that it is legitimate for the states to require the speaker to prove the truth of what he said, and not simply that he acted diligently (with 'good faith') when he checked the truth of what he said.

So, the case law is not sufficiently clear on this point. In general, though, the ECHR seems to be ready to protect journalists when they adduce evidence to support their claim that they checked the information in a diligent way, even if the evidence is not sufficient to prove its truth.

3.2.1.3 The Principle of Proportionality

The third aspect in which the ECHR case law differs from that of the US Supreme Court refers to the principle of proportionality. The ECHR, in comparison to its American counterpart, is more ready to review the nature and the amount of the civil and criminal penalties that state courts impose on speakers, in order to make sure that they are not out of proportion.[24] The

---

and Mr Gijsels had written their articles'. It instead considered that 'the journalists' concern not to risk compromising their sources of information by lodging the documents in question themselves was legitimate' (para. 55).

[23] Judgment of 15 February 2005, No. 68416/01, ECHR 2005.

[24] There have been voices in the United States who have proposed to abandon *New York Times v Sullivan* and to substitute for it some kind of constitutional limit on damages. Justice White, for example, in a concurring opinion in *Dun & Bradstreet, Inc. v Greenmoss Builders*, 472 US 749, 771 (1985), wrote: 'In *New York Times*, instead of escalating the plaintiff's burden of proof to an almost impossible level, we could have achieved our stated goal by limiting the recoverable damages to a level that would not unduly threaten the press.' Some scholars are also in favour of imposing constitutional limits on damages. See, for instance, R. A. Smolla, *Suing the Press: Libel, the Media, and Power* (Oxford: Oxford University Press, 1986), at 241–42.

ECHR has held that freedom of speech is infringed if the state reacts in a disproportionate manner against the speaker, even if he has overstepped the limits of freedom of speech. Such disproportionate reactions unduly discourage the legitimate exercise of this right.

Thus, in *Tolstoy Miloslavsky v The United Kingdom*,[25] the ECHR concluded that the applicant's free speech rights had been infringed to the extent that the damage award granted by an English jury (£1.5 million) was too large, however serious the libellous statements were. (The applicant, a historian, had said in a pamphlet that Lord Aldington was a 'man with the blood of 70,000 men, women or children in his hands', on the grounds that there was overwhelming evidence that he had arranged the perpetration of a major war crime.) The ECHR held that 'an award of the present size must be particularly open to question where the substantive national law applicable at the time fails itself to provide a requirement of proportionality' (para. 49). It also objected to the great latitude that English law gave to the jury at that time: the libel awards could not be set aside by the Court of Appeal simply on the grounds that they were excessive, but only when they were so unreasonable that they must have been arrived at capriciously, unconscionably, or irrationally. The ECHR found that the scope of such judicial control was insufficient (para. 50).

Similarly, in *Cumpana and Mazare v Romania*,[26] the ECHR held that there had been no breach of Article 10 to the extent that the journalists had failed to adduce evidence at any stage of the defamation proceedings to substantiate their allegations or provide a factual basis for them. However, it deemed that the criminal sanctions that had been imposed on them were excessive (they had been sentenced to seven months' imprisonment and prohibited from exercising certain civil rights and from working as journalists for one year). It thus concluded that, because of the lack of proportion of the penalties, there had been a violation of freedom of expression. The ECHR was explicit that the chilling effect argument was the justification for its readiness to review the proportionality of the sanctions that are imposed on the press, even when the press has not acted diligently. It said that states may impose restrictions on the press to protect reputation interests, but 'they must not do so in a manner that unduly deters the media from fulfilling their role of alerting the public to apparent or suspected misuse of public power', and that 'investigative journalists are liable to be inhibited from reporting on matters of general public interest . . . if they run the risk, as one of the standard sanctions imposable for unjustified attacks on the reputation of private individuals, of being sentenced to prison or to a prohibition on the exercise of their profession' (para. 113). 'The chilling effect that the fear of such sanctions poses on the exercise of journalistic freedom of expression is evident' (para. 114). The ECHR transcended the particular circumstances of the case and announced the general rule

---

[25] Judgment of 13 July 1995, Series A No. 316-B.
[26] Judgment of 17 December 2004, [GC] No. 33348/96, ECHR 2004.

that 'the imposition of a prison sentence for a press offence will be compatible with journalists' freedom of expression as guaranteed by Article 10 of the Convention only in exceptional circumstances, notably where other fundamental rights have been seriously impaired, as, for example, in the case of hate speech or incitement to violence' (para. 115).[27]

Given these three differences that I have described, it is a fair question whether the ECHR is sufficiently protective of freedom of the press, and whether the introduction of some of the American rules would be beneficial. Overall, however, it is not clear that the ECHR should basically alter its current approach.

The fact that the ECHR has elaborated a general doctrine, instead of three separate legal regimes, may have the disadvantage that the decisions in the particular cases are more unpredictable. But it has the advantage of flexibility. It is probably too rigid to attach sharply different legal regimes to the distinction between public and private figures, and to the presence or absence of an issue of public interest.

As to the standard of diligence, and the rules on burden of proof, it is true that the position of the ECHR in this matter entails the risk that the press will be discouraged from issuing information that it has good reason to believe is true. But the problem of the chilling effect can be attacked successfully from another angle, as the ECHR does: by making sure that the civil and criminal penalties that are imposed on the press are not excessive. The chilling effect argument depends on the gravity of the penalties, whether criminal or civil, that the speaker is expected to suffer.[28] The ECHR should make clear, however, that States are free to require the press to satisfy relatively demanding standards of diligence, and to impose on them the burden of proof of their diligence, *provided that the domestic courts are especially careful in reviewing the proportionality of the legal consequences that the press has to suffer as a result of its negligence*. It should also hold explicitly that its own readiness to review the proportionality of the civil or criminal sanctions in a particularly careful way is derived from its basic holding that freedom of speech does not prohibit states from placing on the press the burden of proving that it acted diligently.

The ECHR could also qualify explicitly the rules that grant immunity to the press (and to speakers in general) when they have acted in a diligent manner, in the following way: even if, under the European Convention, the domestic law cannot authorize courts to punish the press in such cases for having issued information that turns out to be false, it can nevertheless authorize them to

[27] The Court followed the same line of reasoning in *Steel and Morris v The United Kingdom*, Judgment of 15 February 2005, para. 96, No. 68416/01, ECHR 2005.

[28] This depends, basically, on the material harm that the penalty entails. But one should not disregard the symbolic harm of certain legal consequences. Thus, the ECHR was right in *Lehideux and Isorni v France*, Judgment of 23 September 1998, *Reports of Judgments and Decisions* 1998-VII, when it noted 'the seriousness of a criminal conviction for publicly defending the crimes of collaboration' with the enemy, even if the penalty was a fine of only one franc (para. 57).

make a declaration that such information is false and to require the press to correct it (or to publish the judicial declaration) and to abstain from reproducing it in the future. The chilling effect argument is not compelling when the consequence at stake is merely that.[29]

Also, the regime of legal liability could be less severe when the media outlet offers the victim of an alleged false statement equal space or time to respond. The public can then hear the victim's side of the story. I do not think that this should be sufficient to bar the victim from bringing an action against the media, for it may still be necessary to go to the courts to clarify whose story is right. But the damage award may be reduced when the public has been given both sides of the story. Both the reputation of the victim and the right of the public to get accurate information suffer less when the statement made by the press is challenged immediately by the victim.

3.2.2 Relaxing the Standard of Diligence when the Information Relates to Politicians?

It is sometimes said that the rules of legal liability for false information should be relaxed when the latter refers to politicians. One reason that is often invoked is that politicians have chosen freely to enter the public sphere. The ECHR, for example, said in the *Lingens* case that 'the limits of acceptable criticism are ... wider as regards a politician as such than as regards a private individual. Unlike the latter, the former inevitably and knowingly lays himself open to close scrutiny of his every word and deed by both journalists and the public at large, and he must consequently display a greater degree of tolerance.'[30] The US

---

[29] In *Bladet Tromsø and Stensaas v Norway*, Judgment of 20 May 1999, [GC] No. 21980/93, ECHR 1999-III, the ECHR refers to the law in Norway, where a defamatory statement which is unlawful and has not been proved true may be declared 'null and void' by a court. Such an order is not considered a criminal sanction, but a civil law remedy. The ECHR explains: 'In recent years there has been a debate in Norway as to whether one should abolish the remedy of null and void orders, which has existed in Norwegian law since the sixteenth century and which may also be found in the laws of Denmark and Iceland. Because of its being deemed a particularly lenient form of sanction, the Norwegian Association of Editors has expressed a wish to maintain it' (para. 40). In the United States, there have been proposals to reform libel law in order to arrive at something like the system used in a number of European countries, which deal with the problem of defamation by providing for lawsuits to determine the truth, with awards of only symbolic damages or none at all. For references, see A. Lewis, *Make No Law: The Sullivan Case and the First Amendment* (New York: Vintage, 1992), at 228–29. In Spain, one of the leading experts in freedom of speech has defended the view that the legal system should give more weight to mere declaratory actions in libel cases. Those actions should be granted even if the press was diligent. The important point is that the relevant statement was false, and both the victim and the general public have a right to have that falsehood corrected. See P. Salvador Coderch, *El derecho de la libertad* (Madrid: Centro de Estudios Constitucionales, 1993), at 64–78; and P. Salvador Coderch and M. T. Castiñeira Palou, *Prevenir y castigar. Libertad de información y expresión, tutela del honor y funciones del derecho de daños* (Madrid: Marcial Pons, 1997), at 38–52.

[30] *Lingens v Austria*, Judgment of 8 July 1986 (para. 42), Series A No. 103. The ECHR has made clear that this argument does not apply to civil servants, who cannot be said, in general, to 'knowingly lay themselves open to close scrutiny of their every word and deed to the extent to which

Supreme Court made a similar argument, in connection with public figures in general.[31]

But this is not by itself a justification for relaxing the legal rules on truth. If we are considering which rules should govern the political sphere, it is irrelevant to argue that those who decide freely to participate in it should be prepared to face the consequences. We are discussing precisely what the rules should be. Once we have justified them, but not before we have done so, may we say that those who decide freely to enter the political domain should accept the consequences of applying the rules that govern it. So we must first assess the advantages and disadvantages of having more relaxed rules when the information refers to politicians. In this regard, while strict rules may have a chilling effect on citizens who would like to inform and give opinions about politicians, relaxed rules may have a chilling effect on citizens who would like to become political candidates for public office. As Rodney Smolla has written in the American context, it is already hard enough to attract quality people to public office: 'If public office becomes a libel free-fire zone, good people in office will be even harder to find.'[32]

Another argument that is often made rests on the politicians' greater access to the media to counteract any false information regarding them.[33] But this argument is not conclusive either. Not all politicians have quick access to the

politicians do'. See *Janowski v Poland*, Judgment of 21 January 1999, para. 33, [GC] No. 25716/94, ECHR 1999-I; *Lesnik v Slovakia*, Judgment of 11 March, 2003, para. 53, No. 35640/97, ECHR 2003-IV. Thus, in *Pedersen and Baadsgaard v Denmark*, Judgment of 17 December 2004, [GC] No. 49017/99, ECHR 2004, the ECHR uses this argument to conclude that 'although the Chief Superintendent was subject to wider limits of acceptable criticism than private individuals, being a public official, a senior police officer and leader of the police team which had carried out an admittedly controversial criminal investigation, he could not be treated on an equal footing with politicians when it came to public discussion of his actions' (para. 80). On the other hand, not all civil servants are to be treated similarly for these purposes. They occupy a conceptual space between private individuals and politicians, but some of them are closer to the former while others are closer to the latter. Law enforcement officers or prosecutors are not as close to politicians in the continuum as the managers of an important state-owned company, for example. See *Busuioc v Moldova*, Judgment of 21 December 2004, para. 64, No. 61513/00.

[31] It reasoned in *Gertz v Robert Welch, Inc.*, 418 US 323, 344 (1974), that 'the communications media are entitled to act on the assumption that public officials and public figures have voluntarily exposed themselves to increased risk of injury from defamatory falsehoods concerning them. No such assumption is justified with respect to a private individual. He has not accepted public office nor assumed an "influential role in ordering society" ... He has relinquished no part of his interest in the protection of his own good name, and consequently he has a more compelling call on the courts for redress of injury inflicted by defamatory falsehood.'

[32] R. A. Smolla, *Suing the Press*, above, n. 24, at 243. The Supreme Court of the United States did not go so far in *New York Times v Sullivan* as to grant protection to malicious false statements about public officials. As Lewis explains, *Make No Law*, above, n. 29, at 167, Justice Brennan had in mind the McCarthy period's vindictive efforts to destroy public officials, when he wrote the *Sullivan* opinion.

[33] In the *Gertz* case, for instance, the US Supreme Court, in connection with public officials and public figures in general, stated: 'Public officials and public figures usually enjoy significantly greater access to the channels of effective communication and hence have a more realistic opportunity to counteract false statements than private individuals normally enjoy' (p. 344).

media to make their point of view known. In order to neutralize false information, moreover, politicians must have access to the particular media that published it, as well as the other media that may have republished it. Moreover, a politician may sometimes not be in the position to prove the falsity of a piece of information that ascribes a particular action to him, because it may be impossible or very hard to prove a negative fact. It will be up to the public to decide whether to give more credibility to the speaker or to the politician, but this is not sufficient if truth matters. We should bear in mind that it is not politicians who are principally harmed by false information about them. It is the community of citizens as a whole, whose right to receive accurate information is infringed.

A more convincing justification appeals to the nature of political information as a public good.[34] Because public goods are nonrival and nonexclusive, they tend to be underproduced in ordinary markets. Those who divulge political information (the media, basically) bear the enormous costs of obtaining it and checking its accuracy, but they cannot fully internalize the benefits of their efforts. They cannot exclude others from free riding and enjoying the benefits of their investment. So, if the community wants to encourage the production of political information, the law must compensate for this problem, by giving the media a certain privilege: immunity from legal liability (unless they acted with malice).

This argument, however, underestimates the ways in which the media have been able to internalize the benefits of their efforts in producing political information: by linking political information with advertising, and by packaging political information in entertaining formats, so as to increase the size of their audience. As Lillian Bevier reminds as, 'the news industry regularly generates sizeable revenues and appears to be highly profitable'.[35]

Moreover, even if the quantity of political information is likely to increase if we have a relaxed regime of legal liability, the question is whether we should accept it, given the risk that the information will be of inferior quality (that is, more of it will be false). In this connection, one must take into account that it is hard for citizens to tell by themselves whether or not the political information they receive is true. They cannot easily react, therefore, against those who are offering them a defective product. This is in contrast to what happens with commercial information: consumers can usually have a look at the product before they buy it, or learn about it after the purchase, and can thus use the market to punish the sellers who have given them false information about the product.[36]

---

[34] For a good presentation and critical evaluation of this argument, see Lillian R. Bevier, 'The Invisible Hand of the Marketplace of Ideas', included in L. C. Bollinger and G. R. Stone (eds.), *Eternally Vigilant: Free Speech in the Modern Area* (Chicago, IL: The University of Chicago Press, 2002), at 233–55.   [35] Ibid, at 246.
[36] Ibid, at 249–52.

It is true that, apart from the regime of legal liability, there is another monitoring mechanism that can ensure that the press will tend to give information of a certain quality: competition among journalists and publishers. In particular, some publishers cater to specific groups of citizens who are more interested than others in politics, and who are more demanding as to the quality of the information they get. These alternative information suppliers will have to be more accurate, and they will act as an indirect constraint on the mainstream media.[37]

The problem, however, is that this external incentive is not likely to be sufficient. There is a considerable level of fragmentation in the media market: people are attached to certain newspapers, radios, or TV channels, and they are not likely to know, or to give credibility to, the information that other media, or more specialized sources, are giving in order to counteract false information.[38] It is not clear why a relatively demanding legal regime of legal liability should not be imposed on the press (even when it informs about political matters) in order to reinforce the market incentive, given that (a) the media have been able to find ways to internalize the benefits of their efforts, so there is no special problem of systematic underproduction of political information, and provided that (b) the possible chilling effect of imposing a duty of diligence on the press when it refers to political matters is neutralized through a careful assessment by courts of the proportionality of the sanctions.

So, all things considered, the arguments we have examined do not seem to be powerful enough to justify a special and more protective rule for false information that involves politicians.

3.2.3 The Problem of Partial Truth

An interesting problem arises when the information that someone gives is only partially true. To what extent is the portion of falsehood sufficiently important to disqualify it as protected speech? A certain amount of tolerance is called for in this regard, though much will depend on the context. In political debates, in particular, speakers or writers do not always have sufficient time or space to introduce all the qualifications that would be needed for the information to be completely accurate. Also, given the polemical character of most debates, it is not unreasonable for the different parties to rely on the facts that are helpful to

---

[37] Ibid, at 253–55.

[38] On the problems that the fragmentation of the media gives rise to, and some proposals for remedying the situation, see C. Sunstein, 'The Future of Free Speech', included in Bollinger and Stone (eds.), *Eternally Vigilant*, above, n. 34, at 285–310. He proposes, for example, that the government require especially popular websites to include links to other sites that deal with substantive issues in a serious way, and to impose on highly partisan websites similar links to other sites containing opposing views (at 309). Owen Fiss has also referred to the problem of fragmentation as a result of technological advances, and has emphasized the role of television in creating a shared understanding among the public. See O. Fiss, 'The Censorship of Television', ibid, at 258–60.

support their opinions, while they silence other facts that are disturbing to their causes. The problem of partial truth presents itself in different forms.

One variation of the problem is this: the press discusses a topic of general interest, concerning the practice of certain groups of citizens or officials, and offers a particular story to exemplify those practices. There is good evidence that such practices exist, but the particular story that is reported turns out to be false. The *Bladet Tromso and Stensaas v Norway* case is a good example:[39] there was a very intense debate in Norway (and internationally, too) on whether or not to allow seal hunting, and what limitations should be imposed on it. In this context, a newspaper published a story about the professional behaviour of the crew of a particular vessel, a story that was false. It seemed clear that, however plausible the generalization about the practices of the relevant group of individuals (seal hunters, in this case), the particular false story should not be protected (if the press did not act in a diligent way). Account must be taken of the right to reputation of the individuals who are harmed by the false information. The public may have been more attracted to the debate on the general question by being exposed to that particular story, but the individuals whose reputation was harmed by the false information should not be sacrificed for the benefit of collective discussion. Moreover, it is epistemically relevant that the particular story that the press chose to focus on turns out to be false. It is possible that many other cases could have been reported to corroborate the generalization about the practices of seal hunters, but it is telling that the particular story that was supposed to exemplify those practices was actually false.[40]

Another modality of the problem of partial truth consists in the presence of inaccurate details in the particular story that is being reported. The importance of these details varies from case to case.

The *Schwabe v Austria* case provides an extreme example.[41] Mr Tomaschitz, a city mayor who belonged to the Young Austrian People's Party, was convicted in 1984 for causing a car accident while under the influence of alcohol. Mr Wagner, a leader of the Socialist Party, suggests that he should resign. Mr Schwabe, another politician of the Young Austrian People's Party, agreed, but said that Wagner has no moral authority to suggest that course of action, since he had supported Mr Frühbauer, an important figure of the

[39] Judgment of 20 May 1999, [GC] No. 21980/93, ECHR 1999-III.

[40] The ECHR protected the press in this case, however, on the grounds that it had acted in good faith. A similar problem arises in *Thorgeir Thorgeirson v Iceland*, Judgment of 25 June 1992, Series A No. 239. In the context of a debate about police brutality, a writer published an article in the press criticizing the behaviour of the Reykjavik police. What triggered his decision to publish the article was a widely publicized case of a police officer who had been convicted for treating a journalist in a brutal way. The writer insisted, however, that there had been many other incidents of police brutality, and he mentioned, among others, one case he had learned about while being in a hospital. The problem was that at the defamation trial he did not prove his allegation about this latter case, and was fined. The ECHR, however, protected the writer on the grounds that he had been sufficiently diligent.

[41] *Schwabe v Austria*, Judgment of 28 August 1992, Series A No. 242-B.

Socialist Party, in spite of the fact that he, too, had been convicted (many years before, in 1966) of driving while under the influence of alcohol and causing an accident. Schwabe was convicted under the Criminal Code. One of the reasons was that the factual statement about Frühbauer was not accurate: in Frühbauer's case, the level of alcohol had not reached the level at which intoxication is presumed by the law, so the criminal court did not convict him of driving under the influence of alcohol, though he took that fact as an aggravating circumstance. The Austrian courts deciding the defamation case considered that, by referring to the two criminal convictions in the car accidents as equivalent, Schwabe had misled the audience as to the facts, and harmed Frühbauer's reputation. The ECHR disagreed and found that there had been a violation of freedom of speech in this case. It emphasized that the speaker never said that the two convictions were identical as to the facts. He made a moral judgment about their similarity—a value judgment that was substantially correct in light of the facts (para. 34). It should be noted, however, that even if the speaker had said that the two convictions were exactly the same as to the facts, this would have been a minor mistake: the important factual point is that the two politicians had been involved in car accidents, with significant levels of alcohol in their bodies, and were convicted for the damage caused. It is an irrelevant mistake to have confused an aggravating circumstance with the basic crime. As the ECHR rightly points out, moreover, the writer did not have the space to get into much detail (para. 33).

In contrast, in *Radio France*, the partial error was regarded as too serious to be tolerated.[42] A radio station had broadcast information concerning Michel Junot, who had been deputy mayor of Paris from 1977 to 1995. The station said correctly that *Le Point* (a journal) had informed that Mr Junot had organized the deportation of 1,000 Jews in 1942. But the radio made a partial mistake: it stated wrongly that Mr Junot had acknowledged having organized those deportations. The ECHR found that this was not a minor inaccuracy. Given the extreme seriousness of the facts that were attributed to Mr Junot, and the enormous impact of the news that was broadcast, the radio station should have been more careful.[43]

A third modality of partial truth consists in silencing certain facts that would give a more nuanced and complete picture of a person or event. This form of partiality is illustrated in the case *Lehideux and Isorni v France*.[44] Two French associations had published an advertisement in *Le Monde*, trying to rehabilitate the memory of Marshal Philippe Pétain, who had headed the collaborationist Vichy regime during the Nazi occupation of France in World War II. The ECHR said rightly that it was clear that the political advertisement in favour of Marshall Petáin was unilateral, polemical. It was understandable for the associations that signed the advertisement

---

[42] *Radio France and Others v France*, Judgment of 30 March 2004, No. 53984/00, ECHR 2004-II.
[43] Para. 39.
[44] Judgment of 23 September 1998, *Reports of Judgments and Decisions* 1998-VII.

to have told the facts that place the Marshall under the best light, and silence other facts that would be damaging to his reputation (such as the fact that the Vichy regime approved laws against the Jews).[45] The audience was not misled when it received information and opinions from a source that was explicitly partial in favour of a particular cause.

3.2.4 Historical Facts

Citizens get information about the world through different sources (from the school system to the many different institutions and organizations that are specialized in diverse fields of knowledge), and it would make no sense to ask courts to check the veracity of all the information that is distributed to the public. The sphere of science, for example, has its internal rules of procedure to generate and test theories, and courts are not used regularly to declare that a particular theory is false. The same pattern should apply, in principle, to historical debates.[46] Courts should not intervene in them, since other institutions, organizations, and individuals are sufficiently reliable to consider the evidence and sometimes bring closure to historical controversies, and courts do not have a comparative advantage in this regard.[47]

The ECHR is generally sympathetic to this view. In the *Lehideux and Isorni* judgment that was mentioned above, the Court held that courts should not try to resolve historical controversies that remain open. In that case, the two French associations that wanted to rehabilitate the memory of Marshall Pétain had defended in their advertisement the 'double game' theory, according to which the Marshall had really wanted the victory of the Allies and to save France from the enemy, and had collaborated with Nazi Germany on instrumental grounds only. The ECHR said that it was not its task 'to settle this point, which is part of an ongoing debate among historians about the events in question and their interpretation' (para. 47).

But there are limits to this principle of judicial non-involvement. The ECHR has accepted judicial intervention when the reputation of a person may be tarnished by a historian who fails to respect the fundamental rules of the historical method.[48] More importantly, it considers that the denial of 'clearly established historical facts'

---

[45] Para. 52. See also concurring opinion of Judge de Meyer.

[46] I assume, of course, that there is a fact of the matter about historical events. It is a fact of the matter that the Holocaust existed, for instance. On the difficulty of criticizing revisionist theories about the Holocaust if one does not accept that there can be objectivity in historical debates, see R. Evans, *In Defence of History* (London: Norton & Co, 1997), at 238–43.

[47] As Rodney Smolla argues, 'when we move away from litigation over relatively confined arenas of fact and into litigation over the unbounded causes and effects of history, the normal "fact-finding" function of the jury may break down. At some point on the continuum from raw factual detail to the larger themes of history we move from fact to ideology; we turn jurors into historians and political scientists.' Smolla, *Suing the Press*, above, n. 24, at 249. What Smolla says about jurors is applicable, *mutatis mutandis*, to courts.

[48] See *Chauvy and Others v France*, Judgment of 29 June 2004, paras 69 and 77, No. 64915/01.

is unprotected speech. In *Lehideux and Isorni*, it said that '[the double game theory concerning the strategy of Marshall Pétain] does not belong to the category of clearly established historical facts—such as the Holocaust—whose negation or revision would be removed from the protection of Article 10 by Article 17'. (Article 17 denies protection to the acts that are aimed at the destruction of the fundamental rights of others.)

The Court applied this precedent in the *Garaudy* case,[49] and dismissed the application of Roger Garaudy, a philosopher, writer, and former politician who had been convicted by French courts for the publication of his book, 'The Founding Myths of Israeli Politics'. Garaudy had criticized in that book the Nazi crimes, but had questioned the number of Jews that had been killed (much less than 6 million), the cause of their death (the deportations and the epidemics in the concentration camps, rather than gas chambers), and the interpretation of the 'Final Solution' (not the extermination of the Jews, but their deportation to Madagascar or to Eastern Europe). He said that the major beneficiaries of these myths were the Israeli–Zionist lobbies in France and the United States, whose aim was to place themselves above the law and endanger world unity and peace. The ECHR reasoned that the writer had denied 'clearly established historical facts', instead of contributing to a historical debate in quest for the truth. Since the aim and result of his book was to rehabilitate the Nazi regime, it was not protected speech under the Convention (for Article 17 denies protection to such speech).[50]

This exception to the general principle of judicial non-involvement in historical matters is not easy to justify. We could think of two different types of harm that may be caused when someone denies a clearly established fact. One is epistemic, and the other is emotional. The epistemic harm is difficult to substantiate. It is true that the audience gets wrong information about history if someone publicly denies the Holocaust, for example. But it is hard to argue that much epistemic harm derives from this. Since such a terrible event is a 'clearly established historical fact', not only among historians but among the population at large, it is very unlikely that many people will be misled into falsehood after listening to someone who denies that it happened.[51] Interestingly, it is rather when someone is participating

---

[49] *Garaudy v France*, decision of 24 June 2003, No. 65831/01, ECHR 2003-IX.

[50] See also *Marais v France*, decision by the Commission of 24 June 1996, No. 31159/96, rejecting the application of a French engineer who had been convicted for the publication of an article that had questioned the existence of gas chambers in the concentration camp of Strutof-Natzweiler; *FP v Germany*, decision by the Commission, of 29 March 1993, No. 19459/92, rejecting the application of a German military officer who had been punished for having stated at a private party, in the presence of German and American soldiers, that the Holocaust was a lie of the Zionists while in reality Jews had never been persecuted and killed; and *Witzsch v Germany*, decision by the Court, 20 April 1999, No. 41448/98, rejecting the application of a secondary school-teacher who had sent letters to Bavarian politicians, in which he had complained about a planned amendment of the Penal Code on the punishment of incitement to hatred (expressly penalizing the denial of Nazi mass killing), and to which he had attached a statement denying the existence of gas chambers and the mass killing of Jews.

[51] Of course, this judgment is relative to the different audiences. If such 'clearly established facts' were not secure in the popular culture of a particular country, then it might be dangerous if

in a historical debate *about an open question* (the answer to which has not yet been clearly established), that he can infringe people's right to get accurate information, if he offers a historical theory that he has not properly checked (or, worse than that, that he is aware to be false). We are epistemically harmed, not when someone tells us something we already know to be clearly false, but when he is reckless and tells us something that we are ignorant about, and we believe him. We are not harmed when someone says that the earth is flat (unless we are children and he is a teacher), but we are harmed when someone carelessly says that microwaves produce cancer (to borrow an example from the case law of the ECHR[52]). Similarly, it is when historical debates are still open (and not when they have been completely settled) that the people's right to receive accurate facts is really at stake.

As far as the emotional harm is concerned, it is true that the denial of certain clearly established facts like the Holocaust can cause harm to particular groups of people (which can be defined more or less narrowly: the victims of the Holocaust and their families, or Jews in general, for example). We could say that when someone denies the Holocaust, he is sending a message of contempt to the victims and their families, or to the ethnic group to which they belong. He unsettles the feelings and the sense of dignity of those groups.

The problem with this argument, however, is that it undermines the cardinal principle of free speech, namely, that this right affords protection 'not only to information and ideas that are favourably received or regarded as inoffensive or as a matter of indifference, but also to those that offend, shock or disturb the State or any sector of the population', as the ECHR has said.[53]

Should there be an exception, however, when the historical facts that are being denied meant the violation of the equal dignity of human beings? Unfortunately, there are so many such historical acts, that if we decide that the denial of any of those facts (or the minimization or justification of any of those facts) is not protected speech, we will have to prohibit too much. We may try to confine the prohibition to certain historical events, but we will have to establish the criteria that define the category, which is not an easy task. Is it a matter of

---

revisionist books were published. It is doubtful, however, that prohibiting revisionist books would be part of the best strategy to respond to the problem.

[52] See *Hertel v Switzerland*, Judgment of 25 August 1998, *Reports of Judgments and Decisions* 1998-IV.

[53] *Handyside v The United Kingdom*, Judgment of 7 December 1976, para. 49, Series A No. 24. Thus, in *Giniewski v France*, Judgment of 31 January 2006, No. 64016/00, ECHR 2006, the ECHR protected an article written by a historian and sociologist who claimed that a papal encyclical (*Veritatis Splendor*, published in 1993) advocated a theological principle that favoured an anti-semitic position. The author established causal links between that principle and the Holocaust. The Court rightly held that the fact that many Catholics would be shocked by the article was not a sufficient reason to punish its publication (para. 52). The Court, however, was not coherent with this general free speech principle when it allowed the protection of religious feelings to override free speech claims in *Otto Preminger-Institute v Austria*, Judgment of 20 September 1994, Series A No. 295-A, and *Wingrove v The United Kingdom*, Judgment of 25 November 1996, *Reports of Judgments and Decisions* 1996-V.

degree (the number of people who suffered, or the kind of violence that they suffered, for example)? Should one distinguish between ethnic or racial persecution and other kinds, such as political or religious? These distinctions seem arbitrary. Of course, the scope of freedom of speech is enlarged if we narrow down the category of the relevant historical facts through some arbitrary definitions, but freedom of speech suffers in a different way if the state is not neutral towards the different ideas and positions that are expressed in the public sphere. It is not right, under general principles of freedom of speech, for the state to prohibit the denial of the Holocaust under the Nazis, but permit someone to deny (or minimize, or understand, or legitimate) the violation of human rights performed by any of the many other brutal regimes or institutions that have existed throughout history. (Stalin's Russia and Mao's China easily come to mind.[54])

A better approach could be this: we could acknowledge that prohibiting the denial of the Holocaust is inconsistent with the general principles of freedom of speech, and yet establish that prohibition. We should not try to rationalize that decision, however, presenting it as a more or less ordinary example of a restriction that is imposed on speech on some general grounds (such as the need to protect the feelings of dignity of a group of people). That rationalization is bound to fail: if the reason why the denial of the Holocaust can be forbidden is that such denial is deeply offensive to a group of people, that reason would also apply to many other cases, and we would end up repressing too much speech. Instead, we should say that we have decided to *suspend* the general principles that govern freedom of speech, when it comes to the Holocaust. We have decided to suspend them because, as a community, we want to express our rejection of the Holocaust. We decide to attach a particular cultural meaning to this European tragedy, even if there have been other moral catastrophes in human history.[55] The very fact that we are not applying the general principles,

---

[54] The European Commission of Human Rights, in the case of *BH, MW and GK v Austria* (Decision of 12 October 1989, No. 12774/87), had to examine the complaint of three Austrian citizens who had been convicted under a law that prohibited political activities inspired by National Socialist ideas. They objected that while the law punished those who deny, minimize, or defend Nazi crimes, 'similar sanctions are not provided for those who deny, minimize or defend communist crimes or war crimes of the Allied Powers'. The Commission held that there was no discrimination in this case. 'Insofar as National Socialist activities are treated differently [by the Austrian law] from those of other political groups,' it said, 'this has an objective and reasonable justification in the historical experience of Austria during the National Socialist era, her treaty obligations, and the danger which the activities based on National Socialist thinking may constitute for the Austrian society' (para. 2). It is doubtful, though, that these reasons are weighty enough to justify such an absence of neutrality on the part of the law.

[55] Thus, the Ministers of Education of the European Union declared at their meeting of 18 October 2002, their commitment to establish a day in remembrance of the Holocaust. On the special significance of the Holocaust in human history, see R. Nozick, *The Examined Life: Philosophical Meditations* (Cambridge, MA: The Belknap Press, 1989), at 236–42. He writes that after the Holocaust, 'it now would not be a *special* tragedy if humankind ended, if the human species were destroyed in atomic warfare or the earth passed through some cloud that made it impossible

but suspending them, is what makes it possible for the community to send the pertinent message.[56] The problem with this approach, of course, is that other groups who have suffered extreme cruelty in the past may feel underestimated by the community if only the Holocaust, but not their suffering, leads to the suspension of the general principles.

So, in spite of the unanimous view of the ECHR that the denial of the Holocaust is not protected speech, it is not easy to come up with a plausible argument that justifies this position and that is consistent with the general principles of freedom of speech.

3.3 VALUE JUDGMENTS, OPINIONS, AND INSULTS

3.3.1 The Distinction between Factual Statements and Value Judgments

So far, we have been dealing with the problem of truth in connection with factual statements. In the *Lingens* case, the ECHR held that 'a careful distinction needs to be made between facts and value judgments. The existence of facts can be demonstrated, whereas the truth of value judgments is not susceptible of proof.'[57] The Court said that it is a breach of freedom of speech for the law of a state to require the speaker to prove the truth of a value judgment. It noted, however, that 'the facts on which Mr. Lingens founded his value judgments were undisputed'. In later opinions, the ECHR has been more explicit and has held that even if a value judgment cannot be subjected to the test of truth, it should nevertheless have some factual basis for it to be protected as speech.[58]

The ECHR did not offer an explicit justification for the distinction between facts and value judgments. But here is a plausible one: as citizens, we are interested in forming correct judgments about public matters. And in order to form such judgments, we need to have accurate information. If you give me wrong information, the normative opinions I develop are likely to be wrong. In contrast, if you express a value judgment, and you give me the right facts

---

for the species to continue reproducing itself... There is no point in arguing about comparative cruelties and disasters. (China, Russia, Cambodia, Armenia, Tibet... will this century become known as the age of atrocity?) Perhaps what occurred is that the Holocaust *sealed* the situation, and made it patently clear' (at 238).

[56] From a technical point of view, of course, the decision to prohibit the denial of the Holocaust would still be a special form of restriction of freedom of speech (and not a suspension or derogation of the right, in the sense of Article 15 of the European Convention).

[57] *Lingens v Austria*, Judgment of 8 July 1986, para. 46, Series A No. 103.

[58] *Prager & Oberschlick v Austria*, Judgment of 26 April, 1995, para. 37, Series A No. 313; *De Haes & Gijsels v Belgium*, Judgment of 24 February 1997, para. 47, *Reports of Judgments and Decisions* 1997-I; *Oberschlick v Austria (No. 2)*, Judgment of 1 July 1997, para. 33, *Reports of Judgments and Decisions* 1997-IV; *Feldek v Slovakia*, Judgment of 12 July 2001, para. 76, No. 29032/95, ECHR 2001-VIII.

(or I know the facts myself), you are less likely to mislead me, since I have the factual infrastructure upon which to build my own value judgments. I listen to your judgments, and I can easily test them against the factual evidence I have. I can autonomously decide whether your normative opinion is persuasive or not.

So, for example, to use the *Dichand* case as an illustration, you tell me that while Mr Graff, a politician, was presiding over Parliament's Legislative Committee, a law was amended which brought about big advantages for the companies which Mr Graff represented as a lawyer.[59] If the information is false, you cause me an epistemic harm. If, instead, the information you give me is right, and you then add your own value judgment, I have enough resources to form my own opinion autonomously. If you say that Mr Graff should have given up his law firm when he became the president of the Legislative Committee, and that he is 'immoral' and 'thick-skinned', I may agree, or disagree. I may have different moral standards, or less strict ones than yours, and reach different conclusions as to the evaluation of Mr Graff's conduct. Even if you use strong, polemical language against Mr Graff, and the factual basis for it is slim, you cause me no epistemic harm, since you are conveying the underlying facts in the right way, and you are therefore not misleading me.[60]

Whether a particular utterance is taken to express a factual statement or a value judgment will affect the question whether the evidence the speaker relies upon to justify the utterance is sufficient or not. The *Feldek* case can illustrate this point.[61] A writer referred to an important politician and said that he had a 'fascist past'. The politician sued him for defamation under the Civil Code. To simplify the case, let us say that the basic fact that the writer had in mind to support his statement was the fact that the politician had been a member of a youth organization that was considered fascist. Is this basic fact sufficient? The highest domestic court held the view that a person could be considered as having had a fascist past only if he or she had propagated or practised fascism in an active manner, which was not true in the case of this politician. Mere membership in an organization that was considered fascist did not count as 'fascist past'. So, if the utterance was taken as a factual statement, the evidence the writer offered to justify its truth was not sufficient. The domestic court acknowledged that the utterance about the 'fascist past' could have been understood differently, as a value judgment. But in that case, it said, the speaker should have made clear that the underlying fact he was referring to, and was making a value judgment about, was mere membership in a youth organization. Since the writer had not made this explicit, the court concluded that the utterance was unprotected and defamatory, and ordered him to endure the publication of this conclusion in five newspapers of the plaintiff's choice.

---

[59] *Dichand and Others v Austria*, Judgment of 26 February 2002, para. 13, No. 29271/95.

[60] In the *Dichand* case, the ECHR acknowledged that the factual basis for the polemical value judgments in question was 'slim' (para. 52), but it protected the speaker nevertheless.

[61] *Feldek v Slovakia*, Judgment of 12 July 2001, No. 29032/95, ECHR 2001-VIII.

The ECHR, however, found that this decision had breached the applicant's free speech rights. It rejected the proposition that, as a general principle, a value judgment can only be considered as such if it is explicitly accompanied by the facts on which that judgment is based. 'The necessity of a link between a value judgment and its supporting facts may vary from case to case according to specific circumstances' (para. 86). In this case, the ECHR said, it was not necessary to disclose that link in an explicit manner because the writer had based his judgment on 'information that was already known to the general public' (namely, the information about membership in that youth organization). It is controversial, however, whether the ECHR was right when it considered that in this particular case the context was such that the public already understood what were the underlying facts that the speaker was making a judgment about.[62] In any case, the Court did not seem to deny the importance of being clear what the facts are that one is making a value judgment about, when the context does not by itself determine this.

Actually, one could take a further step and argue that, to the extent that the speaker is explicit about the basic facts he is relying upon, the truth of which he is prepared to defend, *it does not matter whether what he says about those basic facts is a value judgment or a factual statement that he derives from those facts or constructs out of them.* The argument to justify this proposal is as follows.

There is a tendency to make the distinction between facts and values coextensive with the distinction between information and opinions. But this is not right. It is true that one informs about facts. But opinions need not be value judgments: they may amount to factual statements as well. 'In my opinion, the Prime Minister was aware of the cases of corruption that the Minister of Agriculture is involved in' is not an opinion about values, but an opinion about facts. This does not imply that the speaker is here exercising his right to impart information: he is clearly exercising his right to express opinions.

In all cases, what really matters is that the audience gets the right basic facts. Speakers, both when they impart information and when they give opinions, should be prepared to guarantee the truth of the basic facts they are actually reporting (to the extent that they are reporting any facts). If they make a value judgment about those basic facts, or if they express their opinion about the factual conclusions one can draw from those facts, no requirement of truth is applicable, provided that it is clear for the audience what the basic facts are that that judgment, or that factual conclusion, is linked to, and provided those basic facts are indeed true. If, in contrast, the speaker expresses a factual statement and does not disclose the evidence and the sources he has relied upon, then he must be prepared to guarantee its truth. The press typically does this when it publishes information. The readers give more credibility to the press, precisely because they assume that the press has

[62] The dissenting opinion by Judges Fischbach and Lorenzen interpret the context in a different way: they think that the public took it that the writer was referring to *new* facts, different and more serious than the ones that had already been made public.

undisclosed sources that justify the information it has decided to make public. When individuals express opinions, in contrast, they simply speculate about what may be the case, in light of the fragmentary evidence they have. To the extent that it is clear that they do not pretend to have more evidence than the one that is already in the public domain (or the one that they explicitly offer themselves), the audience is not misled and gives less credibility to that opinion than to a statement of fact made by the press with undisclosed evidence.[63]

It is not easy, of course, to distinguish an opinion from a piece of information in each case. The text is a first element to consider: expressions such as 'in my opinion', 'apparently', and 'I think' are textual indications that the speaker is simply giving an opinion. The context is relevant too. The general tone of the article or oral statement helps demarcate an opinion from a piece of information. The format is a useful indicator as well. Editorials, political cartoons, and letters to the editor, for example, will be read differently by the public than 'hard' news printed in the news sections of the newspaper.

The *Castells v Spain* case can illustrate this point.[64] The applicant, a politician, relied on certain basic facts that were indisputably true when he published his newspaper article criticizing the Spanish government. He enumerated a list of murders and attacks carried out in the Basque Country; he evoked the involvement of various extreme right-wing organizations; and he stressed that those crimes still remained unsolved and unpunished. From these facts, which were true, he drew the conclusion that 'behind those acts there can only be the Government, the party of the Government and their personnel'. Given the general tone of the article, and the place where it figured in the newspaper, it was clear that this was just an opinion. The ECHR protected the applicant, on the grounds that the Spanish courts should have allowed him to prove the truth of his conclusion, which was a factual statement. Judges De Meyer and Pekkanen, however, wrote concurring opinions arguing that no test of truth was applicable in this case. The applicant had simply expressed his opinion, on the basis of certain undisputed facts, and it should not matter whether he was right or wrong in his opinion.

I think that the concurring judges had the better argument in this case. The applicant was not reporting new facts beyond those uncontroversial facts that the public was already aware of. He was expressing his opinion as to what factual conclusions one could draw from them (and his value judgment about them). In doing this, he was not misleading the public: the readers were able to judge for themselves whether that opinion was persuasive, given the known facts. The speaker was under no duty to prove his factual conclusion.

The need to disclose the underlying facts and get them right is especially important in politics when it comes to information and criticism about what others have said or written. In particular, the democratic process cannot work well if the

---

[63] A similar position to the one defended here was espoused in the United States by Justices Brennan and Marshall. See their dissenting opinion in *Milkovich v Lorain Journal Co.*, 497 US 1, 23 (1990).   [64] Judgment of 23 April 1992, Series A No. 236.

information concerning statements made by political figures is not accurate. There may be some room for interpretation, but there is some fact of the matter about what a politician has said: there is an oral statement or a text to reproduce or to summarize faithfully. The criticism of a politician should be based on accurate information about what he actually said. In *Lopes Gomes da Silva v Portugal*,[65] for example, the ECHR emphasized the importance of giving readers the exact terms of the statements one is criticizing. The applicant was a journalist and manager of a newspaper who wrote an article attacking the views of a political candidate. He printed alongside the editorial in question numerous extracts from recent articles published by that candidate. As the Court put it: 'while reacting to those articles, he allowed readers to form their own opinion by placing the editorial in question alongside the declarations of the person referred to in the editorial'. And it added: 'The Court attaches great importance to that fact' (para. 35).[66]

Of course, how an utterance is to be characterized depends, in part, on cultural and linguistic conventions. A particular community may tend to exaggerate, and to use words in a metaphorical way. In another community, the same remarks may be taken literally, and the underlying facts may therefore be deemed insufficient to justify the utterance. Courts should try to stress, however, that if it is clear what the facts are that the speaker is referring to, and making a judgment about, there should be ample room for exaggeration and provocation, as the ECHR has said.[67]

Sometimes, however, the ECHR has not given sufficient weight to the need that the underlying facts should be clearly and truly conveyed to the public. It is one thing to exaggerate, once the facts are clear, and quite another to convey wrong factual information through exaggeration. In *Bladet Tromso and Stensaas v Norway*, for example, the newspaper had reported that seals had been 'skinned alive' by the members of the crew of a vessel, and that the inspector had said that he had been 'beaten up by furious hunters, who also threatened to hit him on the head with a gaff if he did not keep quiet'. All this was false. The ECHR considered, however, that such statements 'could be understood by readers as having been presented with a degree of exaggeration' (para. 67). It is difficult to see why. The underlying facts that were being commented upon were not clear to the public, so those exaggerated statements were misleading in this case.

3.3.2 Insults

Insults are a particular form of value judgment. It seems that they should not be protected, since they harm someone's reputation unnecessarily. There is no need to

[65] Judgment of 28 September 2000, No. 37698/97, ECHR 2000-X.
[66] Similarly, *Stoll v Switzerland*, Judgment of 25 April 2006, para. 55, No. 69698/01.
[67] See *Prager and Oberschlick v Austria*, Judgment of 26 April 1995, para. 38, Series A No. 313; *Bladet Tromso and Stensaas v Norway*, Judgment of 20 May 1999, para. 67, [GC], No. 21980/93, ECHR 1999-III.

resort to insults in order to contribute to public debate. The problem with the legal prohibition of insults, however, is that it is very difficult for courts to decide whether a particular expression amounts to it (or whether a particular insult is excessive under the circumstances). It is even more difficult for speakers to predict in advance what courts will decide. This uncertainty can have a serious chilling effect on freedom of speech. It would be better for courts not to get into the business of certifying whether or not a particular remark is an insult in a particular case, or whether or not it is excessive. We should instead rely on social norms: the audience should apply the relevant social standards and judge by themselves whether a particular speaker unduly insulted another person. A speaker undermines the persuasive effect of his own speech if he uses words that are regarded by the public to be insulting.

The ECHR has not gone that far, but seems to have applied a rather strict conception of what counts as an unnecessary insult, and has thus tolerated a high level of harshness, especially when the target is a politician.[68] It has rightly pointed out that 'political invective often spills over into the personal sphere', and that 'such are the hazards of politics and free debate of ideas, which are the guarantees of a democratic society'.[69] It has concluded, for example, that expressions such as 'beasts in uniform', which had been used in the context of a discussion about cases of police brutality, were not excessive;[70] that the words 'grotesque', 'buffoonish', and 'coarse', that a journalist had applied to a political candidate, were protected speech;[71] that it was not excessive for a journalist to react to a very provocative speech by a politician, pointing out his contradiction, and saying that he was an 'idiot'.[72]

Citizens are entitled to feel indignant about a moral or political decision or opinion they strongly disagree with, and should be allowed to react against it with speech that reflects that sentiment.[73] In *Oberschlick v Austria (No. 1)*,[74] for

---

[68] In contrast, the Court has held that public servants cannot be criticized in the same way as politicians: *Janowski v Poland*, Judgment of 21 January 1999, para. 33, [GC], No. 25716/94, ECHR 1999-I. Thus, it was not protected speech for the applicant to have insulted some police officers in the street, while on duty, calling them 'oafs' and 'dumb', even if he was right that the police action he was criticizing was illegal. The ECHR has also been less tolerant of offensive language when it is directed against public figures in connection with aspects of their private life that are of no public concern. See, for instance, *Tammer v Estonia*, Judgment of 6 February 2001, para. 68, No. 41205/98.

[69] *Lopes Gomes da Silva v Portugal*, Judgment of 28 September 2000, para. 34, No. 37698/97, ECHR 2000-X.

[70] *Thorgeir Thorgeirson v Iceland*, Judgment of 25 June 1992, para. 67, Series A No. 239.

[71] *Lopes Gomes da Silva v Portugal*, para. 34.

[72] *Oberschlick v Austria (No. 2)*, Judgment of 1 July 1997, para. 33, *Reports of Judgments and Decisions* 1997-IV.

[73] The United States Supreme Court rightly said in *Cohen v California*, 403 US 15, 25–6 (1971), 'we cannot overlook the fact...that much linguistic expression serves a dual communicative function: it conveys not only ideas capable of relatively precise, detached explication, but otherwise inexpressible emotions as well. In fact, words are chosen as much for their emotive as their cognitive force.' [74] Judgment of 23 May 1991, Series A No. 204.

example, the ECHR reasoned that a politician knew that he was likely to generate a strong reaction against him when he proposed that the family allowances for Austrian women should be increased by 50 per cent in order to obviate their seeking abortions for financial reasons, whilst those paid to immigrant mothers should be reduced to 50 per cent of their current levels. 'A politician who expresses himself in such terms exposes himself to a strong reaction on the part of journalists and the public' (para. 61). It thus protected the counter-speech of a journalist who had published 'criminal information' in a newspaper, accusing the politician of incitement to hatred and of engaging in activities that are supportive of the National Socialist Party. Similarly, in another case, the Court concluded that it was not disproportionate to call Mr Haider an 'idiot', given the indignation knowingly aroused by Mr Haider's speech, glorifying the role of the generation of soldiers who had taken part in the Second World War. He had said that all soldiers, including those in the German army, had fought for peace and freedom.[75]

A special problem arises when a speaker uses a word, one of the meanings of which refers to a legal crime. So, for example, someone says that politician X is in favour of 'murder', since he is in favour of decriminalizing abortion (or in favour of a war, or the death penalty). It would not be reasonable for courts to operate under the presumption that such value judgments are to be understood in a technical sense. Thus, the statement that a politician supports murder (when made in the context of the abortion controversy, for example) cannot be understood to refer to actions that fall under the technical description of 'murder' in the Criminal Code. (If the statement were thus understood, it would be possible to subject it to the test of truth, of course.) It should not be characterized as an offensive or insulting value judgment either. Otherwise, political speech on morally sensitive matters would be unduly chilled.[76]

---

[75] *Oberschlick v Austria (No. 2)*, Judgment of 1 July 1997, para. 34, *Reports of Judgments and Decisions* 1997-IV

[76] So, for example, in *Unabhängige Initiative Informationsvielfalt v Austria*, Judgment of 26 February 2002, No. 28525/95, ECHR 2002-I, the Court held that when a journalist criticized Haider for engaging in 'racist agitation', he was not making a statement of fact that referred to the commission of a crime, but expressing a value judgment that was sufficiently supported by the facts. (Haider's party had organized a poll in favour of 'Austria first' proposals that the journalist considered to be against the rights of immigrants). However, in *Wabl v Austria*, Judgment of 21 March 2000, No. 24773/94, the ECHR considered that it was not protected speech for a politician who had been defamed by an article in a newspaper (which had falsely alleged that he had AIDS) to say that that article was an example of 'Nazi journalism'. The Court reasoned that a special stigma attaches to activities inspired by National Socialist ideas, and it noted in this regard that 'pursuant to constitutional provisions and legislation introduced in Austria after the Second World War, it is a criminal offence to perform such activities' (para. 41). In Germany, a famous and controversial decision of the Federal Constitutional Court held that the expression 'soldiers are murderers', used by some pacifist citizens to criticize war, cannot be taken in a technical criminal sense. See BVerfGE 93, 266–312 10 October 1995.

Once again, what is important in such cases is that the audience have a clear picture of what is the underlying fact the speaker is referring to. If people realize that the speaker is referring to the fact that the politician is in favour of abortion (or war, or the death penalty), the speaker should be protected, even if the word 'murder' is offensive to many people who disagree with the value judgment that is being made. It is even acceptable for speakers to say that politicians who vote in favour of laws that allow women to have an abortion (or who vote in favour of a war, or the death penalty) are themselves 'murderers'. This harsh judgment is sufficiently linked (for purposes of free speech) to the fact that those politicians make it possible with their vote to allow women to extinguish fetuses (or send soldiers to kill and be killed, or to authorize the execution of convicted persons).[77]

It is important to highlight that in these cases the utterance is to be protected, but not at the price of transforming the message into something different, and more moderate, than what the speaker meant to say. When someone says that abortion (or war, or the death penalty) is murder, he may want the audience to take him seriously: he is indeed saying that there is no moral reason to distinguish abortion (or war, or the death penalty) from the paradigmatic instances of murder. Courts should not take the utterance to be metaphorical. They should not impose a charitable interpretation on the utterance, an interpretation that would erode the radical quality of the message that is being conveyed. Speech should be protected in such cases, in spite of its radical quality (that is, in spite of its not being metaphorical).

3.4 THE PRINCIPLE OF SYMMETRY

It seems intuitively right that participants in public discussions should be treated equally under the law. They should be bound by the same rules regarding the limits of free speech. Unless there are good reasons for deviating from this principle, the assumption should be that speakers are to be treated in a symmetrical way.

---

[77] For example, in *Oberschlick v Austria (No. 1)*, Judgment of 23 May 1991, Series A No. 204, the ECHR protected a journalist who had accurately reported the statements made by a particular politician he was criticizing, compared them to certain texts of the National Socialist Party manifesto of 1920, and concluded that that politician expressed ideas that corresponded to those professed by the Nazis. The journalist 'had published a true statement of facts followed by a value-judgment as to those facts', said the Court, and was exempted from proving the truth of that value judgment (para. 63). So, the important thing is that the applicant clearly set out what were the basic facts he was referring to, and that these facts were true. It was up to the readers to decide whether the value judgment was persuasive or not, in light of the undisputed facts. Even if we thought (as dissenting Judge Thor Vilhjalmsson did) that the conclusion that the journalist drew was not a value judgment, but a statement about facts, he should still be protected, since the readers understood that the journalist was not delivering information, but was expressing his own opinion, the rightness or wrongness of which they could independently assess.

There are manifestations of this 'principle of symmetry', as we may call it, in the case law of the ECHR.[78] In *Nilsen and Johnsen v Norway*,[79] for example, the Court had to examine a case where the chairmen of two police associations had been sanctioned in respect of statements they had made in response to certain reports publicizing allegations of police misconduct. The Court held: 'While there can be no doubt that any restrictions placed on the right to impart and receive information on arguable allegations of police misconduct call for a strict scrutiny on the part of the Court... *the same must apply to speech aimed at countering such allegations since it forms part of the same debate.* This is especially the case where, as here, the statements in question have been made by elected representatives of professional associations in response to allegations calling into question the practices and integrity of the profession.'[80] Since there was factual basis for the response given by the representatives of the police (since, indeed, a number of informants about police brutality had been convicted for false accusations against the police), the Court found that their statements were protected speech, however harshly critical they were against the law professor who had done the research and had published a book on police brutality.[81]

The ECHR's position that governments should try to avoid resorting to criminal sanctions to repress speech that is critical of them can also be understood as linked to the principle of symmetry. The Court has said that 'the dominant position which the Government occupies makes it necessary for it to display restraint in resorting to criminal proceedings, particularly when other means are available for replying to the unjustified attacks and criticisms of its adversaries or the media'.[82]

There are some special cases, however, where the principle of symmetry seems to be breached. Two particularly interesting instances involve members of Parliament and judges, for different reasons, and in different ways.

---

[78] As well as in the case law of the US Supreme Court. Thus, one of the reasons the Court gave to support its holding in *New York Times v Sullivan*, 376 U.S. 254, 282–3 (1964), was that ordinary citizens should be treated equally to public officials when it comes to speech. It said: 'It would give public servants an unjustified preference over the public they serve, if critics of official conduct did not have a fair equivalent of the immunity granted to officials themselves.' The Court had earlier held that federal officers enjoy an absolute privilege for defamatory publication within the scope of official duty. See *Barr v Matteo*, 360 US 564, 575 (1959).

[79] Judgment of 25 November 1999, [GC], No. 23118/93, ECHR 1999-VIII.

[80] Para. 44 (emphasis added).

[81] Interestingly, in their dissent, four judges questioned the principle of symmetry. In essence, they reasoned that there was a tension here between two freedoms of speech (that of the professor, and that of the police force), a tension that should be resolved in favour of the former, given the interest in a prompt and impartial investigation of police brutality, an interest that is protected under the 1984 United Nations Convention against Torture and other Cruel, Inhuman and Degrading Treatment or Punishment (to which Norway is a party).

[82] *Castells v Spain*, Judgment of 23 April 1992, para. 46, Series A No. 236. Similarly, *Sürek v Turkey (No. 1)*, Judgment of 8 July 1999, para. 61, [GC], No. 26682/95, ECHR 1999-IV.

3.4.1 Parliamentary Privileges

In most countries, the speech of Members of Parliament (MPs) is privileged: they cannot be made accountable before a judge for the statements made in the legislative chamber. The ECHR has upheld this privilege, against Article 6 objections.[83]

Separation of powers is often invoked as a justification for the speech immunity. Separation of powers is thought to entail that the speech that takes place within Parliament should be immune against decisions made by the executive and the judiciary. But unless we unpack this argument into a more pragmatic argument about the risks for freedom of speech, the principle of separation of powers standing alone will not offer a sufficient basis to justify the privilege. Rather, it seems to go against it: why should certain types of claims (those concerning the speech of MPs) be removed from the ordinary judicial power to adjudicate controversies? Moreover, in some countries the privilege has been given to MPs by Parliament itself (through an internal regulation, a statute, or a Constitution that is approved by Parliament exclusively). One could argue that Parliament is biased when it privileges its members in this manner.[84]

So it is more promising to transform the separation of powers argument into a free speech argument. The basic idea would be that representatives should speak freely in Parliament, and should not be afraid of the possible legal consequences that their speech could give rise to. The only limitations on their speech should be enforced by the internal organs of Parliament. So, for example, the official presiding over the debates may require an MP to stop using particular language that is insulting or offensive, or to retract from the remarks he has made. The advantage of this system is that it does not generate a serious chilling effect on parliamentary speech. The MP can dare to say many things, and he will be warned if he is going too far. He is under no risk that a judge may later find that he overstepped the limits of freedom of speech. The disadvantage

---

[83] See *A v The United Kingdom*, Judgment of 17 December, 2002, No. 35373/97, ECHR 2002-X. In its reasoning, the ECHR does not develop a convincing substantive argument in favour of the privilege. Rather, it is very deferential to the views of most Council of Europe Member States that have decided to keep the privilege (sometimes in broader terms than in the United Kingdom). The members of the Parliamentary Assembly of the Council of Europe, moreover, enjoy a similar protection. The ECHR tries to minimize the consequences of the privilege with the claim that the victim of a defamatory misstatement made in Parliament is not entirely without means of redress. In the United Kingdom, it says, the victims can petition the House with a view to securing a retraction, and, in extreme cases, the statements may be punished by Parliament as contempt (para. 86). But these means of redress are more illusory than effective, as Judge Costa rightly points out in his concurring opinion.

[84] Interestingly, Judge Loucaides, in his dissenting opinion in the case of *A v The United Kingdom*, Judgment of 17 December 2002, does not give much weight to the conclusions reached by a recent review of parliamentary privilege by a joint committee of the House of Commons and House of Lords in support of retaining the rule of absolute parliamentary immunity. One of the reasons Judge Loucaides adduces to justify his skepticism is that the review 'was not carried out by any organ independent of the persons enjoying the privilege in question'.

is that the officer moderating the parliamentary debate may not be as impartial as a judge. And the lack of temporal distance between the speech and the official reaction to it may lead to overreaction.[85]

The problem is that an important asymmetry is then introduced between speech within and without Parliament. Outside Parliament, the free speech system is generally different. Prior restraints are possible, but rare.[86] It is also possible sometimes for courts to issue an injunction prohibiting someone to *repeat* what he said.[87] But the general rule is that the speaker is not prevented from saying whatever he wants to say, and is not officially warned about the limits he may be overstepping. So he runs the risk that a judge will later conclude that he did overstep those limits and will impose him a civil or criminal sanction. If the law were clear when it defined the circumstances under which a court may impose sanctions, the risk would not be great. But the law is inevitably uncertain in many respects, and it is therefore difficult for citizens to

---

[85] An interesting analogy to consider refers to the speech of the lawyers and the parties to a controversy, who must respect certain limits when they make statements in the courtroom. The ECHR has said that the general rule should be for lawyers to be warned immediately, if they are overstepping those limits. See *Nikula v Finland*, Judgment of 21 March, 2002, No. 31611/96, ECHR 2002-II, where it stresses 'the duty of the courts and the presiding judge to direct proceedings in such a manner as to ensure the proper conduct of the parties and above all the fairness of the trial—rather than to examine in a subsequent trial the appropriateness of a party's statements in the courtroom' (para. 53). The ECHR argues that 'the threat of an *ex post facto* review of counsel's criticism of another party to criminal proceedings . . . is difficult to reconcile with defence counsel's duty to defend their clients' interests zealously' (para. 54). That threat would have a chilling effect, it says. However, when a lawyer or party is accused of contempt of court, aimed at the judges personally, the correct course dictated by the requirement of impartiality under Article 6 of the Convention is to have the matter determined by a different bench from the one before in which the problem arose. See *Kyprianou v Cyprus*, Judgment of 15 December 2005, para. 127, [GC], No. 73797/01, ECHR 2005.

[86] The leading case is *Sunday Times v United Kingdom (No. 1)*, Judgment of 26 April 1979, Series A No. 30. The Court has said that Article 10 does not prohibit prior restraints on publication as such, but 'the dangers inherent in prior restraints are such that they call for the most careful scrutiny', especially so far as the press is concerned, 'for news is a perishable commodity and to delay its publication, even for a short period, may well deprive it of all its value and interest'. See *Ekin Association v France*, Judgment of 17 July 2001, para. 56, No. 39288/98. On the other hand, 'the need to interfere with freedom of expression may be present initially yet subsequently cease to exist' (*Éditions Plon (Societé) v France*, Judgment of 18 May 2004, para. 45, No. 58148/00, ECHR 2004-IV). Thus, in this latter case, the ECHR accepted the validity of an interim injunction against the distribution, just after President Mitterand's death, of a book that gave details about the illness that the President had suffered from for many years, and which he had kept secret. But the ECHR rejected the final judicial decision on the merits which had banned the book. The ECHR held that as time elapsed, the public interest in discussing the history of the President's two terms of office had to prevail over privacy interests.

[87] See, for instance, *Wabl v Austria*, Judgment of 21 March 2000, No. 24773/94: a politician is ordered by a court not to repeat the statement that a particular article that had defamed him (falsely saying that he had AIDS) amounted to 'Nazi journalism'. If we have free speech in mind, it is easier to accept that a person is told by a judge not to repeat the expression 'Nazi journalism' in the future than for a judge to punish a person for having used those words in the past. Other examples can be found in *Jerusalem v Austria*, Judgment of 27 February 2001, No. 26958/95, ECHR 2001-II; and *Unabhängige Initiative Informationsvielfalt v Austria*, Judgment of 26 February 2002, No. 28525/95, ECHR 2002-I.

predict the judicial response to their speech.[88] There is the advantage of institutional and temporal distance, since the judge is removed from the controversy the speech refers to, and time allows passions to cool down, which is normally favourable to speech interests. But citizens act under a higher level of uncertainty than MPs concerning the legal sanctions that may be imposed on them for the speech they have engaged in.

This asymmetry between MPs and citizens could make sense if public discourse took place in Parliament exclusively, or even principally. But this is not so. Public opinion is formed through exchanges between citizens, politicians, and the media, and it is important to ensure that these exchanges develop on an equal basis.[89] The asymmetry between MPs and the rest of citizens is particularly worrisome to the extent that political candidates that are challengers may sometimes be less protected in their speech than incumbents.

Moreover, the privilege is deemed in many countries to be restricted to what is said within Parliament, so MPs are not protected when they speak outside. The ECHR has actually held that it is against Article 6 of the Convention for states to extend the privilege to all statements made by MPs outside the legislative chamber.[90] This ruling has the advantage that it minimizes the negative impact that parliamentary immunity may have on the right of access to the courts. But, from the point of view of freedom of speech, it is not very reasonable to limit the privilege in this way, for the most important statements made by MPs are usually made *outside the legislative chamber* (when they give a press conference, or make a speech at an election meeting, for example).[91] It is

---

[88] The ECHR is not very strict when it checks whether the law that defines the conditions for the restriction of freedom of speech is sufficiently clear.

[89] An example of the asymmetry between MPs and ordinary citizens can be found in the *Lingens* case, Judgment of 8 July 1986, Series A No. 103. Bruno Kreisky, President of the Austrian Socialist Party, referred to a Jewish organization and its activities as a 'political mafia' and 'mafia methods'. Indignant with that speech, a journalist (Lingens) wrote an article saying that Kreisky had exhibited 'the basest opportunism' and had acted in an 'immoral' and 'undignified' way. While the Austrian courts found the journalist guilty of defamation, the existing legislation on parliamentary immunity made it impossible for the politician to be prosecuted for defamation (para. 26). It should be noted in this connection that the ECHR has reduced the asymmetry between representative assemblies that technically enjoy immunity and those that do not. In *Jerusalem v Austria*, Judgment of 27 February 2001, the Court says: 'Irrespective of whether the applicant's statements were covered by parliamentary immunity, the Court finds that they were made in a forum which was at least comparable to Parliament as concerns the public interest in protecting the participants' freedom of public expression. In a democracy, Parliament or such comparable bodies are essential fora for political debate. Very weighty reasons must be advanced to justify interfering with the freedom of expression exercised therein' (para. 40). Similarly, *Roseiro Bento v Portugal*, Judgment of 18 April 2006, para. 44, No. 29288/02.

[90] *Cordova v Italy (No. 2)*, Judgment of 30 January 2003, para. 63, No. 45649/99, ECHR 2003-I.

[91] Interestingly, the ECHR said in the *Castells v Spain* case, Judgment of 23 April 1992, Series A No. 236: 'In the case under review, Mr Castells did not express his opinion from the senate floor, as he might have done without fear of sanctions, but chose to do so in a periodical. That does not mean, however, that he lost his right to criticize the Government' (para. 43). It is not difficult to guess the reason why many MPs choose to express their opinions in a periodical: to have better access to the public.

difficult to argue that the speech of politicians in Parliament (an organ that is composed of representatives elected by the people) should be more privileged than the speech expressed by politicians in an electoral meeting, when they address themselves to the people whose sovereignty is the very foundation of Parliament's institutional relevance in a democracy.

So it is not clear that good reasons exist nowadays to maintain this asymmetry between citizens and MPs. Reforms in order to reduce such inequality should be welcomed.[92]

3.4.2 Criticism of Judges

Another source of asymmetry concerns the judiciary. The ECHR has had to face the question whether special considerations apply when speech refers to the judiciary.[93]

There is no doubt that the judiciary is part of the governmental structure. As is also true of the other branches, the risk exists that the judiciary will abuse its powers or will make wrong decisions. Internal corrections (through a system of appeals, and through the institution of dissenting opinions by judges) are insufficient. Public criticism of judicial decisions is necessary as an external check. To the extent that the judiciary is relatively insulated from political checks, it is of fundamental importance to create a culture of public discussion around the judiciary. Judges should know that their powers will be subjected to public scrutiny, and will have to pay reputational costs if their decisions are found wanting.

Whether or not the judicial function should be characterized as a 'political function', there is no doubt that not all cases are easy cases. There is room for interpretative disagreement about the law (even if there may be a single right answer), which means that the judge will have to justify why it concludes that a particular legal solution is to be preferred to its rivals. As judges perform a function that is increasingly relevant in society, their opinions should be subjected to closer inspection and criticism.

---

[92] For example, given the importance of ensuring the truth of the information that is given in public debates, the parliamentary privilege could be eroded through the institution of declaratory actions. The victim of a false statement made by an MP could be entitled to go to the courts and get a declaration that the relevant statement was indeed false. The MP would suffer no sanction. It is difficult to see in what ways parliamentary speech may suffer if the legal system granted this kind of remedy. The public's right to receive accurate information would be honoured. (When it comes to value judgments that are expressed in offensive or insulting language, in contrast, there is probably no need to resort to the courts, since the internal parliamentary checks seem to be sufficient.)

[93] I do not refer here to the problem whether restrictions can be imposed on speech while a judicial process is developing. My focus is on restrictions on speech that is critical of judicial decisions that have already been made. The leading case about speech that refers to pending cases is *Sunday Times v The United Kingdom (No. 1)*, Judgment of 26 April 1979, Series A No. 30. See also, *Worm v Austria*, Judgment of 29 August 1997, *Reports of Judgments and Decisions* 1997-V; *Du Roy and Malaurie v France*, Judgment of 3 October 2000, No. 34000/96, ECHR 2000-X; and *Tourancheau and July v France*, Judgment of 24 November 2005, No. 53886/00.

Actually, in the last decades there has been a tendency in many European countries to enlarge the scope of permissible criticism of judicial decisions.[94] Article 10 of the Convention, however, mentions explicitly the need to maintain 'the authority and impartiality of the judiciary' as a legitimate ground to justify the restriction of freedom of speech. And the ECHR has said there is a special need to protect the public confidence in the judiciary against unjustified attacks, 'especially in view of the fact that judges who have been criticised are subject to a duty of discretion that precludes them from replying'.[95]

The existence of this legal duty of discretion is contingent, however, and its scope and force may vary from country to country. Also, even if judges cannot themselves reply to criticism, court press offices may have been established to help explain the complexities of judgments to the public. These offices may sometimes defend a judgment against criticism that is clearly wrong. Still, to the extent that judges are indeed expected to refrain from replying to criticism, it seems reasonable to subject that criticism to more stringent limitations, as the ECHR has held.

So, for example, the value judgments that are critical of the judiciary may have to be more strongly based on the facts. The ECHR denies protection to 'unfounded attacks' against courts, which seems to require a stronger factual basis for speech to be protected.[96] Similarly, there may be stricter norms regarding insults. The kind of epithets that can legitimately be used to criticize a judge may

[94] See M.K. Addo (ed.), *Freedom of Expression and the Criticism of Judges: A* Comparative *Study of European Legal Standards* (Burlington, VT: Ashgate Publishing Co, 2000), at 3–28.

[95] *Prager and Oberschlick v Austria*, Judgment of 26 April, 1995, para. 34, Series A No. 313. Consistent with this idea, the ECHR permits states to restrict speech by judges (and prosecutors) more intensely than speech by other individuals. Thus, in *Altin v Turkey*, Decision of 6 April 2000, No. 39822/98, the ECHR rejected a complaint filed by a public prosecutor who had been disciplined for conducting himself like a 'professional politician' having regard to his oral and written statements on politically divisive issues such as the fight against terrorism. The ECHR found no violation of freedom of expression, since law officers are under the duty not to impair the confidence of the public in the independent administration of justice. (The duty of judicial discretion has its own limits, however. See *Wille v Liechtenstein*, Judgment of 28 October 1999 [GC], No. 28396/95, ECHR 1999-VII.) On the other hand, if the judge enters political life (for example, if he makes public his intention to become a candidate for election on the list of a particular political party), the limits of acceptable criticism of his decisions are wider (especially when they are related to issues of public concern that are a matter of political debate). See *Hrico v Slovakia*, Judgment of 20 July 2004, paras 45–48, No. 49418/99. One could argue that, as a politician, the former judge will be free to reply to any criticism his judicial decisions may have attracted.

[96] In *Barfod v Denmark*, Judgment of 22 February 1989, Series A No. 149, the ECHR did not protect a citizen who had published an article criticizing the fact that two lay judges who were members of a court and who were at the same time employed by the local government had not disqualified themselves in a tax case that involved the local government as one of the parties. The applicant said that the two lay judges 'did their duty' when they decided the case in favour of the government (meaning that they cast their votes as employees of that government rather than as independent and impartial judges). The ECHR held that the speaker was entitled to criticize the composition of the court, but the fact that two of the judges were government employees 'was certainly no proof of actual bias' (para. 33). Since the speaker had not offered evidence to prove actual bias, his statement was not protected speech.

be more restricted. Also, a sharper contrast may be drawn than in other contexts between criticism of the decision and criticism of the person (the judge) that is responsible for it.[97] And, in general, more exigent standards may be applied to lawyers than to ordinary citizens when they criticize courts and their decisions.[98]

This should not mean, however, that lawyers and citizens are not entitled to criticize a judge for his moral or political beliefs, which may have played a role in the interpretation of the law. The authority of the judiciary should not be preserved at the price of denying that judges are sometimes or often sensitive to moral and political convictions when they interpret the law.[99] It should also be possible to inform about, and express criticism about, the links judges may have, or may have had, with political parties and groups.[100] It is also acceptable to relate their interpretations of the law to the preferences of the social class that judges are members of, or are close to.[101]

---

[97] The ECHR has given weight to this distinction. See, for instance, *Barfod v Denmark*, Judgment of 22 February 1989, para. 35, Series A No. 149.

[98] The ECHR has said that it is legitimate to expect lawyers to contribute to maintain the public confidence in the administration of justice, given the key role they play in this field. When they go to the media to criticize judicial decisions, stricter limitations on their speech seem to apply, especially if they have not yet used the available legal remedies to attack the judicial decision they criticize. See *Schöpfer v Switzerland*, Judgment of 20 May 1998, paras 29–34, *Reports of Judgments and Decisions* 1998-III. Speech by counsel within the courtroom, in contrast, is more strongly protected, especially when the target of the criticism is one of the parties (such as the prosecutor). See *Nikula v Finland*, Judgment of 21 March 2002, paras 49–50, No. 31611/96, ECHR 2002-II.

[99] Arguably, one could distinguish in this regard between the Constitutional Court and ordinary judges, or, more precisely, between decisions by the Constitutional Court that determine whether a statute is valid, and those of ordinary courts enforcing statutes. In the former case it is more difficult to distinguish the legal correctness of the decision from its moral or political desirability, and the social impact of the decision is likely to be larger. In *Amihalachioaie v Moldova*, Judgment of 20 April, 2004, No. 60115/00, ECHR 2004-III, the Court seemed to be considerably protective of speech that was critical of a Constitutional Court's decision rendered in a politically charged proceeding of the abstract review of legislation. The applicant had not offered any legal argument in his speech against the decision of the Court that had struck down a statute that made it compulsory for lawyers to belong to a national bar organization. The applicant had said in a public interview that the decision would lead to total anarchy in the organization of the legal profession, he wondered whether the Constitutional Court was itself constitutional, and stated that the decision showed that, quite probably, the judges did not consider the ECHR and its case law an authority to follow. The ECHR protected his speech nevertheless. In contrast to other cases, it did not examine the question whether the criticism of the Court was sufficiently justified.

[100] In *Perna v Italy*, Judgment of 6 May 2003, [GC], No. 48898/99, the ECHR did not protect a journalist who had been convicted for having said in effect that the head of the Palermo public prosecutor's office (Mr Caselli) had knowingly committed an abuse of authority, in circumstances connected with the indictment of Mr Andreotti, in furtherance of an alleged strategy by the Italian Communist Party of gaining control of prosecutors' offices in Italy. Since the journalist had not even tried to prove the specific conduct imputed to the prosecutor, the ECHR found no violation of freedom of expression. But it noted that the journalist 'did not confine his remarks to the assertion that Mr. Caselli harboured or had manifested political beliefs and that this justified doubts about his impartiality in the performance of his duties' (para. 47). The Court seems to suggest that the latter would have been protected speech.

[101] It is one thing, however, to emphasize the closeness of judges to certain ideological circles in order to explain their preference for certain interpretations of the law, when the law is not clear. It is

Finally, it is important to emphasize that, in a democracy, judicial decisions are and should be criticized, not only by experts on narrow technical grounds, but also by politicians, the media, and ordinary citizens, in the light of general standards of justice. It is not rare for those who lack legal expertise to blame the judge for an outcome in a particular case, when as a matter of fact, it is the existing law, and not the interpretation of the judge, that is to be found wanting. In such cases, it is in some sense an 'unfounded' criticism to attack the judicial decision for the outcome reached. Yet, that criticism should be protected. It is crucial in a democracy that citizens can express their opinions about the decisions made by the organs that make up the governmental structure. The public has the right to express its rejection of what it considers to be an unjust solution to a social problem, no matter whose responsibility it is within the governmental structure. Citizens cannot easily criticize laws in the abstract. They can more effectively object to them as they see how they are applied by courts in particular cases. They are thus entitled to object to the result they see in real cases and bring pressure on the system to introduce the necessary reforms. The system of democratic accountability could not function if this sort of unjustified criticism of judges were banned.

quite another to say that a judge was biased because he was ideologically sympathetic to the views of one of the litigants (in a case where the interpretive legal question is not connected to that ideological affinity). The latter statement should have a stronger factual basis. The ECHR should have been more sensitive to this distinction in *De Haes and Gijsels v Belgium*, Judgment of 24 February 1997, *Reports of Judgments and Decisions* 1997-I, where it protected a journalist who had alleged that the judges deciding a child custody case had been biased in favour of the father (a public notary) as a result of their sharing the same rightist political views. In their dissenting opinions, Judges Matscher and Morenilla are persuasive when they reason that the judicial decision in the custody proceedings could be criticized, but it was not right for the journalist to say that the reason why the judges had protected the father was that his political ideas were similar to those held by them.

4

Freedom of Political Association and the Question of Party Closures

Eva Brems

4.1 INTRODUCTION

The term 'party closure' refers to the prohibition or forced dissolution of a political party by a government authority. This issue will be examined in the perspective of international human rights law. At the domestic law level, both the regulatory framework and state practice with respect to party closure vary widely. It seems that among democratic states adhering to the same international human rights standards, different interpretations exist about the compatibility of the measure of party closure with such standards, in addition to diverging views on the opportunity of this measure. To the extent that opportunity considerations belong to the political realm, they remain outside the scope of this chapter.[1] First, party closure is situated within the context of the scope of the international provisions on freedom of political association, as well as the rules on restrictions of this freedom (4.2). Then, the measure is examined in detail in the light of international norms and case-law (4.3). In a first step, the seriousness of party closure as an interference in the freedom of political association is measured against that of other restrictive measures against political parties (4.3.1). Next, the different grounds that are invoked to justify party closure are studied (4.3.3), followed by the modalities of the measure (4.3.4), and some matters of procedure (4.3.5).

4.2 FREEDOM OF POLITICAL ASSOCIATION: INTERNATIONAL LEGAL FRAMEWORK

The examination of the provisions dealing with the freedom of political association in UN and regional texts will concern first the scope of that freedom

---

[1] See, for example, J. Finn, 'Electoral Regimes and the Proscription of Anti-Democratic Parties', in D. C. Rapoport and L. Weinberg (eds.), *The Democratic Experience and Political Violence* (London/Portland, OR: Frank Cass, 2001), 51, at 65–67.

under those provisions (4.2.1), followed by an analysis of acceptable and mandatory restrictions of the freedom (4.2.2).

4.2.1 Scope

In the context of the study of party closures, the relevant aspect of the freedom of political association is the right to form and join political parties. Yet many other types of associations have a 'political' character. Some organizations offer support to a particular political party, others lobby for their own platform with one or several political parties or with governmental bodies, still others try to influence directly public opinion with regard to certain issues that are 'political' in that they are in the general interest. In this broad sense, for example, human rights NGOs can be seen as exercising the freedom of political association. The same holds for trade unions, which are mentioned specifically in several provisions on the freedom of association.[2] Nevertheless, trade union freedoms as such—being a human rights chapter of their own, reaching into the field of economic and social rights, and the work of the International Labour Organization—are not dealt with in this chapter. This section attempts to give an overview of international provisions on the freedom of association and their applicability to political parties, both in the main human rights conventions of the United Nations and in regional human rights treaties.

4.2.1.1 The United Nations System

Article 22(1) of the International Covenant on Civil and Political Rights (ICCPR) provides that: 'Everyone shall have the right to freedom of association with others, including the right to form and join trade unions for the protection of his interests.' During the drafting process, a proposal providing for the suppression of certain political organizations was rejected. But on the other hand, an express provision excluding the possibility of outlawing political parties was equally rejected.[3] From these procedures we may derive, firstly, that the drafters worked on the assumption that political parties fell within the scope of Article 22 ICCPR; and secondly, that in their mind party closures did not automatically constitute a violation of that provision. The applicability of Article 22 ICCPR to political parties results furthermore from the general wording of the text, and from the practice of the Human Rights Committee, that never questioned the application of Article 22 ICCPR to political parties. For example, it considers a one-party system to be incompatible with Article 22 ICCPR.[4]

---

[2] E.g., Article 22(1) (ICCPR), Article 11(1) ECHR, Article 26(1) ICMW.

[3] K. J. Partsch, 'Freedom of Conscience and Expression, and Political Freedoms', in L. Henkin (ed.), *The International Bill of Rights. The Covenant on Civil and Political Rights* (New York/Guildford: Columbia University Press, 1981), 209, at 235.

[4] Concluding Observations of the Human Rights Committee: Viet Nam, 26 July 2002, CCPR/CO/75/VNM, § 20: '... the Committee is concerned at the absence of specific legislation on

Article 25 ICCPR protects political rights in the strict sense, including the right to vote and to be elected, but does not mention political parties. Yet in its General Comment on Article 25,[5] the Human Rights Committee stressed the strong link with the freedom of political association: 'It [the full enjoyment of rights protected by Article 25] requires the full enjoyment and respect for the rights guaranteed in Articles 19, 21 and 22 of the Covenant, including freedom to engage in political activity individually or through political parties and other organizations...'[6] and '[t]he right to freedom of association, including the right to form and join organizations and associations concerned with political and public affairs, is an essential adjunct to the rights protected by Article 25. Political parties and membership in parties play a significant role in the conduct of public affairs and the election process. States should ensure that, in their internal management, political parties respect the applicable provisions of Article 25 in order to enable citizens to exercise their rights thereunder.'[7] In concluding observations with regard to state reports, the Committee goes a step further, by considering that restrictions on political parties may violate not only Article 22 ICCPR, but also Article 25 ICCPR.[8]

As one of the main goals of political parties is the expression of political opinions, restrictive measures against political parties in most cases entail restrictions of the freedom of expression, protected amongst others in Article 19 ICCPR. Hence, when dealing with party closure or other restrictions on political parties, provisions on freedom of expression may function as a fallback option in cases where provisions on freedom of association may not be used. For example, in 1995 the Human Rights Committee dealt with an individual complaint by a Korean citizen who had been convicted for his membership and participation in a political organization that was qualified under National Security Law as an 'anti-State organization'. The claim before the Committee could not be brought under Article 22 ICCPR, because Korea had made a reservation under that provision. Yet the Committee did find a violation of Article 19 ICCPR, on the basis of a reasoning stating that the conviction and sentence were based on the fact that through his activities in the organization,

---

political parties and at the fact that only the Communist Party is permitted... The state party should take all necessary steps to enable... political parties to function without hindrance'.

[5] Human Rights Committee, General Comment No. 25: The right to participate in public affairs, voting rights and the right of equal access to public service (Art. 25), 12 July 1996, CCPR/C/21/Rev.1/Add.7. [6] Ibid, § 25.

[7] Ibid, § 26.

[8] E.g. Concluding Observations of the Human Rights Committee: Republic of Moldova, 26 July 2002, CCPR/CO/75/MDA, § 16: 'The Committee is concerned that certain requirements that the state party places upon the registration of political parties, such as conditions with respect to the extent of their territorial representation, may violate Article 25 of the Covenant by restricting the right of individuals to full expression of their political freedoms. The state party should review its law and policy concerning the registration of political parties, removing those elements which are inimical to the full exercise of Covenant rights, in particular Article 25.'

the person involved had expressed his support or sympathy to certain political slogans and positions.[9]

Article 7(c) of the Convention on the Elimination of all forms of Discrimination Against Women (CEDAW) protects the right of women, on equal terms with men, 'to participate in non-governmental organizations and associations concerned with the public and political life of the country'. This provision does not in the first place offer a basis for protecting political parties against restrictive measures. It concerns rather the rights of individual women in the political sphere, which is one of many fields in which women are underrepresented. Yet this Article can be invoked when women become the victim of specific restrictive measures concerning political parties. Moreover, it may be invoked against political parties that would discriminate against women in their internal organization. The CEDAW Committee mentioned in a General Comment that amongst others 'political parties have an obligation to demonstrate their commitment to the principle of gender equality in their constitutions, in the application of those rules and in the composition of their memberships with gender-balanced representation on their executive boards so that these bodies may benefit from the full and equal participation of all sectors of society and from contributions made by both sexes'.[10] In recent Concluding comments, it has commended a State Party for a system of public funding of political parties in proportion to the number of women elected,[11] and invited another State Party to encourage political parties to use quotas in order to increase the number of women.[12] Hence, Article 7(c) CEDAW may function as a restriction of the freedom of political association of the party, while furthering the freedom of political association of women.

Article 15 of the Convention on the Rights of the Child (CRC) protects in general terms the right of the child to freedom of association. Yet given the fact that minors as a rule do not have the right to vote, one may wonder whether this automatically includes political association. The CRC Committee answers this question in the affirmative. In its comments on a report by Georgia, the Committee showed concern about a law prohibiting minors from becoming members of political parties, stating that 'this prohibition limits the opportunity for youth to learn about the political process, delays their preparation for political leadership, and denies their full right to freedom of association. In light of Article 15 of the Convention, the Committee recommends that the State Party amend its legislation to ensure that youth are allowed to join political parties and that they fully enjoy their right to freedom of association.'[13] Like Article 7(c) CEDAW, this provision is not likely to serve as a basis for the

---

[9] Human Rights Committee, Communication 628/1995, *Tae Hoon Park, v Republic of Korea*, views of 20 October 1998.
[10] CEDAW Committee, General Comment No. 23 (Sixteenth Session, 1997), A/52/38/Rev.1, § 34.   [11] CEDAW Committee, Concluding Comments: Mali, 3 February 2006, § 6.
[12] CEDAW Committee, Concluding Comments: Thailand, 3 February 2006, § 30.
[13] Concluding Observations of the Committee on the Rights of the Child: Georgia, 28 June 2000, CRC/C/15/Add.124, §§ 30–31.

protection of political parties against restrictive measures, although it may be invoked when minor members of political parties become the victims of specific restrictive measures. Moreover, in the light of the CRC Committee's position, it can be invoked against political parties that would discriminate against minors in their internal organization.

Finally, Article 26(1) of the International Convention on the Protection of the Rights of all Migrant Workers and members of their families (ICMW) recognizes the right of migrant workers and members of their families: '(a) To take part in meetings and activities of trade unions and of any other associations established in accordance with law, with a view to protecting their economic, social, cultural and other interests, subject only to the rules of the organization concerned; (b) To join freely any trade union and any such association as aforesaid, subject only to the rules of the organization concerned; (c) To seek the aid and assistance of any trade union and of any such association as aforesaid.' This is a specific right of these persons to participate in associations, including political parties, for the defence of their interests. These need not be their specific interests: the interests of migrant workers coincide to a large extent with those of members of the non-immigrant population; but these can be such specific interests. Although the right to *form* such associations is not mentioned, it seems to be a necessary corollary of the right to join an association and to take part in its activities. In any event, when the activities of a political party are restricted or the party is prohibited, this affects also the rights to join and to take part in the activities of the party. In the debate on party closures, this provision may come into play in a situation in which migrant workers have their own political party that is prohibited, or when they would want to have such a party, but this is not allowed, for example because it is not allowed to organize a political party on the basis of ethnicity (cf. *infra*). It is to be noted that this applies only in those states where (some) foreign nationals have the right to vote, since immigrants who acquire the nationality of the host state, fall outside the scope of this Convention.

4.2.1.2 Regional Systems

Article 16 of the American Convention on Human Rights (ACHR) specifies that freedom of association includes association for political purposes. There can be no doubt that this provision applies to restrictions of the activities of political parties, including party closure. Yet there has as yet not been any case before the Inter-American Commission or Court on Human Rights dealing directly with this issue.

Article 10 of the African Charter on Human and Peoples' Rights (ACHPR) provides: '1. Every individual shall have the right to free association provided that he abides by the law. 2. Subject to the obligation of solidarity provided for in Article 29 no one may be compelled to join an association.' Given the general scope of the first paragraph, political associations and political parties in particular are included. The African Commission on Human and Peoples' Rights has interpreted Article 10 in this sense.[14] The reference to law should not be so interpreted as if the legislator has unfettered power to restrict the right. The second paragraph contains a reference to Article 29 of the Charter, the provision on duties. The concept of 'solidarity' is mentioned in § 4 of this Article, which stipulates the duty of every individual 'to preserve and strengthen social and national solidarity, particularly when the latter is threatened'. Applied to political parties, this suggests that in some circumstances, individuals could be compelled to join a political party of national unity. Moreover, the reference to Article 29 need not be restricted to § 4, since all individual duties in Article 29 may be linked to the principle of solidarity, even though they do not all mention that term. Hence there may be other reasons than 'social and national solidarity' justifying compulsion in the matter of association, for example the obligation 'to serve his national community by placing his physical and intellectual abilities at its service' (§ 2), and the duties 'not to compromise the security of the state whose national or resident he is' (§ 3), 'to preserve and strengthen the national independence and the territorial integrity of his country and to contribute to its defence in accordance with the law' (§ 5), 'to preserve and strengthen positive African cultural values in his relations with other members of the society, in the spirit of tolerance, dialogue and consultation and, in general, to contribute to the promotion of the moral well-being of society' (§ 6), and 'to contribute to the best of his abilities, at all times and at all levels, to the promotion and achievement of African unity' (§ 8). Obviously, these individual duties may also be a basis for the restriction of individuals' positive freedom of association, in the sense that restrictions (and maybe even closure) may be imposed on political parties that for example threaten state security, territorial integrity or African unity, or even those that contradict 'positive African values'. Yet it should be kept in mind that the African Commission on Human and Peoples' Rights will most likely submit restrictions on both the positive and negative aspects of freedom of association to a proportionality test.

Article 8 of the African Charter on the Rights and Welfare of the Child provides that '[e]very child shall have the right to free association and freedom of peaceful assembly in conformity with the law'. This is quite similar to Article 15 CRC (cf. above).

The 2003 Protocol to the African Charter on Human and Peoples' Rights on the Rights of Women in Africa, provides in its Article 9 for affirmative action measures to strengthen women's political participation: '1. States Parties shall take specific positive action to promote participative governance and the equal

---

[14] African Commission on Human and Peoples' Rights, Communication 212/98, *Amnesty International v Zambia*, § 49, Twelfth Annual Activity Report, 1998–1999, in R. Murray and M. Evans (eds.), *Documents of the African Commission on Human and Peoples' Rights* (Oxford/ Portland, OR: Hart Publishing, 2001), at 752.

participation of women in the political life of their countries through affirmative action, enabling national legislation and other measures to ensure that: a. women participate without any discrimination in all elections; b. women are represented equally at all levels with men in all electoral processes; c. women are equal partners with men at all levels of development and implementation of state policies and development programmes. 2. States Parties shall ensure increased and effective representation and participation of women at all levels of decision-making.' Since state commitments under this provision are significantly stronger than those under Article 7 CEDAW, what has been said with regard to the potential use of that provision will apply a fortiori to this provision when it enters into force.

Article 11 of the European Convention for the protection of Human Rights and fundamental freedoms (ECHR) protects freedom of association in general terms. Yet within this scope, the freedom to form and join political parties is considered particularly important. In 1998, the European Court of Human Rights examined for the first time whether political parties fell within the scope of application of Article 11: 'The Court considers that the wording of Article 11 provides an initial indication as to whether political parties may rely on that provision. It notes that although Article 11 refers to "freedom of association with others, including the right to form . . . trade unions . . . ", the conjunction "including" clearly shows that trade unions are but one example among others of the form in which the right to freedom of association may be exercised . . . However, even more persuasive than the wording of Article 11, in the Court's view, is the fact that political parties are a form of association essential to the proper functioning of democracy. In view of the importance of democracy in the Convention system . . . there can be no doubt that political parties come within the scope of Article 11'.[15] Later it added: 'In view of the role played by political parties, any measure taken against them affects both freedom of association and, consequently, democracy in the state concerned.'[16]

According to the Court, political parties differ in an important respect from other political organizations: 'It is in the nature of the role they play that political parties, the only bodies which can come to power, also have the capacity to influence the whole of the regime in their countries. By the proposals for an overall societal model which they put before the electorate and by their capacity to implement those proposals once they come to power, political parties differ from other organisations which intervene in the political arena.'[17] Hence the Court suggests that the freedom of association of political parties has an ambivalent meaning for democracy: on the one hand it is a crucial

---

[15] *United Communist Party of Turkey and Others v Turkey* ECHR (1998), Reports 1998–I, §§ 24–25.

[16] *Refah Partisi (The Welfare Party) and Others v Turkey* ECHR Grand Chamber (2003), Reports 2003-II, § 87, referring to *United Communist Party of Turkey*, o.c., § 31.

[17] *Refah Partisi (Grand Chamber)*, o.c., § 87.

prerequisite for the functioning of a democratic regime, while on the other hand it poses a particular risk for democratic values and institutions.

Recently, the Court recognized the existence of positive state obligations with respect to the freedom of association of political parties. The authorities must protect the functioning of a political party, for example against hostilities from citizens. Otherwise, other political parties might be dissuaded to openly express themselves on controversial issues.[18]

The European Court of Human Rights consistently links the freedom of association of political parties to their freedom of expression (protected in Article 10 ECHR), inasmuch as the activities of political parties form part of a collective exercise of the freedom of expression. Articles 10 and 11 ECHR are strongly linked, because in the eyes of the Court, 'protection of opinions and the freedom to express them within the meaning of Article 10 of the Convention is one of the objectives of the freedoms of assembly and association enshrined in Article 11. That applies all the more in relation to political parties in view of their essential role in ensuring pluralism and the proper functioning of democracy.'[19]

The Council of Europe's Framework Convention for the Protection of National Minorities includes some provisions that affect the freedom of political association of members of minorities. The crucial question that may be asked in this regard is whether this convention allows states to prohibit political parties based on for example ethnic minority allegiance, or political parties whose agenda consists of the promotion of minority concerns, which may include regional autonomy or even separatism. The text of the Convention does not give a clear answer to that question. Article 7 protects in general terms the freedom of association of persons belonging to national minorities. Article 15 stipulates: 'The Parties shall create the conditions necessary for the effective participation of persons belonging to national minorities in cultural, social and economic life and in public affairs, in particular those affecting them.' The explanatory report mentions in this respect the 'effective participation of persons belonging to national minorities in the decision-making processes and elected bodies both at national and local levels',[20] hence this seems to include a potential role of minority political parties. Article 17(2) provides: 'The Parties undertake not to interfere with the right of persons belonging to national minorities to participate in the activities of non-governmental organizations, both at the national and international levels.' The concept of NGOs may or may not include political parties. Article 21 states: 'Nothing in the present framework Convention shall be interpreted as implying any right to engage in any activity or perform any act

[18] *Ouranio Toxo and Others v Greece* ECHR (2006), not reported, § 37.

[19] *Refah Partisi (Grand Chamber)*, o.c., § 88, referring to *United Communist Party of Turkey*, o.c. §§ 42–43.

[20] Framework Convention for the Protection of National Minorities, Strasbourg, February 1995, Explanatory Report at § 80.

contrary to the fundamental principles of international law and in particular of the sovereign equality, territorial integrity and political independence of States.' It is not clear whether the reference to territorial integrity in this provision could form a basis for a state to prohibit political parties promoting separatism. The interpretative question in this respect is whether promoting separatism in a party programme is in itself an activity or act contrary to territorial integrity or not.

The Charter of Fundamental Rights of the European Union in its Article 12, on freedom of association, explicitly includes association in political matters, and moreover mentions political parties in its second paragraph (corresponding to Article 191 of the EC Treaty): 'Political parties at Union level contribute to expressing the political will of the citizens of the Union.' This is not a phrase that grants any additional right, but it brings the political parties at Union level explicitly within the scope of protection of freedom of association, thus protecting them against interferences from the EU institutions.

In the 1990 Copenhagen Document of the OSCE, the freedom of association with regard to political parties is explicitly included: '[T]o ensure that the will of the people serves as the basis of the authority of government, the participating States will (7.5.) respect the right of citizens to seek political or public office, individually or as representatives of political parties or organizations, without discrimination; (7.6.) respect the right of individuals and groups to establish, in full freedom, their own political parties or other political organizations and provide such political parties and organizations with the necessary legal guarantees to enable them to compete with each other on a basis of equal treatment before the law and by the authorities.'

Although the texts of the OSCE on the 'human dimension' are not formally binding, they do have political importance and they guide the work of this organization, amongst others in the field of election monitoring and assisting democracy and the rule of law, especially in former communist states.

4.2.2 Restrictions

The standard justification of a measure restricting a fundamental freedom is that which is given within the framework of a restriction clause (4.2.2.1). In addition, in the specific context of the fight against racism, restrictions of the freedom of political association may be mandatory (4.2.2.2). Moreover, the context in which party closure is considered may be such that abuse clauses (4.2.2.3) or derogation clauses (4.2.2.4) become relevant.

4.2.2.1 Restriction Clauses

Article 22 (2) ICCPR, Article 11(2) ECHR, Article 16(2) ACHR, Article 15(2) CRC, and Article 26(2) ICMW are restriction clauses that are similarly phrased. A restriction of the freedom of (political) association is justified if three conditions are met. Firstly, the restriction must be 'prescribed by law', i.e. it must be based on a general rule that is accessible and foreseeable. Secondly, the restriction must serve a legitimate purpose, from among those enumerated in the restriction clause. The legitimate purpose can be either the protection of the rights and freedoms of others (which is included in all of the above-mentioned provisions), or the protection of a general interest. The general interests which may justify a restriction of the freedom of (political) association differ slightly among the conventions and include national security (ICCPR, ECHR, ACHR, CRC, and ICMW), public safety (ICCPR, ECHR, ACHR, and CRC), public order (ICCPR, ACHR, CRC, and ICMW), the protection of public health or morals (ICCPR, ECHR, ACHR, and CRC), and the prevention of disorder or crime (ECHR). Finally, the restriction must be 'necessary in a democratic society' for this legitimate purpose. This is the crucial element in the test, encompassing a proportionality requirement: the weight of the individual freedom must be balanced against the weight of the interest invoked for its restriction.

The Charter of Fundamental Rights of the European Union contains a general restriction clause in Article 52(1), which is formulated somewhat differently from those that are mentioned above: 'Any limitation on the exercise of the rights and freedoms recognised by this Charter must be provided for by law and respect the essence of those rights and freedoms. Subject to the principle of proportionality, limitations may be made only if they are necessary and genuinely meet objectives of general interest recognised by the Union or the need to protect the rights and freedoms of others.' Yet the substance of this provision is the same as that of the other restriction clauses, mentioned above, especially since Article 52(3) of the Charter stipulates: 'In so far as this Charter contains rights which correspond to rights guaranteed by the Convention for the Protection of Human Rights and Fundamental Freedoms, the meaning and scope of those rights shall be the same as those laid down by the said Convention. This provision shall not prevent Union law providing more extensive protection.'

Hence, in order to be compatible with any of these restriction clauses, a party closure must have a legal basis, and must serve one of the enumerated legitimate aims. Moreover, the measure must be proportionate to that aim. Since party closure is a very restrictive measure, the proportionality requirement will not easily be met.

The restriction clauses in the ICCPR, the ECHR, and the ACHR also make an exception for 'the imposition of lawful restrictions' (in the ACHR it is added 'including even deprivation of the exercise of the right of association') on members of the armed forces and of the police, and in the ECHR also the administration of the state. A literal interpretation suggests that the legislator has unfettered power to restrict the freedom of association of these persons, and that the other conditions of the restriction clause do not apply.[21] Yet the

---

[21] See *Rekvényi v Hungary* ECHR (1999), Reports, 1999-III, about a ban on political activities and membership of political parties for members of the police, the armed forces, and the security

Eva Brems

'legitimate purpose' requirement is implicit in these cases: the good functioning and the neutrality of the armed forces and the police (and the administration) may justify restrictions on the political freedoms of their members. Moreover, since most measures that restrict the freedom of political association also restrict the freedom of expression, and no exception for the same categories of people is made in the provisions on the latter freedom, a proportionality requirement needs to be respected anyway. Yet the specific mention of these categories justifies a proportionality control that is less strict.

Finally, Article 16 ECHR states: 'Nothing in Articles 10, 11 and 14, shall be regarded as preventing the High Contracting Parties from imposing restrictions on the political activity of aliens.' This suggests that the ordinary conditions for restriction do not apply to the freedom of political organization of aliens, which could be limited without any conditions attached. There seems to be a consensus, however, about the outdated character of this provision. The Parliamentary Assembly of the Council of Europe called for its deletion in 1977.[22] The provision has never been applied by the European Commission[23] or the European Court of Human Rights.

4.2.2.2 *Mandatory Restrictions*

In rare cases, human rights treaties make it compulsory or strongly recommended for states parties to impose certain restrictions on individual rights. This is normally explained by an underlying conflict of human rights, which the drafters decided to solve by giving priority to one right over the other. In the context of the freedom of political association, a provision of this type is Article 4 of the Convention on the Elimination of All Forms of Racial Discrimination (CERD), where it stipulates that states parties should condemn all propaganda *and all organizations* which are based on ideas or theories of superiority of one race or group of persons of one colour or ethnic origin, or which attempt to justify or promote racial hatred and discrimination. Among the action states are to undertake in this respect, point (b) states that they 'shall *declare illegal and prohibit organizations*, and also organized and all other propaganda activities, which promote and incite racial discrimination, and shall recognize participation in such organizations or activities as an offence punishable by law'. Hence, unless they made a reservation to this provision, the 170 states that are parties to this Convention are obliged to prohibit racist political parties. Nevertheless,

---

forces. The European Court of Human Rights left the question of the applicability of the general conditions of the restriction clause unresolved, but did not accept that a legal basis alone was sufficient for these restrictive measures, of which it examined the severity as well as the political and historical context.

[22] Parliamentary Assembly of the Council of Europe, Recommendation 799 (1977) on the Political Rights and Position of Aliens, § 10(c).

[23] In its report in the *Piermont* case, the European Commission on Human Rights interpreted the term 'alien' restrictively, in order to avoid application of Article 16 ECHR: *Piermont v France* (1994) Series A, No. 313, §§ 58–69.

while most states parties to CERD enacted criminal legislation against racist hate speech in order to implement their obligations under this convention, a smaller number enacted legislation providing for the prohibition of racist organizations.[24] This is related to the framing of Article 4 CERD, which states that the measures to be taken by the states should be taken 'with due regard to the principles embodied in the UDHR', which include for example freedom of association. Hence, despite the very concrete language under Article 4(b) CERD, states interpret this in the sense that they are entitled to make their own balancing between on the one hand freedom of association and the freedom of expression, and on the other hand the prohibition of racial discrimination, meaning that they are allowed to go less far in restricting racists' political freedoms than prescribed by Article 4 CERD. The Committee on the Elimination of Racial Discrimination, however, insists that the specific obligations under Article 4 have a mandatory character.[25] In a 1993 General Comment, it stated, 'When the International Convention on the Elimination of All Forms of Racial Discrimination was being adopted (1966), Article 4 was regarded as central to the struggle against racial discrimination. At that time, there was a widespread fear of the revival of authoritarian ideologies. The proscription of the dissemination of ideas of racial superiority, and of organized activity likely to incite persons to racial violence, was properly regarded as crucial. Since that time, the Committee has received evidence of organized violence based on ethnic origin and the political exploitation of ethnic difference. As a result, implementation of Article 4 is now of increased importance.'[26] The Committee stressed that what was needed was not only appropriate legislation, but also to ensure that it is effectively enforced.[27] With regard to the obligation to prohibit racist organizations under Article 4(b) CERD, the Committee added: 'Some States have maintained that in their legal order it is inappropriate to declare illegal an organization before its members have promoted or incited racial discrimination. The Committee is of the opinion that Article 4(b) places a greater burden upon such States to be vigilant in proceeding against such organizations at the earliest moment. These organizations, as well as organized

---

[24] E.g. Albania: Article 9(2) Constitution 1998 (political parties); Austria: prohibition of National Socialist or similar organizations in Article 9 Treaty of Vienna of 1955 and § 1 Prohibition Statute; Belarus: Article 5 (3) Constitution 1994; Bulgaria: Article 44(2) Constitution; France: Article 10 Law 10 January 1936 (as amended in 1972) on combat groups and private militias; Italy: XIIth final provision of the Constitution and Section 1 of Act No. 645 of 1952 (ban on reconstitution of Fascist Party), Section 3 of Act 654/75; 'former Yugoslav Republic of Macedonia': Law on Political Parties (1996) Article 4; Moldova: Article 4 Association Code; Netherlands: Article 20 Civil Code; Poland: Article 13 Constitution (political parties); Portugal: Article 46 Constitution and Law No. 64/78; Spain: Articles 174 and 515 Criminal Code; Turkey: Article 69 Constitution and Act on Political Parties 2820/1983 (political parties); Articles 5 and 76 Act 2908/1983 (associations); Ukraine: Article 37 Constitution (political parties).
[25] Committee on the Elimination of Racial Discrimination, General Comment No. 4, adopted on 24 August 1985 and General Comment No. 15, Adopted on 17 March 1993.
[26] General Comment No. 15, o.c., § 1.   [27] Ibid, § 2.

and other propaganda activities, have to be declared illegal and prohibited. Participation in these organizations is, of itself, to be punished.'[28] This is unambiguous: as soon as an association—including a political party—promotes or incites racial discrimination, it must be prohibited outright. The same concern appears in the concluding observations of the Committee under state reports, for example the comments with regard to the report of Belgium in 2002. Belgium has criminal legislation against racist speech and propaganda, and has made support and membership of racist organizations an offence,[29] but the prohibition of such organizations is not provided for. At the same time, several political parties in Belgium advocate a racist agenda, amongst whom is the Vlaams Belang, a political party that gets more than 20 per cent of the Flemish vote. Belgium made a reservation to Article 4 CERD, stating that it will take care to reconcile Article 4 with the freedom of expression, assembly, and association. Hence Belgium reserved the right to determine how far to go in the restriction of these rights. Nevertheless it was criticized by the Committee: 'The Committee is concerned that there is no legislation prohibiting racist organizations and propaganda activities. It is also concerned about the increasing influence of xenophobic ideology on political parties, especially in Flanders... Taking into account the mandatory nature of Article 4 of the Convention, the Committee also recommends that the state party enact legislation that declares illegal and prohibits any organization which promotes or incites to racism and racial discrimination and consider withdrawing its reservation to this Article.'[30]

4.2.2.3 *Abuse Clauses*

Article 5 § 2 ICCPR provides that: 'Nothing in the present Covenant may be interpreted as implying for any State, group or person any right to engage in any activity or perform any act aimed at the destruction of any of the rights and freedoms recognized herein or at their limitation to a greater extent than is provided for in the present Covenant.' Similar provisions are found in the ECHR (Article 17), the ACHR (Article 29(a)), the ICMW (Article 81(2)) and the Charter of Fundamental Rights of the European Union (Article 54). These 'abuse clauses' exclude abusive use of fundamental rights from the scope of protection of these rights.[31] Abuse clauses are relevant in the context of party

---

[28] Ibid, § 6.

[29] Act of 30 July 1981 on the punishment of certain acts motivated by racism or xenophobia, Article 3.

[30] Concluding observations of the Committee on the Elimination of Racial Discrimination: Belgium, 21 May 2002, CERD/C/60/CO/2, § 14. Cf. also Concluding Observations of the Committee on the Elimination of Racial Discrimination: Netherlands, 1 May 2001, CERD/C/304/Add.104, § 4, in which the Committee 'welcomes the judicial proceedings that have led to the prohibition of a racist political party'.

[31] Abuse clauses have been criticized by some commentators. E.g. according to Vasak, they contain 'a not too democratic principle inherited from the Robespierre period of the French Revolution: No freedom for the enemies of freedom' (Vasak, 'Democracy, Political Parties and International Human Rights Law' (1996) 26 *Israel Yearbook on Human Rights* 15, at 27).

closure when the desire to prohibit a political party is motivated by the threat this party poses to human rights. When a political party and the people who compose it use their freedom of political association for example to promote a political agenda that includes serious human rights violations, they cannot rely on their fundamental right when the state imposes rights-restrictive measures (such as party closure) on them. From a technical legal viewpoint, an abuse clause may operate in different ways. A first possibility is its use as an inter-pretative guideline in the balancing exercise that is to decide whether or not a restrictive measure is proportionate to a legitimate aim. In this case, evidence of rights abuse will almost automatically lead to the restrictive measure being considered proportionate.[32] An alternative is the use of the abuse clause on its own. In that scenario, evidence of rights abuse leads to a finding of inadmiss-ibility and the proportionality issue is not even examined.[33]

4.2.2.4 *Derogation Clauses*

Article 4 ICCPR, Article 15 ECHR, and Article 27 ACHR provide for the derogation of some human rights, including the freedom of association, in time of war or emergency. These provisions may be relevant to the issue of party closures to the extent that among the measures that are judged necessary to cope with an emergency situation may be restrictions on the activities of political parties, and even party closure. For example, when the emergency is caused by the threat of civil war, it may be desirable to prohibit a political party inciting to war. Likewise, when the emergency is caused by terrorist attacks, it may be desirable to prohibit a political party that supports the terrorists.

A state of war or emergency has to be officially notified to the Secretary-General of the United Nations (ICCPR), the Council of Europe (ECHR), or the Organization of American States (ACHR). The notification must indicate the provisions the application of which are suspended, the derogative measures that are taken, the reasons for the suspension and under the ACHR also the date set for the

---

[32] This approach is adopted in a number of cases before the European Commission on Human Rights: *J. Glimmerveen and J. Hagenbeek v The Netherlands* (1979) DR 18, at 187; *X v Federal Republic of Germany* (1982), DR 29, at 198; *T v Belgium* (1983), DR 34, at 171; *Hendrikus Van Der Heijden v The Netherlands* (1985) DR 41, 264; *Felderer v Sweden* (1985) 8 European Human Rights Reports (1986) 91; *Michael Kühnen v Federal Republic of Germany* (1988) DR 56, at 210; *H, W, P and K v Austria* (1989) DR 62, at 220; *FP v Germany* (1993), not published; *Walter Ochensberger v Austria* (1994), not published; *Udo Walendy v Germany* (1995) DR 80-A 99; *Otto EFA Remer v Germany*, (1995), DR 82-A 117; *Gerd Honsik v Austria* (1995) not published; *Nationaldemokratische Partei Deutschlands, Bezirksverband München-Oberbayern v Germany* (1995) DR 84-A 154; *Friedrich Rebhandl v Austria* (1996) not published; *DI v Germany* (1996) not published; *Pierre Marais v France* (1996) DR 86-B 190; *Karl-August Hennicke v Germany* (1997) not published; *Herwig Nachtmann v Austria* (1998) not published. See also some cases of the European Court of Human Rights: *Hans Jürgen Witzsch v Germany*, ECHR (1999) not published; *Hans Jörg Schimanek v Austria* ECHR (2000) not published.

[33] Recently, the European Court of Human Rights adopted this approach: *Garaudy v France* ECHR (2003), not published. See also some early cases of the European Commission on Human Rights: *X v Austria* (1963) YB 6, at 424, and *X v Italy* (1976) DR 5, at 83.

termination of the suspension. Derogative measures remain subject to a limited proportionality check: the restrictions must be 'strictly required by the exigencies of the situation', both with regard to their severity and with regard to their duration. Moreover, the measure must be compatible with the other obligations of the state under international law (for example international humanitarian law) and may not be discriminatory.[34]

Under the ECHR, the use of derogation is rare, and has never involved derogation from the freedom of association. In the ICCPR system, the derogation clause has frequently been invoked and derogations have regularly involved the freedom of association. This is to be expected, since the threat inspiring the state of emergency often comes from organized people (armed militias, guerilla groups, conspiracies . . .). Sometimes these measures have included the adoption of new legislation facilitating party closure. An example is the state of emergency in two cities in Azerbaijan in 1994 as a reaction to political violence. The state of emergency decree amongst other measures outlawed political parties that 'obstruct normalization of the political situation'.[35]

4.2.3 International Cases on Party Closure: Brief Overview

The case law of international human rights supervisory bodies about the issue of party closure consists of one case before the Human Rights Committee, a few inadmissibility decisions of the former European Commission on Human Rights, and a series of judgments of the European Court of Human Rights, dealing mainly with party closure in Turkey.

The Human Rights Committee's case of *MA v Italy*[36] dealt with the application of an Italian penal law adopted in 1952, prohibiting 'reorganizing the dissolved fascist party'. Hence the case did not concern the dissolution of the fascist party as such, but rather one of the consequences attached to it: the fact that the same party can not be re-created. Proceedings against MA were initiated in 1974, when he was only seventeen years old. He was sentenced in 1976 to four years imprisonment, yet after half a year he was released on mandatory daily supervision. The young man appealed, and the judgment was confirmed, but in the meantime he went into exile to France, from where he was later extradited. The Human Rights Committee was very brief about this case: it applied the abuse clause of Article 5 § 2 ICCPR and held that the complaint was

---

[34] The prohibition of discrimination is mentioned in Article 4 ICCPR and Article 27 ACHR, but not in Article 15 ECHR. Yet the requirement of respect for other international legal obligations entails that for states that are a party to both treaties, the prohibition of discrimination from Article 4 ICCPR is valid also in the context of Article 15 ECHR.

[35] Human Rights Watch, *World Report 1995* (www.hrw.org/reports/1995/WR95/HELSINKI-02.htm).

[36] Human Rights Committee, Communication 117/1981, *MA v Italy*, inadmissibility decision of 10 April 1984.

inadmissible, because it was incompatible *rationale materiae* with the provisions of the Covenant.

The first party closure case of the European Commission on Human Rights concerned the prohibition of the German Communist Party in application of Article 21(2) of the German Constitution that was enacted after the Second World War: 'Parties which, by reason of their aims or the behaviour of their adherents, seek to impair or abolish the free democratic basic order or to endanger the existence of the Federal Republic of Germany are unconstitutional. The Federal Constitutional Court decides on the question of unconstitutionality.' This provision has been applied only twice. In 1952, the Sozialistische Reichspartei (very similar to Hitler's NSDAP) was prohibited and in 1955 so, too, was the Kommunistische Partei Deutschlands. The latter applied to the European Commission on Human Rights, arguing that this prohibition violated its freedom of association. The Commission however held that there was no reason to examine this case in the light of Article 10 or 11 ECHR, because of the application of Article 17, the abuse clause. The Commission stated that the motives of the German legislator drafting Article 21(2) of the Constitution were the same as those of Article 17 ECHR, namely safeguarding human rights by protecting the free functioning of democratic institutions. The German Communist Party aimed at the establishment of a communist social order through a proletarian revolution and the dictatorship of the proletariat. The Commission stated that recourse to dictatorship to install a regime is incompatible with the Convention and entails the destruction of numerous rights and liberties it protects. Hence the organization and functioning of the German Communist Party was an activity in the sense of Article 17; therefore the application was ruled inadmissible because it was incompatible with the provisions of the Convention.[37]

The 1976 European Commission case of *X v Italy*[38] concerned an application of the same Italian law that later came before the Human Rights Committee in *MA v Italy* (cf. above). The applicant founded in 1968 a political movement whose doctrine and platform were inspired by those of the fascist party, of which he even copied the symbol. He had been convicted for this, and claimed that this was a violation of his freedom of speech and of association, as well as discrimination. In this case, the Commission did not apply the abuse clause, but simply the limitation clauses of Articles 10 and 11 ECHR, stating that the conviction of the applicant was a measure that was necessary in a democratic society in the interests of public safety and the protection of the rights and freedoms of others. Neither was it a prohibited discrimination under Article 14 of the Convention, since 'the difference in treatment under the Italian legislation to persons inspired by the fascist ideology is justified by the fact that it pursues a legitimate aim, that of protecting democratic institutions'. Hence, the application was declared inadmissible because it was 'manifestly ill-founded'.

[37] *Application 250/57 v FRG*, YB 1, 222.   [38] *Application 6741/74 v Italy*, DR 5, 83.

Finally, the European Commission on Human Rights examined in 1979 the case of *Glimmerveen and Hagenbeek v the Netherlands*.[39] Mrs Glimmerveen and Hagenbeek were the president and vice-president of the Nederlandse Volks Unie, a political party that in 1978 was declared a prohibited association by a Dutch court, in application of a provision of the civil code, stating that an association can be prohibited if its activities or its goal violate the public order. In this case, the reason was that the party propagated a racist platform. One month later, the applicants and a third person, who was the secretary of the prohibited party, submitted a list of candidates—including their own names— for the municipal elections of Amsterdam. It was a list without a name. The Central Voting Board declared the list invalid, arguing that it was against the Dutch legal order to accept a list of a prohibited party, whilst the candidates on the list shared the views of this party and had in no way dissociated themselves from its racist opinions. Hence, the complaint in Strasbourg was not about the prohibition of the party, but about the consequences of the prohibition, i.e. the refusal of the lists of the party. The claim was not made under Article 11 ECHR, but rather under Article 3 of the First Additional Protocol to the ECHR, protecting the freedom to take part in elections. However, according to the Commission, the applicants could not rely on this right, because they wanted to use it for a purpose that was unacceptable in light of Article 17, the abuse clause. Hence, the applications were incompatible with the provisions of the Convention and therefore inadmissible.

Starting in 1998, the European Court of Human Rights issued eleven judgments about party closure in Turkey. The Turkish Constitution[40] as well as the Law on the regulation of political parties[41] provide that political parties can be dissolved by the constitutional court, for a number of reasons, including a programme that wants to change the republican form of the Turkish state, or the integrity of its territory and unity of its nation, abolish fundamental rights and freedoms, or defend the domination of one social class or community. Political parties may neither assert the existence of national minorities in Turkey, nor include in their names certain terms such as 'communist', 'anarchist', 'fascist', 'theocratic', 'national socialist', the name of a religion, language, race, sect, or region. On the basis of this law, the Turkish Constitutional Court has dissolved more than thirty political parties in the past fifty years;[42] at least eighteen in recent times.[43] In ten cases, the political party

---

[39] *J. Glimmerveen and J. Hagenbeek v The Netherlands* (1979) DR 18, at 187.

[40] Article 69 of the Turkish Constitution.

[41] Law No. 2820 on the regulation of political parties, in particular Section 101.

[42] E. Yuksel, 'Cannibal Democracies, Theocratic Secularism: The Turkish Version' (1999) 7 *Cardozo J Int'l & Comp L* 423.

[43] Cf. *Refah Partisi (The Welfare Party) a.o. v Turkey* ECHR (2001), not reported, Joint Dissenting Opinion of Judges Fuhrmann, Loucaides and Sir Nicolas Bratza, citing Refah as 'the fifteenth political party to have been compulsorily dissolved by the Turkish Constitutional Court in recent times'.

fought the dissolution in the European Court of Human Rights. Eight of the ten political parties won their case in Strasbourg. The other two are the *Refah* case, which gave rise to two judgments, by an ordinary chamber and a Grand Chamber, and the *Fazilet* case, which was struck from the role. Through these cases, the European Court of Human Rights had the occasion to develop clear standards about the situations in which it considers the prohibition or forced dissolution of a political party to be allowed.

The first case was that of the *United Communist Party a.o. v Turkey*.[44] This party was formed in June 1990. To conform with the requirements of the law, it immediately submitted its constitution and programme to the office of the Principal State Counsel at the Court of Cassation for assessment of their compatibility with the Constitution and the law on the regulation of political parties. A few days later, the State Counsel applied to the Constitutional Court for an order dissolving the party. The Constitutional Court dissolved the party in July 1991. There were several reasons for doing this, amongst which the use of the word 'Communist' in its name and the fact that the constitution and programme referred to two nations: the Kurdish nation and the Turkish nation, which was seen as encouraging separatism. The European Court of Human Rights saw no reason to invoke Article 17 ECHR in this case, because nothing in the constitution and programme of the party pointed at the conclusion that it was engaging in activity to destroy any of the rights and freedoms of the Convention. Rather, it evaluated the dissolution under the restriction clause of Article 11 ECHR, and concluded that the measure was not proportionate, and therefore violated that provision.

Four months later, the Court reached the same conclusion in the case of the *Socialist Party a.o. v Turkey*.[45] This party had been formed in February 1988 and in this case as well the State Counsel had applied for dissolution immediately after receiving notification of its constitution and programme. He accused the party of seeking to establish the domination of the working class with a view to establishing a dictatorship of the proletariat. Yet in December 1988, this first application for dissolution was dismissed. In November 1991, the State Counsel applied again for dissolution, this time accusing the party of having carried on activities likely to undermine the territorial integrity of the state and the unity of the nation, relying on extracts from its publications and from oral statements made at public meetings and on television. In July 1992, the party was dissolved as a result. The reasoning of the European Court of Human Rights was parallel to that in the first case: there was no reason to invoke Article 17 ECHR, and under Article 11 § 2 ECHR, the prohibition measure was disproportionate.

---

[44] *United Communist Party of Turkey and Others v Turkey* ECHR (1998), Reports 1998-I. For a comment, see B. Duarté, 'Les partis politiques, la démocratie et la Convention européenne des droits de l'homme' (1999) *Rev Trim Dr H* 314.

[45] *Socialist Party and Others v Turkey* ECHR (1998), Reports 1998-III.

At the end of 1999, this was reconfirmed in the case of the *Freedom and Democracy Party (ÖZDEP) v Turkey*.[46] This party was founded in October 1992, and again the State Counsel filed for dissolution on the basis of its constitution and programme. While the Constitutional Court proceedings were pending, the founding members dissolved the party. Yet a few months later, in July 1993, the Constitutional Court still made an order dissolving it. The arguments were again that the party sought to undermine the territorial integrity and the unity of the nation. Again the European Court of Human Rights found a violation of Article 11 ECHR.

The next judgment came in April 2002, in the case of *Yazar, Karataş, Aksoy and the People's Labour Party (HEP) v Turkey*.[47] HEP was founded in June 1990, and two years later the State Counsel filed for dissolution. The party was dissolved in July 1993. On the basis of publications, statements, slogans, etc., the Constitutional Court concluded that this party also threatened national unity and territorial integrity. The European Court of Human Rights judged again that the measure was disproportionate and violated Article 11 ECHR.

Then there was the case of *Dicle for the Democratic Party (DEP) v Turkey*.[48] DEP was the successor of HEP, and was dissolved for the same reasons. Once again, the European Court of Human Rights judged that this was a violation of Article 11 ECHR.

It was followed by the case of the *Socialist Party of Turkey (STP) a.o. v Turkey*.[49] This party was created in November 1992 and dissolved one year later on the basis of its programme, again because it threatened the territorial integrity and national unity, by mentioning a Kurdish nation and even Kurdish self-determination. The European Court of Human Rights again found a violation of Article 11 ECHR.

The most recent cases in this series are *DDP (Party of Democracy and Evolution) v Turkey*[50] and *EP (Labour Party) and Şenol v Turkey*.[51] These parties were founded in 1995 and 1996, respectively, and dissolved soon thereafter on grounds of threatening territorial integrity and national unity, based on reference to Kurdish rights in their programmes. In both cases, the European Court pronounced a violation of Article 11 ECHR.

All these judgments were taken by a unanimous Court. In the meantime, however, on 31 July 2001, the Court had been divided over the prohibition of a different type of Turkish party: the case of the *Welfare Party (Refah Partisi) a.o. v Turkey*.[52] This party was founded in 1983, and gradually became more and

---

[46] *Freedom and Democracy Party (ÖZDEP) v Turkey* ECHR (1999), Reports 1999-VIII.
[47] *Yazar, Karataş, Aksoy and the People's Labour Party (HEP) v Turkey* ECHR (2002), Reports 2002-II. [48] *Dicle for the Democratic Party (DEP) v Turkey* ECHR (2002), not reported.
[49] *Socialist Party of Turkey (STP) a.o. v Turkey* ECHR (2003), not reported.
[50] *DDP (Party of Democracy and Evolution) v Turkey* ECHR (2005), not reported.
[51] *EP (Labour Party) and Şenol v Turkey* ECHR (2005), not reported.
[52] *Refah Partisi (The Welfare Party) a.o. v Turkey* ECHR (2001), not reported. For comments, see, S. Sottiaux and D. De Prins, 'La Cour européenne des droits de l'homme et les organisations

more successful, especially in the mid nineties under chairman Necmettin Erbakan, when it obtained around 22 per cent of the votes in the 1995 general election and about 35 per cent of the votes in the 1996 local elections. These 22 per cent made Refah the largest political party in the Turkish parliament. As a result, it formed a coalition government with the centre-right True Path Party (Tansu Ciller), under the premiership of its leader, Necmettin Erbakan. While the Refah Party was in the government, the State Counsel applied for its dissolution, which was pronounced in January 1998. The argument was in this case, that the party threatened the secular nature of the state. This conclusion was not based on the party programme, but on certain statements of Erbakan and other party representatives. In this case a narrow majority of four against three of a chamber of the European Court of Human Rights held that the dissolution of Refah was not a violation of Article 11 ECHR. They did not however invoke Article 17. Refah appealed before a Grand Chamber (seventeen judges) of the European Court of Human Rights, and the judgment was confirmed by a unanimous Court on 13 February 2003.[53]

The case of *Fazilet Partisi (Virtue Party) and Kutan v Turkey*[54] concerns one of the successor parties of Refah, that was dissolved on the same grounds. Displeased with the Court's case-law on 'Islamic' matters (including in particular the *Refah* case), the applicants withdrew their complaint and the case was struck from the role in April 2006.

In October 2004, the Court examined two complaints about the dissolution of Russian parties. In 1995 the Russian State Duma adopted a new Federal Law on Public Associations. It required public associations registered before its entry into force to ensure that their Articles of Association complied with the new law and to re-register. A party called 'Mordovian All-Republican Socio-Political Association— the Presidential Party of Mordovia' applied for re-registration in June 1999. The Minister of Justice of Mordovia refused to renew its registration, stating that the party had failed to create branches in more than half of the districts and cities of Mordovia to quality for the title 'All-Republican', and that its Articles of Association did not comply with the requirement to include among its objectives participation in the political life of society and in elections. Later, the party was

antidémocratiques' (2002) 13 *Rev Trim Dr H* 1008; C. M. Zoethout, 'Het verbieden van dissidente politieke partijen', in N. F. van Manen (ed.), *De multiculturele samenleving en het recht* (Nijmegen: ArsAequi Libri, 2002), 277.

[53] *Refah Partisi (The Welfare Party) and Others v Turkey* ECHR Grand Chamber (2003), Reports 2003-II. For comments, see D. Kugelmann, 'Die streitbare Demokratie nach der EMRK', (2003) 30 *EuGRZ* 533; S. Sottiaux, 'Anti-Democratic Associations: Content and Consequences in Article 11 Adjudication' (2004) 22 *NQHR* 585. On the totality of the European Court of Human Rights' case-law on party closure: M. Koçak and E. Örücü, 'Dissolution of Political Parties in the Name of Democracy: Cases from Turkey and the European Court of Human Rights' (2003) 9 *European Public Law* 399; P. Vanden Heede, 'Het Europees Hof voor de Rechten van de Mens en het partijverbod: dansen op een slap koord', in M. Adams and P. Popelier (eds.), *Recht en democratie* (Antwerp: Intersentia, 2004), 193.

[54] *Fazilet Partisi (Virtue Party) and Kutan v Turkey* ECHR (2006), not reported.

dissolved by court order on the basis of its failure to re-register. Afterwards, the Presidium of the Supreme Court of the Republic of Mordovia quashed this court decision, holding the refusal to renew the registration unlawful. Yet in the meantime, the Law on Political Parties of 2001 had changed the requirements for establishing political parties. Under the new law no regional political parties were accepted. Hence the party could not be registered. The European Court of Human Rights did not pronounce on the validity of the substance of the law. Since it was not disputed that the refusal to renew registration of the party and its subsequent dissolution were unlawful under domestic law, the Court found a violation on the basis that the interference was not 'prescribed by law'.[55]

The second case concerns a regional branch of the Vatan Party, a Tatar nationalist party. In 1998, a court suspended the party's activities for six months, on the grounds that it had called for violence in a particular text. In 2000, the branch was dissolved by court on account of its failure to bring its Charter in compliance with new legislation. The complaint before the European Court of Human Rights concerned the suspension order. Yet it was held inadmissible on formal grounds, because the applicant was the Vatan Party itself, whereas the victim of the alleged violation was its regional branch, which is a different legal entity.[56]

In October 2005, a unanimous Court held that Bulgaria had violated Article 11 ECHR through the dissolution of the United Macedonian Organization Ilinden–PIRIN. This political party, which claimed that Bulgaria's Pirin region should belong to Macedonia, was dissolved in 2000 on the grounds of threatening the territorial integrity of the country. Yet the Court found that in the absence of any evidence of violent or undemocratic intentions, secessionism is not a valid basis for party closure.[57]

The crucial paragraph recurring throughout these judgments is the one establishing the grounds on which a political party can be legitimately dissolved according to the European Court of Human Rights: 'a political party may promote a change in the law or the legal and constitutional structures of the state on two conditions: firstly, the means used to that end must be legal and democratic; secondly, the change proposed must itself be compatible with fundamental democratic principles. It necessarily follows that a political party whose leaders incite violence or put forward a policy which fails to respect democracy or which is aimed at the destruction of democracy and the flouting of the rights and freedoms recognised in a democracy cannot lay claim to the Convention's protection against penalties imposed on those grounds.'[58]

In two judgments, the European Court applied these same criteria to the refusal of registration of political parties. The 'Party of Communists who have not been members of the Romanian Communist Party' was refused registration

[55] *Presidential Party of Mordovia v Russia* ECHR (2004), not reported, § 32.
[56] *Vatan v Russia* ECHR (2004), not reported, §§ 38–54.
[57] *UMO Ilinden–PIRIN and Others v Bulgaria* ECHR (2005), not reported.
[58] *Refah (Grand Chamber)*, § 98.

as a political party because its communist doctrine would threaten the constitutional and legal order.[59] The 'Communist Party of Bulgaria' founded in 1996 was not registered for several reasons, amongst which was the use of the term 'revolutionary'.[60] In both cases, the refusal of registration was held contrary to Article 11 ECHR.

In one case, the Court found a temporary ban on the activities of a political party in violation of Article 11 ECHR.[61]

Finally, it is worth mentioning the role of the European Commission for Democracy through Law, also known as the Venice Commission. This is a body of independent experts that serves as an advisory body on constitutional matters to the Council of Europe and an influential international legal think-tank. In the area under consideration, the Venice Commission has issued general guidelines,[62] based on surveys of comparative law as well as on the Commission's reading of international legal standards. Moreover, it has also given its advice on several texts of domestic (draft) legislation concerning, amongst others, party closure. The rules and rulings of the Venice Commission will be used and quoted in the analysis below whenever appropriate.

4.3 PARTY CLOSURE AND THE FREEDOM OF POLITICAL ASSOCIATION

4.3.1 Party Closure as a Measure Restricting Freedom of Political Association

In this section, the seriousness of party closure as a rights-restrictive measure is appreciated. First, party closure is situated among alternative measures that may be taken against political parties or the persons involved in them (4.3.1). Next, party closure as such is put on the scales (4.3.2).

4.3.1.1 Party Closure and Other Restrictive Measures Against Political Parties

The main subject of this chapter is the dissolution or prohibition of a political party by a court or other authorities. Yet for similar reasons, authorities may resort to other restrictive measures against political parties. Some of those, such as the refusal to register a political party or the systematic disqualification of its lists, are

---

[59] *Partidul Comunistolor (Nepeceristi) and Ungureanu v Romania* ECHR (2005), not reported.
[60] *Tsonev v Bulgaria* ECHR (2006), not reported.
[61] *Christian Democratic People's Party v Moldova* ECHR (2006), not reported.
[62] In particular the guidelines on 'Prohibition of political parties and analogous measures', adopted by the Commission at its 35th plenary meeting (Venice, 12–13 June 1998), CDL-INF (1998)014e, and the Guidelines on legislation on political parties: some specific issues, adopted by the Venice Commission at its 58th Plenary Session (Venice, 12–13 March 2004), CDL-AD (2004) 007rev, B. See www.venice.coe.int.

measures of a preventive nature that lead to the same result as the a posteriori measure of party closure. Other measures restrict the freedom of association to a lesser degree, and may therefore in some circumstances be a commendable alternative to party closure.

4.3.1.1.1 Refusal of Registration

Several states require political parties to be registered, yet the legal consequences of registration differ. The more important those consequences are, the more restrictive the refusal of registration is as an interference with the freedom of political association. Registration may sometimes be a mere formality, but can also be used as a means to exercise control over the programme and activities of the party. In those states where registration is a requirement for a political party to function and in particular to take part in elections, its effect comes close to that of party closure. The main difference is that an association that was refused registration as a political party may still exist and function as an association. The distinction between the preventive effect of the refusal of registration and the repressive effect of party closure is sometimes merely theoretical, since party closure is sometimes used as a preventive measure, for example in Turkey (cf. above), where newly erected parties are obliged to submit their constitution and programme to the office of the Principal State Counsel at the Court of Cassation for assessment of their compatibility with the Constitution and the law on the regulation of political parties, and the State Counsel in many cases immediately institutes proceedings for dissolution.

The European Court of Human Rights applies the same standards in cases of refusal of party registration as in cases of party closure.[63]

The Venice Commission's Guidelines on Prohibition and Dissolution of Political Parties and Analogous Measures (1998) stipulate that the requirement to register political parties will not in itself be considered to be in violation of the freedom of political association (§ 1). The 2004 Guidelines on legislation on political parties confirm this (4.3.2): 'Registration as a necessary step for recognition of an association as a political party, for a party's participation in general elections or for public financing of a party does not *per se* amount to a violation of rights protected under Articles 10 and 11 of the European Convention on Human Rights. Any requirements in relation to registration, however, must be such as are "necessary in a democratic society" and proportionate to the objective sought to be achieved by the measures in question. Countries applying registration procedures to political parties should refrain from imposing excessive requirements for territorial representation of political parties as well as for minimum membership. The democratic or non-democratic character of the party organization should not in principle be a ground for denying registration of a political party. Registration of political parties should

---

[63] *Partidul Comunistilor (Nepeceristi)* ECHR (2005), o.c., § 46; *Tsonev* ECHR (2006), o.c., § 50.

be denied only in cases clearly indicated in the Guidelines on prohibition of political parties and analogous measures, i.e. when the use of violence is advocated or used as a political means to overthrow the democratic constitutional order, thereby undermining the rights and freedoms guaranteed by the constitution. The fact alone that a peaceful change of the Constitution is advocated should not be sufficient for denial of registration.' This criterion is not entirely clear. Whereas the final sentences refer to the very restrictive 'violence' criterion the Venice Commission uses for party closures (cf. *infra*), the preceding sentences suggest that registration may also be refused in other circumstances, for example on the grounds of formal requirements such as territorial representation and minimum membership, as long as these are compatible with the proportionality requirement under the restriction clauses of Articles 10 and 11 ECHR.

At the United Nations level, the Human Rights Committee recognizes in its Concluding observations on state reports the risk of abuse of registration requirements leading to violations of the freedom of association of opposition parties.[64]

It should be noted that the risk of abuse of registration requirements may be greater than that of abuse of party closure, because the latter is usually in the hands of the judiciary (cf. *infra*), whereas the former is frequently in the hands of the executive.[65]

4.3.1.1.2 Temporary Ban on Party Activities

The restrictive character of a temporary ban on party activities depends amongst others on the duration and timing of the ban. Yet the European Court of Human Rights takes this measure very seriously, finding a violation in a case where the ban had been lifted and had never been enforced. It held that 'the temporary nature of the ban is not of a decisive importance in considering the proportionality of the measure, since even a temporary ban could reasonably have a "chilling effect" on the Party's freedom'.[66] This was even more so in this case, as the ban was adopted on the eve of the local elections.[67] The Moldovan Christian Democratic People's Party, an opposition party representing about 10 per cent of the votes, had been imposed a temporary ban as a sanction for the organization of several unauthorized demonstrations against a particular

---

[64] Concluding observations of the Human Rights Committee Azerbaijan, 12 November 2001, CCPR/CO/73/AZE, § 23; Concluding Observations of the Human Rights Committee Equatorial Guinea, 30 July 2004, CCPR/CO/79/GNQ, § 12; Concluding Observations of the Human Rights Committee Uzbekistan, 26 April 2005, CCPR/CO/83/UZB, § 21.

[65] E.g. in Albania it is the competence of the Ministry of Justice, in the Czech Republic and Slovakia of the Ministry of the Interior, in Canada of the Director General of Elections (a civil servant), and in Ireland of the Clerk of the Dail (also a civil servant): information from the European Commission for Democracy through Law (Venice Commission), 'Prohibition of political parties and analogous measures', Report adopted by the Commission at its 35th Plenary Meeting, Venice, 12–13 June 1998.   [66] *Christian Democratic People's Party* ECHR (2006), o.c., § 77.

[67] *Christian Democratic People's Party* ECHR (2006), o.c., § 77.

government proposal. The Court held that 'only very serious breaches such as those which endanger political pluralism or fundamental democratic principles could justify a ban on the activities of a political party'.[68]

4.3.1.1.3 Disqualification of a List Submitted for Elections

The disqualification of electoral lists is a somewhat less restrictive measure, since a party whose list has been refused is allowed to function normally apart from participating in the elections. Moreover, the disqualification is normally only valid for one particular election. Nevertheless, it is a very serious measure, since it is the main purpose of a political party to compete in elections.

The most well-known example of a state that uses this approach, is Israel. Section 7a of the Israeli Basic Law: The Knesset, provides that: '1. A list of candidates will not take part in the elections to the Knesset nor shall an individual person be a candidate for the Knesset if the goals or deeds of the list or the deeds of the person explicitly or implicitly, are one of the following: (a) reject the existence of the State of Israel as a Jewish and democratic state; (b) incite to racism; (c) support the armed struggle of an enemy state or terrorist organization against the State of Israel 2. A decision of the Central Elections Committee preventing a candidate's participation in the elections is subject to approval by the Supreme Court.'

The Central Elections Committee is not a court, but a partly political body: it is composed of Members of Parliament and chaired by a Supreme Court judge. The Israeli experience has shown the importance of the supervision by the Supreme Court. It has several times overturned decisions of the Central Elections Committee to disqualify a list.[69] Starting in the 1960s, several parties have been disqualified from participating in Israeli elections.[70]

---

[68] *Christian Democratic People's Party* ECHR (2006), o.c., § 76.

[69] In 1984, it concerned the right extremist Kach Party, and the left extremist 'Progressive List for Peace' (an Arab List): E.A. 2/84. *Neiman & Avneri v Chairperson of the Central Committee for the Elections to the 11th Knesset.* PD 39 (ii), 237. In 2003, it concerned the Bald-National Democratic Assembly (an Arab List): Judgment of 9 January 2003, EA 11280/02, 50/03, 55/03, 83/03, 131/03, 57 (4) IsrSC 1, included in CODICES database: http://codices.coe.int.

[70] It concerned one Arab party, 'Socialists List', in 1965 (*Yeridor v Chairman of the Central Elections Committee*, 19(3) PD 365 (1965)), and several times a racist list: Kach in 1988 (EA 1/88, *Neiman & Kach v Chairperson of the CEC to the 12th Knesset*, 194) and Kach and 'Kahane Is Alive' in 1992 (EA 2805/92, *Kach v Chairperson of the CED to the 13th Knesset*; EA 2858/92, *Kahane Is Alive Movement v Chairperson of the CEC to the 13th Knesset*). In a number of other cases, applications for the disqualification of lists were turned down by the Central Elections Committee. For a discussion on the disqualification of political lists in Israel, see R. Cohen-Almagor, 'Disqualification of Political Parties in Israel: 1988–1996' (1997) 11 *Emory Int'l L Rev* 67; D. Gordon, 'Limits on Extremist Political Parties: A Comparison of Israeli Jurisprudence with that of the United States and West Germany' (1987) 10 *Hastings Int'l and Comparative Law Review* 337; M. Kremnitzer, 'Disqualification of Lists and Parties: The Israeli Case', conference paper, 11th Annual Conference on The Individual vs. The State: Conference on Militant Democracy (Budapest, 5–6 December, 2003); A. Pedahzur, 'Struggling Challenges of Right-Wing Extremism and Terrorism within Democratic Boundaries: A Comparative Analysis', Paper for Workshop on 'Democracy and the New Extremist Challenge in Europe', ECPR Joint Session, Grenoble, 6–11 April 2001: www.essex.ac.uk/ECPR/events/jointsessions/paperarchive/grenoble/ws14/pedahzur.pdf.

4.3.1.1.4 The Criminal Conviction of a Political Party for Dissemination of Certain Proposals from its Party Programme

In states where political parties have legal personality and where legal persons can be held criminally responsible, criminal procedures—for example under hate speech legislation—may be a less restrictive alternative to party prohibition if the motive for measures against the party lies in its programme.

4.3.1.1.5 Exclusion of a Political Party from State Subventions

In a system where party funding is very strictly regulated and state subventions to political parties are generous, the exclusion of a political party from such subventions may seriously limit the functioning of a political party in practice. Opinions may differ on whether or not this is a more restrictive measure than a criminal conviction of the party. When the measure is based on the party's programme, a withdrawal of subventions nevertheless leaves the party free to continue to disseminate that programme. In that respect, the measure is less restrictive as a matter of principle. Yet in practice, the financial cost of the with-drawal—or even temporary suspension—of state subventions is normally infinitely higher than the cost of the fine that is to be paid as a result of a criminal conviction.

The suspension or withdrawal of public funding for organizations promoting extremism is a measure that is recommended by the Parliamentary Assembly of the Council of Europe, which appears to have had in mind mainly racist and right-wing extremist political parties.[71] Moreover, the European Commission against Racism and Intolerance, an expert body of the Council of Europe, advises that '[w]here a system of public financing of political parties is in place, such an obligation should include the suppression of public financing of political parties which promote racism'.[72] An example is the legislation on party financing in Belgium, which contains a provision stipulating that federal state subventions to a political party can be temporarily withdrawn (for a period between three months and one year) 'when the party itself, or its components, lists, candidates or elected officials show clearly and repeatedly their hostility toward the rights and freedoms protected in the European Convention on Human Rights and its additional protocols'.[73] The decision is taken by the Council of State (the highest administrative court), but no case has been decided yet. In Belgium, this is generally perceived as a very restrictive measure, because party financing makes up a very substantial part of a party's total budget.[74] While the bill implementing this measure was being considered in the

---

[71] Parliamentary Assembly of the Council of Europe, Resolution 1344 (2003): Threat posed to democracy by extremist parties and movements in Europe.

[72] ECRI general policy recommendation No. 7 on national legislation to combat racism and racial discrimination, adopted by ECRI on 13 December 2002, § 16.

[73] Act of 4 July 1989 (as amended in 1999) on the determination and control of electoral expenditure for the elections of the federal chambers, the financing and open accounting of political parties, Article 15*ter*.

[74] Party subventions granted at the regional Flemish level, can be withdrawn by a decision of the Board of the Flemish Parliament, whenever the federal subventions have been withdrawn, or

Belgian Parliament, the Human Rights Committee expressed its concern 'that political parties urging racial hatred can still benefit from the public financing system', and urged Belgium to have the bill passed as soon as possible.[75]

4.3.1.1.6 The Criminal Conviction of Individual Party Members for Acts or Speech Related to the Party Programme

This is an alternative to a similar conviction of the party as such. In terms of relative severity, this measure seems less severe, because the public image of the party is less affected when the responsibility is born by specific individuals only. Although in legal terms, a conviction of the members does not directly concern the party itself, in practice when the conviction is based on the party programme, the party will be forced to change its programme to avoid systematic convictions of all those promoting the party programme.

If the intention behind the prosecution of members is to indirectly convict the party, it will be most effective if the procedure is aimed at the party leaders. Yet when these are elected Members of Parliament, they will in many cases enjoy parliamentary immunity. Even where it is possible to lift the immunity, the procedure this requires provides an obstacle against effective prosecution.

An example is the conviction of the leader of a Norwegian political party called 'White Election Alliance' for disseminating hatred through the distribution of the party programme. This programme contained statements concerning sterilization and compulsory abortion addressed to the dark-skinned part of the population. Before the Norwegian Supreme Court, it was argued that the freedom to formulate a political programme should not be subjected to any restrictions. A minority of five judges followed this reasoning, but was overruled by the majority who stated that statements encompassing such serious violations of the most fundamental human rights could not be protected by the Constitution.[76]

4.3.1.1.7 The Criminal Conviction of Individual Party Members for their Membership of the Party

In some legal systems that do not provide for party closure, membership of certain political parties may nevertheless be an offence. In terms of comparative

whenever a final judgment has found that several clear expressions of a political party violate the legislation prohibiting racist speech and Holocaust denial (Article 9 (6)(b), Internal Rules of the Flemish Parliament. After the conviction of the party Vlaams Blok had become final (cf. *infra*), and the party changed its name to 'Vlaams Belang', this issue was tabled, but the Bureau decided against the withdrawal of funding. In any event, the procedure in the Flemish Parliament can be questioned in terms of due process, since representatives of political parties have to decide about the financial interests of a competing party. At least the appearance of impartiality is compromised in such a case.

[75] Concluding observations of the Human Rights Committee Belgium, 12 August 2004, CCPR/CO/81/BEL, § 27.

[76] Norwegian Supreme Court, 28 November 1997, Norsk Retstidende, 1997, 1821, included in CODICES database: http://codices.coe.int.

severity, this is a more rights-restrictive measure than individual convictions on the basis of the acts or speech of these individuals. In this case, the conviction of individuals is indirectly a conviction of the party. Moreover, such a conviction will strongly discourage membership of the party (if membership is an offence for one individual, it is an offence for everybody), and not just active promotion of its programme. An example of this type of legislation is found in Belgium, where membership of or support for an organization that incites and propagates racism is an offence.[77] Party closure does not exist in Belgium and political parties do not have legal personality and can therefore not be prosecuted, for example under hate speech legislation. On 21 April 2004, three supporting associations of the Vlaams Blok party were convicted for this offence.[78] This did not diminish popular support for this party. In the elections that took place less than two months later, it obtained a record 24 per cent of the vote in the Flemish region. In order to avoid future convictions, the party was required to renounce racist proposals. Yet instead it decided to change its name (Vlaams Blok–Flemish Block became Vlaams Belang–Flemish Interest), and to keep most of its programme intact.[79] The example shows the limitations of this approach.

In a system where party closure does exist, closure is the logical next step after this type of conviction, given the fact that a conviction of the party is already implied in that of the members. This is illustrated by the case of the Centrumpartij '86, a not very successful racist party in The Netherlands. In 1997, some of its leading members were convicted for 'participation in a criminal organization'.[80] Next, a civil court dissolved the party on the basis of the general law on associations, which gives the court the power to dissolve associations that are incompatible with the public order.[81]

4.3.1.1.8 Annulling the Election Result after the Victory of an Undesirable Party

Party closure is a very restrictive measure. Yet on a scale of possible measures, it is not the most restrictive that one may conceive. When a political party is considered as a real threat, for example to democracy or to public security, extreme measures may sometimes be taken to prevent its coming to power. An example is the cancellation of the December 1991 general elections in Algeria after the first round, when this indicated a victory for the Islamic Salvation Front, an Islamist party that aimed for the creation of an Islamic state. A state of emergency was declared and the constitution was suspended. Only then was the

---

[77] Act of 30 July 1981 (several times amended) on the punishment of certain acts motivated by racism and xenophobia.

[78] Court of Appeal Ghent, 21 April 2004, at: www.antiracisme.be. Cassation appeal was rejected: Court of Cassation, 9 November 2004, at: www.juridat.be.

[79] Presumably the party will at the same time avoid renouncing the programme on which its electoral success is based, and repeating the racist proposals contained in it, for fear of future convictions.   [80] Hoge Raad, 30 September 1997.

[81] Civil Court Amsterdam, 18 November 1998.

Islamic Salvation Front prohibited, and in the new constitution, a provision was included prohibiting political parties based on religion.[82]

Compared to such extremely far-reaching interferences with the democratic process and individual political rights, it would have been desirable had the constitution of Algeria provided for party closure, and if a procedure to prohibit the Islamic Salvation Front had been instituted before its participation in the elections.

4.3.2 Weighing up the Seriousness of the Interference

Are restrictions of the rights of political parties more serious than restrictions in respect of other associations or individuals? For the European Court of Human Rights, they are. Among the different functions of the freedom of expression, the European Court privileges the 'political function': free speech about matters in the general interest as both an individual and a collective good, enabling citizens' participation and central in the functioning of control mechanisms in a democracy.[83] In this context, the freedom of expression of a political party deserves even more protection than that of an individual, because it is situated at the core of the political debate, and because of its multiplier effect: one party may express the opinion of thousands or even millions of citizens. Moreover, in the Turkish cases the European Court of Human Rights put forward a stricter test for restrictions of the freedom of association of political parties than for that of other groups; put in the balance with competing interests, the freedom of association of political parties will thus weigh heavier: ' . . . the exceptions set out in Article 11 are, where political parties are concerned, to be construed strictly; only convincing and compelling reasons can justify restrictions on such parties' freedom of association. In determining whether a necessity within the meaning of Article 11 § 2 exists, the Contracting States have only a limited margin of appreciation. Although it is not for the Court to take the place of the national authorities, which are better placed than an international court to decide, for example, the appropriate timing for interference, it must exercise rigorous supervision embracing both the law and the decisions applying it, including those given by independent courts. Drastic measures, such as the dissolution of an entire political party and a disability barring its leaders from carrying on any similar activity for a specified period, may be taken only in the most serious cases.'[84]

On the other hand, it may also be argued that whenever restrictions of the political freedoms of individuals or groups are justified, similar restrictions are a fortiori justified with respect to political parties. This is due to the leverage of

---

[82] Constitution of Algeria, Article 42(3).

[83] See P. Mahoney, 'Universality versus Subsidiarity in the Strasbourg Case Law on Free Speech: Explaining Some Recent Judgments' (1997) 4 *EHRLR* 364, at 372.

[84] *Refah (Grand Chamber)*, o.c., § 100.

political parties: their speech is always an attempt to persuade the largest number of people, and their projects are intended to become state policies. The European Court of Human Rights described this characteristic of political parties as follows: 'It is in the nature of the role they play that political parties, the only bodies which can come to power, also have the capacity to influence the whole of the regime in their countries. By the proposals for an overall societal model which they put before the electorate and by their capacity to implement those proposals once they come to power, political parties differ from other organizations which intervene in the political arena.'[85] Hence, when prohibition or other restrictive measures are based on the threat an association poses by seeking to realize its aims, there may be better reasons to prohibit a political party than there are to prohibit another type of peaceful association, because political parties in many cases have a more direct potential to realize their goals in practice. Yet in specific situations, this argument may be outweighed by other considerations. In particular when the same political programme is also promoted by other groups that are even more threatening (for example violent groups), the prohibition of a political party may lead to increased support for such underground groups. Moreover, it may stand in the way of a negotiated solution to the problems that are at the basis of the conflict, by eliminating the only more or less acceptable negotiating partner.[86]

Many national legal systems do not provide for party closure. This choice is based on the one hand on the enormous value that is put on the freedoms of political parties in a democracy. On the other hand, in most cases it is also based on a minimization of the threat posed by political parties. Spain is a good example of a state that enacted party closure legislation only when a specific political party began to be seen as a real threat.[87] Nevertheless, from a democratic viewpoint it is preferable to have legislation in place *in tempore non suspecto*. There may not always be time to act after a threat arises except by using extreme measures (cf. the Algerian example). Moreover, when majority political parties vote restrictive legislation that is clearly aimed at a particular opposition party, they burn themselves in the eyes of public opinion. The 'underdog' position may result in increased support for the targeted group, expressed in electoral terms when the measure remains short of party closure,[88] or in terms of support for underground organizations. Hence, it may be preferable to provide the possibility of restrictive measures (of which party closure may be a part) regardless of the existence of a threat, and to make the assessment about the threat posed by a specific party at the time of the application of the measures.

---

[85] *Refah (Grand Chamber)*, o.c., § 87.
[86] Cf. L. Turano, 'Spain: Banning political parties as a response to Basque terrorism' (2003) 1 *International Journal of Constitutional Law* 730, at 739.   [87] Cf. *infra*.
[88] Cf. the electoral victory of the Vlaams Blok in the Belgian parliamentary elections of 2004, shortly after a court had determined that the party manifestly and repeatedly propagated discrimination and hatred (cf. above).

Another motive underlying the rejection of party closure is the belief in the working of the ordinary checks and balances in contemporary democracies functioning in an international environment. If an extremist party comes to power and proposes laws that conflict with the constitution, there is in most cases a constitutional court that may redress this. In Europe, the European Court of Human Rights will convict states that violate the European Convention on Human Rights. Moreover, such states may be shunned in international relations, and if the violations are gross and systematic, totally or partially excluded from international organizations such as the European Union.[89] At the bottom of this assessment is again an assessment of the threat posed by democratic parties, that is confident that no party will gain a sufficient majority to change the constitution or will be bold enough to disregard international relations.

When a party's political programme threatens human rights, prohibiting this party may not only be allowed under human rights provisions, but may even be an obligation. Article 4(b) CERD stipulates this explicitly with regard to organizations (including political parties) that promote and incite racial discrimination (cf. above). This is repeated in the United Nations Model Legislation for the Guidance of Governments in the Enactment of Further Legislation Against Racial Discrimination, that was promulgated in the context of the Third Decade to combat racism and racial discrimination (1993–2003):[90] 'Any organization which undertakes to promote, incite, propagate or organize racial discrimination against an individual or group of individuals shall be declared illegal and prohibited' (§ 30). At the level of the Council of Europe, the European Commission against Racism and Intolerance advised in its General policy recommendation on national legislation to combat racism and racial discrimination:[91] 'The law should provide for the possibility of dissolution of organisations which promote racism' (§ 17). Beyond the issue of racism, the Parliamentary Assembly of the Council of Europe asked states parties to provide for the possibility of prohibition of parties promoting 'extremism'.[92] With respect to parties that otherwise threaten human rights through their actions (e.g. violence) or through their programme, a similar argument can be

---

[89] Cf. Article 7 TEU: The Council, meeting in the composition of the Heads of State or Government and acting by unanimity on a proposal by one third of the Member States or by the Commission and after obtaining the assent of the European Parliament, may determine the existence of a serious and persistent breach by a Member State of the principles of liberty, democracy, respect for human rights and fundamental freedoms, and the rule of law. The Council, acting by a qualified majority, may then decide to suspend certain of the rights deriving from the application of the EU Treaty to the Member State in question, including the voting rights of the representative of the government of that Member State in the Council.

[90] www.unhchr.ch/html/menu6/2/pub962.htm.

[91] ECRI general policy recommendation No. 7 on national legislation to combat racism and racial discrimination, adopted by ECRI on 13 December 2002.

[92] Parliamentary Assembly of the Council of Europe, Resolution 1344 (2003): Threat posed to democracy by extremist parties and movements in Europe.

made, based on the state's *obligation to protect*. States are not only required to abstain from action that would violate human rights (obligation to respect), but must also take some action in order to protect individuals and groups against violations by private actors. This includes preventive as well as repressive action. The protective framework normally includes legislative measures criminalizing certain behaviour. It could be argued that in order to complete the protective framework, the ultimate measure of party closure should be available, so that in those cases where other means are not sufficient to avert a risk of human rights violations, it can or even must be used.[93] In the *Refah* case, a Grand Chamber of the European Court of Human Rights remarked about the measure of party closure: 'The Court takes the view that such a power of preventive intervention on the state's part is also consistent with Contracting Parties' positive obligations under Article 1 of the Convention to secure the rights and freedoms of persons within their jurisdiction. Those obligations relate not only to any interference that may result from acts or omissions imputable to agents of the state or occurring in public establishments but also to interference imputable to private individuals within non-State entities... A Contracting State may be justified under its positive obligations in imposing on political parties, which are bodies whose *raison d'être* is to accede to power and direct the work of a considerable portion of the state apparatus, the duty to respect and safeguard the rights and freedoms guaranteed by the Convention and the obligation not to put forward a political programme in contradiction with the fundamental principles of democracy.'[94] The Court stopped short of saying that party closure may be an obligation for the state. In the context of their positive obligations to protect human rights, states are as a rule granted a margin of appreciation with regard to their choice of means. The Court's ruling in the above quote is limited to stating that party closure is one among several options for a state confronted with a party that threatens human rights, in the context of its obligation to protect human rights.

4.3.3 Grounds for Party Closure (and Other Restrictive Measures)

Given the importance of political parties' freedom of association, a decision to prohibit or dissolve a political party, or to otherwise restrict its operation, must be based on good reasons. Those reasons reside in the harm that is caused by the party. In this respect a distinction can be made between actual harm and potential future harm. The actual harm that is caused by a political party—in

---

[93] Among German constitutionalists, the question on the existence of 'discretion' to decide whether or not to initiate party closure proceedings, has long been the subject of debate. According to some, the legislative and executive bodies that have the power under Article 21(2) of the German Constitution to initiate such proceedings, have the duty to do so whenever a party threatens the free democratic basic order. On this debate, see J. Ipsen, 'Parteiverbot und "politisches" Ermessen', in *Staat-Kirch-Verwaltung: Festschrift für Hartmut Maurer zum 70. Geburtstag* (Munichi: Beck, 2001), 163.

[94] *Refah (Grand Chamber)*, o.c., § 103.

particular a party that is not in power—is in many cases similar to the actual harm that may be caused by another type of association (for example inciting hatred or violence). The potential future harm on the other hand is typical for political parties: it is the harm that would be caused if the party's political programme were to be realized.

4.3.3.1 Protecting Democracy Against Anti-Democratic Ideologies

Party closure may be one of the measures available in a democracy that is conscientiously defensive or militant[95] vis-à-vis ideologies or political programmes that would undermine its tenets. Particularly in Europe it is common to label 'anti-democratic' a tendency that threatens human rights. This has to be situated in a substantive conception of democracy.[96] Whereas a formal or procedural concept of democracy defines democracy as a set of procedures for political decision-making, a substantive model of democracy includes in its definition the underlying reasons for those procedural arrangements, i.e. the protection of fundamental rights. In this view, a democratic government does not operate only within the procedural restrictions of majority rule and respect for higher law. Democracy and the rule of law also entail substantive requirements for decision making: the rules have to respect and protect the fundamental rights and freedoms of the citizens. Under a model of substantive democracy, proposals of political parties propagating discrimination or otherwise denying the fundamental rights of part of the population are 'liberticidal' and therefore anti-democratic. They become a threat to democracy when their advocates gain so much support that the perspective that they may be able to put their proposals into practice becomes a realistic one.

Party closure as a reaction to anti-democratic ideologies in the broad sense (including incitement to hatred, racism, etc.) exists in many states. In Europe these include Germany, Albania, the Czech Republic, Slovakia, Moldova, Portugal, Poland, France, Spain, Belarus, Ukraine, Bulgaria, and Russia.[97]

Positions in favour or against defensive democracy, including the measure of party closure, appear to rely to a large extent on assessments of the seriousness of the risk of this anti-democratic threat. In Europe, such assessments vary widely. While some consider that it is absurd to think that democracy and the rule of law would be seriously threatened in the foreseeable future, others think that there is a real risk that in one or more European states, a political party would

---

[95] See K. Loewenstein, 'Militant Democracy and Fundamental Rights' (1937) 31 *American Political Science Review* 417, at 638, and 'Legislative Control of Political Extremism in European Democracies' (1938) 38 *Columbia Law Review* 591, at 725, including several examples of party closure in Europe in the 1930s, faced with the threat of fascism.

[96] On the distinction between substantive and procedural conceptions of democracy, see G. H. Fox and G. Nolte, 'Intolerant Democracies' (1995) 36 *Harvard International Law Journal* 1, at 14–21.

[97] Information from European Commission for Democracy through Law (Venice Commission), 'Prohibition of political parties and analogous measures', Report adopted by the Commission at its 35th Plenary Meeting, Venice, 12–13 June 1998.

win a majority on a platform, including proposals that seriously violate the human rights of (part of) the population. The crucial factor of the assessment of the risk is largely subjective, intuitive, and susceptible of different interpretations. As a result, it is difficult to express in objective legal terms. In this debate, the European Court of Human Rights has taken position among the believers in a real threat to European democracy. In the *Refah* judgment, a Grand Chamber stated: 'The possibility cannot be excluded that a political party, in pleading the rights enshrined in Article 11 and also in Articles 9 and 10 of the Convention, might attempt to derive therefrom the right to conduct what amounts in practice to activities intended to destroy the rights or freedoms set forth in the Convention and thus bring about the destruction of democracy ... In view of the very clear link between the Convention and democracy ..., no-one must be authorised to rely on the Convention's provisions in order to weaken or destroy the ideals and values of a democratic society. Pluralism and democracy are based on a compromise that requires various concessions by individuals or groups of individuals, who must sometimes agree to limit some of the freedoms they enjoy in order to guarantee greater stability of the country as a whole ... In that context, the Court considers that it is not at all improbable that totalitarian movements, organised in the form of political parties, might do away with democracy, after prospering under the democratic regime, there being examples of this in modern European history.'[98]

4.3.3.1.1 Anti-Democratic Ideologies

The reference to modern European history is a strong argument for the reality of the risk. This reference evokes in the first place the fight against Nazism/fascism on the one hand and against communism on the other. In some states that take the anti-democratic threat very seriously, this is based on their experience of the overthrow of democracy in the relatively recent past. In Italy[99] and Austria,[100] the law specifically prohibits the recreation of the party (respectively the Fascist Party and the Nazi Party NSDAP) that was in power during the Second World War. Arguably, the lesson to be learned from a historical experience of the overthrow of democracy concerns the vulnerability of democracy vis-à-vis its enemies in general, rather than the threat posed by one specific anti-democratic ideology. Hence, an effective translation of this lesson into legal provisions requires measures of a more general nature. For example in Germany, the experience with the NSDAP inspired a broader clause[101] providing for the possibility to prohibit all parties threatening the free democratic constitutional order. As described above, this has been applied not only against a Nazi Party,[102] but also outside the context

---

[98] *Refah (Grand Chamber)*, o.c., § 99.
[99] Cf. above, Law No. 645 of 1952 ('Legge Scelba').
[100] Prohibition law of 1947 ('Verbotsgesetz').
[101] Cf. above, Article 21 of the German Constitution.
[102] SRP Judgment of 23 October 1952, *BverfGE* 2,1.

of the fight against (neo-)Nazism, in the case leading to the prohibition of the German Communist Party.[103]

The experience of communist parties with party closure measures offers a good illustration of the relative character both in time and in place of the perception of the threat posed to democracy by a particular ideology. Looking back, one may say that the KPD did not constitute a serious threat to West German democracy.[104] Yet in the aftermath of the Second World War, when the Eastern part of the country was 'lost' to communism, this may have been perceived differently. Even more striking is the persecution of communism in the United States during the 1950s, including a specific act, the Communist Control Act of 1954, which, however, stopped short of outlawing the Communist Party of the United States.[105] From a twenty-first century perspective, it seems absurd that the US should ever have taken the threat of domestic communism so seriously, yet in the midst of the Cold War, perceptions were very different. On the other hand, only some of the former

[103] KPD Judgment of 17 August 1956, *BverfGE* 5, 85. On party closure in Germany, see P. Franz, 'Unconstitutional and Outlawed Political Parties: A German–American Comparison' (1982) 5 *Boston College Int' Comparative Law Review* 51, at 69–82; D. Gordon, 'Limits on Extremist Political Parties: A Comparison of Israeli Jurisprudence with that of the United States and West Germany' (1987) 10 *Hastings Int'l and Comparative Law Review* 347, at 365–71; K. Groh, 'Der NPD-Verbotsantrag—eine Reanimation der streitbaren Demokratie?' (2000) *ZRP* 500; J. Ipsen, 'Parteiverbot und "politisches" Ermessen', in *Staat-Kirch-Verwaltung: Festschrift für Hartmut Maurer zum 70. Geburtstag* (Munich: Beck, 2001), 163; C. Leggewie and H. Meier, *Republikschutz* (Reinbek: Rowohlt, 1995), 60–81; C. Leggewie and H. Meier (eds.), *Verbot der NPD oder Mit Rechtsradikalen leben?* (Frankfurt: Suhrkamp, 2002); H. Meier, *Parteiverbote und demokratische Republik* (Baden-Baden: Nomos, 1993); H. Meier, 'In der Nachfolge der NSDAP? Das SRP-Verbotsurteil und das Verfahren gegen die NPD' (2003) *Blätter für deutsche und internationale Politik* 485; M. Morlok, 'Parteiverbot als Verfassungsschutz—Ein unauflösbarer Widerspruch?' (2001) *NJW* 2931; W. F. Murphy, 'Excluding Political Parties: Problems for Democratic and Constitutional Theory', in *Germany and its Basic Law* (Baden-Baden: Nomos, 1993) 173, at 185–87; P. Niesen, 'Anti-Extremism, Negative Republicanism, Civic Society: Three Paradigms for Banning Political Parties' (2002) 3 *German Law Journal* at: www.germanlawjournal.com; Peter Niesen, 'Banning Parties in Germany—Towards a New Paradigm?' Conference Paper, ECPR Conference, Marburg, 18–21 September 2003: www.essex.ac.uk/ECPR/events/generalconference/ marburg/papers/10/7/niesen.pdf; K. Pabel, 'Parteiverbote auf dem europäischen Prüfstand' (2003) 63 *ZaöRV* 921; A. Pedahzur, 'Struggling Challenges of Right-Wing Extremism and Terrorism within Democratic Boundaries: A Comparative Analysis', Paper for Workshop on 'Democracy and the New Extremist Challenge in Europe', ECPR Joint Session, Grenoble, April 6–11 2001: www. essex.ac.uk/ECPR/events/jointsessions/paperarchive/grenoble/ws14/pedahzur.pdf; U. Rommelfanger, 'Die PDS: Eine zu verbietene politische Partei?' (1992) *ZRP* 213; M. Sichert, 'Das Parteiverbot in der wehrhaften Demokratie' (2001) *Die Öffentliche Verwaltung* 16; M. Thiel, *Wehrhafte Demokratie* (Tübingen: Mohr Siebeck, 2003), at 173–207.

[104] In 1953, the KPD represented 2.2 per cent of the votes. Moreover, it did not make any attempts to translate its revolutionary programme into actions (H. Meier, 'In Nachfolge der NSDAP?' (2003) *Blätter für deutsche und internationale Politik* 485, at 490).

[105] Pub L 83–637, 68 Stat 775. On this topic, see P. Franz, 'Unconstitutional and Outlawed Political Parties: A German–American Comparison' (1982) 5 *Boston College Int' & Comparative Law Review* 51, at 69–82; D. Gordon, 'Limits on Extremist Political Parties: A Comparison of Israeli Jurisprudence with that of the United States and West Germany' (1987) 10 *Hastings Int'l and Comparative Law Review*, 347, at 365–71; W. F. Murphy, 'Excluding Political Parties: Problems for Democratic and Constitutional Theory', in Paul Kirchhof and Donald Kommers (eds.), *Germany and its Basic Law* (Baden-Baden: Nomos, 1993), 173, at 185–7.

communist states of Central and Eastern Europe have outlawed the communist party after the transition to democracy,[106] and post-communist constitutional courts have been reluctant to support such bans.[107] Some of these parties are still functioning, after undergoing some transformations.[108] Whether a prohibition of the Communist Party is more justified in contemporary Albania than in the US of the fifties, is open to debate. If 'threat' is the main criterion, there are good reasons to argue that the threat of communism is more serious in today's post-communist states, where communist parties may still have a substantial basis of support among the population, or a potential of easily winning it back, for example in times of severe economic crises. In the US on the other hand, it was always a very small movement, hence restrictive measures are more readily qualified as disproportionate. Yet on the other hand, one may also argue that in states where democracy is new, there should be less room for restrictive measures, because those give the wrong signal. The first few years of democracy after transition have an educational function, and radical measures such as party closure may give a repressive impression and suggest that in terms of political freedoms, the new regime is not all that different from the old one. The European Court of Human Rights has shown a reluctance to accept bans on post-1989 communist parties in former communist states. In the absence of indications concerning violence or undemocratic means or ends, communism as such is not a sufficient basis for party closure. In *Partidul Comunistilor*, the Court stated that it was prepared to take into account Romania's

[106] E.g. Article 13 of the Polish Constitution provides: 'Political parties and other organizations whose programmes are based upon totalitarian methods and the modes of activity of nazism, fascism and communism, as well as those whose programmes or activities sanction racial or national hatred, the application of violence for the purpose of obtaining power or to influence the state policy, or provide for the secrecy of their own structure or membership, shall be forbidden.' On the one hand, communism is put on the same footing as Nazism and fascism. Yet on the other hand, the formulation of this provision leaves room for parties with a communist programme that would not use communist or totalitarian methods. In Albania, the law prohibits 'fascist, communist, antinational, totalitarian and Stalinist' parties. In Byelorussia, the communist party was prohibited in 1991, but the prohibition was lifted in 1993 (P. Esplugas, 'L'interdiction des partis politiques' (1998) 36 *Revue française de Droit constitutionnel* 675, at 680). In Latvia, the prohibition of the communist party was not based on communism as such, but rather on two attempted *coups d'etat* by that party after the transition to democracy. In Ukraine as well, the ban on the Communist Party of Ukraine was based on its support of the August 1991 coup against USSR President Mikhail Gorbachev. This ban was later invalidated by the Ukrainian Constitutional Court (see A. Trochev, 'Ukraine: Constitutional Court invalidates ban on Communist Party' (2003) 1 *International Journal of Constitutional Law* 534). In Russia, President Yeltsin banned the Communist Party in 1991 by decree. In 1992, the Constitutional Court upheld this ban, restricting it however to the leading organs of the party (for a comment, see Y. Feofanov, 'The establishment of the Constitutional Court in Russia and the Communist Party Case' (1993) 19 *Review of Central and East European Law* 623).
[107] A. Trochev, 'Ukraine: Constitutional Court invalidates ban on Communist Party' (2003) 1 *International Journal of Constitutional Law* 534, 540, referring in particular to Ukraine, Russia, and Poland.
[108] Examples include the German PDS (Party of Democratic Socialism) and the Bulgarian Socialist Party. It has been argued that as a successor of the Communist Party, the PDS would qualify for prohibition and confiscation of its property under Germany law: U. Rommelfanger, 'Die PDS: Eine zu verbietene politische Partei?' (1992) *ZRP* 213.

historical experience of totalitarian communism, but 'that context by itself cannot justify the need for the interference, especially as communist parties adhering to Marxist ideology exist in a number of countries that are signatory to the Convention'.[109]

In the *Refah* case, the threat to democracy came from Islamic fundamentalism. According to the Chamber judgment, 'The Court . . . finds . . . that the establishment of a theocratic regime, with rules valid in the sphere of public law as well as that of private law, is not completely inconceivable in Turkey, account being taken, firstly, of its relatively recent history and, secondly, of the fact that the great majority of its population are Muslims.'[110] The Grand Chamber developed this further: 'The Court must not lose sight of the fact that in the past political movements based on religious fundamentalism have been able to seize political power in certain States and have had the opportunity to set up the model of society which they had in mind. It considers that, in accordance with the Convention's provisions, each Contracting State may oppose such political movements in the light of its historical experience. The Court further observes that there was already an Islamic theocratic regime under Ottoman law. When the former theocratic regime was dismantled and the republican regime was being set up, Turkey opted for a form of secularism that confined Islam and other religions to the sphere of private religious practice. Mindful of the importance for survival of the democratic regime of ensuring respect for the principle of secularism in Turkey, the Court considers that the Constitutional Court was justified in holding that Refah's policy of establishing sharia was incompatible with democracy.'[111] Hence the Court's assessment of the justifiability of Turkey's defensive democracy relies to a large extent on its assessment of the reality of the risk for democracy based on the country's historical experience, strengthened by the contemporary experience of other states (regardless of the similarities and differences those present with respect to Turkey).

It should not automatically be assumed that the programme that a political party itself labels 'fascist' or 'communist' or 'Islamist' is necessarily at odds with democracy or human rights. This has to be examined in the specific circumstances of each case. In particular, many contemporary 'communist' parties work within the parameters of parliamentary democracy, and also accept the human rights framework. They make proposals that would challenge the existing order, yet would not violate human rights, such as state ownership of companies and land, or the redistribution of wealth through taxes and social allowances. Similarly, right-wing extremist parties may, despite their roots in old nazism or neo-nazism, become more moderate and promote a programme that, while conservative and rights-restrictive, remains within the limits of the

---

[109] *Partidul Comunistilor* ECHR (2005), o.c., § 58.
[110] *Refah (Chamber)*, o.c., § 65.   [111] *Refah (Grand Chamber)*, o.c., §§ 124–125.

human rights framework. Measures such as the return of most illegal immigrants, zero tolerance for street crime, the abolition of voting rights for non-EU nationals and stringent conditions for the acquisition of nationality do not as such violate human rights.

The same holds for a political party that proposes the introduction of shari'a (Islamic law), which was one of the reasons for the prohibition of the Turkish Refah Party. Shari'a is not a fixed or homogeneous concept. There are numerous schools of interpretation of the same rules of the Qur'an and the traditions of the Prophet. In some interpretations, some of these rules are difficult to reconcile with human rights, in particular gender equality and religious freedom. Yet progressive interpretations are possible; for example there are feminist Muslims who offer a feminist interpretation of the holy sources. Moreover, no state has introduced 'shari'a' as such; usually it is only introduced for some parts of the law, which may then be written into a code which becomes the legal basis (rather than the holy sources directly); hence there is a possibility to make a selection among shari'a rules. For these two reasons, violations of human rights are not a necessary feature of the introduction of shari'a. In order to conclude to a violation of human rights, one has to examine the specific rule that is being proposed. In this respect, the *Refah* judgment of the European Court of Human Rights may be criticized. The speeches that served as a basis for the prohibition of the party contained only general references to 'shari'a'. The Court concluded simply, without any nuances, that shari'a is incompatible with democracy: 'Like the Constitutional Court, the Court considers that sharia, which faithfully reflects the dogmas and divine rules laid down by religion, is stable and invariable. Principles such as pluralism in the political sphere or the constant evolution of public freedoms have no place in it. The Court notes that, when read together, the offending statements, which contain explicit references to the introduction of sharia, are difficult to reconcile with the fundamental principles of democracy, as conceived in the Convention taken as a whole. It is difficult to declare one's respect for democracy and human rights while at the same time supporting a regime based on sharia, which clearly diverges from Convention values, particularly with regard to its criminal law and criminal procedure, its rules on the legal status of women and the way it intervenes in all spheres of private and public life in accordance with religious precepts... In the Court's view, a political party whose actions seem to be aimed at introducing sharia in a State party to the Convention can hardly be regarded as an association complying with the democratic ideal that underlies the whole of the Convention.'[112] Moreover, it seems that the proposals that were made did not concern the introduction of shari'a for all citizens, but rather a system of 'legal pluralism', whereby Muslim citizens would be subjected to Muslim law. Again, the

---

[112] *Refah (Grand Chamber)*, o.c., § 123, quoting *Refah (Chamber)*, o.c., § 72.

references are very vague, so we lack crucial information, such as whether this would apply only in the sphere of personal law, or for example also criminal law, and whether this would be mandatory for all Muslims, or rather optional (i.e. a choice between, for example, the civil marriage system and Islamic marriage system). Again, the Court condemned without any nuances the idea of a plurality of legal systems (regardless of the fact that it concerned Islamic law) in general: '... the Court considers that Refah's proposal that there should be a plurality of legal systems would introduce into all legal relationships a distinction between individuals grounded on religion, would categorize everyone according to his religious beliefs and would allow him rights and freedoms not as an individual but according to his allegiance to a religious movement. The Court takes the view that such a societal model cannot be considered compatible with the Convention system, for two reasons. Firstly, it would do away with the state's role as the guarantor of individual rights and freedoms and the impartial organizer of the practice of the various beliefs and religions in a democratic society, since it would oblige individuals to obey, not rules laid down by the state in the exercise of its above-mentioned functions, but static rules of law imposed by the religion concerned. But the state has a positive obligation to ensure that everyone within its jurisdiction enjoys in full, and without being able to waive them, the rights and freedoms guaranteed by the Convention... Secondly, such a system would undeniably infringe the principle of non-discrimination between individuals as regards their enjoyment of public freedoms, which is one of the fundamental principles of democracy. A difference in treatment between individuals in all fields of public and private law according to their religion or beliefs manifestly cannot be justified under the Convention, and more particularly Article 14 thereof, which prohibits discrimination. Such a difference in treatment cannot maintain a fair balance between, on the one hand, the claims of certain religious groups who wish to be governed by their own rules and on the other the interest of society as a whole, which must be based on peace and on tolerance between the various religions and beliefs.' This is remarkably blunt,[113] and does not take into

---

[113] Yet see the concurring opinion of the Russian Judge Kovler under the Grand Chamber judgment: 'I also regret that the Court, in reproducing the Chamber's conclusions (paragraph 119), missed the opportunity to analyse in more detail the concept of a plurality of legal systems, which is linked to that of legal pluralism and is well-established in ancient and modern legal theory and practice (see, in particular, the proceedings of the international congresses on customary law and legal pluralism organised by the International Union of Anthropological and Ethnological Sciences, and J. Griffiths: "What is legal pluralism?" *Journal of Legal Pluralism and Unofficial Law* 1986, no. 24). Not only legal anthropology but also modern constitutional law accepts that under certain conditions members of minorities of all kinds may have more than one type of personal status (see, for example, P. Gannagé, "Le pluralisme des statuts personnels dans les Etats multi-communautaires—Droit libanais et droits proche-orientaux", Bruxelles, éd. Bruylant, 2001). Admittedly, this pluralism, which impinges mainly on an individual's private and family life, is limited by the requirements of the general interest. But it is of course more difficult in practice to find a compromise between the interests of the communities concerned and civil society as a whole than to reject the very idea of such a compromise from the outset.'

account the fact that in several leading democratic societies today, systems of legal pluralism exist, and that moreover they are considered a very appropriate tool for the protection of minority rights. This may include room for personal law based on traditional customary law, or for religon-based law. For example in India, there is Hindu Personal Law, Muslim Personal law, Parsi Personal Law, and even a Christian Marriage Act.[114] Also, in post-apartheid South Africa, one of the most progressive states in the world when it comes to human rights protection, a process is on its way to recognize Muslim marriages (including efforts to make sure that the interpretation of the Islamic law is compatible with fundamental rights).[115]

In the letter announcing the withdrawal of their case, the applicants in the *Fazilet* case—the other case concerning charges of anti-secularism—stated among other things, that the Court's judgment in the *Refah* case shows that it is prejudiced against Muslim communities, and that they have lost confidence in the justice done by the Court.[116]

It is worth noting that the criterion 'party programme including human rights violations' is not necessarily easy to apply in practice. Human rights are dynamic and open to diverse interpretations. Clearly, a party proposing the expansion of an airport regardless of the noise that this would create for the inhabitants of the area should not be prohibited on this basis. Yet, the European Court of Human Rights has held that in some cases, the increase in (night) noise caused by airport activity violates human rights.[117] This difficulty was recognized by Judge Ress in his concurring opinion in the *Refah* case. Discussing the Court's position that party closure is justified when a party puts forward a policy 'which fails to respect democracy or which is aimed at the destruction of democracy and the flouting of the rights and freedoms recognised in a democracy',[118] he stated: 'In my view it cannot be interpreted to the effect that any campaign to change rights and freedoms recognised in a democracy amount to a situation where a political party would lose protection. In this respect also all depends on the specific rights and freedoms which a political party aims to change and furthermore what kind of change or modification is envisaged.'[119]

After finding that certain political parties may constitute a threat to democracy, the question remains: how should a democracy react to such a threat? The measures that states may take in defence of democracy and human rights are

---

[114] These include the: Hindu Marriage Act of 1955, Hindu Succession Act of 1956, Hindu Guardianship and Minorities Act of 1956, Hindu Adoption and Maintenance Act of 1956, Shari'a Act of 1937, Muslim Women's Dissolution of Marriage Act of 1939, Muslim Women's (Protection of Rights on Divorce) Act of 1986, Christian Marriage Act.

[115] See South African Law Reform Commission, 'Islamic Marriages and Related Matters', Project 106 Report (July 2003).   [116] *Fazilet Partisi* ECHR (2006), o.c., § 9.

[117] *Hatton v The United Kingdom (Chamber)* ECHR (2001), not reported and *Hatton v The United Kingdom (Grand Chamber)* ECHR (2003), Reports 2003-VIII.

[118] *Refah (Grand Chamber)*, o.c., § 98.

[119] *Refah (Grand Chamber)*, o.c., concurring opinion of Judge Ress, joined by Judge Rozakis.

usually of a rights-restrictive nature, including in particular the restriction of the expression of anti-democratic views and the regulation of the activities of anti-democratic associations and individuals. Party closure in particular is a far-reaching restriction of the freedom of political association. This question is known as the 'democratic dilemma': paradoxically, fundamental rights will be restricted for the purpose of protecting fundamental rights. Is the cure then not as dangerous, or maybe even more so, than the illness? This may appear so especially because party closure is intended as a preventive measure, and the harm it is aimed at is a potential future harm. If an anti-democratic political party comes to power and realizes its programme, human rights will be seriously violated. Yet as long as it does not, and its programme remains a dead letter, human rights remain intact. If this party is barred from participating in the elections or even outlawed, the only interference with human rights is the responsibility of those claiming to defend human rights, i.e. the restriction of the freedoms of the political party and its members. Through the insertion of an abuse clause in human rights conventions (cf. above), international law not only allows the militant version of democracy, but even seems to encourage it. When the threat comes from a racist party, the UN system goes even further to promote party closure as an appropriate reaction (cf. above).

Yet in *Refah*, the European Court of Human Rights does not use the abuse clause of Article 17 ECHR. It considers the measure of party closure legitimate under Article 11(2) ECHR, when it 'puts forward a policy which fails to respect democracy or which is aimed at the destruction of democracy and the flouting of the rights and freedoms recognised in a democracy',[120] even when the party is peaceful and uses only legal means to promote its programme. It is noteworthy that the Venice Commission does not consider party closure to be a legitimate measure in cases where the party does not advocate or use violence (cf. *infra*). The Parliamentary Assembly of the Council of Europe in this debate sided with the European Court of Human Rights. In a 2002 resolution, it stated that 'restrictions on or dissolution of political parties should be regarded as exceptional measures to be applied only in cases where the party concerned uses violence or threatens civil peace and the democratic constitutional order of the country',[121] and in a 2003 resolution it called on states to introduce and apply the dissolution of extremist parties and movements, saying at the same time that it should be an exceptional measure, which, however, is justified in the case of a threat to a country's constitutional order.[122]

---

[120] *Refah (Grand Chamber)*, o.c., § 98.
[121] Parliamentary Assembly of the Council of Europe, Resolution 1308 (2002): 'Restrictions on political parties in the Council of Europe Member States'. It is however not clear what is meant by 'threatens civil peace'. It is noteworthy that the Parliamentary Assembly applies the same strict criteria not only to party closure, but also to other restrictions on political parties.
[122] Parliamentary Assembly of the Council of Europe, Resolution 1344 (2003): 'Threat posed to democracy by extremist parties and movements in Europe'.

4.3.3.1.2 Internal Democracy

Several states have adopted constitutional or legal provisions in the sense that political parties must necessarily be democratic in their internal organization. For example, Article 71(c) of the Constitution of Uganda (1995) stipulates: 'the internal organisation of a political party shall conform to the democratic principles enshrined in this Constitution'. In Finland, Spain, and Armenia, the party's internal structure and functioning must be democratic.[123] In the Czech Republic and Slovakia, party statutes must be democratic and their organs must be democratically established.[124] In Albania, freedom of expression must be guaranteed within the party, as well as the right to join and leave the party as one pleases.[125] The Portuguese constitution requires political parties to be run according to the principles of transparency, democratic organization, and management and participation by all their members.[126] In Argentina, the party bodies and candidates presented for elections must be periodically elected.[127]

Under the criteria put forward by the European Court of Human Rights and the Venice Commission, the lack of democracy in the internal party organization cannot justify party closure. The Venice Commission's 2004 Guidelines on legislation on political parties add that: 'The democratic or non-democratic character of the party organization should not in principle be a ground for denying registration of a political party.'[128] In its General Comment on Article 25 ICCPR, the UN Human Rights Committee, on the other hand, stated that 'States should ensure that, in their internal management, political parties respect the applicable provisions of Article 25 in order to enable citizens to exercise their rights thereunder'[129] (cf. above). Freedom of internal organization is an aspect of freedom of association. On the one hand, it appears disproportionate to prohibit a political party because its chairperson is appointed by its predecessor rather than being elected by the party members, or because members can join only after being accepted by an all-powerful executive board. Yet on the other hand, the importance of internal democracy in political parties for the exercise of individual political rights should not be underestimated. Most contemporary democracies are particracies. Citizens can de facto only exercise their right to participate in democratic decision-making through political parties. Hence the accessibility and internal democracy of political parties becomes a crucial factor determining the effective exercise of that right. Most justifications of party closure rely on a negative protection of democracy against attempts to destroy it. The requirement of internal democracy is different in that it concerns the positive protection of democracy: the state is

---

[123] Information from European Commission for Democracy through Law (Venice Commission), 'Prohibition of political parties and analogous measures', Report adopted by the Commission at its 35th Plenary Meeting, Venice, 12–13 June 1998.   [124] Ibid.
[125] Ibid.   [126] Ibid.   [127] Ibid.   [128] Ibid.
[129] Human Rights Committee, General Comment No. 25: The right to participate in public affairs, voting rights and the right of equal access to public service (Art. 25), 12 July 1996, CCPR/C/21/Rev.1/Add.7, § 26.

obliged—conform General Comment 25—to impose internal democracy on political parties in order to make the state's democratic system and the citizens' political rights more effective. Yet this does not necessarily imply that a state is entitled to take the far-reaching measure of party prohibition against a party whose internal organization is not democratic. Other types of sanctions are probably sufficient.

An exception is the hypothetical case of a political party that refuses members on the basis of race. Such a party is a racist organization, and its prohibition is mandated by Article 4 CERD (cf. above). A difficult question arises with respect to a political party that refuses members on the basis of other grounds of discrimination, for example gender. Such political parties exist. An example is the Staatkundig Gereformeerde Partij in The Netherlands, a political party that aims at government on the basis of the Bible, currently represented with four members in the Dutch Parliament. On the basis of their religious beliefs, they do not accept female members. In its most recent Concluding Observations on The Netherlands, the CEDAW Committee wrote: 'The Committee notes with concern that, in The Netherlands, there is a political party represented in the Parliament that excludes women from membership, which is a violation of Article 7 of the Convention. The Committee recommends that the State Party take urgent measures to address this situation, including through the adoption of legislation that brings the membership of political parties into conformity with its obligations under Article 7.'[130] In 2005, a Dutch court held that state subventions to this party should be discontinued, as they violated Article 7 CEDAW.[131] In its General Comment under Article 23 CEDAW, the Committee goes even further to impose on political parties and other organizations gender-balanced representation on their executive boards (cf. above).[132] International provisions prohibiting gender discrimination require that measures be taken against a party that excludes female members. Yet the question remains whether among possible measures the state has the freedom to choose for party closure on this basis. On the one hand, it may be argued that party closure would be a disproportionate measure, since less restrictive measures would most likely be effective in forcing the party to open membership to women. Yet on the other hand, the fact that party closure is not only allowed but even mandated under CERD when the discrimination is on the basis of race, makes it hard to justify that the same sanction would not be allowed in the fight against gender discrimination. This would require arguments to the effect that the—actual and/or potential—harm involved in racial discrimination is significantly stronger than that involved in other types of discrimination.

---

[130] Concluding Observations of the Committee on the Elimination of Discrimination Against Women: The Netherlands, 31 July 2001, A/56/38, §§ 219–20.
[131] Court of The Hague, 7 September 2005; Busstra and Vrielink, 'Geen vrouwen, geen geld', *Tijdschrift voor Mensenrechten* (2006) 7–10.
[132] CEDAW Committee, General Comment No. 23 (Sixteenth Session, 1997), A/52/38/Rev.1, § 34, quoted above, text accompanying footnote 10.

4.3.3.1.3 Party Name

Some states provide for the possibility of party closure on the basis of the party name alone. For example, Section 96 (3) of the Turkish Law No. 2820 on the regulation of political parties, as applied in the *United Communist Party* case,[133] reads: 'No political party shall be formed with the name "communist", "anarchist", "fascist", "theocratic" or "national socialist", the name of a religion, language, race, sect or region, or a name including any of the above words or similar ones.' In this case, the Turkish government argued: 'By choosing to call itself "communist", the TBKP perforce referred to a subversive doctrine and a totalitarian political goal that undermined Turkey's political and territorial unity and jeopardised the fundamental principles of its public law, such as secularism. "Communism" invariably presupposed seizing power and aimed to establish a political order that would be unacceptable, not just in Turkey but also in the other member States of the Council of Europe.'[134] Yet the European Court of Human Rights rejected this line of reasoning: 'The Court considers that a political party's choice of name cannot in principle justify a measure as drastic as dissolution, in the absence of other relevant and sufficient circumstances.'[135] The Turkish Constitutional Court had admitted that despite the name, this party was not seeking to establish the domination of one social class over the others, and that on the contrary, it satisfied the requirements of democracy. The Court pointed out that in that respect it differed clearly from the German Communist Party, which was dissolved in 1956, and whose application before the European Commission on Human Rights was found inadmissible.[136] Clearly, a party's name is not the equivalent of a party programme. Hence, if the justification for party closure resides in the actual or potential harm caused by the party, it is to be noted that a party's name is not a source of potential future harm.

Yet in some cases, the choice of a party name may cause actual harm. In the first place, a name may in itself constitute hate speech or incite violence. For example a hypothetical 'Kill All Women Party'. In principle, a party with such a name also has an unacceptable programme, and party closure would be justified on the basis of its programme. If this is not the case, the name alone does not justify party closure, since a less restrictive measure would probably suffice to effectively eliminate the harm, i.e. prohibit the use of this name. Yet under Article 4 CERD, prohibition is allowed and even mandated when the name incites racism, since this would make the political party an organization inciting racism. A party name may also cause another type of harm, for example because it strongly resembles the name of another political party. In such a case it is self-evident that dissolution of the party is a disproportionate measure; changing the name is sufficient. In states where registration of political parties is required, a

---

[133] *United Communist Party of Turkey and Others v Turkey* ECHR (1998), o.c.
[134] Ibid, § 20.   [135] Ibid, § 54.   [136] *Application 250/57 v FRG*, YB 1, 222.

control of the name with a view to avoiding confusion may happen on that occasion. For example, in Estonia, a party may be denied registration if its name resembles that of an existing party or one which existed in the past.[137]

In most cases, restrictive measures against political parties on the basis of the party name take the shape of preventive measures, for example the refusal of registration, rather than party closure. In that respect, they may not fall under the strict criteria of the European Court of Human Rights with regard to party closure. This is not problematic, since it is indeed a less restrictive measure. In most cases, it will not be a major obstacle for a starting political party to choose a different name.[138] If the authorities can advance a good reason for the ban of certain names, and if it comes at a time when it does not cause huge problems for the party, such a preventive measure will normally not be disproportionate. Examples of restrictions on party names[139] include Canada, where party names may not include the word 'independent', and Slovenia, where party names must not include the names of foreign states, parties, or natural or legal persons. In Argentina, political party names may not contain personal names or the words Argentine, national, international, or derivatives thereof. Under the Portuguese Constitution, a political party is not allowed to use a name that directly refers to a religion or church or to use emblems that are liable to be mistaken for national or religious emblems. The Constitutional Court of Portugal in 1995 refused to register a political party that wanted to call itself the Social Christian Party and to have as its emblem a white fish on a blue background. The Court ruled that it was not permissible for Christian doctrine to be appropriated by any one political party, and that the historical significance of the fish as symbol of Christ might mislead the electorate.[140] The political party changed its name and emblem within the legally prescribed two-day time limit and was then registered.

4.3.3.2 *Fighting (Political) Violence and Societal Unrest*

According to the Venice Guidelines, the fight against violence is the only legitimate justification for party closure: 'Prohibition or enforced dissolution of political parties may only be justified in the case of parties which advocate the

---

[137] Information from European Commission for Democracy through Law (Venice Commission), 'Prohibition of political parties and analogous measures', Report adopted by the Commission at its 35th Plenary Meeting, Venice, 12–13 June 1998. The same source notes that restrictions on names that may create confusion exist also in Canada, Portugal, and Slovenia.

[138] Cf. *Gorzelik and Others v Poland* ECHR (2004): with respect to an association to whom registration had been refused, the Court held that no violation of Article 11 ECHR had taken place and noted that 'the decisive factor for us in the present case was the fact that the association would not only have existed, but also have been registered, if it had changed its name and amended paragraphs 10 and 30 of its memorandum of association, as it had been asked to do . . .'.

[139] Information from European Commission for Democracy through Law (Venice Commission), 'Prohibition of political parties and analogous measures', Report adopted by the Commission at its 35th Plenary Meeting, Venice, 12–13 June 1998.

[140] Constitutional Court of Portugal, 23 February 1995, No. 107/95, Diário da República (Official Gazette) (Series II), 78, 1 April 1995 summary in CODICES database: http://codices.coe.int.

use of violence or use violence as a political means to overthrow the democratic constitutional order, thereby undermining the rights and freedoms guaranteed by the constitution' (§ 3). The Explanatory Report adds: 'prohibition or dissolution of political parties can be envisaged only if it is necessary in a democratic society and if there is concrete evidence that a party is engaged in activities threatening democracy and fundamental freedoms. This could include any party that advocates violence in all forms as part of its political programme or any party aiming to overthrow the existing constitutional order through armed struggle, terrorism or the organisation of any subversive activity.'[141] Under this criterion, one incidence of violence does not justify party closure, since that is not sufficient to indicate that the party intends to use violence as a political means to overthrow democracy. Nevertheless, the criterion of the Venice Commission is somewhat ambiguous, since in the explanations accompanying a different paragraph of the Guidelines, the Explanatory Guidelines put forward a very broad definition of 'violence': 'As was indicated . . . the competent bodies should have sufficient evidence that the political party in question is advocating violence (including such specific demonstrations of it such as racism, xenophobia and intolerance), . . . ' The part between brackets seems to equate the advocacy of racism with the advocacy of violence. Maybe the drafters wanted to bring their text in line with the CERD. Yet the open-ended formulation leaves open the question of whether the propagation of other human rights violations may also be qualified as 'violence'.

For the European Court of Human Rights, the promotion or the use of violence is one of the grounds justifying party closure (and an anti-democratic party programme is another ground, cf. above). The prohibition of the Refah Party was partly based on its promotion of violence through ambiguous references to jihad. An example that was quoted in the case is a speech of party leader Erbakan to the Refah group in Parliament: 'The second important point is this: Refah will come to power and a just [social] order (adil düzen) will be established. The question we must ask ourselves is whether this change will be violent or peaceful; whether it will entail bloodshed. I would have preferred not to have to use those terms, but in the face of all that, in the face of terrorism, and so that everyone can see the true situation clearly, I feel obliged to do so. Today Turkey must take a decision. The Welfare Party will establish a just order, that is certain. [But] will the transition be peaceful or violent; will it be achieved harmoniously or by bloodshed? The 60 million [citizens] must make up their minds on that point.'[142] According to the Court, discussing this speech as well as other samples, 'there was ambiguity in the terminology used to refer to the method to be employed to gain political power. In all of these speeches the possibility was mentioned of resorting 'legitimately' to force in order to

---

[141] European Commission for Democracy through Law (Venice Commission), Explanatory report to guidelines on the prohibition of political parties and analogous measures, § 10.
[142] *Refah (Grand Chamber)*, o.c., § 31.

overcome various obstacles Refah expected to meet on the political route by which it intended to gain and retain power. Furthermore, the Court endorses the following finding of the Chamber: '... While it is true that Refah's leaders did not, in government documents, call for the use of force and violence as a political weapon, they did not take prompt practical steps to distance themselves from those members of Refah who had publicly referred with approval to the possibility of using force against politicians who opposed them. Consequently, Refah's leaders did not dispel the ambiguity of these statements about the possibility of having recourse to violent methods in order to gain power and retain it.'[143] Hence the Court takes a broad approach in its appreciation whether or not a party promotes violence: explicit calls for violence are not required, ambiguity may suffice. Such ambiguity exists in a strong form when members advocate violence and the party does not promptly react against this.

In the Turkish cases concerning pro-Kurdish parties, the Turkish government argued in several cases that the targeted party supported the PKK. Under the criteria put forward by the European Court of Human Rights, support for a terrorist organization would be a cause for dissolution, because it would mean that the means used by the party are no longer democratic (since they include support for violence). Yet there was never sufficient proof of this. In several cases, the Court stated that a political party's promotion of Kurdish rights can not by itself be interpreted as supporting terrorism. Otherwise, armed movements would monopolize these issues and it would become impossible to deal with these matters in the framework of a democratic debate.[144]

It came close, however, in the *DEP* case. The dissolution of the DEP Party was based on a number of statements and speeches. One speech, by a former president of the DEP, held in Kurdish before a Kurdish party in North Iraq, clearly supported violence as a way of achieving Kurdish autonomy. For example: 'Whoever does whatever it is for the independence and liberation of Kurdistan, deserves our respect. Everything is for the Kurdish State ... O armed soldiers of the Democratic Party of Kurdistan, the cause of your party represents your name ... The Kurds have sworn an oath. Our oath is death. O, homeland, we sacrifice our lives for you. Shrouds are our clothes. We do not ask for gifts. You can sell our blood to buy back Kurdistan, that would be the realisation of our dreams.'[145] The European Court of Human Rights considered that measures against the author of this speech were justified, because it incites to profound hatred against those presented as the enemies of the Kurds, and because it creates the impression that the use of violence is a liberation measure that is necessary and justified in the face of the enemy.[146] Yet the dissolution of the entire party on the basis of this speech is not a proportionate measure.

---

[143] *Refah (Grand Chamber)*, o.c., § 130.
[144] *Yazar* ECHR (2002), o.c., § 57: *DDP (Party of Democracy and Evolution)* ECHR (2005), o.c., § 25; *EP (Emek Partisi)* ECHR (2005), o.c., § 28.
[145] *Dicle for the Democratic Party (DEP) v Turkey* ECHR (2002), § 20.   [146] Ibid, § 62.

Besides the dissolution procedure, a criminal procedure had been started against the author. In the eyes of the Court, one single speech by a former leader held abroad in another language than Turkish and before an audience that was not directly concerned with the Turkish situation had a very limited potential impact on national security, public order, or territorial integrity in Turkey.[147] In this case, the conclusion is that the Court considered only the harm caused by the speech itself, while refusing to look at it as an element potentially indicating the 'true violent nature' of this party.

The possibility to prohibit parties that resort to or encourage violence exists in several states, including[148] Denmark, Portugal, Albania, Georgia, and Latvia. In France, this is limited to 'terrorist acts'.[149] The Croatian Constitutional Court in 1998 rejected the complaint of the president of 'The New Croatian Right' against the refusal of the Ministry of Administration to register his party, confirmed by an Administrative Court. The programme contained a presentation of Croatian boundaries that included parts of Bosnia and Herzegovina and FR Yugoslavia. It declared as its party's aims and activities on these 'Croatian territories under Serbian occupation': 'general destabilization', 'diversions', 'subversions', 'assassinations', 'devastations', and 'conflicts'.[150]

In Spain,[151] the continued attacks by the Basque terrorist organization, ETA,[152] led in 2002 to the adoption of a new Statute on Political Parties[153] aimed in particular at the Batasuna political party[154] that was widely perceived

---

[147] Ibid, § 64.

[148] Information from European Commission for Democracy through Law (Venice Commission), 'Prohibition of political parties and analogous measures', Report adopted by the Commission at its 35th Plenary Meeting, Venice, 12–13 June 1998.

[149] Act of 10 January 1936 on combat groups and private militias, Article 7.

[150] Constitutional Court of Croatia, 16 December 1998, Narodne novine (*Official Gazette*) 1/99, 18–19, Summary in CODICES database: http://codices.coe.int.

[151] See V. Ferreres Comella, 'The New Regulation of Political Parties in Spain, and the Decision to Outlaw Batasuna', Conference Paper, 11th Annual Conference on The Individual vs. The State: Conference on Militant Democracy (Budapest, 5–6 December 2003); M. Revenga Sánchez, 'The Move Towards a (and the Struggle for) Militant Democracy in Spain', Conference Paper, ECPR Conference, Marburg, 18–21 September 2003 www.essex.ac.uk/ECPR/events/generalconference/marburg/papers/10/7/sanchez.pdf; K. Sawyer, 'Rejection of Weimarian Politics or Betrayal of Democracy? Spain's Proscription of Batasuna under the European Convention on Human Rights' (2003) 52 *Am UL Rev* 1531; G. Tardi, 'Political Parties' Right to Engage in Politics: Variations on a Theme of Democracy,' Conference Paper, 11th Annual Conference on The Individual vs. The State: Conference on Militant Democracy (Budapest, 5–6 December 2003); U. L. Turano, 'Spain: Banning political parties as a response to Basque terrorism' (2003) 1 *International Journal of Constitutional Law* 730.

[152] In its thirty years of existence, ETA killed more than 800 people. Its goal is Basque independence. Its targets include Basque politicians belonging to non-nationalist parties.

[153] Ley Orgánica 6/2002 de Partidos Políticos, 27 June 2002, BOE No. 154 of 28 May 2002, 23600–23607.

[154] The name 'Batasuna' was adopted in June 2001 by the party formerly named 'Herri Batasuna'. This party was formed in 1978 in the autonomous Basque region within Spain. Its goal is the creation of an independent Basque state. The party scored over 10 per cent of the Basque electorate in regional elections and had a large number of municipal councillors.

as its political arm.[155] Within a week of its entry into force, the Spanish Parliament passed a motion urging the government to bring a case against Batasuna on the basis of this law. The motion was promoted by Batasuna's refusal to condemn ETA's terrorist action on 4 August 2002 in which a car bomb killed two bystanders. Batasuna was declared illegal in March 2003.[156] In May 2004, the lists of another party, Herritarren Zerrenda, for the elections of the European Parliament, were refused because it was seen as a continuation of Batasuna. An appeal before the Constitutional Court against this judgment was rejected.[157] Since this is the most recently adopted European legislation concerning party closure (coming moreover after the first *Refah* judgment), it is worth citing its core provisions concerning the grounds of prohibition. Section 9(2) provides that a political party shall be outlawed when its activity violates democratic principles, in particular when it seeks to deteriorate or destroy human rights or democracy through any of the types of behaviour enumerated in that section, when this behaviour is serious and repeated. These include 'a) violating fundamental rights by promoting, justifying, or excusing attacks on the life or dignity of the person or the exclusion or persecution of an individual by reason of ideology, religion, beliefs, nationality, race, sex, or sexual orientation; b) encouraging or enabling violence to be used as a means to achieve political ends or as a means to undermine the conditions that make political pluralism possible; and c) assisting and giving political support to terrorist organizations with the aim of subverting the constitutional order'.[158] Section 9(3) specifies that the conditions of the previous paragraph concur in a political party in case of the repetition or accumulation of several of the following activities: 'a) giving express or tacit political support to terrorism, and thus legitimizing terrorist actions by seeking to minimize the importance of human rights and their violation; b) creating a culture of confrontation linked to the actions of terrorists and thereby seeking to intimidate, deter, neutralize, or socially isolate anyone who opposes such actions, forcing them to live with the daily threat of coercion and fear and depriving them of the fundamental right of freedom of expression and participation in public life; c) including regularly in its directing bodies and on its electoral lists persons who have been convicted of terrorist crimes and who have not publicly renounced terrorist methods and aims, or maintaining among its membership a significant number of "double militants" (i.e. those who also belong to groups with links to terrorist organizations), except where there are attempts by the party to expel or discipline such persons; d) using in an official way symbols, slogans, or other representational

---

[155] On the variety of relationships that may exist between political parties and terrorist groups, see L. Weinberg (ed.), *Political Parties and Terrorist Groups* (London: Frank Cass, 1992).

[156] Tribunal Supremo, Sala Especial, 17 March 2003 (available at: www.poderjudicial.es/tribunalsupremo).

[157] Tribunal Constitucional, 99/2004, 27 May 2004 (available at: www.tribunalconstitutional.es).

[158] Translation by L. Turano, 'Spain: Banning political parties as a response to Basque terrorism' (2003) 1 *International Journal of Constitutional Law* 730, at 733.

elements that are normally identified with a terrorist organization; e) conceding
to a terrorist organization or to those who collaborate with one of the same
rights and prerogatives that electoral law concedes to parties; f) collaborating
habitually with groups that act systematically in accordance with terrorist or
violent organizations or that protect and support terrorism and terrorists;
g) giving institutional support, administratively or economically, to any of the
groups mentioned in the preceding subparagraph; h) promoting, giving cover
to, or participating in activities that have as their objective rewarding, paying
homage to, or honouring violent or terrorist actions and those who commit or
collaborate with them; and i) giving cover to actions that socially intimidate,
coerce, or disrupt public order and that are linked to terrorism or violence.'[159]
The case against Batasuna was based on double militancy, refusals to condemn
terrorist acts, as well as explicit support to ETA and creating an atmosphere of
terror and intimidation, including threats against politicians supporting a ban
of the party. Hence it seems likely that this falls under the European Court of
Human Rights' *Refah* criteria. However, the scope of the law is so broad that it
may lead to prohibitions that cannot be justified under these criteria.[160]

A state's concern with the prevention of violence may lead it to restrict the
activities of groups that do not use or advocate violence, yet that create or
exacerbate divisions within a society which it fears may lead to societal unrest,
tensions, aggression, and ultimately violent conflict. In states that are characterized by ethnic or religious divisions within society, provisions are regularly
encountered to the effect that political parties based on ethnic or religious
identity may be prohibited.[161] In Georgia, the State Authorities Act prohibits
parties based on geographical or regional criteria. In Kyrghyzstan, the law does
not permit the existence of parties founded on religious principles. In Bulgaria,[162]
as well as in Turkmenistan, the Constitution proscribes parties founded on
religious principles, and also on ethnic or racial principles. Political parties
based on ethnicity are also illegal in Ukraine. Likewise in Senegal, political
parties created for ethnic, linguistic, or religious reasons are prohibited.[163] In the
new Constitution of Afghanistan (Article 35), the 'formation and functioning of

[159] Ibid.
[160] Yet the Spanish Constitutional Court held that the law does not violate Spanish constitutional provisions on freedom of association and the right to participate in public affairs: Tribunal
Constitucional, 48/2003, 12 March 2003 (available at: www.tribunalconstitucional.es).
[161] Information on European states from European Commission for Democracy through Law
(Venice Commission), 'Prohibition of political parties and analogous measures', Report adopted by
the Commission at its 35th plenary meeting, Venice, 12–13 June 1998.
[162] On this basis, a challenge was brought against the Turkish-based Movement for Rights and
Freedoms. In addition to the argument that it was based on ethnic and religious lines, it was argued
that the party threatened national sovereignty and integrity and incited ethnic or religious enmity,
in violation of Articles 11(4) and 44(2) of the Bulgarian Constitution. Six justices found the party
unconstitutional, five disagreed. Since a decision of unconstitutionality required a qualified
majority of seven justices, the party was allowed to continue to exist (E. Konstantinov, 'Turkish
Party in Bulgaria Allowed to Continue' (1992) *East European Constitutional Review* 11.
[163] Concluding observations of the Committee on the Elimination of Racial Discrimination:
Senegal, 4 August 1994, 1/49/18, § 347.

a party based on ethnicity, language, Islamic school of thought and region is not permissible'.[164]

Under the criterion used by the European Court of Human Rights and that of the Venice Commission, party closure on these grounds is not permissible. On the one hand, the risk that political parties based on group allegiance would create tensions in society is to be taken seriously. Yet on the other hand, there are real issues in ethnically or religiously divided societies about the way in which communities are to live together, which need to be discussed politically. The formation of such political parties may be a good way to bring these issues into the political forum. Hence it is worth exploring less restrictive measures than party closure that would serve to avert the risk that is feared, such as in particular legislation prohibiting incitement to hatred and violence.

4.3.3.3 *Protecting the Present Order*

Providing the possibility of party closure in the event that a political party's programme contradicts a state's Constitution, is an extremely rights-restrictive measure. As a rule, a Constitution provides for a procedure for its amendment. Amending the Constitution is the work of Parliament, and hence of politicians. It is therefore a normal feature of political party programmes to include proposals that are not compatible with the current Constitution and that can only be realized through constitutional amendments. In most cases, constitutional amendments require special majorities, hence very often a political party—even if it has an ordinary majority—will need the support of at least one other party in order to be able to effectively amend the Constitution.

The European Court of Human Rights ruled, with respect to a party's proposal to introduce a federal state structure: 'In the Court's view, the fact that . . . a political programme is considered incompatible with the current principles and structures of the Turkish State does not make it incompatible with the rules of democracy. It is of the essence of democracy to allow diverse political programmes to be proposed and debated, even those that call into question the way a state is currently organised, provided that they do not harm democracy itself.'[165] Hence the above-mentioned formulation of the conditions for legitimate party closure: 'a political party may promote *a change in the law or the legal and constitutional structures of the State* on two conditions . . .'.[166]

The Venice Guidelines provide explicitly that: 'The fact alone that a party advocates a peaceful change of the Constitution should not be sufficient for its prohibition or dissolution' (§ 3). In 2003, the Venice Commission examined the Law on Political Parties of the Republic of Armenia. This law provided that the registration of a party might be rejected if the Charter of the Party of provisions

---

[164] Constitution of Afghanistan, Year 1382 (2004).
[165] *Socialist Party of Turkey (STP) a.o. v Turkey* ECHR (2003), § 47.
[166] *Refah (Grand Chamber)*, o.c., § 98

of its programme contradicts the Constitution and laws of the Republic of Armenia. The Commission stated that this needed to be changed, because 'such a provision might be used to prevent registration of political parties aiming for peaceful change of the constitutional order'.[167] Similar provisions can be found in the legislation of other states. For example in Lithuania, a political party can be banned when it violates the Constitution or the Law on Political Parties, after having repeatedly seen its activity suspended on those grounds.[168]

Under the criteria of the European Court of Human Rights and the Venice Commission, a party promoting peaceful separatism cannot be prohibited either. In several Turkish cases before the European Court, the promotion of separatism was one of the grounds for dissolution, even though in fact the parties concerned did not expressly promote separatism but rather advocated Kurdish autonomy within the borders of the Turkish state. The European Court never accepted dissolution on this ground. With respect to the Kurdish issue in Turkey, it stated that 'there can be no justification for hindering a political group solely because it seeks to debate in public the situation of part of the State's population and to take part in the nation's political life in order to find, according to democratic rules, solutions capable of satisfying everyone concerned'.[169] The Court was even more explicit in *UMO Ilinden–PIRIN*: 'The mere fact that a political party calls for autonomy or even requests secession of part of the country's territory is not a sufficient basis to justify its dissolution on national security grounds.'[170]

At the same time, the European Court in these cases pointed out that the programme of the Turkish parties concerned did not explicitly include Kurdish independence,[171] whereas the Bulgarian party did not have 'any real chance of bringing about political changes which would not meet with the approval of everyone on the political stage'.[172] The fact that the Court points this out explicitly

---

[167] European Commission for Democracy through Law (Venice Commission), Opinion on the Law on political parties of the Republic of Azerbaijan, adopted by the Venice Commission at its 59th Plenary Session, Venice, 18–19 June 2004, § 28.

[168] Article 7, Law on Political Parties of Lithuania, see E. Sileikis, 'Das Parteienrecht in Litauen' (1998) 44 *Osteuroparecht* 133, at 155.

[169] *United Communist Party of Turkey and Others v Turkey*, ECHR (1998), o.c., § 57 .

[170] *UMO Ilinden–PIRIN* ECHR (2005), o.c., § 61.

[171] *United Communist Party of Turkey and Others v Turkey*, ECHR (1998), o.c., § 57; *Socialist Party and Others v Turkey*, ECHR (1998), o.c., § 47; *Freedom and Democracy Party (ÖZDEP) v Turkey*, ECHR (1999), o.c., § 41; *Socialist Party of Turkey and Others v Turkey*, ECHR (2003), § 43. In the case of *Dicle for the Democratic Party of Turkey (DEP) v Turkey*, ECHR (2002), the Court finds that a number of remarks made by an ex-president of the party reflected an aspiration for the founding of a Kurdish state (§ 52), yet focused on the arguments that 'in the circumstances of the case' the party's demands for 'autonomy or separatism' could not be summarized as support for terrorist activities (§ 54) and that there was no evidence that the DEP had a real chance to install a system of government that would not be approved by all actors on the political scene (§ 55). Given the facts of the case, in which it is not clear to what extent the call for separatism can be attributed to the party as such, and in which the party is not considered really threatening, this cannot be interpreted in the sense that a separatist programme could never justify the dissolution of a political party. [172] *UMO Ilinden–PIRIN*, ECHR (2005), o.c., § 61.

might suggest that it might judge differently a case in which independence is an explicit project and moreover there is a real chance that the party may gain sufficient power to realize this. The fact that the limitation clause in Article 10(2)—yet not that in Article 11(2)—includes the protection of 'territorial integrity' as a legitimate restriction ground indicates that at least at the time of the drafting of the Convention, the states parties agreed that this was a legitimate basis for the restriction of political rights. Nevertheless, party closure is a very strong restriction, hence even if the aim is considered legitimate, it may not justify such a strong measure, and the *Refah* criterion (only undemocratic means or goals justify party closure) may hold. Moreover, the qualification of party closure as a disproportionate reaction when applied to peaceful separatist parties is strengthened by the use of the 'consensus criterion': since parties striving for separatism within a democratic framework are an accepted feature of contemporary multiparty democracies throughout Europe,[173] the European Court of Human Rights is not likely to hold that a democratic separatist programme can be sufficient reason for dissolution. A final argument is the fact that international law recognizes a right to self-determination of peoples (e.g. Article 1 ICCPR). While this is not a right to unilateral secession, the formation of political parties that seek to achieve independence of part of the territory through the democratic process is a normal exercise of the right to self-determination. Hence, in an international legal context, 'territorial unity' is not a principle at the same level as democracy or human rights. A far-reaching measure such as party closure may be justified for the protection of the latter, but not for that of the former.[174]

The French Conseil d'Etat in 1962 accepted the prohibition of a pro-independence party on the basis of the threat it constituted for the territorial integrity of France (including its overseas territories).[175]

4.3.3.4 Regulating Access to the Democratic Process

Under the legislation of some states, political parties can only legitimately exist if they have a minimum number of members. This formal requirement exists mostly at the level of preventive measures, for example as a condition for registration, rather than as grounds for dissolution. The underlying rationale is that parties with very few members are not important enough; i.e. that in a representative democracy they do not represent a sufficient number of people. For

---

[173] Examples include the Lega Nord in Italy, whose slogan is 'Per l'indipendenza de la Padania' (For the independence of Padania, a virtual Northern Republic), and the Nieuw-Vlaamse Alliantie in Belgium (Striving for the independence of Flanders).

[174] In addition, considerations of political opportunity may in some cases include the risk that excluding separatist parties from the democratic process may lead to violence, when these tendencies have significant support that cannot be expressed through the political forum. See A. Dufseth, 'Indonesia's 1999 Political Laws: The Right of Association in Aceh and Papua' (2002) 11 *Pac Rim L & Pol'y* 613.

[175] Conseil d'Etat, *Dame Tapua and Others*, 15 July 1964, Recueil Lebon 407 (Tahiti Independence Party).

example,[176] under Estonian law a party must in principle have at least 1,000 members; in Latvia, the minimum number of founders is fixed at 200,[177] in Lithuania at 400, in Belarus at 500, in Romania at 25,000. Such a formal requirement may have an important impact in practice. For example, in April 2004, Human Rights Watch launched a report on 'Political Freedoms in Kazakhstan',[178] in which it highlighted the effect of a restrictive new Law on Political Parties. This law raised the minimum number of member signatures to obtain registration from 3,000 to 50,000, arguing that 'any party that claims it represents the interest and speaks on behalf of the people of Kazakhstan should have a legitimate basis for that'. As a result, only eleven of the previous nineteen parties applied for re-registration, and only seven were granted it. HRW alleges that the number of signatures and other minor technical problems were used as pretexts to deny registration to opposition parties. According to HRW, the remaining parties were widely perceived as either pro-President Nazarbaev or moderate and unlikely to produce candidates who would realistically challenge the president.

A variant of the minimum membership requirement is a requirement of a minimum number of candidates to be presented for elections. In Canada, the rule used to be that a political party could only be registered if it was able to submit fifty candidates for the elections, anywhere in the 295 Canadian constituencies.[179] The Communist Party of Canada had been registered since 1974, but for the elections of 1993 it was able to find only eight candidates. As a result, it was deregistered and could not compete in those elections. It contested the measure in court, however, up to the highest level, the Supreme Court of Canada. The Supreme Court declared the fifty-candidate threshold unconstitutional, for violation of the fundamental right to run for public office, as protected in Section 3 of the Canadian Charter of Rights and Freedoms. In the eyes of the Court, this right included a right of effective representation, which was to be seen as the right of every citizen to play a meaningful role in the selection of elected representatives. The Supreme Court argued as follows:[180] 'the ability of a political party to make a valuable contribution to the electoral process is not dependent upon its capacity to offer the electorate a genuine "government option" . . . Irrespective of their capacity to influence the outcome of an election, political parties act as both a vehicle and an outlet for the

---

[176] Information from European Commission for Democracy through Law (Venice Commission), 'Prohibition of political parties and analogous measures', Report adopted by the Commission at its 35th Plenary Meeting, Venice, 12–13 June 1998.

[177] A report in 1998 mentioned that in Latvia, eight political parties had been struck off the register for having insufficient members (European Commission for Democracy through Law (Venice Commission), 'Prohibition of political parties and analogous measures', Report adopted by the Commission at its 35th Plenary Meeting, Venice, 12–13 June 1998).

[178] Human Rights Watch, 'Political Freedoms in Kazakhstan', April 2004, at: www.hrw.org.

[179] RSC 1985, c. E-2, s.28 (2). See on this topic G. Tardi, 'Political Parties' Right to Engage in Politics: Variations on a Theme of Democracy', Conference Paper, 11th Annual Conference on The Individual vs. The State: Conference on Militant Democracy (Budapest, 5–6 December 2003).

[180] Supreme Court of Canada, *Figueroa v Canada (Attorney General)* (2003) 227 DLR (4th) 1.

meaningful participation of individual citizens in the electoral process... In each election, a significant number of citizens vote for candidates nominated by registered parties in full awareness that the candidate has no realistic chance of winning a seat in Parliament—or that the party of which she or he is a member has no realistic chance of winning a majority of seats in the House of Commons. Just as these votes are not "wasted votes", votes for a political party that has not satisfied the 50-candidate threshold are not wasted votes either. As a public expression of individual support for certain perspectives and opinions, such votes are an integral component of a vital and dynamic democracy.' As a result of this judgment, in May 2004 new legislation was passed, replacing the fifty-candidate requirement with a one-candidate requirement, and adding as a requirement for registration the need to have 250 support letters of members.[181]

In Portugal, the Constitutional Court ruled in 2003 that a rule requiring dissolution of a political party that fails to put up candidates at two successive parliamentary elections is an unconstitutional restriction on parties' freedom of activity.[182]

A related criterion concerns the activities of a political party. For example, in Romania, a political party may be dissolved for inactivity (by the municipal court of Bucharest at the request of the Attorney General's Department) if it fails to present candidates in at least ten constituencies (alone or as part of an alliance) in two successive election campaigns, or if it has held no general assembly for five years.[183] In Croatia, a party ceases to exist when the time lapse between two meetings of its governing body is twice as long as that provided for in its statutes.[184] In Hungary, a party may be dissolved if it has not functioned for at least a year and the number of its members has constantly been below the legal minimum.[185]

Can these measures be justified in light of the freedom of political association? The Constitutional Court of Romania held that a representativity threshold consisting amongst others of a requirement of a minimum number of founding members, does not violate the freedom of association, since its purpose is only to ensure that the association of citizens in political parties has the significance of an institutionalized political stream without which the party cannot fulfil its constitutional role.[186] However, if the application of these

---

[181] Act of May 14, 2004 to amend the Canada Elections Act and the Income Tax Act, Statutes of Canada 2004, c.24.

[182] Constitutional Court Portugal, 18 June 2003, Diário da República, 165 (Serie I-A), 19 July 2003, 4208–4216, available in CODICES database: www.codices.coe.int.

[183] Information from European Commission for Democracy through Law (Venice Commission), 'Prohibition of political parties and analogous measures', Report adopted by the Commission at its 35th Plenary Meeting, Venice, 12–13 June 1998.   [184] Ibid.

[185] Ibid.

[186] Constitutional Court of Bulgaria, Decision No. 35 of April 2, 1996, *Monitorul Oficial*, Part I, No. 75/1996 and Decision No. 147 of October 27, 1998, *Monitorul Oficial*, Part I, No. 85 of March 1, 1999, cited in M. Constantinescu and I. Vida, 'Closing Down the Activity of Political Parties in Romania by Way of a Court of Law Decision' (1998) 5 *Journal of Constitutional Law in Eastern and Central Europe* 43, at 49.

formal criteria is grounds for party closure, this is clearly a disproportionate measure, for example under the criteria of the European Court of Human Rights and the Venice Commission. Yet even if the consequences are of a less restrictive nature, there are strong arguments to conclude that the imposition of such rules on political parties violates their freedom of political association. In order to reach this conclusion, a balancing exercise is needed between on the one hand this freedom and on the other the reasons for its restriction. It has to be granted that the weight of the freedom of political association is largely related to the essential role of parties in the functioning of a democracy, which is not a strong argument when applied to very small parties that have never won representation in Parliament. Yet this general interest perspective should not obliterate the importance of the freedom of political association for individuals. The individual importance of the right to form and join a political party as a means of political expression is not dependent upon the size or importance of the party. At the same time, the reasons invoked for restricting the freedom of political association seem not very compelling in this case. When miniature parties cannot be excluded from the political process, there will be some public expenses involved, related for example to printing their names on the ballots. In a system that grants other favours (such as broadcasting facilities or state finances) to political parties, there may be implications in those fields, but usually such facilities will be restricted to parties of a certain size, measured for example by their representation in Parliament. That type of restriction can easily be justified, yet preventing a party from participating in elections or from functioning in general only because of its size or low level of activities seems a disproportionate measure.

Sometimes requirements with respect to nationwide territorial representation are imposed as a way of preventing regionalist political parties from operating. It is highly questionable whether such measures are compatible with the freedom of political association. In 2002, the Venice Commission expressed an opinion on the Ukrainian legislation on political parties, upon a request from the Parliamentary Assembly of the Council of Europe. Ukrainian law included the requirement that parties had to be active nationwide, not only in a region of the country. The Commission concluded that this requirement should be loosened in the text of the law and pointed out that in many European democracies, established regional and local parties are active.[187] The UN Human Rights Committee has also expressed concern that conditions with respect to the extent of a political party's territorial representation may violate individuals' political freedom.[188]

---

[187] European Commission for Democracy through Law (Venice Commission), Opinion No. 183/2002 on the Ukrainian legislation on political parties, adopted by the Venice Commission at its 51st Plenary Session (Venice, 5–6 July 2002), CDL-AD (2002) 17, §§ 9–15.

[188] Concluding observations of the Human Rights Committee: Republic of Moldova, 26 July 2002, CCPR/CO/75/MDA, § 16, quoted above (footnote 8).

Several of the above-mentioned formal requirements may occur in combination. For example, in 2003, the Venice Commission gave an opinion on a proposed amendment to the Law on Parties and other socio-political organizations of the Republic of Moldova. The amendment provided that the Ministry of Justice would be able to request the Supreme Court to order the suspension of activity of a party or other socio-political organization for a number of essentially formal reasons: if the party has not convened a conference or congress during a period of four years, if it has failed to present its membership lists in any particular year, if it is established at the annual verification of the membership lists that the number of members of the party has fallen below the required number of 5,000 members, domiciled in at least half of the administrative and territorial units,[189] or if the party has not established structural sub-divisions (also with a minimum number of members) in at least half of the administrative territorial units. The Venice Commission concluded that this amendment was incompatible with the freedom of association under Article 11 ECHR.[190] Also in 2003, the Venice Commission gave an opinion on the Law of the Republic of Armenia on Political Parties, providing that a party is 'subject to liquidation' if it either does not participate in two subsequent parliamentary elections or does not receive at least 1 per cent of the votes in either of two subsequent parliamentary elections (as a result their property is transferred to the state). The Commission stated that this is problematic and that 'unsuccessful parties should be able to continue to exist at least as non-governmental organisations without the special rights and privileges of a political party'.[191] The 2004 Venice Commission Guidelines on legislation on political parties provide that: 'Countries applying registration procedures to political parties should refrain from imposing excessive requirements for territorial representation of political parties as well as for minimum membership',[192] and 'Public authorities should refrain from any political or other excessive control over activities of political parties, such as membership, number and frequency of party congresses and meetings, operation of territorial branches and subdivisions.'[193] Hence, the Venice Commission deems some formal requirements

---

[189] The Venice Commission noted that this threshold is very high in a state whose population is only 4 million: European Commission for Democracy through Law (Venice Commission), Opinion No. 233/2003 on the proposed amendment to the law on parties and other socio-political organisations of the Republic of Moldova, adopted by the Venice Commission at its Plenary Session (Venice, 14–15 March 2003), CDL-AD (2003) 8, § 15.   [190] Ibid, § 21.
[191] European Commission for Democracy through Law (Venice Commission), Opinion No. 197 on the law of the Republic of Armenia on political parties, adopted by the Commission at its 54th Plenary Session (Venice, 14–15 March 2003), CDL-AD (2003) 5, § 8. Given the fact that NGOs cannot participate in elections (which is the essential function of political parties), this is an only slightly less restrictive measure. It is remarkable that the Venice Commission seems to accept this as compatible with the freedom of political association.
[192] European Commission for Democracy through Law (Venice Commission), Guidelines on legislation on political parties: some specific issues, adopted by the Venice Commission at its 58th Plenary Session (Venice, 12–13 March 2004), CDL-AD (2004) 007rev, B.   [193] Ibid, C.

of this type acceptable. It is not clear, however, what would count as 'not excessive', especially given the recommendation in the same text that registration should be denied only in the cases in which dissolution is allowed by the Venice Commission, i.e. when a party advocates or uses violence.[194]

In some states, the violation of rules regarding the financing of political parties may lead to the dissolution of the party. For example in Albania, a party may be banned for failing to publish its financial resources or to submit them for inspection.[195] Likewise in the Czech Republic, a court may close down a political party for failure to present its annual financial report to the Parliament.[196] And in Ukraine, systematic violations of the rules on party financing may lead to the dissolution of the party concerned.[197] Moreover, if a political party or its leaders have been convicted for a crime such as large-scale corruption, it may appear appropriate to prohibit that party. Yet party closure on such grounds is not permissible under the criterion used by the European Court of Human Rights, nor that of the Venice Commission. It should indeed be considered a disproportionate measure. Rather, when a party commits a criminal offence, ordinary criminal sanctions must be applied. When the crime is of a financial nature, financial sanctions are particularly appropriate. For example in Argentina, the penalty for illegal party financing is a fine that is twice the size of the illegal contribution.[198]

4.3.4 Modalities of Party Closure

4.3.4.1 Timing

To the democratic dilemma inherent in the choice for party closure on the basis of a potential future harm (cf. above), is added another dilemma: that of the right timing of party closure. Both when it comes too early and when it comes too late, a measure of party closure that would otherwise be justified may become disproportionate. First of all, party closure may come too early. If a party is not successful, or attracts only a small percentage of voters, the chances that it can ever realize its programme are very small. Hence the threat it poses to democracy (the potential future harm) is small. As a result it may be outweighed by the threat

---

[194] Ibid, B.

[195] Information from European Commission for Democracy through Law (Venice Commission), 'Prohibition of political parties and analogous measures', Report adopted by the Commission at its 35th Plenary Meeting, Venice, 12–13 June 1998.

[196] S. Balík, 'Law and facts in cases pertaining to the constitutionality of activities of political parties', Venice Commission document CDL-JU (2005)023, 4.

[197] Ibid. These rules are particularly strict: political parties do not have the right to receive funds from foreign states or their citizens, international organizations, stateless persons, or firms in which the state holds more than a 20 per cent stake.

[198] Information from European Commission for Democracy through Law (Venice Commission), 'Prohibition of political parties and analogous measures', Report adopted by the Commission at its 35th Plenary Meeting, Venice, 12–13 June 1998.

posed by the use of such a strong rights-restrictive measure as party closure. This is in particular the case when a party has never won a seat in Parliament and there are no reasons to assume that it is likely to win any in the foreseeable future. Yet in an electoral system based on proportional representation, a political party that has even just one seat, may be asked to join a coalition government. In such a case, this small party will obviously not be able to realize its entire programme, yet it is likely to sell its support at a high price, requiring that some crucial elements of its programme figure in the new government's programme. Hence, if certain proposals in the platform of a political party seriously threaten democracy or human rights, there is a risk of them being realized as soon as a party has sufficient votes to be represented in Parliament. Yet on the other hand, party closure may also come too late. The broader the popular support for a particular political party, the less its prohibition is supported by a consensus in society, and therefore the less democratic it seems as a measure. Moreover, in practical terms, prosecutors and judges—who themselves in most societies do not have a direct mandate from the electorate—may be hesitant to prosecute and convict a party that attracts a large number of voters. This is illustrated by the case of the Belgian Vlaams Blok, a racist party against which the public prosecutor never took the initiative of prosecution on the basis of hate speech legislation. Moreover, when procedures were initiated at the initiative of non-governmental organizations, several courts used remarkably creative interpretations of the law to deny jurisdiction, until finally the party was convicted.[199] Yet the same theory is belied by the *Refah* case, where the prosecution was initiated against the party of the Prime Minister. Another problem is that once a set of ideas or a group of persons has gathered significant support, the prohibition of the party will not stop them from pursuing their goals, either through another party, or if this is not possible, underground, which may cause a much greater threat. Another risk is that the prohibition of a widely supported party may cause turmoil in society, maybe even violence, and destabilize the country. But these are arguments in favour of an early intervention, rather than against a later intervention when there has not been an early one. In the human rights balance, late prohibition is a very restrictive measure, because it disregards the political choice of a large number of voters; it infringes not only the rights of the party leaders, but of an increasing number of people. Yet on the other side of the balance, the reasons for intervening become increasingly urgent, because as the voting percentage rises, so do the chances of the party coming to power and realizing its programme. In other words: the threat increases. The

---

[199] Both the Brussels Court of first instance (Judgment of 29 June 2001) and the Brussels Court of Appeal (Judgment of 26 February 2003) denied competence, holding that the case concerned a 'political offence', for which the Belgian Constitution prescribes a jury trial. In their innovative interpretations of the concept of 'political offence', both courts set aside consistent case law of the Court of Cassation. Only after the Court of Cassation (Judgment of 18 November 2003)) had quashed the Brussels appeal judgment on this basis, did the Ghent Court of Appeal examine the case on the merits, and find a violation (Judgment of 21 April 2004). The texts of the judgments can be found at: www.antiracisme.be.

balancing exercise remains very difficult, since the certainty of a serious restriction of a fundamental human right (party closure) is to be balanced against what remains only a possibility of serious human rights violations—after all, it remains uncertain whether the party will come to power, and if it does, whether it would not be prevented from carrying out its anti-democratic programme, for example through international pressure or the intervention of a constitutional court. It appears that prohibition of a political party enjoying broad voter support (for example 25 or 30 per cent of the votes) is justified only when the uncertainty on the one end of the balance becomes a probability, for example due to clear statements by party leaders about their intentions after acceding to power, and to the incapacity of other mechanisms to stop this.

It seems very difficult to regulate the appropriate timing of party closure in terms of a minimum or maximum percentage of the votes obtained by the party. First of all, there is a practical problem involved, since it is not possible to know how much support a political party has at a given moment, except immediately after elections. Moreover, it may be debated which elections are to be taken as a reference: do local or European elections count? What if the results vary widely across the country? More importantly, in most cases neither a bottom percentage nor a top percentage seems advisable. The appropriate bottom percentage under which a party is too small to justify its prohibition depends on the electoral system. Yet as explained above (cf. above), even the perspective of one seat in Parliament may constitute a threat in some circumstances. Hence the bottom percentage would have to be so low as to cast doubt on its usefulness. On the other hand, the use of a top percentage, above which party closure is no longer justified in a democracy, seems irresponsible. If the threat is serious, it is better to react late than not to react at all.

In the *Refah* case, the dissolution of the party came late, since the party was represented in the government. Yet even there it might be argued that it came too early, since even if the party had the power, it had not done anything to harm democracy or human rights. Under the heading 'The appropriate timing for dissolution', the European Court of Human Rights stated that: 'the Court considers that a state cannot be required to wait, before intervening, until a political party has seized power and begun to take concrete steps to implement a policy incompatible with the standards of the Convention and democracy, even though the danger of that policy for democracy is sufficiently established and imminent. The Court accepts that where the presence of such a danger has been established by the national courts, after detailed scrutiny subjected to rigorous European supervision, a state may reasonably forestall the execution of such a policy, which is incompatible with the Convention's provisions, before an attempt is made to implement it through concrete steps that might prejudice civil peace and the country's democratic regime.'[200] Ruling more specifically on

---

[200] *Refah (Grand Chamber)*, o.c., § 102.

the *Refah* case, the Court examined 'whether Refah could have presented a threat to the democratic regime at the time when it was dissolved'.[201] It recalled the figures: 22 per cent of the votes in the 1995 general elections, 35 per cent of the votes in the 1996 local elections, 37 per cent in an opinion poll in 1997 and a forecast of 67 per cent for the next elections in four years. According to the Court, 'those figures bear witness to a considerable rise in Refah's influence as a political party and its chances of coming to power alone. The Court accordingly considers that at the time of its dissolution Refah had the real potential to seize political power without being restricted by the compromises inherent in a coalition.'[202] 'While it can be considered, in the present case, that Refah's policies were dangerous for the rights and freedoms guaranteed by the Convention, the real chances that Refah would implement its programme after gaining power made that danger more tangible and more immediate. That being the case, the Court cannot criticize the national courts for not acting earlier, at the risk of intervening prematurely and before the danger concerned had taken shape and become real. Nor can it criticize them for not waiting, at the risk of putting the political regime and civil peace in jeopardy, for Refah to seize power and swing into action, for example by tabling bills in parliament, in order to implement its plans. In short, the Court considers that in electing to intervene at the time when they did in the present case the national authorities did not go beyond the margin of appreciation left to them under the Convention.'[203] The Court did not consider the argument that given the success of this party, its dissolution had harmed large numbers of people. The arguments only considered the question of a minimum threshold justifying prohibition. Since this was a very successful party, the threshold that was proposed was a very high one, i.e. not in terms of percentage of success, but the criterion that the party should have started implementing its programme. This was rejected. The Court explicitly allowed preventive intervention. It should be noted, however, that this was in the context of a case in which the party had held power only as part of a coalition government and at the same time the Court estimated that there was a real threat that the party would come to power alone.

A specific hypothesis arises when a party elected on a platform including anti-democratic proposals comes to power alone, yet does not realize any anti-democratic measure nor announces any intention to do so. An argument may be made that in such a case, the party should be judged on the basis of its current policies rather than its past proposals and closure is no longer justified. This hypothesis is not extremely far-fetched, since one of the factors causing change in political parties, is their rise to power. For example, in an international context that puts high value on democracy and human rights, the desire of a government to be a respectable member of the international community

---

[201] *Refah (Grand Chamber)*, o.c., § 107.   [202] *Refah (Grand Chamber)*, o.c., § 108.
[203] *Refah (Grand Chamber)*, o.c. § 110.

may outweigh its desire to deliver the anti-democratic measures promised during the electoral campaign.

Another specific matter that concerns timing, is the question of whether it is allowed to dissolve a political party when elections are near. In case of an unjustified dissolution, appeal may in such cases come too late to undo the effect of the dissolution on the election results. In the Czech Republic, a party cannot be dissolved in the period from the date on which the (local, regional or national) elections have been announced until the tenth day after the final date of these elections.[204]

4.3.4.2 Uncovering the Hidden Agenda

In many cases, party closure is based on the fear for a potential future harm inherent in the party programme. Yet this issue is complicated by some of the characteristics of political parties. First, it is common sense that parties change. For example, many communist or hard-line socialist parties have transformed into social democrats seemingly without much difficulty. Similarly, extreme-right—even racist—parties may transform into mainstream conservative parties. If party closure is a measure to prevent the realization of a potential future harm, the past has only limited relevance. Hence, it may be argued that when party closure is based on a party's programme, this must necessarily be its most recent programme. Second, parties are not necessarily homogeneous. This is equally common sense. For example, a party may have the ambition to be a 'people's party', addressing all layers of the population. Often this results in a party composed of different factions, representing different target groups (e.g. women, farmers . . .) or different ideological foci. For example, in a party that identifies mainly with a particular social-economic programme, there may be widely diverging opinions on ethical matters and vice versa. As a result, it may not always be easy to identify the party programme. One option is to rely only on the party constitution and on the most recent election programme, assuming that these express a consensus within the party. In that sense, this is a correct way to assess the potential future harm, as long as power relations within the party do not change. But what if other—worse—things are proposed in other publications of the party, either at the lower level, of local party branches, or in campaign materials of individual politicians or public statements made by party members? This could be an indication that the real threat is stronger than the official programme suggests, either because the consensus around the official programme is not so solid, or due to a deliberate attempt to hide the party's true intentions. This brings up a third characteristic of political parties: parties do not necessarily act in good faith. If a party is really dangerous, it is likely to want to hide this. Whereas some anti-democratic proposals (for example those

---

[204] S. Balík, 'Law and facts in cases pertaining to the constitutionality of activities of political parties', Venice Commission document CDL-JU (2005) 023, 3.

restricting the rights of immigrants) are unfortunately the reason of a party's popularity, other elements of the same party's agenda may be less pleasing to its electorate (for example the restriction of women's rights or labour union rights, or the abolition of parliamentary democracy). Yet the most important incentive for hiding 'dangerous' proposals is the existence of legislation providing for restrictions of the rights of political parties making such proposals. The threat of persecution, and even prohibition, leads those parties to be very careful in formulating such proposals in their official documents and publications. At the same time, if these proposals are the reason why people vote for this party, it is not in the party's interest to be entirely silent on them, so it is likely that these proposals will still emerge in oral statements, and in publications of a less official nature. When one takes into account the possibility that parties may act in bad faith, one may also want to reconsider the idea that only the most recent texts issued by the party can be an appropriate basis for repressive action. In a context where over time increasingly repressive legislation applicable to political parties has been adopted, or where this legislation has been applied with increasing severity, a party may choose to be careful in its recent documents, but without formally taking a distance from the old ones. The reasoning is that people already know what the party stands for, without the need for it to confirm this too explicitly. Hence, there appear to be good arguments to look beyond the official party programme and constitution, and to include other publications and statements. Likewise there seems to be reason to look at older proposals that have never been rejected afterwards. A crucial guarantee for political parties, however, is that they must have the chance to reject older proposals or texts as well as viewpoints expressed by individual party members and local branches. Yet when the party leadership is aware of such statements and does not reject them, there is no reason not to hold the party accountable for them.

The finding of a violation in the *Refah* case was not based on official proposals in the party programme or constitution, but rather on speeches by the chairman (Necmettin Erbakan), vice-chairman, individual MPs and a local governor, made between 1993 and 1997, when the procedure for dissolution was initiated. The official programme, on the contrary, expressly recognized the fundamental nature of the principle of secularism. The European Court of Human Rights took a clear position in this respect: 'The Court further considers that the constitution and programme of a political party cannot be taken into account as the sole criterion for determining its objectives and intentions. The political experience of the Contracting states has shown that in the past political parties with aims contrary to the fundamental principles of democracy have not revealed such aims in their official publications until after taking power. That is why the Court has always pointed out that a party's political programme may conceal objectives and intentions different from the ones it proclaims. To verify that it does not, the content of the programme must be compared with the actions of the party's leaders and the positions they defend. Taken together, these acts and stances may be relevant in proceedings for the dissolution of a political party, provided that as a whole they disclose its aims and intentions.'[205]

Moreover, the Court also addressed the issue of the use of older material: 'As regards the applicants' argument that Refah was punished for speeches by its members made several years before its dissolution, the Court considers that the Turkish courts, when reviewing the constitutionality of Refah's acts, could legitimately take into consideration the progression over time of the real risk that the party's activities represented for the principles of democracy. The same applies to the review of Refah's compliance with the principles set forth in the Convention. Firstly, the programme and policies of a political party may become clear through the accumulation of acts and speeches by its members over a relatively long period. Secondly, the party concerned may, over the years, increase its chances of gaining political power and implementing its policies.'[206] It should be noted that this statement addresses only the hypothesis that older statements are used in combination with recent statements. It is not clear how the Court would evaluate a party closure case based only on older material.

The Court in the *Refah* case examined with respect to all the statements it used whether statements by this particular person were imputable to the party, and concluded that they all were. With respect to the chairman/prime minister (Mr Erbakan), this was because of his function: 'The Court considers that the statements and acts of Mr. Necmettin Erbakan, in his capacity as chairman of Refah or as the Prime Minister elected on account of his position as the leader of his party, could incontestably be attributed to Refah. The role of a chairman, who is frequently a party's emblematic figure, is different in that respect from that of a simple member. Remarks on politically sensitive subjects or positions taken up by the chairman of a party are perceived by political institutions and by public opinion as acts reflecting the party's views, rather than his personal opinions, unless he declares that this is not the case. The Court observes on that point that Mr. Erbakan never made it clear that his statements and stances did not reflect Refah's policy or that he was only expressing his personal opinion.'[207] The Court leaves some room for personal opinions of a chairperson that would not be credited to the party, yet this should be made explicit. According to the Court, the same reasoning applies to the vice-chairman.[208] Yet it is more nuanced about other party members: 'Moreover, the Court considers that, inasmuch as the acts and remarks of the other Refah members who were MPs or held local government posts formed a whole which disclosed the party's aims and intentions and projected an image, when viewed in the aggregate, of the model of society it wished to set up, these could also be imputed to Refah. These acts or remarks were likely to influence potential voters by arousing their

[205] *Refah (Grand Chamber)*, o.c., § 101.   [206] *Refah (Grand Chamber)*, o.c., § 109.
[207] *Refah (Grand Chamber)*, o.c., § 113.   [208] *Refah (Grand Chamber)*, o.c., § 114.

hopes, expectations or fears, not because they were attributable to individuals but because they had been done or made on Refah's behalf by MPs and a mayor, all of whom had been elected on a Refah platform. Such acts and speeches were potentially more effective than abstract forms of words written in the party's constitution and programme in achieving any unlawful ends. The Court considers that such acts and speeches are imputable to a party unless it distances itself from them. But a short time later Refah presented those responsible for these acts and speeches as candidates for important posts, such as member of parliament or mayor of a large city, and distributed one of the offending speeches to its local branches to serve as material for the political training of its members. Before the proceedings to dissolve Refah were instituted no disciplinary action was taken within the party against those who had made the speeches concerned on account of their activities or public statements and Refah never criticized their remarks. The Court accepts the Turkish Constitutional Court's conclusion on this point to the effect that Refah had decided to expel those responsible for the acts and speeches concerned in the hope of avoiding dissolution and that the decision was not made freely, as the decisions of leaders of associations should be if they are to be recognized under Article 11 . . .'[209] The first part of this statement is somewhat ambiguous: it suggests that isolated statements that are at odds with the general image a party represents cannot be a basis for dissolution, but this is different when there are several and they coincide in the message they convey. Then a different and much clearer criterion is put forward: statements of individual members are imputable to the party unless it distances itself from them. Moreover, this distancing must be spontaneous. Refah did in fact expel three MPs, yet the Court refused to take this into account since it happened only after the institution of the party closure proceedings.

Three dissenting judges in the Chamber judgment in the *Refah* case proposed a stricter burden of proof when party closure is not based on the programme, but on individual statements: 'Whereas here the grounds relied on . . . relate not to the programme and activities of the political party itself but rather to actions or statements of individual leaders or members of the party, we consider that particularly convincing and compelling reasons must be shown to justify a decision to dissolve the entire party. This is all the more so where, as in the present case, the acts or statements complained of were not linked in terms of time or place but were isolated events occurring in very different contexts over a period covering some six years and in certain cases long before Refah came to power.'[210]

Moreover, the Venice Guidelines put forward a much stricter criterion than that used by the European Court of Human Rights in *Refah*: 'A political party

---

[209] *Refah (Grand Chamber)*, o.c., § 115.
[210] *Refah (Chamber)*, o.c., Joint Dissenting Opinion of Judges Fuhrmann, Loucaides, and Sir Nicolas Bratza.

as a whole cannot be held responsible for the individual behaviour of its members not authorised by the party within the framework of political/public and party activities' (§ 4). The Explanatory Report states: 'Any restrictive measure taken against a political party on the basis of the behaviour of its members should be supported by evidence that he or she acted with the support of the party in question or that such behaviour was the result of the party's programme or political aims. In the case that these links are missing or cannot be established the responsibility should fall entirely on the party member.'[211] In the view of the Venice Commission, it is for the prosecutor or the party suing for dissolution to prove that individual views are imputable to the party. In the *Refah* perspective, the burden of proof is on the party, and the only acceptable kind of evidence is evidence that it spontaneously distanced itself from the views of the members.

Finally, the Parliamentary Assembly of the Council of Europe stated in its Recommendation 1308 (2002) on 'Restrictions on political parties in the Council of Europe Member States' that: 'a party cannot be held responsible for the action taken by its members if such action is contrary to its statute or activities'.[212] This view resembles that in the *Refah* case in that as a rule, a party is responsible for action by members. Yet it differs from it in that proof of the opposite does not require explicit distancing, but rather reference to the party statute or 'activities'. This difference is crucial: under this rule, it would not have been possible to hold the Refah Party responsible for individual statements going against its statute, which explicitly supported the principle of secularism.

4.3.4.3 Last Resort?

If one accepts that party closure is a very far-reaching measure, and that it should be used with caution, this may lead to the conclusion that it should be a measure of last resort, to be used only when less restrictive alternatives have been exhausted or prove insufficient. The 'last resort' reasoning is one that is not automatically inherent in any proportionality test under an ordinary restriction clause (cf. above). According to one view, there is a line separating acceptable measures from unacceptable measures. This line must not necessarily be fixed, but may be determined partially by contextual circumstances. A state is not allowed to take any of the measures above that line, but is free to choose from any of the measures below the line, including more or less restrictive measures. This freedom of policy choice disappears in another view, which puts forward the criterion of the 'less restrictive alternative'. In this perspective, a state is not free to choose a more restrictive measure if a less restrictive measure is sufficient to reach the goal. Two variants may be distinguished. It may be a substantial test, implying an obligation of result for

[211] European Commission for Democracy through Law (Venice Commission), Explanatory report to guidelines on the prohibition of political parties and analogous measures, § 13.
[212] Parliamentary Assembly of the Council of Europe, Resolution 1308 (2002): Restrictions on political parties in the Council of Europe Member States, § 11, iv.

the authorities to effectively choose the least restrictive option. Or it may be a procedural test, resulting in an obligation of means: the authorities must thoroughly examine the situation and explore the different options, and make a choice based on a concern to minimize the interference with individual rights. In this version, the controlling body (e.g. the European Court of Human Rights) will not put its own idea of what is least restrictive in the place of that of the state, but only examine whether sufficient attempts were made to explore alternatives. Reasons to choose for a 'least restrictive alternative' criterion are based on an appreciation of the seriousness of the restrictive measure (in this case party closure). For example the conviction that a particularly important right is concerned, and that restrictions may have far-reaching consequences, for example not only for the individuals directly concerned, but also for others or even society in general (cf. above). One of the ways to implement a 'least restrictive alternative' criterion, is by a 'last resort' criterion, implying, first, that less restrictive measures must be available; and second, that these must be tried first, and only if they have failed to achieve the desired result, the more restrictive measure can be used.

In the *Refah* case, the European Court of Human Rights did not follow this line of reasoning. The Refah Party was prohibited amongst others for 'being a centre of anti-secular activities'. Yet in 1991, i.e. six years before the start of proceedings against Refah, the Criminal Code had been amended, so that anti-secular activities in itself no longer constituted a criminal offence under Turkish law. Yet at the same time, a political party could be prohibited for being a centre of such—legitimate— activities.[213] This is therefore a clear case where less restrictive measures were not taken. This issue was highlighted by the three dissenting judges in the Chamber judgment: 'In judging the proportionality of the measures taken to dissolve the entire party on the grounds that it was a centre of anti-secularism, we consider it to be significant that, with the repeal of section 163, the acts and statements which are relied on as evidence of this, are no longer themselves contrary to the law. In this regard we cannot accept that, in terms of Article 11, the use of the blunt instrument of dissolving a party is to be seen as a genuine alternative to the taking of steps against the individual person responsible.'[214]

Contrary to the European Court of Human Rights, the Venice Guidelines do promote a 'less restrictive alternatives' criterion: 'The prohibition or dissolution of political parties as a particularly far-reaching measure should be used with utmost restraint. Before asking the competent judicial body to prohibit or dissolve a party, governments or other state organs should assess, having regard to the situation of the country concerned, whether the party really represents a danger to the free and democratic political order or to the rights of individuals and whether other, less radical measures could prevent the said danger' (§ 5). In the Explanatory Report, some examples of less restrictive measures are

---

[213] Cf. *Refah (Chamber)*, o.c., § 79.
[214] *Refah (Chamber)*, o.c., Joint Dissenting Opinion of Judges Fuhrmann, Loucaides, and Sir Nicolas Bratza.

given: fines, 'other administrative measures', and bringing to justice individual members of the political party involved in the prohibited activities.[215]

The same view is taken by the Parliamentary Assembly of the Council of Europe in its Resolution 1308 (2002) on 'Restrictions on political parties in the Council of Europe Member States': 'as far as possible, less radical measures than dissolution should be used', and 'a political party should be banned or dissolved only as a last resort'.[216]

4.3.5 Procedural Matters

4.3.5.1 *Whose Power?*

There have been instances when a parliament has prohibited a particular political party, for example the Nazi Party NSDAP in Austria in 1947,[217] the Australian Communist Party in 1950,[218] and in the early 1990s the Communist Party in Latvia,[219] Ukraine,[220] and Byelorussia (in 1991, but lifted in 1993). This is somewhat problematic in the sense that a parliament is by definition a political body, composed mostly of representatives of political parties. Hence a party closure by parliament means that the decision is taken by 'competitors', which gives at least an impression of partiality. With respect to a very strong rights-restrictive measure such as the prohibition of a political party, such an impression is to be avoided. Hence it is preferable to limit the role of the parliament to the enactment of a law laying down the criteria for party closure in general terms, and to leave the application of these criteria to specific parties in the hands of the judiciary.

For the same reasons, it is not satisfactory to leave party closure in the hands of the executive power. This is, for example, the case in France, where the dissolution of a political party (as of any other association) is pronounced by decree of the President of the Republic adopted at a meeting with the Cabinet. This can be contested before the Council of State (the highest administrative court).[221] In Russia, the Communist Party was banned by presidential decree

---

[215] European Commission for Democracy through Law (Venice Commission), Explanatory report to guidelines on the prohibition of political parties and analogous measures, § 15.

[216] Parliamentary Assembly of the Council of Europe, Resolution 1308 (2002): Restrictions on political parties in the Council of Europe Member States, § 11, iii and v.

[217] Article 1 Verbotsgesetz 1947.

[218] Communist Party Dissolution Act 1950. This Act was invalidated by the Australian High Court: *Australian Communist Party v Commonwealth* (1951) 83 CLR 1.

[219] This party was declared anticonstitutional by a decision of 23 August 1991 of the Supreme Council (Parliament). See *Ždanoka v Latvia* ECHR (2004), § 19.

[220] The Communist Party of Ukraine was banned by decree of the Presidium of the Verkhovna Rada, a permanent body of the Ukrainian Parliament, in 1991. In 2001, this ban was invalidated by the Ukrainian Constitutional Court (A. Trochev, 'Ukraine: Constitutional Court invalidates ban on Communist Party' (2003) 1 *International Journal of Constitutional Law* 534).

[221] Act of 10 January 1936 (several times amended on combat groups and private militias. For an excellent discussion of this law and its applications, see P. Esplugas, 'L'interdiction des partis politiques' (1998) 36 *Revue française de Droit constitutionnel* 675.

in 1991.[222] In Germany, the system is such, that ordinary associations can be subject to administrative dissolution by the Minister of the Interior, but political parties can only be dissolved by the Constitutional Court. This is called the 'party privilege'.[223] As a result, many associations are prohibited,[224] but until now only two political parties have been prohibited (cf. above). Several states leave less restrictive measures than party closure, such as the refusal of registration[225] or the temporary suspension of activities of a political party,[226] in the hands of the executive.

The Venice Commission's Guidelines on Prohibition and Dissolution of Political Parties and Analogous Measures provide in § 7: 'The prohibition or dissolution of a political party should be decided by the Constitutional court or other appropriate judicial body in a procedure offering all guarantees of due process, openness and a fair trial.'

For less restrictive measures than party closure, it may be necessary to at least provide for judicial supervision of the decisions that may be taken by an administrative body. The Inter-American Commission on Human Rights held that the protection of political rights was not guaranteed under Peruvian law, because the National Elections Board, competent for the registration of lists of candidates for the National Congress, is a non-judicial body, whose decisions are not subject to review or control of any kind. In the Commission's opinion, 'recourse to specialized electoral judges or members of the judiciary, or any other effective recourse, is essential to protect the rights set forth in the Convention, including the rights to political participation'.[227]

4.3.5.2 Whose Initiative?

Whereas it is not desirable to leave the decision to outlaw a political party in the hands of a political body, the legislative and the executive may nevertheless play

---

[222] This ban was upheld as far as the central party organs were concerned by the Russian Constitutional Court in a Judgment of 30 November 1992.

[223] The German Constitutional Court is reluctant to qualify small groups with little activity as political parties. Those are considered ordinary associations, without the party privilege. For example, in 1994 the Court dismissed two applications for the prohibition of two right-wing extremist parties: the Free German Workers' Party and the National List, on the ground that these were not political parties, hence their prohibition was not the competence of the Court, but of the Executive: BVerfG, Judgments of 17 November 1994, 2 BvB 1/93 and 3/93, *BverfGE* 91, 262 and 276; W. Wietschel, 'Unzulässige Parteiverbotsanträge wegen Nichtvorliegens der Parteieigenschaft' (1996) *ZRP* 208; J. Wise, 'Dissent and the Militant Democracy: The German Constitution and the Banning of the Free German Workers Party' (1998) 5 *U Chi L Sch Roundtable* 301.

[224] Between 1951 and 1995, at least 350 associations were prohibited. Amongst them 30 that can be characterized as right-wing extremist (J. van Donselaer, *De staat paraat? De bestrijding van extreem-rechts in West-Europa* (The Hague: Babylon-DeGeus, 1995), 119.

[225] Cf. above, footnote 65.

[226] E.g. in Denmark, Kyrghyzstan, and Lithuania (information from European Commission for Democracy through Law (Venice Commission), 'Prohibition of political parties and analogous measures', Report adopted by the Commission at its 35th Plenary Meeting, Venice, 12–13 June 1998).

[227] Inter-American Commission on Human Rights, Report No. 119/99, *Susana Higuchi Miyagawa v Peru*, 6 October 1999, § 57.

a role as initiators of a procedure leading to party closure.[228] In a 2003 Opinion, the Venice Commission advised that 'in order to achieve a thorough and comprehensive examination of a possible case at an early stage, the decision to initiate court proceedings aiming at prohibition or dissolution of a political party or other political organization should be made, not by the Security Service, but by a political instance such as the parliament, the government or a minister. Requests to prohibit or dissolve other organizations should be made by the public prosecutor or by an administrative agency, which is independent of the Security Service.'[229] Hence, in the eyes of the Venice Commission, it is advisable to leave the initiative to a political body, rather than to the public prosecutor. Yet in the Turkish cases, the European Court of Human Rights did not object to the initiative of the public prosecutor as initiator of party closure proceedings. Would it be acceptable to give individual citizens the right to initiate closure proceedings? It seems that such a broad access might easily lead to abusive procedures. Given the importance of the freedom of association of political parties, party closure proceedings with a very low threshold will likely constitute a disproportionate restriction of that freedom.

4.3.5.3 Procedure

It hardly needs mentioning that a procedure that may lead to a serious restriction of fundamental rights, such as party closure, must respect the most stringent standards of the right to a fair trial. These standards are soundly established in international human rights conventions (e.g. Article 14 ICCPR, Article 6 ECHR, Article 8 ACHR), and have been developed in some detail by their supervising bodies, as well as by domestic laws and case law in many states. Moreover, the highest standard of care and of respect for human rights must also apply during the investigation preceding the trial and with respect to the gathering of evidence.

Recently, a combined initiative of the German Parliament and Government to ban the extremist right National Democratic Party of Germany (NPD), failed as a result of shortcomings of this type. In March 2003, the Constitutional Court halted the case because of the high number of spies in the NPD's

---

[228] For example in Spain, the government and the minsterio fiscal have standing to apply for a party ban before the Constitutional Court; they must do so at the request of either chamber of Parliament (Article. 10(1) Statute on Political Parties of 27 June 2002, cf. above). In Germany, a case concerning the prohibition of a political party can be brought before the Constitutional Court only by a chamber of the federal Parliament (*Bundestag* or *Bundesrat*), by the federal government, or by the government of a *Land* (a federated entity) if the party operates only on the *Land* level (Article 43 Law on the Bundesverfassungsgericht).

[229] European Commission for Democracy through Law (Venice Commission), Opinion No. 241/2003 on the draft law on prohibition of extremist organizations and unions in Georgia, adopted by the Venice Commission at its 55th Plenary Session (Venice, 13–14 June 2003), CDL-AD (2003) 11 rev, § 23.

190

Eva Brems

ruling bodies.[230] Apparently there were as many as twenty in the party's national and regional leaderships alone.[231]

4.3.6 Consequences of Party Closure

The measure of party closure is usually accompanied by a number of other measures. Some of these are designed to guarantee the effectiveness of the measure (e.g. the prohibition to continue the activities of the prohibited party in a new party), others are simply additional sanctions (e.g. criminal sanctions for party leaders). Most of those measures have a hybrid nature, i.e. they may be defended as necessary to reach the goal aimed at by the party closure (e.g. stop the risk caused to democracy by the propaganda or activities of the party); yet depending on the circumstances, they may be too broad or too stringent for this purpose. Some of those measures will be examined below in light of international human rights standards.

4.3.6.1 Prohibition to Continue the Activities of the Prohibited Party

When a party is prohibited because it causes an actual or potential harm, it seems essential for the effectiveness of this measure to associate it with a prohibition to continue the activities of this party, for example by creating a new party. In particular in Turkey,[232] experience shows that when a party is prohibited, its leaders and members will want to create a new party with the same goals. Hence, this accessory measure exists in many states that provide for party closure.[233]

The necessity of this measure is pointed out by the Parliamentary Assembly of the Council of Europe. In its Resolution 1344 (2003) on the 'Threat posed to democracy by extremist parties and movements in Europe', it invites states 'to monitor, and if necessary to prevent, the reconstitution of dissolved parties or movements under another form or name'.[234] The European Commission

---

[230] BverfG, 18 March 2003 (2003) *NJW* 1577. On the NPD case, see K. Groh, 'Der NPD-Verbotsantrag—eine Reanimation der streitbaren Demokratie?' (2000) *ZRP* 500; H. Meier, 'In der Nachfolge der NSDAP? Das SRP-Verbotsurteil und das Verfahren gegen die NPD' (2003) *Blätter für deutsche und internationale Politik* (Frankfurt: Suhrkamp, 2003), at 485; and C. Leggewie and H. Meier (eds.), *Verbot der NPD oder Mit Rechtsradikalen leben?* (Frankfurt: Suhrkamp Verlag, 2002).

[231] T. Wild, 'State spies prevent NPD ban,' *Searchlight*, May 2003.

[232] For example, among the parties whose case came before the European Court of Human Rights, DEP was the successor of HEP (cf. above). The dissolved Refah (Welfare) Party was succeeded by the Fazilet (Virtue) Party, which was also dissolved by the Turkish Constitutional Court in 2001.

[233] E.g. Article 33 of the German Law on Political Parties prohibits 'ersatz organizations' of parties that have been prohibited by application of Article 21(2) Constitution. A new party will not be considered as an 'erszatz organization' if it clearly renunciates the antidemocratic goals of the prohibited party. As a result, despite the prohibition of the KPD in 1956, a new Communist Party (DKP) was created in West Germany in 1968, and was allowed to operate (H. Meier, *Parteiverbote und demokratische Republik* (Baden-Baden: Nomos, 1993), at 220).

[234] Parliamentary Assembly of the Council of Europe, Resolution 1344 (2003), o.c.

against Racism and Intolerance likewise assumes that the prohibition to create organizations promoting racism includes a prohibition on maintaining or reconstituting a group that has been prohibited.[235]

This may extend to the use of symbols, emblems, and the like. For example in 2004, the Turkish Constitutional Court issued a warning to the Happiness Party (Saadet Partisi) for using the symbol SP, used by the dissolved Socialist Party.[236]

4.3.6.2 Confiscation of the Assets of the Party

After the dissolution of the Refah party, its assets were automatically transferred to the Treasury, in accordance with Section 107(1) of the Turkish Law No. 2820 on the regulation of political parties. This was mentioned in the European Court of Human Rights' assessment of the proportionality of the interference with Refah's freedom of association: 'In view of the low value of Refah's assets, their transfer to the Treasury can have no bearing on the proportionality of the interference in issue.'[237] This suggests that the measure might be considered disproportionate when a party has significant assets.

In an opinion of the Venice Commission, which concerned Armenian legislation that provided for dissolution on formal grounds, it rejected the idea that as a consequence of the liquidation of a political party, its property should be transferred to the state: 'It should be up to each party to determine in its Charter the fate of party property following liquidation or, failing a provision in the Charter, this should be up to a decision by the party conference.'[238]

It may be concluded that confiscation of the assets of a dissolved political party should be seen as an additional sanction. When dissolution is based on formal grounds, this sanction is almost certainly not justified. Yet in other cases, this additional sanction may be appropriate, depending on the circumstances. Hence, when this sanction is provided for by the legislator, it is good practice not to make it automatic upon party dissolution, but rather to leave some discretion to the judges.[239]

4.3.6.3 Loss of Seats in Parliament and in Other Elected Bodies

When a political party is dissolved, its elected Members of Parliament need not necessarily lose their seats in Parliament. After all, while elected on a party list,

---

[235] European Commission against Racism and Intolerance, General Policy Recommendation No. 7 on national legislation to combat racism and racial discrimination, adopted by the ECRI on 13 December 2002, explanatory memorandum, § 43.
[236] Constitutional Court Turkey, 10 February 2004, *Resmi Gazzete*, 13 March 2004, 25401, available in CODICES database: www.codices.coe.int.
[237] *Refah (Grand Chamber)*, o.c., § 134.
[238] European Commission for Democracy through Law (Venice Commission), Opinion No. 197 on the law of the Republic of Armenia on political parties, adopted by the Commission at its 54th Plenary Session (Venice, 14–15 March 2003), CDL-AD (2003) 5, § 8.
[239] For example in Germany, confiscation of the goods of the party after prohibition is possible, but not automatic (Article 46 Law on the Bundesverfassungsgericht).

they were elected as individual representatives of the people. They may continue to serve as Members of Parliament without party affiliation, or join another political party. Under Turkish law, loss of a seat in Parliament is provided for as an additional sanction for some Members of Parliament: according to Article 84 of the Turkish Constitution, 'The term of office of a member of parliament whose words and deeds have, according to the Constitutional Court's judgment, led to the dissolution of his party, shall end on the date when that judgment is published in the *Official Gazette*...' After the dissolution of the Refah party, only five of its Members of Parliament temporarily forfeited their parliamentary office. The 152 remaining MPs continued to sit in Parliament and pursued their political careers normally. The European Court of Human Rights held that this measure was not disproportionate.[240]

Yet when the loss of seats in Parliament is an automatic consequence of the dissolution of a political party, this is in the eyes of the European Court of Human Rights a disproportionate measure in violation of the right to participate in elections (Article 3 Protocol 1 ECHR). Such was the Court's finding in the *Sadak* case, upon a complaint of thirteen MPs of the dissolved DEP.[241] At that time, Turkish law provided for the loss of seats in Parliament as an automatic measure. The Court held unanimously that the restriction of Article 3 Protocol 1 was disproportionate, referring to the 'extreme harshness' of the measure, which occurred automatically and regardless of the personal activities of the individuals.[242]

4.3.6.4 *Loss of Political Rights of Party Leaders, MPs, or Candidates*

The United Nations Human Rights Committee dealt in 1981 with an individual application by five Uruguayan citizens, who had lost their right to vote and to be elected for a term of fifteen years as a result of having been candidates on the list for the 1966 and 1971 elections of Marxist political groups that were later declared illegal by a decree issued by a new government in 1973. An Act of 1976 provided this sanction for all candidates of these parties for these elections. The government of Uruguay attempted to justify this measure on the basis of the powers of derogation they have in a state of emergency. But even in a state of emergency, derogative measures must respect a proportionality requirement. In this case, the Committee did not accept that valid reasons for derogation existed, but stated that 'even on the assumption that there exists a situation of emergency in Uruguay, the Human Rights Committee does not see what ground could be adduced to support the contention that, in order to restore peace and order, it was necessary to deprive all citizens, who as members of

---

[240] *Refah (Grand Chamber)*, o.c., §§ 133–34.
[241] *Sadak and Others v Turkey* ECHR (2002), Reports 2002-IV. The dissolution of the DEP was later found to be a violation of Article 11 ECHR: *Dicle for the Democratic Party of Turkey (DEP) v Turkey* ECHR (2002).   [242] *Sadak*, o.c, § 38.

certain political groups had been candidates in the elections of 1966 and 1971, of any political right for a period as long as 15 years. This measure applies to everyone, without distinction as to whether he sought to promote his political opinions by peaceful means or by resorting to, or advocating the use of, violent means. The Government of Uruguay has failed to show that the interdiction of any kind of political dissent is required in order to deal with the alleged emergency situation and pave the way back to political freedom.'[243] The reason why the Human Rights Committee judged that this was a human rights violation resides not so much in the nature of the measure, but rather in the long term of the suspension of political rights as well as in its blanket application disregarding the specific aspects of each individual case.

An example of a provision that leaves room for those specific aspects, is Article 69 § 8 of the Turkish Constitution: 'Members and leaders whose declarations and activities lead to the dissolution of a political party may not be founder members, leaders or auditors of another political party for a period of five years from the date on which the reasoned decision to dissolve the party is published in the *Official Gazette*...' On this basis, the suspension of political rights was pronounced for five leading members of the Refah party. The European Court of Human Rights held that this was not a disproportionate measure.[244]

In *Ždanoka v Latvia*, the European Court of Human Rights accepted even a much broader and permanent loss of political rights.[245] After two attempted *coups d'état*, a decision of the 'Supreme Council' (the legislative power) of Latvia in 1991 declared the Communist Party of Latvia unconstitutional and dissolved it. A law of 1995 on the parliamentary elections stipulated that persons who actively participated in this political party after 13 January 1991 (the date of the first attempted coup) could not be candidates for the elections. The application of this rule was challenged in this case, by a woman who as a Member of Parliament had held an important position within the prohibited party, but who had not had an active role in the coups, as separate investigations had shown. Whereas the Chamber had found a violation of Article 11 ECHR and Article 3 Protocol 1, the Grand Chamber ruled otherwise, granting a wide margin of appreciation to the State, in light of the 'very special historico-political context'.[246] If found that the intention of the Latvian legislature was motivated by prevention rather than by punishment,[247] and that the acts of a party are imputable to its members (particularly the leading figures) unless they distance themselves from those acts.[248] The Court did however warn the

---

[243] Human Rights Committee, Communication No. 34/1978, *Jorge Landinelli Silva et al. v Uruguay*, Views of 8 April 1981, § 8.4.   [244] *Refah (Grand Chamber)*, o.c., §§ 133–34.

[245] *Ždanoka v Latvia* ECHR Grand Chamber (2006), not reported.

[246] *Ždanoka v Latvia* ECHR Grand Chamber (2006), o.c., §§ 121 and 133–34.

[247] *Ždanoka v Latvia* ECHR Grand Chamber (2006), o.c., § 122.

[248] *Ždanoka v Latvia* ECHR Grand Chamber (2006), o.c., § 123.

Latvian Parliament that it should keep the measure under constant review, 'with a view to bringing it to an early end'.[249] This suggests that the Court does not fully accept the permanent character of the measure.

4.3.6.5 Criminal Sanctions for the Party Members or Leaders

Article 4 CERD not only obliges states to prohibit and declare illegal organizations that promote or incite racial discrimination, but also requires them to recognize participation in such organizations or activities as an offence punishable by law. Moreover, the dissemination of racist ideas and the incitement to racial discrimination must also be declared an offence. In a racist political party, it is likely that most party leaders have committed this offence. The same requirements are found in the United Nations Model Legislation Against Racial Discrimination,[250] which moreover establishes a presumption against directors or executive officers (or persons in an equivalent position) in the organization, that they were guilty of an offence of racial discrimination.[251] This implies a shift of the burden of proof: these persons have to provide evidence to the effect that either they did not know about the racial discrimination or did not consent to it, or that they acted with due diligence to take the steps available to them which might have prevented it. Hence, when such legislation is enacted, it seems normal that a procedure for party closure against a racist party would be accompanied by a procedure against the party leaders.

When the measure of party closure concerns a party that is not racist, there are no comparable international texts. Hence, the proportionality of criminal sanctions against members or leaders of the party is to be evaluated in the light of the facts of each case.

4.4 CONCLUSION

In the area of political freedoms, party closure is one of the most restrictive measures to be practiced by democratic states. International human rights law does not consider party closure as a human rights violation per se. The clearest legal criteria concerning the conditions under which party closure may be an acceptable restriction of the freedom of political association, may be found in the case law of the European Court of Human Rights. Yet useful elements may be deduced also from other sources, such as the work of the UN Human Rights Committee and CERD Committee, as well as recommendations and resolutions of the Parliamentary Assembly of the Council of Europe, the texts of the

---

[249] *Ždanoka v Latvia* ECHR Grand Chamber (2006), o.c., § 135.
[250] Cf. above. This text was prepared in 1996 in the context of the Third Decade to Combat Racism and Racial Discrimination, under the auspices of the Secretary General of the United Nations, on the basis of an analysis of domestic and international provisions, in order to serve as a guideline for national legislation.   [251] Ibid, §§ 32–33.

European Commission Against Racism and Intolerance, and the rules and rulings of the Venice Commission. Even within the context of a single organization such as the Council of Europe, different bodies apply different standards in this field. Moreover, research about the rules concerning party closure and their application in domestic law reveals examples of good practices, alongside practices that are hard to reconcile with international norms, as these are developing presently.

5

The Role of Political Rights in the Democratization of Central and Eastern Europe

Jiří Přibáň and Wojciech Sadurski

5.1 INTRODUCTION

The communist totalitarian state and its legal system seemed to contradict the very principle of the rule of law. The enforcement of law, both according to legal rules and arbitrary political interests, was a typical characteristic of communist regimes, which systematically violated the principles of legal generality, non-retroactivity, and in particular, of equality before the law. Nevertheless, these regimes underwent significant changes in the course of their historical development. Their character changed and communist governments gradually shifted away from the practice of open political terror, common in the early 1950s, to that of public noninterference in political affairs in the 1970s and 1980s, accompanied by a limited private autonomy and the socialist consumerist lifestyle. The totalitarian state thus eliminated any possibility of *polis* but gradually recognized the limited autonomy of *oikos*.

Political terror had not vanished from the region of Central and Eastern Europe (CEE) by the 1970s and 1980s, but was limited and exercised only against a tiny minority of dissident groups and human rights activists. This 'limited use of terror'—limited, that is to say, in its intensity and social targets—nevertheless had a significant political function because it reminded the population that it had to ritually approve the system as the instruments of political violence and that open repression still existed. At this stage, the CEE communist systems had a modicum of legal stability and the arbitrary use of political violence was not their dominant mode of governance.

The post-1989 political and legal transformations did not therefore have to confront openly repressive and violent systems. Rather, they were faced with a political and legal structure giving the state ultimate social control and which treated citizens as powerless and entirely dependent entities. This unbalanced relationship between the state and the individual citizen needed to be changed by incorporating those political rights necessary for the establishment of democratic elections, decision-making, and control. The creation of such catalogues of political rights in postcommunist legal systems was meant to constitute the normative and operative framework for the liberal democratic system.

Political rights, therefore, have to be perceived both as a system of rules protecting the individual citizen or different groups from interference by the state, and also as a structural precondition of the liberal democratic system. The first, traditional, aspect of political rights refers to individual or collective autonomy and the limits of democratic political power. It recalls the general principle that *everything is permitted that is not prohibited by law* which, if vigorously upheld and enforced by independent courts, has always been the most effective remedy against all forms of political oppression and despotic governmental tendencies. Political rights guarantee private autonomy and limit the extent to which power-holders within the state can determine the lives of individual citizens. They represent juridico-institutional limits imposed on a government's goal of enforcing its own political interests.

The second aspect emphasizes the regulative function of political rights within the democratic political system and the participation of citizens in public political life. Political rights thus protect the interests of individuals but also open avenues for their involvement in political life. Most of these rights are participatory; they are individual rights, the use of which results in the formation of a democratic political unity. At the same time, it is vitally important that right-holders have the power to enforce them in their personal and political lives. Political rights empower individuals and provide them with access to democratic decision-making and the redistribution of social and political resources. Their minimum structural precondition is that of courts independent from government and ready to implement specific political rights against government wishes. The process of establishing political rights cannot thus be isolated from structural and institutional reform of the legal system. Substantive political rights have to be synchronized with judicial reform and implementation of the due process of law.[1]

In this chapter we do not claim exhaustively to have covered all significant developments regarding political rights in the CEE but will focus on what we consider to be the central transformations: central both in terms of their importance to the overall political systems of the countries in question and in terms of their contested, controversial nature. We will show these developments as emerging within a context affected by two principal factors: the legacy of communist systems and pressure from the outside, in particular from the European Community/ European Union. This 'Europeanization' factor can be seen as having provided

---

[1] See V. Ganev, 'Judicial Independence and Post-Totalitarian Politics' (1996) 3 *Parker School of Law Journal of East European Law* 227.

crucial political resources in support of those local elites and social movements who were then convinced that the only available path towards democratization was to emulate (what was seen to be) the clear and correct model of establishing citizens' political rights within liberal, constitutional democracies. The prospect of a 'return to Europe', operationalized via the specific goal of accession to the European Union (EU), provided political actors in the CEE with a set of incentives, templates, and aims: incentives, through the mechanism of so-called 'conditionality'; templates in the form of the dominant models of political rights; and aims encapsulated in the much-coveted prospect of accession to the EU.

5.2 DEMOCRATIZATION, LEGAL TRANSFORMATIONS, AND HUMAN RIGHTS IN POSTCOMMUNIST COUNTRIES: AN OVERVIEW

Postcommunist legal transformations were significantly influenced by the specific forms of political negotiation and power transfers occurring in individual countries of the former Soviet bloc in the late 1980s and early 1990s. Specifically, the mechanism of round-table talks facilitated the transformation of communist systems into liberal democracies. Different models, and the role of round-table talks in the former communist countries, must therefore be considered in any analysis of political and legal changes in the CEE in the 1990s.

In some countries round-table talks extended over a longer period. Here the talks played a central role because they facilitated communication between a communist government and the political opposition, recognized as a legitimate partner. In other countries this form of political negotiation was employed only after an outbreak of public protest and therefore within a much wider and faster revolutionary process. Here, because they were arranged only after communist governments had been challenged by revolutionary crowds, round-table talks had a much more limited impact on the nature of postcommunist constitutional and legal transformations.[2]

Poland and Hungary were more liberal and reform-oriented than other communist states and undoubtedly fall within the first of these two groups, i.e. those in which round-table talks played a central role. These two countries experienced evolutionary and gradual, rather than revolutionary and sudden, political change. Their respective political transition periods were informed, to a greater extent than countries in the second group, by ideas of negotiation and political bargaining. The gradual transfer of power thus facilitated was commonly described as a process of regulated and self-limiting revolution,[3] or even

---

[2] For a general overview, see K. von Beyme, *Transition to Democracy in Eastern Europe* (London: Macmillan, 1996).

[3] See, for instance, J. Přibáň, *Dissidents of Law: On the 1989 velvet revolutions, legitimations, fictions of legality and contemporary version of the social contract* (Aldershot: Ashgate, 2002), at 88–90; A. Arato, *Civil Society, Constitution, and Legitimacy* (Lanham, MD: Rowman and Littlefield, 2000).

'refolution',[4] impacting deeply on the character of constitutional and legal transformations, and the perception of the rule of law in the process of political change. For instance, the Hungarian political *rendszervaltozas* (regime change) occurred entirely through constitutional acts and democratic procedures, and sought to avoid political divisions and to establish a new national unity. It was a transformation of communism into liberal democracy entirely shaped and controlled by the existing constitutional and legal framework. Similarly, Poland's constitutional transformation took place gradually, with the communist Constitution of 1952 first amended by the interim 'Small Constitution' of 1993, and its comprehensive redesign postponed until enactment of the 1997 Constitution.

Round-table negotiations in Hungary and Poland proceeded according to specific rules somewhat resembling the procedures and principles of the rule of law. The Hungarian transformation was depicted as a *constitutional amendment* based on the idea of legislated-for regime change.[5] Although politically much more dynamic and less consensual than the Hungarian post-1989 changes, the Polish transformation can also be seen as following this 'amendment' model.

By contrast, the political and constitutional impact of round-table talks was much weaker in both Czechoslovakia and the German Democratic Republic, which underwent more radical revolutionary transformation. In these countries, round-table talks channelled a revolutionary situation and guaranteed the peaceful character of the revolutionary change. Until the last minute, the Czechoslovak and East German communist leaderships remained steadfastly committed to the neo-Stalinist form of political rule, including the practice of persecuting political opponents, continuing to enact repressive legislation and orchestrating political trials. Unlike Hungary and Poland, Czechoslovakia and East Germany experienced high political tension and revolutionary politics. The idea of the self-limiting revolution was weakened, opening a much greater space for the birth of a radical politics of decommunization and alternative interpretations of basic and political rights.[6]

5.2.1 Democratic Constitutionalism, Rights and Retrospective Justice

Round-table talks and the notion of self-limiting or legalistic revolution naturally raise issues of the temporal emergence of the rule of law, legal continuity, and

---

[4] M. Brzezinski, H. Hausmaniger, and K.L. Scheppele, 'Constitutional "Refolution" in the Ex-Communist World: The Rule of Law' (1997) 12 *American University Journal of International Law and Policy* 87.

[5] See P. Paczolay, 'The New Hungarian Constitutional State: Challenges and Perspectives', in A. E. Dick Howard (ed.), *Constitution Making in Eastern Europe* (Baltimore, MD: John Hopkins University Press, 1993), at 21.

[6] R. Dahrendorf, *Reflections on the Revolution in Europe* (New York: Times Books, 1990). See also J. Přibáň, 'Constitutional Justice and Retroactivity of Laws in Postcommunist Central Europe',

retrospective legislation in postcommunist societies. The idea of a revolution delimited and shaped by the existing constitutional and legal system was understood as helping to secure political stability and legal certainty and was accordingly supported by all parties to round-table talks in Poland and Hungary. It contributed fundamentally to the establishment of democratic institutions, constitutional separation of powers, and an independent system of justice protecting constitutional rights and freedoms. Constitutional transformations benefited from this idea because they could use the negotiated political consensus of round-table talks and because they could implement principles of democratic constitutionalism, human rights, and the rule of law—political goals shared by all parties to the talks.[7]

This shared understanding of political and legal transformation resulted in the persistence of the communist constitutional framework both in Hungary and Poland, whose constitutions' substantive and formal character changed only gradually, after democratically elected governments and independent judiciaries had been established. Catalogues of human rights were incorporated into these emerging constitutional systems as a result of round-table talks, despite the fact that the deployment of communist legal systems to specify the new systems of democratic constitutionalism, was truly 'squaring the circle'.[8]

The goal of reconstructing human rights based democratic constitutionalism was accompanied by an examination of breaches of human rights, political crimes, and injustices committed by communist officials, often with the backing of the wider communist government and justice systems. The prospective programme of creating a system of liberal democracy and human rights protection was thus mirrored by the task of addressing past crimes and injustices.

Some politicians, lawyers, and legal scholars supported the notion that the very occurrence of negotiations and round-table talks already indicated the existence of the democratic rule of law so that discriminatory or retrospective laws dealing with communist political crimes and injustices would not be justifiable.[9] Retrospective legislation or adjudication would, it was argued, amount to the breach of basic constitutional rights and due process of law. The idea that the system already existed at a time when it was actually being negotiated and its consensual agreement sought by communists and opposition made it much harder, later, to apply retrospective measures in dealing with past human rights abuses.

in J. Přibáň, P. Roberts, and J. Young (eds.), *Systems of Justice in Transition: Postcommunist Experiences in Central Europe since 1989* (Aldershot: Ashgate, 2003), 29, at 38–40.

[7] See G. Casper, 'European Convergence' (1991) 58 *The University of Chicago Law Review* 442.

[8] A. Arato, 'Dilemmas Arising from the Power to Create Constitutions in Eastern Europe' (1993) 14 *Cardozo Law Review* 674.

[9] In Poland, one of the supporters of this idea of the 'democratic revolution', which rules out any chance of retrospective legislation as unjust and contradicting the existing rule of law, is Ewa Letowska, the first Ombudsperson of Poland and currently a judge on the Constitutional Tribunal. For her general views, see E. Letowska and J. Letowski, *Poland: Towards the Rule of Law* (Warsaw: Scholar, 1996).

Different dynamics of political transformation therefore had a fundamental impact on the implementation, protection, and, especially, the 'reading' of different human rights principles in postcommunist countries.[10] While the rule-bound, round-table transformations supported unconditional implementation of the principle of equal treatment of all citizens before the law, revolutionary change opened greater space for retrospective legislation as well as both punitive and restorative historical justice. The Polish Constitutional Tribunal ruled that departure from the principle *lex retro non agit* would be authorized only in exceptional legal circumstances,[11] and the Hungarian Constitutional Court declared retrospective justice unconstitutional as an infringement of the principle of legal security and therefore of the rule of law.[12] However, the German prosecution of communist political crimes rehabilitated retrospective and supra-positive law based on Radbruch's formula in order to avoid obstacles of legal formalism.[13] Similarly, the Czech Constitutional Court ruled that, despite formal legal and constitutional continuity, there was substantive discontinuity between the pre-1989 communist totalitarian and the post-1989 liberal democratic legal systems.[14]

The Czech and German interpretations of legal and political changes after 1989 contradict those provided by the Hungarian Constitutional Court, and expand the range of legal possibilities in dealing with aspects of the past, such as lustration law, natural restitution of property to individuals, or public access to secret police files.[15] Hungarian and Polish constitutional adjudication clearly favoured the principle of unconditional equality before the law. This, as a cornerstone of the human rights based rule of law, ruled out extraordinary legal and discriminatory measures against former communist officials. On the other hand, Czech or German legislative and judicial approaches to dealing with past crimes and injustices have often preferred an alternative interpretation of the equality principle, according to which equality before the law means that no person stands above the law and all crimes are punishable, even

[10] See further A. J. McAdams (ed.), *Transitional Justice and the Rule of Law in New Democracies* (Notre Dame, IN: University of Notre Dame Press, 1997).

[11] Judgment of the Constitutional Tribunal of the Republic of Poland S 6/91, 25 September 1991, Orzecznictwo Tryb. Konst. 290, at 294.

[12] Judgment of the Constitutional Court of Hungary No. 11 of 1992, (III.5) AB.

[13] See R. Alexy, 'A Defense of Radbruch's Formula', in D. Dyzenhaus (ed.), *Recrafting the Rule of Law* (Oxford: Hart Publishing, 1999), at 15.

[14] Judgment of the Constitutional Court of the Czech Republic, No. 19/93.

[15] Laws prohibiting former communist officials and secret police agents from holding office in the new democratic administration were generally much more restrictive in Germany and the Czech Republic. Similarly, the Czech Republic eventually followed the German model of making communist secret police files accessible to the public. The Parliament of the Czech Republic enacted the Act of Public Access to Files Connected to Activities of Former Secret Police, No. 140/1996, in 1996 and amended it in 2002 so that the main registers of the communist secret police would be accessible to the general public. For more on the issues mentioned in this and in the preceding paragraphs, see W. Sadurski, *Rights Before Courts: A Study of Constitutional Courts in Postcommunist States of Central and Eastern Europe* (Dordrecht: Springer, 2005), at 224–49.

if disguised as lawful acts, at the time of their commission, by unjust totalitarian laws.

5.2.2 The Human Rights Culture and its Emergence in the 1990s

Despite different priorities in reconstructing the democratic rule of law and
protection of human rights, there has been common ground in human rights
discourses in the postcommunist countries of Central and Eastern Europe. A
significant influence in this respect was exerted by political dissidents and their
use of international human rights law texts in the struggle against communist
totalitarian systems. In this regard, the 1989 revolutions can even be described
as 'rights revolutions'.[16] European and international human rights documents
took on a central role in the constitutional and legal transformations in the
CEE, being adopted to provide a normative framework for emerging liberal
democracies.

Dissidents thus won a long-term struggle for human rights by incorporating
international and European standards into reconstructed constitutional systems.
They denounced the 'socialist concept of human rights' of official communist
propaganda, which denied basic political rights, assaulted liberal democratic
values, and focused principally on the egalitarian distribution of limited social
welfare. The communist legal system was based on the notion of the individual's
duties towards the state, compensated for by socialist welfare rights, such as the
right to employment (accompanied by an individual duty to contribute to
society's wealth, translating on a practical level into a legally enforceable duty to
work), the right to housing (in effect creating a feudal system, with employees
made legally dependent on their employers for housing), access to free health care
(seriously compromised by corruption among doctors and health care execu-
tives), etc. Typically, socialist constitutions listed a great number of rights on
paper, presenting these as the socialist 'historically superior alternative' to the
Western 'bourgeois' concept of rights. Nevertheless, these rights could never
protect the individual's interests and autonomy because the very concept of
'socialist' rights was based on the supremacy of collective interests formulated by
the totalitarian state and enforced by more or less explicit constitutional clauses
prohibiting the use of rights for 'anti-socialist' purposes.

The significance of civil and political rights in the struggle against the
communist regime was enormous and international human rights documents
provided highly useful argumentative support. Moreover, as Polish legal sociologist Jacek Kurczewski has proved, civility and liberal values had always been
intrinsic to the history of political protest against the communist regime.[17]

---

[16] For a description of this concept, see C. R. Epp, *The Rights Revolution* (Chicago, IL:
University of Chicago Press, 1998).
[17] J. Kurczewski, *The Resurrection of Rights in Poland* (Oxford: Oxford University Press, 1993).

Political rights were one of the normative projects of dissent long before their culmination in the politically organized and discursively systematized demands of the Solidarnosc movement in the 1980s. Far from being mere imports from Western constitutional and political systems, arguably political rights rather represented a local political tradition 'resurrected' with the help of international human rights discourse and liberal democratic politics.

From a human rights perspective, 1989's political changes proved that basic human and political rights were inseparable from the distribution of social welfare and required to be made a fundamental pillar of subsequent constitutional transformations.[18] The constitutional rights chapter of the Hungarian Constitution was entirely revised during round-table talks in 1989. Similarly, the first democratically elected Czechoslovak Parliament enacted *The Charter of Fundamental Rights and Freedoms* as early as January 1991. The legislator effectively established the Charter as the country's ultimate legal document, stating that all other laws, including the Constitution, had to be consistent with the Charter's provisions. The Charter also tied the Czechoslovak constitutional and legal order into the international system of human rights protection: Article 10 incorporated the principle of the priority of provisions of ratified international human rights covenants over ordinary laws. Moreover, the dissident human rights discourse left its characteristic 'natural rights' and 'democratic value-oriented' mark in the emerging constitutional systems of Central and East European countries. Thus, the Czechoslovak Charter invoked the natural rights principle in its Preamble and, later, the same principle was made part of the oath of office for judges of the Czech Republic's Constitutional Court.[19]

The binding force of international human rights covenants and the principles of 'humanity' and 'human dignity' also heavily influenced an historic judgment of the Hungarian Constitutional Court abolishing capital punishment in 1990.[20] This judgment has often been criticized as a political decision, whose main purpose was to support Hungary's accession to the Council of Europe. Though its reasoning has been considered very weak in formal legal terms,[21] the judgment was undoubtedly a landmark both in establishing the commitment of constitutional justice to human rights and in signalling the extent of the Hungarian Constitutional Court's judicial activism that continued throughout

---

[18] W. Osiatynski, 'Rights in New Constitutions of East Central Europe' (1994) 26 *Columbia Human Rights Law Review* 111.

[19] See Article 85 of the Constitution of the Czech Republic enacted by the Czech Parliament in December 1992.

[20] Judgment of 24 October 1990, No. 23/1990. Discussed in L. Sólyom and G. Brunner (eds.), *Constitutional Judiciary in a New Democracy: The Hungarian Constitutional Court* (Ann Arbor, IL: University of Michigan Press, 2000), at 130–31.

[21] See W. Sadurski, 'Rights-Based Constitutional Review in Central and Eastern Europe', in T. Campbell, K. D. Ewing and A. Tomkins (eds.), *Sceptical Essays on Human Rights* (Oxford: Oxford University Press, 2001) 315, at 323–24.

the 1990s: it declared capital punishment unconstitutional, due to its arbitrary character and as a violation of certain international covenants regulating respect for human rights, including the right to life.[22] Like the Czechoslovak Charter, the Hungarian Constitutional Court indicated that 'the ideological tide was turning'[23] in Hungary in the 1990s. Under Justice Sólyom's presidency, the Court proceeded on the basis of an extraordinarily activist model for the protection of human rights, which endured until the replacement of most of the first bench of Constitutional Court judges in 1998.[24]

5.3 THE IMPACT OF 'EUROPEANIZATION' ON POLITICAL RIGHTS IN THE CEE

Changes in the dominant understandings of human rights in general and, more specifically, of political rights, as outlined in the previous section, neither occurred overnight nor in a geographical vacuum: they had a very clear point of reference encapsulated in the word 'Europe'. The 'return to Europe' rhetoric implied at least two things: that the demise of the artificial East/West division freed up possibilities for the CEE to deploy the positive consequences of hitherto Western-only democratic developments (hence the emulation aspect of Europeanization); and that the adoption of European norms was not really a matter of extrinsic pressure, but should rather be seen as primarily responding to ever-present indigenous needs which had merely been overshadowed during Soviet domination. These two themes were closely interconnected, with 'Europe' portrayed as a positive and liberating factor, but for intrinsic reasons. In this sense 'Europeanization' performed an ideological function in CEE states' domestic politics, often relieving political actors of the need to develop their own comprehensive programmes; 'Europe' also serving as an easily recognizable shorthand description of what the party or a politician stood for, referred to in the hope of eliciting a favourable response from the domestic audience. In contrast, reactions against 'Europeanization' served as rallying cries for authoritarian and nationalistic groups who used the spectre of Europe to engender fears of cosmopolitanism, loss of national traditions, and of surrender to foreign rule. In both positive and in negative terms, 'Europeanization' made a fundamental imprint on political discourse in CEE states.

---

[22] See Article 54 of the Hungarian Constitution. Its Section 1 reads: 'In the Republic of Hungary everyone has the inherent right to life and to human dignity. No one shall be arbitrarily denied of these rights.' This wording also affected the Court's ruling in the abortion law case. See C. Dupre, *Importing the Law in Post-Communist Transitions: The Hungarian Constitutional Court and the Right to Human Dignity* (Oxford: Hart Publishing, 2003), at 73.

[23] G. Fletcher, 'Searching for the Rule of Law in the Wake of Communism' (1992) 17 *Brigham Young University Law Review* 145, at 154.

[24] For more details, see Sólyom and Brunner, above, n. 20.

5.3.1 Europeanization and Conditionality

Here we focus on the impact of EU conditionality (understood as the monitoring of compliance by candidate states with EU accession criteria) on the consolidation of political rights in the CEE. Nevertheless, it is important to note that 'Europeanization' is a term with a scope exceeding the issue of EU conditionality. This is for at least two reasons. First, and most obviously, the EU is only one of a number of sources of 'conditionality' which have effected, through compliance mechanisms, the adoption of rules and standards concerning political rights in CEE postcommunist states. The Council of Europe and NATO, among other entities, ranked as equally important sources of norms comprising membership conditions for newly democratized states. Second, and more importantly, 'conditionality' (regardless of its source) is just one of a number of forms of effecting norm adoption and emulation. In the literature, conditionality is often contrasted to 'social learning' or 'lesson drawing', where European rules are adopted and internalized, not because they are prerequisite to joining a particular European grouping, but rather through processes of acculturation and socialization into (real or perceived) 'European norms'.[25] The difference this suggests largely concerns *motives* for rule adoption, but it should be noted that, contrary to appearances, it does not correspond to a distinction between voluntary and involuntary rule adoption. After all, rule adoption through the conditionality process may also be perfectly voluntary. In the conditionality processes, however, voluntariness attaches to the decision to apply for membership and the obligation to adopt rules merely follows this original decision.

By Europeanization, in this context, we refer to the way in which domestic legal and political structures and institutions respond to changes in the interests, norms, and preferences (perceived or real) of European international and supranational structures in which they become embedded, either in joining, or aspiring to join or ally themselves with, those structures.[26] This definition is broad enough not to pre-empt any substantive theory about the character of the dynamic involved in Europeanization. In contrast to definitions of Europeanization, which stress the impact or the effect of European on domestic structures,[27] neither does this definition preclude (and indeed it should not) Europeanization being seen as a 'two-way street', as opposed to a 'top-down' process in which 'European' norms are merely emulated by Member States of

---

[25] See, e.g. F. Schimmelfennig and U. Sedelmeier, 'Introduction: Conceptualizing the Europeanization of Central and Eastern Europe', in F. Schimmelfennig and U. Sedelmeier (eds.), *The Europeanization of Central and Eastern Europe* (Ithaca, NY: Cornell University Press, 2005), 1–28, at 8–25.

[26] This definition tracks (though does not fully replicate) a concept of Europeanization expounded in R. Ladrech, 'Europeanization of Domestic Politics and Institutions: A Case of France' (1994) 32 *Journal of Common Market Studies* 69, at 71–72.

[27] On 'Europeanization' in this sense, see R. Stawarska, 'EU Enlargement from the Polish Perspective' (1999) 6 *Journal of European Public Policy* 822, at 831–34.

the Council of Europe (CoE) or the EU. It is clear that Member States are not passive recipients of norms, but that they also project their own norms and preferences upwards with a view to promoting their adoption as European norms. The dynamic of Europeanization is subtle and complex. While more detailed discussion of this dynamic would go beyond the confines of this chapter, it should be emphasized that the advantage of our chosen definition (in contrast to those focusing on the 'impact' or the 'effect' of European norms and institutions) is that it orients attention to the active role of the domestic institutions, and sees their response to perceptions of external expectations as key. The importance of this becomes evident below.

These introductory observations suggest that patterns of 'Europeanization' need to be viewed in conjunction with the 'democratic transition' paradigm, and that the disciplinary boundaries between 'Europeanization scholars' and 'transitologists' (to use an ugly but widely-adopted neologism) are artificial and need to be transcended. Democratic transition coincided in time, and was functionally interrelated with aspects of Europeanization. Consolidation of democracy was seen as supported by accession of formerly communist systems into broader structures (CoE, NATO, EU) with their own norms, expectations and conditions of eligibility. *Vice versa*, the embedding of these states into pan-European structures, even if partly driven by other than consolidation-of-democracy motives, created its own dynamic for the entrenchment of democratic and liberal standards. An attempt to disentangle one from the other (that is, 'Europeanization', from democratic transition) would distort the reality of their mutual and tight connection.

With these general insights in mind, we will deliberately focus on one specific aspect of Europeanization, namely the impact of EU conditionality on the structure of political rights in the CEE. While we believe that EU conditionality played a central role with respect to the design of and respect for political rights in the CEE, conditionality was only one aspect of a broader process of Europeanization, and the EU was just one of a number of sources of conditionality. Compared to CoE conditionality, EU conditionality had some special features, however, and awareness of these should be maintained when contemplating their respective effectiveness. To simplify, in order to sharpen the contrast, one may say that there was a fundamental structural difference between CoE and EU conditionality, with the former largely incentive-based, and followed by serious post-accession monitoring,[28] and the latter mainly compliance-based and focused on a

---

[28] In this context, B. de Witte notes with disapproval a 'rather lax' admissions policy of the CoE, reflected in 'the lack of serious scrutiny prior to the accession of certain countries,' B. de Witte, 'The Impact of Enlargement on the Constitution of the European Union,' in M. Cremona (ed.), *The Enlargement of the European Union* (Oxford: Oxford University Press, 2003), 209, at 229. Note that the formal CoE conditionality was also explicitly articulated in 1993 (before this it remained implicit), and included free and fair elections, freedom of expression and of the media, rights of minorities, and signing of the ECHR: see K. Smith, 'The Evolution and Application of EU Membership Conditionality', in M. Cremona (ed.), *The Enlargement of the European Union* (Oxford: Oxford University Press, 2003), at 115, n. 28.

strict pre-admission scrutiny. This difference corresponded to the two organizations' differing logics. While the CoE has a more 'pedagogic' mission, linked to its aspiration to spread standards of democracy and human rights to as many European states as possible, the EU's is a more inward-related logic, concerned to service the interests and preferences of those countries already 'in', and admitting outsiders only if insider interests are not adversely affected. This, though, is a highly stylized (and partly unrealistic) picture. In practice, the difference between the two types of conditionality has not been as sharp as suggested: for example, the inevitable vagueness of EU political conditionality criteria rendered strict-compliance logic partly illusory. We return to this point below.

5.3.2 EU Political Conditionality in Action

Political conditionality within the EC dates to April 1978 when the European Council determined representative democracy and human rights as conditions for membership of the European Communities, with the intention of encouraging democratization in Greece, Portugal, and Spain.[29] With respect to the CEE, in the years immediately after the fall of communism, EC conditionality focused mainly on human rights and general democratic stability; this was the period in which CEE states established their basic institutional frameworks. Conditionality operated via cooperation and association agreements with CEE states and through the assistance programme, PHARE. Even at this very early stage, the European Parliament demanded that 'reference to human rights should figure' in such agreements, and should be mentioned specifically in the Commission's negotiating mandates.[30] Fundamentally, however, the EC/EU's role at this stage consisted of *responding* to the rapid changes occurring in the CEE.

The turning point was the Copenhagen summit of June 1993, which established, as political criteria to be met by new entrants, the 'stability of institutions guaranteeing democracy, the rule of law, human rights and respect for and protection of minorities'. This can be seen as the canonical statement of 'political conditionality', though it must be emphasized that the conditions for entry related to political rights have a strong Treaty basis. Article 49 TEU, which deals with eligibility criteria, talks of a European state which 'respects the principles' set out in Article 6(1); this lists, inter alia, the principles of liberty, democracy, and respect for human rights and fundamental freedoms (though not, significantly, minority protection). Nevertheless, in the period 1993–97 the principal focus of conditionality was on the internal market *acquis*, with the main pre-accession strategy determined at the Essen European Council in 1994. Political conditionality acquired real bite only after 1997, when the Commission began evaluating the

---

[29] See Smith, above, n. 28, at 109–10; de Witte, above, n. 28, at 229.
[30] Quoted in Schimmelfennig, Engert, and Knobel, 'The Impact of EU Political Conditionality', in Schimmelfennig and Sedelmeier (eds.), above, n. 25, 29–50, at 30.

progress of all candidates in its annual reports, which included sections on 'Democracy and the rule of law' (with sub-sections on parliament, executive, judicial system, and anti-corruption measures) and on 'Human rights and the protection of minorities' (with sub-sections on civil and political rights, economic, social, and cultural rights, and minority rights and the protection of minorities).[31]

At the start of that monitoring cycle, in 1997, the Commission determined that some countries had already fulfilled the democracy criterion (Estonia, Poland, Hungary, Slovenia, and the Czech Republic). Others were on their way (Bulgaria, Romania, Lithuania, and Latvia), while one had not fulfilled it (Slovakia) and was accordingly excluded from accession negotiations. The Commission's *avis* of July 1997 referred to 'the instability of Slovakia's institutions, their lack of rootedness in political life and the shortcomings in the functioning of its democracy'.[32] It was only at the Helsinki summit of December 1999 that the new Slovak government of Dzurinda (elected in 1998) won agreement to open negotiations commencing in February 2000.

The Commission's annual reports constitute the most significant available evidence of EU decision-makers' thinking about the application of political standards to candidate states. Though partial and indirect, these nonetheless provide a valuable indication as to how EU conditionality may have affected the CEE states' progress in articulating, entrenching, and implementing political rights. Close reading of the sections of the reports dealing with political rights suggests that their impact should not be exaggerated. Their structure and phraseology is rather formulaic, suggesting a 'one size fits all' approach, and revealing a bureaucratic, rather than critical-reflective, attitude towards their contents. As Gwendolyn Sasse observes, the reports' explicit intention was to review the rate at which a country was adopting the *acquis*, rather than to assess the actual political and social conditions of a given country, therefore 'once the accession negotiations began the emphasis was not on the monitoring of the broadly stated normative conditions of the political Copenhagen criterion'.[33] The same author also observes that there was a certain anti-critical bias written into the reports' production, as the EU's avowed priority was to maintain the enlargement process already set in motion by that time, to which harsh criticism was not seen as conducive.[34] One can perhaps draw an analogy with a pedagogical system, whereby criticism of a student is seen as a motivating and assisting device; while particularly severe criticism is viewed as counterproductive, even if pinpointing failures and mistakes may be necessary.

---

[31] On the minority-protection aspect of political conditionality based on Copenhagen criteria, see Gwendolyn Sasse's chapter in this volume.

[32] See G. Pridham, 'The European Union's Democratic Conditionality and Domestic Politics in Slovakia: The Mečiar and Dzurinda Governments Compared' (2002) 54 *Europe-Asia Studies* 203, at 224, n. 3.

[33] Gwendolyn Sasse, 'EU Conditionality and Minority Rights: Translating the Copenhagen Criterion into Policy', EUI Working Paper RSCAS No.2005/16, at 6.   [34] Ibid, at 6.

Ultimately, it must be remembered that the reports were primarily political documents, produced by bureaucrats/politicians for politicians, rather than dispassionate pieces of political and legal analysis. Anticipated reactions must clearly have informed their wording which, along with their level of criticism, was determined by the overall goal behind the whole exercise. And part of this goal was the overall commitment by the EU (specifically by the Commissioner for Enlargement) to the successful completion of enlargement negotiations.

5.3.3 Assessing the Impact of Conditionality

To what extent was the consolidation of democracy and entrenchment of political rights in the CEE the result of EU political conditionality, forced on candidate states as a club entry-fee? It is important when assessing the consolidation of democracy and strengthening of political rights in the CEE, to maintain the right balance between the relative impact of domestic and external factors (mainly EU conditionality). It must also be kept in mind that some of the most important institutional innovations, especially in the initial period of democratic change, resulted predominantly from domestic public pressure. This included pressure from democratic opposition elites who made their demands heard, either at round-tables (as in Poland or Hungary) or on the streets (as in Czechoslovakia or Romania). Often members of these groups were themselves motivated by fundamental ideas concerning liberal democracy, such as free elections to parliament, independence of the judiciary, a free press, etc., absent any outside persuasion. These ideas coincided with perceived European 'norms' and CEE elites more often than not found it perfectly natural to base their own systems on models they saw successfully practiced in Western Europe. Emulation designs were often developed by dissident élites in anticipation of the fall of Communism and so could be put in place soon after transition. Indeed, institutional innovation sometimes *preceded* transition—installed, though in a carefully limited way, by the old regime, as in the case of the establishment of Poland's Constitutional Tribunal. Similarly, moves towards regionalization in some countries predated EU interest in this process, the latter driven largely by the Union's own rules for management of the structural funds.[35]

Many institutional changes introduced later during the 1990s were driven by the need, felt locally, to modify the political system in response to the experience of lapses in democracy. For instance, reforms introduced after 1998 by the Slovak Dzurinda government drew lessons from the authoritarianism of the Mečiar era. Decentralization and regionalization serve as further examples of

[35] See M. Brusis, 'Instrumentalized conditionality: Regionalization in the Czech Republic and Slovakia', paper presented at the workshop 'The Europeanization of Eastern Europe: Evaluating the Conditionality Model', Robert Schuman Centre for Advanced Studies at the European University Institute, Florence, 4–5 July 2003, at 9.

this type of action.[36] Similarly, in 1993, and prior to the EU's announcement of the Copenhagen criteria, Hungary passed a progressive law on the rights of national and ethnic minorities, granting collective rights and cultural autonomy to thirteen specified minorities (and had already before this constitutionally proclaimed the right to representation in local and national institutions). This stemmed not from EU pressure, but rather out of concern for Hungarian minority populations in neighbouring Slovakia, Romania, and Serbia—and the hope that protecting minority rights at home would confer added legitimacy in its demands for Hungarian minorities abroad. Hungary thus found itself well ahead of the standards of minority protection in place in EU countries and eventually became a leading (though ineffectual) proponent of writing minority and ethnic rights into the EU Constitutional Treaty.

None of this is to say that conditionality lacked importance: rather, conditionality can be seen to have worked best where it resonated with domestic preferences and political aims. Consequently, its importance varied across policy domains and countries. One major factor affecting the efficiency of rule adoption was the extent to which an 'imported' rule or institution fitted with public opinion and prevailing values within a given community. The relative ineffectiveness throughout the CEE region of measures aimed at protecting members of the Roma minority are largely attributable to broad social hostility and prejudice with respect to this group, and so to a lack of resonance between externally required anti-discrimination measures and local consensus.[37] Another factor was the 'density' of previously established rules, practices, and institutions in any given area in each candidate state: the greater the degree of entrenchment, the higher the resistance to rules imported from the EU.

A further factor, clearly related to those two already mentioned, was the magnitude of the social cost likely to be incurred by domestic political elites in adopting a rule exogenously advocated or imposed in the form of 'conditionality'. In a series of case studies, Frank Schimmelfennig and his collaborators have shown how changes in domestic socio-political settings crucially influenced the effectiveness of rule adoption. For example, under the Dzurinda government in Slovakia, the costs of rule adoption were significantly lower than under the former Mečiar government. Among other reasons, this was because Dzurinda's governing coalition had made EU accession its overarching, uniting policy goal. Previously, by contrast, EU rule-adoption costs were high because acceding to the requirements of EU political conditionality, in particular those pertaining to the position of the Hungarian minority, would have endangered the coalition of Mečiar's party (Movement for a Democratic Slovakia, HZDS) with the nationalist Slovak National Party (SNS).[38] Following the change of government in 1998, Slovakia quickly set about adopting

---

[36] Ibid, at 11.

[37] This factor is emphasized by G. Schwellnus, 'The Adoption of Nondiscrimination and Minority Protection Rules in Romania, Hungary, and Poland', in Schimmelfennig and Sedelmeier (eds.), above, n. 25, at 51–70.   [38] Schimmelfennig, Engert, and Knobel, above, n. 30, at 39.

the rules dictated by political conditionality, starting with a new law on national minority languages (which allowed the use of minority languages in local public administration if the minority population exceeded 20 per cent in a given area).[39] In light of this particular case study, Schimmelfennig *et al.* conclude that a change in government 'can itself be partially attributed to a credible policy of conditionality, which caused a prowestern and prodemocratic electorate to reassess the costs of having a government, which proved to be an obstacle to the western integration of their country'.[40]

Finally, it needs to be emphasized that the influence of conditionality rarely took the form of suggestions of specific institutional solutions and devices— perhaps for the simple reason that there is no single model of democracy and rights-protection in the EU itself, much less in the 'West'. The absence of a common political-constitutional blueprint has recently been given emphatic expression in the principle of constitutional autonomy, enunciated in the draft Constitutional Treaty of the EU: 'The Union shall respect the equality of Member States before the constitution as well as their national identities of the Member States, inherent in their fundamental structures, political and constitutional, inclusive of regional and local self-government . . .'[41] This merely makes explicit what has been obvious throughout the process of European integration. Conditionality's influence on candidate states more often took the form of general templates or thresholds, with certain minimal conditions to be fulfilled, than the installation of specific institutional designs. The very fact, however, of the generality of these templates or the minimalist nature of the thresholds renders it very difficult to trace the 'emulation' to one specific source—or even to determine whether it was indeed emulation in the first place. Certainly, the degree of specificity of EU political conditionality varied from one domain to another. Conditionality may have been more effective given a determinate set of rules candidate states were expected to observe, as opposed to cases in which the criteria laid down could at best be characterized as a vague template.[42] Additionally, legitimacy of conditionality demands corresponded to the extent to which the EU was holding existing Member States to those standards. In areas where the EU set political conditions extrinsic to the EU legal system *and which in addition* were not in place among current Member States (such as minority rights), conditionality's credibility and effectiveness must have been suspect. Aside from the problem of 'double standards', candidate states, even when acting in good faith, could not know exactly what

[39] Ibid, at 39.   [40] Ibid, at 40.

[41] Article I–5.1 of the draft Treaty establishing a Constitution for Europe.

[42] Compare, for example, Dimitrova's finding of the high effectiveness of conditionality in the area of civil service reform (A. Dimitrova, 'Europeanization and Civil Service Reform in Central and Eastern Europe', in Schimmelfennig and Sedelmeier (eds.), above, n. 25, at 71–90) with the Brusis' conclusion that if conditionality had been an important factor, we would not be able to explain the significant differences in the regionalization policies between the Czech Republic and Slovakia (Brusis, above, n. 35, at 13–14).

was expected of them, as neither Member States' current practice nor the *acquis* provided clear guidance.

The case of minority rights offers a particularly significant example. '[T]he respect for and protection of minority rights' figures prominently as the first Copenhagen criterion, but sadly lacks any basis in EU law and is not directly translatable into the *acquis communautaire*. It may be hypothesized that this criterion's inclusion mainly reflected widespread Western perceptions and security concerns vis-à-vis the CEE where 'the salience of minority issues and the potential for ethno-regional conflict amidst multi-facetted transition processes' appeared to be high.[43] Nevertheless, the absence of clear standards, both in EU law and EU Member States' law and practice exposed conditionality to the charges of hypocrisy and double standards, as well as creating difficulties in gauging the real meaning of this criterion. While the Maastricht Treaty recognizes respect for fundamental rights as one of the underlying values of the EU, and the Treaty of Amsterdam incorporated *almost* all of the values set out by the EU in the Copenhagen political criteria, any reference to minority protection is conspicuously absent from the Treaties. Clearly, there is no consensus between older EU Member States as to standards of minority protection. Some officially recognize the existence of minorities in their population, while others (France, Greece) do not; some reserve the term 'minority' to the immigrant population (UK), while in others it attaches to historical ethnic groups (the Slovenes in Austria); some have ratified the CoE Framework Convention for the Protection of National Minorities of 1995, yet others have not.[44] If one analyses the Commission's annual Regular Reports with respect to progress in fulfilling the 'minority protection' criterion, one notices ambiguities and inconsistencies in the scrutiny of practice in candidate states. As Sasse observes, the Reports consistently emphasize only the plight of two minority groups in the region (the Roma population and the Russian-speaking population in Baltic states) notwithstanding the pervasive nature of the majority-minority problems in the CEE.[45] Such selectivity suggests that the main concerns informing the drafting of these Reports were extrinsic (a fear of uncontrollable migration to Western countries in the case of Roma, and concern for Russia's political sensibilities in the case of the Baltic states) and not intrinsically related to the plight of disadvantaged minorities.

5.4 POWER TO THE PEOPLE: POLITICAL RIGHTS AND DEMOCRATIC STATEHOOD

Returning to the institutional framework, the early stage of constitutional transformations includes the incorporation of human rights principles into

---

[43] Sasse, above, n. 33, at 2. See also Sasse's chapter in this volume.
[44] Belgium, Greece, and Luxembourg have not ratified, and France has not even signed, the Framework Convention.   [45] Sasse, above, n. 33, at 7.

postcommunist constitutional and legal systems. The concept of human rights defended by political dissidents involved moral and natural rights based arguments. It represented a confluence of politics, morality, and law that was yet to be incorporated into the structural framework of democratic constitutional statehood emerging in Central and Eastern Europe in the 1990s. The concept of human rights was both *morally evaluative* and *politically instrumental*. Human rights, therefore, had to be transformed from moral and political ideals into the legal capabilities of a democratic polity. After the successful removal of communists from state power and the ideological victory of the liberal democratic concept of human rights over the communist notion of class-based historical justice, it was important to convert *human rights into constitutional rights* that would be enforceable by legal means.

5.4.1 Constitution-Making and Human Rights: Between Political and Social Rights

All postcommunist countries engaged in the enactment of legislation protecting human rights and the embedding of this in the constitutional system. Before addressing specific problems related to this process, it is important to distinguish the respective roles played by different rights in the 1990s' constitutional transformations. Postcommunist transformations exhibited a distinct trajectory regarding human rights issues. Socialist welfare rights were diminished, due to free-market reforms, while basic and political rights had to be newly constituted, to establish the structural preconditions of a liberal democratic polity. At the same time, social and economic rights could not be entirely dismantled, given the risk of provoking political and economic instability in new, fragile democracies. The concept of 'social peace' therefore played a central part in balancing the structural necessity of thoroughly transforming the social welfare system, on the one hand, with public trust in emerging democratic power, on the other. Granting political rights to economically dispossessed citizens could have been a suicidal policy for new democratic governments, given the likelihood it would have undermined democratic trust and encouraged political populism and authoritarianism.

Post-1989 human rights-oriented constitutional reforms therefore incorporated both basic and political rights *and* extensive social welfare entitlements. Traditional negative rights of the individual vis-à-vis the state—in particular, freedom of expression and association, the right to vote, the right to petition, and the right to free assembly—were thus accompanied by positive rights[46] seeking to satisfy basic social and economic needs, such as rights to a minimum wage, clean environment, housing, education, health care, pensions, and even annual paid holidays and hygienic labour conditions.[47] Such entitlements entail

---

[46] These rights are commonly referred to as 'positive rights' or 'entitlements'. See C. Sunstein, 'Against Positive Rights' (1993) 2 *East European Constitutional Review* 35.

[47] Some provisions regulating social and economic rights seem to be residual elements of the communist rights discourse. See, for instance, Article 70D of the Constitution of the Republic of

duties on the state, carry implications for its budgetary policies, and interfere with the free-functioning of the market economy. The structural risk of undermining the emerging rule of law, due to the economic inability of new democratic governments to implement constitutionally guaranteed social and economic rights was politically subordinate to the goal of safeguarding social and political stability during the early stages of transformations in the 1990s.

This tendency was marked in the Czechoslovak Charter of Fundamental Rights and Freedoms, the provisions of which, following the split of the Czech and Slovak Federal Republic in 1992, were incorporated into both Czech and Slovak constitutional systems.[48] The Hungarian 'revolution by Constitution' employed the old catalogue of communist constitutional rights, reconfiguring these within the new liberal democratic system—a job made easier by the ratification, by the former communist government, of international human rights documents, such as the United Nations Covenants. The austere text of the Constitution outlined the protection of human rights in Article 8 of its first chapter, and listed a small catalogue of basic, political, and social rights in the twelfth chapter, so providing the Constitutional Court with substantial scope to grant and interpret constitutional rights.[49] In Poland, due to political rivalries and fundamental conflicts within the opposition, the situation was different. The 1952 Communist Constitution remained in force and, like his other constitutional reforms of the early 1990s, President Walesa's proposal for a charter of rights did not materialize. A constitutional format for the protection of human rights eventually materialized with the 1997 Constitution, which incorporated the protection of fundamental rights and freedoms in its second chapter and included a number of provisions regarding socio-economic rights supported by both the postcommunist left and the collective rights-oriented right. It is also noteworthy that the Polish Constitution outlined citizens' duties (in section VI of the second chapter), such as political loyalty (Article 82), observance of the laws (Article 83), the duty to pay tax (Article 84), national defence (Article 85), and care for the environment (Article 86).[50]

Hungary, which states: '(1) Everyone living in the territory of the Republic of Hungary has the right to the highest possible level of physical and mental health. (2) The Republic of Hungary shall implement this right through institutions of labour safety and health care, through the organization of medical care and the opportunities for regular physical activity, as well as through the protection of the urban and natural environment.' See also Article 68 of the Constitution of the Republic of Poland, the fourth and fifth sections of which state: '(4) Public authorities shall combat epidemic illnesses and prevent the negative health consequences of degradation of the environment. (5) Public authorities shall support the development of physical culture, particularly amongst children and young persons.'

[48] While the Czech Republic incorporated the Charter as an independent document to the Czech constitutional order, Slovakia incorporated its provisions in the second chapter of the Constitution of the Republic of Slovakia.

[49] Sólyom and Brunner, above, n. 20.

[50] See a critique by W. Sadurski, 'Rights and Freedoms under the New Polish Constitution', in M. Krygier and A. Czarnota, (eds.), *The Rule of Law after Communism* (Aldershot: Dartsmouth, 1999), 176, at 183–84.

5.4.2 Representative and Direct Democracy: Separation of Powers, Electoral Systems, and Referenda

Regarding the structural aspect of democratization and constitution-making in the CEE in the 1990s, three political rights marked an exit strategy from the communist system: the right to freedom of expression, the right to freedom of association, and the right to vote. Little wonder that the first 'transformative' demands were free elections and the abolition of censorship, accompanied by opposition access to public media (primarily state television and radio). Securing the communist government's concession on these demands was the biggest success of the Polish Solidarnosc movement in the early stages of round-table talks in 1989. The same demands were given more radical formulation by the New Forum in East Germany and the Civic Forum in Czechoslovakia during the revolutionary events of 1989, in these cases conceded by communist governments under political pressure from revolutionary crowds.

The abolition of censorship initially resulted in a spontaneous eruption of free expression, yet to be regulated by new legislation. This 'Big Bang' had a formative effect on emerging political parties, movements, programmes, and propaganda. The one-party system could be dismantled only by opening up public space to free discourse and competition between different political views, to result in the structuration[51] of the pluralistic political system. Developing political pluralism was a necessary first step in building a democratic political system based on the majority-minority distinction. Free democratic elections make sense only if the free expression of different political views, leading people to associate in different parties and movements, is granted inside the polity.

Democratic political representation could thus be achieved only after the state's withdrawal from the public sphere of ideas and worldviews, opening up opportunities for new political agency to arise, for example, in the form of political parties, movements, and civil campaign groups. At the same time, these agents' political practice was fundamental to the constitution of democratic political systems in the CEE postcommunist countries. Legislating for freedom of expression therefore established the necessary framework for the growth of liberal democratic politics and institutions, which could in turn create other rights and rules necessary to democracy. Free elections and the right to vote and be elected allowed the origination of democratic political institutions which, because elected in free general elections, possessed democratic legitimacy to outline and implement further political, economic, and legal reforms. At the national level, parliaments shaped new policies, contributing significantly to the structuration of new political alliances, parties, and elites.

---

[51] For the dual dynamics and general aspects of the theory of structuration elaborated by Anthony Giddens, see A. Giddens, *A Contemporary Critique of Historical Materialism, Vol. 1: Power, Property and the State* (Berkeley, CA: University of California Press, 1981), at 26–29. See also A. Giddens, *The Constitution of Society* (Berkeley, CA: University of California Press, 1984).

Postcommunist countries established systems of parliamentary democracy
which, despite incorporating many elements of the republican system of checks
and balances and the separation of powers, were based on Parliamentary
supremacy. Constitutional debates regarding parliamentary elections, closely
linked to institutional reform, were therefore essential and led to the establishment of very different electoral systems in different countries. Hungary
opted for a one-chamber Parliament and, inspired by the German model, a
mixture of the majority and proportional representation system. Following the
division of Czechoslovakia, Slovakia preferred a one-chamber Parliament and
the old Czechoslovak tradition of the proportionally representative vote; on the
other hand, the Czech Republic favoured a new design, establishing a bicameral
Parliament with the Assembly of Deputies elected on a proportional vote and
the Senate elected by majority. Poland retained its bicameral Parliament and
opted for a proportional voting system.

All of these institutional and systemic changes reflected political struggles and
the distribution of power within the new democratic regimes. President
Walesa's fight to enact a new constitution granting more power to the President
and making the country a semi-presidential republic was unsuccessful and the
effect of the 'Small Constitution' of 1993, granting limited extra powers to the
President, was eventually marginalized by the Constitution of 1997. President
Havel's futile attempts to change the ineffective constitutional framework of the
Czechoslovak federation also involved a plan to strengthen the President's
constitutional role.[52] Nevertheless, such attempts at constitutional change
always tried to avoid destabilizing the new democratic regime as such. The risk
of anti-democratic populism damaging the institutional framework of representative democracy, including the protection of rights, was too high even for
populist democrats like Lech Walesa.

The classic question of how to protect a democratic system against anti-
democratic forces and preserve democratic power for democrats haunted
constitution-makers in postcommunist countries. In their attempts to resolve it,
they resorted to different cocktails of institutional reform and systems of the
popular vote. The complicated Hungarian electoral system and the Czech
bicameral Parliament are illustrative of the attempts made to ensure greater
diversity in political representation and to limit the role of big, centralized
political parties, as well as Robert Michels' iron law of the party oligarchies.[53] In
the different context of the exceptional Slovak political situation during Prime
Minister Mečiar's 1994–98 government, the political opposition made a pre-
election promise to implement a law on general elections for the presidential
post, despite the fact that the President had very limited powers within the

[52] See especially E. Stein, *Czecho/Slovakia: Ethnic Conflict, Constitutional Fissure, Negotiated Breakup* (Ann Arbor, IL: University of Michigan Press, 1997), at 139–53.
[53] See R. Michels, *Political Parties: A Sociological Study of the Oligarchial Tendencies of Modern Democracy* (London: Jarrold and Sons, 1915).

constitutional system of Slovakia. The promise was driven by the belief that a general election was the best protection against the vicious political agenda of Mečiar and his party, and a nationalist populism threatening the constitutional bodies of the state.

In the ethnically heterogeneous and divided regions of the CEE, the political participation and administrative autonomy of ethnic and national minorities were further important issues permeating the sphere of political rights. Although ethnic and national minority rights, are technically separate from the classic set of political rights, they can nevertheless seriously affect the quality of the democratic political process. The relationship between ethnic or national majorities and minorities can result in international tensions, such as the controversial Hungarian out-of-citizenship 'status law' enacted by the Orbán government in 2001 and criticized by the Council of Europe.[54] They can create serious political crises, as did the nationalist policies of the Mečiar government in Slovakia between 1994 and 1998, sometimes even leading to violent clashes and civil war, as in the former Yugoslavia in the 1990s.

Due to its specific historical circumstances, it is no surprise that Hungary granted a special constitutional right for ethnic and national minorities to be represented and form local and national bodies for self-government. The state is thus obliged to ensure the collective participation of minorities in public affairs and rights to use of their languages and education.[55] Accordingly, in 1993 Parliament passed the Act on the Rights of Ethnic and National Minorities (Act LXXVII) and, two years later, appointed a Minorities Ombudsman. Two-thirds of the votes of the Members of Parliament present are necessary to enact legislation regarding ethnic and national minorities.[56] Though not so extensive as the Hungarian model, most other CEE countries have also afforded constitutional protection to the use of minority languages in public administration and education and the cultural identity of ethnic and national minorities.[57] Despite constitutional guarantees, however, the level of political participation of minorities and their trust in political institutions have varied significantly and have often been affected by citizenship and language legislation, such as in the Baltic states in the 1990s.[58]

[54] See 'Constitutional Watch: the report on the "status law" enacted by the Act of Parliament of the Republic of Hungary on June 19, 2001' (2001) 10 *East European Constitutional Review*, No. 2/3.
[55] See Article 68 of the Constitution of the Republic of Hungary.
[56] See Article 68(5) of the Constitution of the Republic of Hungary.
[57] See, for example, the Constitution of the Republic of Slovakia guaranteeing ethnic and national minorities 'the right to use their language in dealings with the authorities' (Article 34(2)(b)) or 'the right to participate in the solution of affairs concerning national minorities and ethnic groups' (Article 34(2)(c)).
[58] For further details, see, for instance, A. Pabriks, 'Ethnic Limits of Civil Society: The Case of Latvia', in N. Götz and J. Hackmann (eds.), *Civil Society in the Baltic Sea Region* (Aldershot: Ashgate, 2003), at 133; also see A. Semjonov, 'Ethnic Limits of Civil Society: The Case of Estonia', in N. Götz and J. Hackmann (eds.), *Civil Society in the Baltic Sea Region* (Aldershot: Ashgate, 2003), at 145.

The expansion of forms and areas of political participation by citizens in general elections and public administration often strengthened the political system and typically did not result in the growth of populism undermining the democratic institutions.[59] At the same time, it is interesting to note how different the attitudes towards referenda as a form of direct democracy have been in individual postcommunist CEE countries and the extent of their influence by different political traditions and contemporary developments.

In Poland, the referendum was first used by the Communist Party in 1946, when results were falsified to strengthen the emerging totalitarian regime. The second national referendum was held in 1987, and marked the beginning of the end of communist power: the government failed to secure an overall majority amongst those eligible with respect to two questions concerning political democratization and pro-market economic reforms. This referendum amounted to a vote of no-confidence and the communist leadership consequently invited the opposition to round-table talks. After a regime change, the Constitution was amended and laws concerning referenda were enacted to support the notion of direct democracy.[60] The 1997 Constitution recognizes three different types of referenda—the constitutional, the national, and the local—and though their use is limited, they had become a common element of democratic decision-making in Poland by the 1990s.

In Hungary in the 1980s, the opposition movement issued demands for referenda which culminated in the Gabčíkovo-Nagymaros giant hydroelectric power plant campaign. The referendum law of 1989 was a direct outcome of the anti-plant campaign and the Constitutional Court called on Parliament several times subsequently to amend various parts of the law to ensure its constitutionality. Parliament responded by drafting a new law, enacted in 1997. Referendum rules are currently regulated by the Constitution and two statutes.[61] In Hungary, the referendum is part of the 1980s legacy of the democratization movement, and its legal regulation is influenced by the Constitutional Court.

Czechoslovakia represents a polar opposite to Hungary and Poland. Under its parliamentary tradition the referendum was a marginal element of local democracy: there was not a single nationwide referendum during Czechoslovakia's existence. The referendum law enacted in 1991 was designed to remedy the growing constitutional crisis of the Czechoslovak federation in the early 1990s. This law required a very strict voting majority in both republics, and the

---

[59] For a discussion of the fear of political populism and 'premature political participation' see A. Sajo, 'Rights in Post-Communism', in A. Sajo (ed.), *Western Rights? Post-Communist Application* (Hague: Kluwer, 1996), 139, at 156.

[60] See S. Gebethner, 'Poland', in A. Auer and M. Bützer (eds.), *Direct Democracy: The Eastern and Central European Experience* (Aldershot: Ashgate, 2001), 129, at 130.

[61] See M. Deszö and A. Bragyova, 'Hungary', in A. Auer and M. Bützer (eds.), above, n. 60, 63, at 68–70.

Czechoslovak state broke up without citizens ever having the chance to express their opinion in a referendum vote.[62] After the split, Slovakia adopted the referendum law and actually organized several nationwide referenda, while the Czech legislator retained its traditional suspicion towards this element of direct democracy, enacted the referendum law ultimately only to pave the way for accession to the European Union.

5.5 MILITANT DEMOCRACY, FREEDOM OF SPEECH, AND FREEDOM OF ASSOCIATION

5.5.1 Liberal Freedoms and Political Extremism

Apart from promoting democratic pluralism, the abolition of political censorship naturally resulted in the growth of political extremism and hate speech. In this respect, postcommunist societies were uniquely situated because they had just dismantled a political system founded on the extremist totalitarian ideology of communism. At the same time, all CEE countries permitted the continued existence and activity of communist parties, with only some assets confiscated. Because political transformation legitimized these elements of communist political extremism it was much harder to fight any other forms of extremism and violent political programmes within the new liberal democratic system.

This argumentatively complicated and paradoxical situation, together with strong resentment for any form of censorship in the early 1990s, was effectively exploited by right-wing extremists. All postcommunist societies experienced the revival of anti-Semitism and racism. In the 1990s, though Central and East European countries were only gradually moving towards harmonization of their national economies, law, and political systems with European Union standards, they had been 'fully integrated' into the dark spirit of European racism and nationalism. Political extremists in CEE countries successfully cooperated with EU extremist organizations, such as the Liberal Party in Austria, the National Front in France, and the Republican Party in Germany. The Czechoslovak Republican Party, a right-wing extremist party with a racist and anti-immigration agenda, for instance, drew heavily on the political programmes and campaign strategies of the German 'Reps'. Jean-Marie Le Pen lent support to the Slovak National Party, an extreme ethno-nationalist party, in national elections in the 1990s. Elements of ethno-nationalism and anti-Semitism, though limited in their impact on mainstream politics, were also present in Hungary and Poland throughout the 1990s.

---

[62] See M. Gillis, 'Czech Republic', in A. Auer and M. Bützer (eds.), above, n. 60, 39, at 40–42; see also E. Stein, above, n. 52, at 262–65.

How did legal systems in CEE states respond to these dangers? Did legal responses achieve an appropriate balance between, on one hand, the need to respect the freedom of speech and association crucial for a well-ordered democratic state and, on the other, the need to counter threats to democracy stemming from extremist, violence-propagating parties and from hateful, extremist speech? As is clear from the chapter by Eva Brems in this book, this is a problem transcending the CEE region; dilemmas stemming from so-called 'militant democracy' are of universal character, though they manifest differently in different countries. For the purposes of this chapter we will use the concept of militant democracy (MD) in its most basic meaning, as a system which allows (indeed, mandates) restrictions on the human rights of anti-democratic actors on the grounds of the need to protect democracy itself.[63] In the European context, the call for MD is often accompanied by an invocation of the most traumatic European experience of weak democracy unable to cope with anti-democratic enemies within—that of the fall of the Weimar Republic, and the emergence of an undemocratic system through the exploitation of democratic freedoms by parties and politicians committed to destroying democracy itself. However, the very idea of restricting the rights of those opposed to a democratic constitutional system, to protect the values and survival of democracy, is of course paradoxical and troubling. Democracy may be just as easily undermined by the excessive use of the 'anti-democratic' label to ban the political opponents of those currently controlling the executive and/or legislature as by underestimating dangers posed by the enemies of democracy.[64] If we assign to political rulers the authority to define 'true' democracy and consequently to deny those who depart from their criteria the right to exercise freedom of speech and association, are we not undermining the very premises of democracy we claim to protect? Further, in denying non-democratic parties the right to function freely in a democratic environment, are we not disregarding the potentially civilizing effect of democracy upon legal political parties who may be drawn away from extremism through participation in the democratic political game?[65]

These dilemmas were forcefully manifested in the CEE after the fall of communism and, as our discussion will show, none of the countries of the region can plausibly claim to have struck just the right balance in protecting the political liberties of all political agents, on one side, and the overall system of liberties, against the dangers posed by anti-democratic movements, on the other. Two issues encapsulating the dilemmas of MD with particular salience, discussed further below, are freedom of political speech and the right to political

[63] The literature on militant democracy is voluminous; apart from the references given in the chapter by Eva Brems in this volume, and also the discussion contained in Michel Rosenfeld's chapter here, we wish to acknowledge an excellent recent treatment of the problem in the context of the examination of the jurisprudence of the European Court of Human Rights: P. Harvey, 'Militant Democracy and the European Convention on Human Rights' (2004) 29 *ELRev* 407–20.
[64] Ibid, at 409.   [65] Ibid, at 410.

association (in particular, freedom of political parties). It should be noted from the outset that dangers posed by the MD concept are not necessarily equal in both these cases. One may well argue for differential standards of scrutinizing MD with respect to freedom of speech and freedom of political parties. One may, legitimately, be *more* suspicious of MD-motivated restrictions on freedom of speech than on freedom of political parties. This is because a prohibition on a party on the basis of its pursuit of a particular idea does not exclude other, non-party-related channels for the public expression of this ideal, hence the effect of such a ban on the free circulation of ideas may be less restrictive than limits on freedom of speech in general.[66] One may also say that 'preventive restrictions' on political parties, based on their programmes, more closely resemble the regulation of 'conduct' than of speech, and so warrant less stringent scrutiny than the regulation of speech as such. Since 'conduct' may have a number of non-expressive effects that collide with other important social goals, its regulation is less objectionable, according to the usual rationales applied to the protection of political speech.[67]

5.5.2 Militant Democracy and Hate Speech

The limits of freedom of political speech are painfully tested when the speech in question can be seen as inciting hatred, discrimination, or violence against certain groups in society. Restrictions on such extremist speech create a strong clash of values: the value of freedom of public speech (including speech hurtful to some groups and having the potential to promote hostility towards those groups) encounters the value of maintaining equal dignity and social peace among the members of different groups. All CEE legal systems contain restrictions upon (variously defined) incitement to hatred on racial and ethnic grounds. In their willingness to control racist or other hate speech, the CEE countries follow suit with the European tradition of readiness to restrict speech in the interests of social peace or to protect the dignity of victims of racism (a contrasting approach is adopted in the United States). Such restrictions are also consistent with the International Convention on the Elimination of All Forms of Racial Discrimination (CERD) of 1969, to which all CEE countries are parties. None has lodged any reservation regarding CERD Article 4(a) which obliges states to declare, as an offence punishable by law, all dissemination of and incitement to racial hatred and discrimination.[68] In some countries, such restrictions on freedom of speech are pronounced constitutionally.[69]

[66] See A. Sajo, 'Hate Speech for Hostile Hungarians' (1994) 3:2 *East Europ Constit Rev*, 82–87, at 82.
[67] See W. Sadurski, *Freedom of Speech and its Limits* (Dordrecht: Kluwer, 1999), at 43–58.
[68] See http://www.unhchr.ch/html/menu3/b/treaty2_asp.htm.
[69] For example, the Lithuanian Constitution explicitly provides that freedom of speech does not cover 'the instigation of national, racial, religious, or social hatred, violence, or discrimination...', Article 25(3).

Significantly, the basic propriety of such restrictions, whether constitutional or statutory, has never been subject to any fundamental challenge in the CEE. The responses of constitutional courts in cases where relevant laws have been questioned have, by and large, been supportive of the idea of such restrictions, with the exception of the Hungarian Constitutional Court, which has gradually moved towards a radically libertarian position.

This evolution in Hungary is interesting and worth discussing in some detail because it may offer a template for broader developments in the CEE region. The Hungarian Court first dealt with incitement to hatred in 1992 when it considered two provisions of the Criminal Code, both significant from the point of view of the limit of the right to free political speech: the prohibition of the denigration of the Hungarian nation and the offence of incitement to hatred.[70] The former was struck from the Code while the latter survived on the grounds of the need to maintain public peace. The decision was as important for its actual outcome as for the theory of freedom of expression that it developed quite explicitly. In the process of considering arguments for the invalidation and preservation of the two provisions, the Court presented an impressive array of constructions supporting a very robust conception of freedom of expression. It noted freedom of expression's 'special place among the constitutional rights';[71] that it is described as a condition 'of a truly vibrant society capable of development';[72] that laws restricting it must be strictly construed;[73] and that it should be interpreted in a content-neutral manner, so as to protect opinions 'irrespective of the value or veracity of [their] content'.[74] This amounts to an expansive, strongly libertarian theoretical construction, although, as one critic noted, under the provision upheld by the Court '[i]t is not necessary...that the incitement to racial hatred result in any clear and present danger'.[75] It is one thing to incite to 'hatred' but another to incite to 'violence', and the distinction between the two marks the important point at which speech ceases to be merely a carrier of ideas and becomes dangerous conduct. This distinction, however, is not evident in the judgment. Indeed, incitement to hatred is characterized as 'emotional preparation for the use of violence' and, as such, 'an abuse of the freedom of expression'.[76]

The Hungarian Parliament reacted to this decision by modifying the surviving provision against incitement to hatred, adding a provision that prohibited any act 'capable of triggering incitement to hatred'. The Court invalidated this modification[77] and, in effect, the relevant provision of the Criminal Code

---

[70] Decision No. 30/1992 (V.18) AB, of 18 May 1992, reprinted in *E Europ Const Case Rep* 2 (1995) 8–26.   [71] Ibid, at 12.
[72] Ibid, at 13.   [73] Ibid, at 22.   [74] Ibid, at 23.
[75] A. Sajo, above, n. 65, at 84; see also G. Halmai, 'Criminal Law as Means Against Racist Speech? The Hungarian Legal Approach' (1997) 4 *Journal of Constitutional Law in Eastern and Central Europe* 41–52, at 45.   [76] Decision 30/1992, at 16.
[77] Decision 12/199.

was reduced to a prohibition on incitement to hatred against the Hungarian nation or against any national, ethnic, racial, or religious group taking place in front of a large audience. In the wake of this decision, the Parliament did not attempt to reintroduce a wider prohibition, perhaps because it was not in the interests of the then ruling Young Democrats to alienate the extreme right-wing and xenophobic Hungarian Justice and Life Party, which had entered Parliament in 1998. Most recently, in 2003, the Parliament enacted a new law on hate crimes which the President refused to sign, referring it to the Constitutional Court. On 24 May 2004, the Court in turn declared it invalid as violating freedom of expression. The law would have provided for imprisonment of up to three years for all persons who 'publicly incite hate against a nation, race, national, ethnic or religious minority or call for acts of violence against such groups'.[78]

This Hungarian saga, and specifically the tension between Parliament and public opinion on the one hand, and the Constitutional Court on the other, is revealing. While liberal lawyers (whose influence is dominant in the Constitutional Court) tend to accept highly libertarian criteria and push legislation towards a less speech-restrictive design, public opinion is largely indifferent or hostile to abuses of freedom of speech in the form of violent, hateful, or provocative public expression. It is safe to say, liberal approaches to freedom of speech have hardly intruded on broader public opinion in the CEE. On the other hand, it is clearly the case that the various legal devices available to prosecute hateful or vilifying speech have been under-enforced, with examples very rare in the region discussed here. One well-publicized instance, however, concerned a recent publication of Adolf Hitler's *Mein Kampf* in the Czech Republic and Slovakia. In both countries the affair led to criminal investigations and the prosecution of the publishers. In the public controversies which ensued, some claimed that if the original text had been accompanied by a short commentary (in which the editors clearly distanced themselves from the book's message, as was true of the Slovak version) its publication would have been legally acceptable and legitimate for purely historical reasons. The authorities did not agree (even for the Slovak version with the commentary).[79] Another rare

---

[78] http://www.iht.com/articles/521549.html; see also: http://www.origo.hu/itthon/20040524 gyuloletbeszed.html.

[79] The Czech edition of Hitler's *Mein Kampf* was published by Michal Zítko, the owner of the Otakar II. Publishers, on 21 March 2000. In addition to an initial conflict with the Bavarian Finance Ministry regarding publication rights, Zítko was found guilty of inciting racial hatred and was sentenced to three years' imprisonment suspended for five years and was fined 2 million Czech crowns (EUR 65,000) by the first instance Court of Prague 7 District in December 2000. This ruling was upheld by the Appeal Court of the City of Prague in February 2002. In July 2002, the Supreme Court (Decision 5 Tdo 337/2002 of 24 July 2002) referred the case back to the first instance court to complete the fact-finding procedures. While the lower court subsequently sentenced Zítko to 22 months' imprisonment suspended for five years, the appeal court changed the judgment, qualified the publication not as a mere incitement but as a support and propaganda of racist movements, and sentenced the publisher to three years' imprisonment suspended for five

instance of the prosecution of an author of hateful propaganda was in Latvia, a country plagued by xenophobic and anti-Semitic publications. Mr Landmanis was convicted in 2002, under the Criminal Code's prohibition of incitement to national and racial hatred, and sentenced to eight months' imprisonment for spreading hatred by publishing the anti-Semitic paper *Patriots*. Although prolonged on appeal, this sentence was subsequently softened by suspension for one year.[80]

All in all, the picture in the CEE is of a combination of (a) general unwillingness (subject to certain exceptions, in Hungary and, to a lesser extent, the Czech Republic)[81] to launch a direct constitutional challenge against statutory prohibitions of hateful, violent, group-vilifying speech, and (b) very marked under-enforcement of these laws. Both parts of this picture are, of course, interrelated because general awareness of under-enforcement diminishes the incentive to launch strong constitutional challenges to anti-hate speech laws. Further, in some countries in the region (e.g. Lithuania) such a constitutional challenge would anyway be ineffective because relevant constitutional provisions themselves envisage limits to freedom of speech based, among other things, on the prevention of 'the instigation of national, racial, religious or social hatred'.[82] Another reason such laws are rarely questioned may be that a preponderance of countries opt for prosecution for racial hate speech, Holocaust denial, and other insulting and provocative speech, although the West European example is mixed. Under-enforcement is probably best explained by a composite of four factors: a genuinely liberal belief that prosecution for hateful speech may spill over into the silencing of speech which, though controversial, is a legitimate contribution to public discourse; an understandable aversion, based on experiences in the 'bad old days', to any restrictions on speech; an unwillingness to provide racists and other extremists with 'free publicity' in the form of a public trial; and a degree of deplorable public tolerance for anti-Semitic and other racist or xenophobic opinions.

5.5.3 Restrictions on Political Parties

A similar observation can be made, *mutatis mutandis*, with respect to restrictions on the establishment and operation of 'extremist' political parties. While CEE

years, in January 2004. The case was finally heard by the Supreme Court of the Czech Republic which, on 10 March 2005, ruled that the publisher, Zítko, did not commit a criminal offence of incitement of racial hatred and propaganda of racist movements by publishing the book. For details, see Decision 3 Tdo 1174/2004 of the Supreme Court of the Czech Republic.

[80] Human Rights in Latvia in 2002 (Latvian Centre for Human Rights and Ethnic Studies Riga: 2003), at: 26.http://www.politika.lv/polit_real/files/lv/LCESC2002en.pdf.

[81] In 1992 the Czech Constitutional Tribunal examined the Criminal Code's prohibition on hate speech and upheld it (except for a very minor constitutional defect which is of no special relevance here), Decision No. 5/92, reprinted in *East Europ Const Case Rep* 6 (1999) 1–17.

[82] Constitution of Lithuania, Article 25(3).

constitutional systems provide relatively wide-ranging means of regulating parties based on their potential to threaten democracy, these provisions have been used extremely sparingly. It is perhaps understandable that, after a long and unfortunate experience with one-party rule, CEE countries have responded particularly adversely to attempts to place restrictions on political parties, and have celebrated the principle of party pluralism (at times, even proclaiming this principle in their constitutions).[83] On the other hand, social dislocation combined with the ideological vacuum left by the demise of an all-encompassing orthodoxy posed fertile ground for anti-democratic, often extremist organizations, aiming to cater for the needs of large numbers of disillusioned and impoverished voters.

It is against this background that the framing of rights to form and belong to a party of one's choice must be considered. As a result of the combination of these two factors, the CEE constitutions' treatment of the role of political parties is relatively comprehensive. Some of the constitutions provide succinct 'definitions' of the purposes of political parties, perhaps a somewhat didactic motive in a society not perfectly used to such institutions: the Bulgarian Constitution informs citizens that parties 'facilitate the formation and expression of the citizens' political will' (Article 11.3); the Hungarian Constitution, that 'Political parties shall participate in the development and expression of the popular will' (Article 3.2); and the Polish Constitution, that the purpose of parties 'shall be to influence the formulation of the policy of the state by democratic means' (Article 11). At the same time, however, most constitutions in the region set limits on political pluralism and, consequently, on political parties. The Hungarian Constitution demands, quite clearly, that parties 'respect the Constitution and laws established in accordance with the Constitution' (Article 3.1); the Constitution of the Czech Republic, that they 'respect the fundamental democratic principles' and 'renounce force as a means of promoting their interests' (Article 5). The Polish Constitution adds that parties must be founded on 'the principle of voluntariness and upon the equality of Polish citizens' (Article 11).

Most constitutional and statutory restrictions addressing political parties are in fact purely formal ones, concerning the name of the party,[84] the minimum

---

[83] The Bulgarian Constitution states that 'Politics in the Republic of Bulgaria shall be founded on the principle of political plurality' (Article 11), the Czech and Slovak Constitutions announce the principle of 'free competition' among political forces (Articles 5 and 31, respectively), etc.

[84] In Lithuania, for example, legislation provides for the registration of only parties or organizations whose names or symbols differ from those of existing political parties and organizations, Articles 3 and 4 of Law on Political Parties and Political Organizations, amended 20 June 1995; in Estonia a party may be denied registration if its name resembles that of an existing party or one which existed in the past. Article 9(2) Estonian Political Parties Act, 11 May 1994. In Slovenia the names, abbreviations, or symbols of political parties must not resemble those of state or regional institutions, Article 8, Political Parties Act, *Uradni list RS*, Nos 62/94.

number of members[85] and/or the continuity of its activities,[86] documents required to be submitted at registration,[87] etc. In addition, certain rules also incorporate requirements as to the parties' internal organization. The Polish Constitution, for instance, states that parties act on the basis of 'voluntariness and equality of Polish citizens' (Article 11.1). This has been further interpreted by the Constitutional Tribunal as providing, more generally, that a political party's 'internal organization' must correspond to 'democratic principles' and that the violation of one of those principles, either by its membership rules or internal structure, must result in disqualification.[88] This type of requirement may be indirectly linked to the party's programme, as parties that are undemocratic in ideology tend also to be less internally democratic.

More important from the point of view of this chapter, however, are requirements that are openly substantive. The most common restrictions apply to parties whose activities may endanger fundamental freedoms, to those which attempt to use violence in order to gain power, or to those that foster discrimination, hatred, and violence. The Polish Constitution, for instance, includes an express ban on parties with programmes which 'appeal to totalitarian methods and practices of nazism, fascism and communism' and those whose programmes or activities are based on racial or nationalistic hatred.[89] According to the Bulgarian Constitution, parties may be prohibited both for pursuing fascist ideals and for formenting racial, national, religious, or ethnic unrest.[90] Latvian parties may be prohibited for fostering violence through propaganda. Peculiarly to postcommunist countries, and explicable with reference to their recent past, some postcommunist countries decided to include regulations that would help avoid any confusion between a political party and the state. For example, the Hungarian Constitution prohibits political parties from exercising political power.[91] In Slovakia, parties will not be registered if their statutes assume the

---

[85] In Estonia, a party must in principle have at least 1,000 members; in Latvia and Lithuania the minimum number of founders is fixed at 200, 400, and 500, respectively.

[86] In Romania, at the request of the Attorney General's department, the municipal court of Bucharest may dissolve a party for inactivity if it fails to present candidates in at least ten constituencies, alone or as part of an alliance, in two successive election campaigns, or if it has held no general assembly for five years. In Hungary a party may be dissolved if it has not functioned for at least a year and the number of its members has constantly been below the legal minimum, Article 3 (3) Law No. XXXIII of 1989 on the operation and financial functioning of political parties.

[87] In Estonia, for example, applications for registration must contain the party statute, the names, addresses, and telephone numbers of party leaders, the political programme, a list of party members with their names and addresses and, where appropriate, the party emblem.

[88] Decision W. 14/95 of 24 April 1996, OTK 1996, Vol. 1, item 16, 223–40, at 229. Note that this decision was handed down before the new Constitution entered into force (in 1997). However, the new Constitution virtually replicated the older constitutional and statutory rules regarding political parties so the 1996 interpretation by the Constitutional Tribunal remains applicable to the 1997 Constitution.

[89] Article 13 of the Constitution of the Republic of Poland of 2 April 1997. For other constitutional and sub-constitutional bans on communist and/or fascist, totalitarian, etc. parties, see Eva Brems, in this book, n. 107.

[90] Article 11(4) of the Constitution of the Republic of Bulgaria of 13 June 1991.

[91] Article 2(3) of the Constitution of Hungary.

conduct of activities exclusively the preserve of state authorities, and the Constitution provides that political parties 'shall be separate from the state'.[92]

As is clear from the above brief overview, CEE postcommunist legal systems envisage rather far-reaching grounds for the control, indeed prohibition, of political parties, with their bases in various vague criteria concerning conflicts with constitutional values.[93] Definitions of permissible restrictions are sufficiently broad to allow highly restrictive interpretations of the programmes, the practices, or the internal structures of parties, making it possible to ban parties falling out of favour with a current ruling elite or, more benignly, which indeed pose a threat to democratic consolidation. Restrictions may operate both *ex ante*, as in the case of bans on forming a political party or refusal to register one, or *ex post*, in the form of party dissolution.

There is a fine line between parties advocating undemocratic *aims* (that is, aims found undemocratic by the interpreters and enforcers of the rule) and those which use undemocratic *means* to achieve their aims, whatever those aims may be.[94] Such a dividing line is, however, sustainable and should be maintained, at least as a rule of thumb for the legitimate limit on state interference with political parties. This is because intervention against parties using violent and undemocratic methods to achieve their aims may be necessary to protect democracy, while interference with a party on the basis of its aims is much more questionable from the point of view of the principles of liberal democracy. Thus a particularly dangerous situation is presented when a party renounces extra-constitutional, non-democratic means and uses only political methods to seek as many supporters as possible in elections, in order to achieve aims which may be seen as democratic (democracy must have built-in devices of political change, including of constitutional change); here, a ban on the party on the basis that its aims are unconstitutional may simply be a disguised attempt to entrench the political status quo by those benefiting most from current constitutional arrangements. One defect, from the point of view of liberal-democratic principles, of many postcommunist constitutional restrictions on political parties is that they do not clearly distinguish between the two grounds for restrictions. Characteristically, the Polish constitutional catalogue of grounds on which

---

[92] Article 29(4) of the Constitution of the Slovak Republic.

[93] Note that denial of registration or dissolution are not the only measures which can be used to restrict parties. Milder but often quite effective means may include heightening the required number of signatures for a party to stand for election, making conditions for eligibility for state funding and introducing election thresholds. These work on the theory that measures which make it more difficult for a party to get into parliament effectively undermine the viability of these parties. They are a double-edged sword, however, because they adversely affect all small and unpopular parties, not necessarily just the undemocratic ones.

[94] The distinction corresponds, roughly, to the German distinction between the 'radical' organizations, which are *verfassungsfeindlich* (opposed to constitutional principles), and the extremist ones which are *verfassungswidrig* (unconstitutional). The practical consequence is that the latter ones are closely monitored by state security while the former are not. See C. Mudde, 'Liberal Democracies and the Extremist Challenges of the Early 21st Century', http://www.extremismus.com/texte/demo2.ht.

parties may be restricted lists in one breath, in Article 13, grounds relating to parties' methods of action and to ideas they propagate or embrace.

In reality, however, the 'militant democracy' model has hardly become established in the CEE—to the point that one knowledgeable observer concluded that postcommunist constitutional states are 'rather defenceless against emotionally manipulative politics and challenges that exploit constitutional opportunities'.[95] Even if, at the constitutional level, there may seem to be ample grounds for sanctioning anti-democratic parties, at the level of statutes and the practice of law enforcers, CEE postcommunist states have been extremely reluctant, or lax, in putting 'militant democracy' into practice.[96] Over the last decade, political parties have been refused registration in countries in Central and Eastern Europe in a number of cases. Yet most often this has stemmed from a failure to comply with formal regulations. In Poland in just one case has the constitutionality of a political party's statute been questioned; the Constitutional Tribunal rejected the motion.[97]

The infrequency of party dissolution on the grounds of the programme or activities in CEE countries arises not because of a lack of extremist parties and associations in those countries. In Poland, for instance, a very small but vocal neo-Nazi group pursues an openly anti-Semitic programme. In the words of Rafal Pankowski, leader of a Polish NGO which monitors extreme right-wing organizations: 'What is specific for Poland is not so much a degree of support for nationalistic views but rather the scope of general social acceptance and also the inaction by the authorities.'[98] As an example in this context he cites the radical organization, Narodowe Odrodzenie Polski (National Revival of

---

[95] Sajo, above, n. 66, at 78.

[96] The most important cases, and in particular those which reached the European Court of Human Rights, are described in the chapter by Eva Brems in this volume, including the dissolution of a Macedonian party in Bulgaria, see the chapter by Brems, text accompanying footnotes 58–59, communist parties in Romania and Bulgaria, text accompanying footnotes 60–61, and in Latvia, text accompanying footnotes 247–51, a Moldovan Christian Democratic party, text accompanying footnotes 67–68, etc.

[97] In its decision of 8 March 2000, the Constitutional Tribunal decided to uphold the statute of a party called 'Christian Democracy of the Third Polish Republic' even though the lower court charged with the task of the registration of parties objected to what it saw as undemocratic internal rules, such as the authority of the party's leader to appoint and dismiss regional leaders. In a wide-ranging argument the Tribunal adopted a presumption in favour of respect for discretion in internal organization considering it to be an aspect of the freedom to form political parties. It indicated that rules of internal party organization can be taken into account in decisions about a party's registration only if they indicate a party's use of undemocratic means of influencing the government, see Decision Pp 1/99 of the Constitutional Tribunal (on file with the authors). There was also another, more recent occasion in which the Constitutional Tribunal could have reviewed the statute of a party from the point of view of its inconsistency with constitutional principles (at stake was the statute of the Party Samoobrona which, effectively, established a system of Führerprinzip). However, on the basis of procedural technicalities, the Tribunal refused to enter into a discussion on the merits of the case, see Decision Pp 1/02 of 16 July 2003 (on file with the authors).

[98] See 'Krajobraz brunatnieje', Interview with Rafal Pankowski, *Tygodnik Powszechny* (Cracow) No. 9/2004 of 29 February 2004: http://tygodnik.onet.pl/1547,1151807,0,324079,dzial.html.

Poland), which is openly racist and which is unobstructed in disseminating its neo-fascist propaganda. Parties of this type operate in most countries in the region and, at times, they come close to being elected, the percentage of votes they acquire varying from under 1 per cent of the popular vote for parties like the Bulgarian National Radical Party (BNRP) to around 5 per cent for parties like the Hungarian Justice and Life Party (MIÉP). If anything, militant democracy measures have been under-utilized in the CEE. How can this be explained?

As in the case of restrictions on hate speech, there is more than one reason for the under-enforcement of MD measures towards extremist parties. First, there is a clear and legitimate aversion to illiberal measures (even if employed for the right reasons), based on the special experience of a recent totalitarian past. There is also a widespread perception that political means of combating anti-democratic parties are better and more effective than legal ones, a perception based partly on the fear of adding to the popularity of extremists by creating 'martyrs', and by providing them with a judicial forum for spreading their ideologies, etc. There is also in CEE countries, however, a perception (often reflecting hidden, indirect sympathy for the programmes of extremist parties and movements) that such parties are not dangerous, and that there are 'more important problems' for courts and the prosecutorial system to address, especially in the face of a surge in ordinary criminality.

The borderline between these different motivations are fluid, and condemnable leniency towards dangerous extremism is often presented as a principled liberal policy. However, genuine commitment to the latter cannot be excluded altogether, and there have been some good-faith disagreements within post-communist states on the limits of justified tolerance for extremists and those who are themselves intolerant. To be sure, such controversies have more usually emerged with regard to restrictions on freedom of speech than with respect to party closures. The latter, it has been argued, are less objectionable because they do not close all avenues of political expression.[99] On the other hand, it should be noted that party closures, compared to limits on speech, are a particularly dangerous instrument in societies which do not demonstrate any reticence to speak freely, but which do suffer from weaknesses in civil society and self-organization, including in party formation. Party closures should be undertaken as a last resort and with great care, because of the direct threat to basic political processes that they pose, and the corollary risk of increasing social cynicism about the self-serving usage of the law by political elites.

Moreover, a widespread perception has taken hold in CEE countries that there is no clear line between dangerous 'extremism' and legitimate parties, and that 'extremists' should be politically shunned but legally tolerated or even included within the system rather than kept out of it. In the CEE, as universally, tolerating the intolerant is often not based on a principled liberalism but driven

---

[99] Sajo, above, n. 66, at 82 and 85.

by purely pragmatic considerations (better having them inside than outside the system) or on a degree of identification with the intolerant (and if not identification, then at the very least only mild condemnation). In some countries, such as Slovakia, extremists have simply been co-opted into government. In others, such as Hungary, though kept out of government, they have at various points been courted to secure their support for particular legislation.

5.6 LUSTRATION, DECOMMUNIZATION, AND THE EQUALITY OF POLITICAL RIGHTS

5.6.1 'Let Bygones Be Bygones'?

Right at the outset of their transition to democracy, the postcommunist countries of the CEE had also to handle some difficult problems concerning their immediate past. The peaceful, negotiated form of transition that prevailed in the region meant that many individuals responsible for authoritarian rule, indeed sometimes for outright crimes, remained politically active in the newly democratized states. One fundamental question thus raised was whether legal tolerance towards such people is reconcilable with the requirements of political justice as well as the exigencies of a democratic society. Should the public sphere be 'cleansed' of those discredited by direct involvement with a communist regime, at the risk of creating a category of second-class citizenship, and even, given the danger, of disloyalty towards the democratic state? Or should an attitude of 'letting bygones be bygones' be adopted for the sake of national reconciliation—a policy of forgiveness, if not of forgetting?

From the point of view of the political rights of citizens, the most controversial and troubling issue emerging in the CEE in the context of 'dealing with the past' was that of 'lustration' (or purges) of public officials for past involvement in communist regimes, in particular for collaboration with the secret police. 'Lustration' is seen by its proponents as the main device of 'decommunization', that is, of cleansing the public sphere of the newly democratized society of those who have shown their utter disregard for the values of democracy and liberty. It is based on the idea that certain individuals cannot be trusted due to their position and activities in the past regime and should therefore be excluded from access to certain public offices. By its opponents, in turn, lustration is viewed as a tool of division that applies the principle of collective responsibility.

A host of moral, political, and practical concerns rendered the issues of 'lustration' and 'decommunization' (understood as the exclusion of certain defined categories of ex-communist officials from the right to run for, and occupy, certain public positions in the new democratic system) particularly controversial and troubling. Can a break with the past be made in a way that does not itself compromise the legal and constitutional attributes of a democratic state: the rule of law, equality before the law, the individualization of guilt, the non-retroactivity of legal sanctions, etc? Significantly, many thoroughly democratically-oriented, non-communist participants in the debate have expressed strong reservations concerning the policies of lustration and decommunization. Vojtech Cepl, an eminent Czech legal scholar and later a judge of the Constitutional Court, admitted right at the outset of the post-communist era to his own 'deep ambivalence about lustration'. On the one hand, he recognized the need to know about the evil committed in the past and the need, inter alia, to preclude the possibility of 'entrusting our future to people who can be continually blackmailed'; on the other, he expressed concern both about 'careless and indiscriminate lustration', and also about the direction of lustration's main thrust at the low-level executioners of orders rather than against those issuing them.[100]

An important theme in debates around lustration concerned its consequences for a newly democratized society. Is it wise to reopen old wounds and create divisions in a society that needs a high degree of coherence to handle the challenges facing it? Those answering this question in the negative relied heavily on the divisiveness of the effects of lustration. Lustration was embarked upon to clear up the secrets of the past and make for greater transparency and openness, but its immediate consequence was the exclusion of some people from the first category of citizenship. Further, there was a fundamental problem with the reliability of evidence used for 'lustration' purposes, namely, the files of the former secret police apparatus. Much of this documentation is incomplete, with parts destroyed during transition (in Czechoslovakia around 90 per cent of secret police registers were destroyed after the Velvet Revolution, as the unreformed secret service controlled the archives until June 1990; similar situations have been reported in many other CEE countries).[101] More importantly, those documents remaining often do not make clear whether a person was an informer/collaborator or merely a candidate for such a role. Further, police agents often inflated the numbers of collaborators co-opted, according to official records, in order to improve their status and financial rewards. As a result, material in police archives is likely to be both over-inclusive (including the names of many phoney agents) and under-inclusive (missing the files of many genuine collaborators).

The evolution of 'lustration' has also been affected, to some degree, by its external context. The stance of Western democratic governments and commentators after the fall of communism was quite opposite to that following the Second World War, when Western allied powers pressured Germany to conduct a wide-ranging denazification of its state apparatus. Indeed, some Western observers of the CEE came to view the idea of 'corrective justice' as antithetical

[100] V. Cepl, 'Ritual Sacrifices' (1992) 1:1 *East Europ Constit Rev* 24–26, at 25.
[101] A. Tucker, 'Paranoids May Be Persecuted: Post-Totalitarian Retroactive Justice' (1999) 40 *Arch europ social* 56–100, at 64.

to constitutionalism itself. This argument is nicely encapsulated in Bruce Ack-erman's assertion: 'An emphasis on corrective justice will divide the citizenry into two groups—evildoers and innocent victims . . . Constitutional creation unites; corrective justice divides.'[102] Another commentator of Eastern European back-ground recently complained that 'seeing lustration with "Western eyes", namely from a democratic and liberal viewpoint but lacking an understanding of the totalitarian experience, became extremely popular among centre and left-wing politicians, who persuaded their electorates that "doing nothing" was the best and most prudent strategy of breaking with the legacy of the past'.[103]

A resolution adopted in 1996 by the Parliamentary Assembly of the Council of Europe, outlining how lustration procedures should be designed in order to be compatible with the principles of the rule of law, is very interesting in this regard.[104] This resolution does not condemn the idea of lustration outright; indeed, it acknowledges, without sounding any disapproval, that 'some states have found it necessary to introduce administrative measures, such as lustration or decommunization laws'.[105] But amongst the criteria it specifies such laws must meet to be compatible with 'a democratic state under the rule of law', the most important is that lustration laws must be based on the principle of individual, rather than collective guilt, which 'must be proven in each indi-vidual case'.[106] Rejecting the collective approach, the resolution appears to go further than it would claim to, and can be read as delegitimizing the very principle of decommunization. Further, it is made clear that lustration may only be used for the protection of the democratization process, and not for 'punishment, retribution or revenge'.[107] This serves to emphasize even more strongly its preference for an individual approach, given the inherent tension between the utilitarian purpose of lustration and the collective identification of the persons to be removed from public office. A collective approach to lustra-tion serves well the purpose of emphatic retribution for the sins of the past, but it is exactly this that the resolution (and most official rhetoric concerning lus-tration in the CEE) specifically prohibits.

5.6.2 'Lustration' Regimes

There is a considerable spectrum of approaches to 'lustration' and 'decom-munization' in CEE countries. Three variables appear to be the prime determinants of the severity and seriousness of methods used to 'settle old

---

[102] B. Ackerman, *The Future of Liberal Revolution* (New Haven, CT: Yale University Press, 1992), at 71.
[103] N. Letki, 'Lustration and Decommunization in East-Central Europe' (2002) 54 *Europe-Asia Studies* 529–52, at 539, footnote omitted.
[104] Resolution of the Parliamentary Assembly of Council of Europe No. 1096 of 27 June 1996 on measures to dismantle the heritage of former communist totalitarian systems, http://stars. coe.fr/Main.asp?link = http%3A%2F%2Fstars.coe.fr%2FDocuments%2FAdoptedText%2Fta96% 2FERES1096.htm.   [105] Ibid, section 11.
[106] Ibid, section 12.   [107] Ibid, section 12.

accounts'. First, the more repressive was the past regime, the harsher and more pervasive, the more robust is the ensuing decommunization process. Second, the manner of the old regime's 'exit' matters. In negotiated transitions, ex-officials of the communist regime played an important role as interlocutors and collaborators with former dissidents, and it was both politically impossible and socially awkward to propose measures aimed at disabling them from performing official political roles in the new system. In addition, forgiveness could be seen as a form of reward for good behaviour during the transition period. Third, the political strength and influence of parties connected to the old regime in the early years after transition has been significant, as those participating in governing coalitions (or even in opposition parties with a high degree of influence) could, and did, use their clout to obstruct effective lustration measures.

A fourth factor (and a secondary one, because heavily influenced by the three just mentioned) has to do with timing. When, due to political circumstances, lustration was placed on the agenda relatively late (as in Poland, where the first successful lustration law was enacted only in 1997), measures adopted have been weaker—partly because of the increasing unreliability of the files on which lustration determinations could be made, and partly because public emotions became, with time, less pronounced.

In the Czech Republic a relatively harsh position on decommunization and lustration was adopted. The Czechoslovak lustration law of 4 October 1991 stated that those who had collaborated with the security services of the communist regime, or had held a position within the regime (defined very broadly and covering even such people as secretaries of the Party at district level), could not now hold high position in governmental bodies and organizations for a period of five years. Even rather low-level former functionaries of the Party, from township and district levels up, were barred from holding certain positions, irrespective of whether they had collaborated with state security agencies, or been involved in criminal activities, or not.[108] Offices from which such persons were barred included positions in state institutions, and also key positions in the military, judiciary, universities, state-run media, and many other state-run enterprises (including joint-stock companies with the state as main shareholder). Despite the subjection of a wide range of public offices to the lustration procedure, positions contested in general democratic elections were not affected by the law. Each employee or prospective employee within the range of categories covered by lustration was required to ask for a certificate of 'negative lustration' that would be submitted to an employer, or in the case of elected officials, to parliament.

Though initially set to expire at the end of 1996, the 1991 Czechoslovak law was in 1995 extended in the Czech Republic until the end of 2000, and again in

---

[108] H. A. Welsh, 'Dealing with the Communist Past: Central and East European Experiences after 1990' (1996) 48 *Europe-Asia Studies* 413–28, at 415.

2000, indefinitely. The initial 1991 law was challenged before the Constitutional Court of the Czech and Slovak Republic, in what was easily the most important case considered by that Court before the 'divorce' of the two constituent entities of the Republic and the first Court's substitution by its two successors.[109] The Court found the lustration law in general to be constitutional, justifying it on grounds of security and democracy and noting the extraordinary nature of the transition period during which there is a greater susceptibility to relapse towards a totalitarian system. The key argument was that former members of the security services may try to influence or reverse democratic developments. The Court did, however, find one provision to be unconstitutional, which included in the scope of lustration those who were merely *candidates* for clandestine collaboration.

Later, the Czech Constitutional Court upheld the amendments of 2000 which had removed time restrictions on the validity of the lustration provisions. The challenge was based on the argument that the main rationale for the earlier law, namely that it countered 'the risk of subversion or a possible return of totalitarianism',[110] was no longer valid after the consolidation of democracy, and that there was no reason to extend transitional measures, extraordinary *par excellence*. The Czech Constitutional Court admitted that part of the earlier decision was based on the extraordinary nature of the moment of transition and the short-lived effect of the law. However, it held that these were not crucial, central justifications for the decision, which was based on the fact that in all democratic systems the state should be able to require loyalty to democratic principles, to set requirements to protect the security of its citizens, and to further democratic development. Nevertheless, the Court's ruling also emphasized that political circumstances change, and the relevance of the lustration law decreases with the passage of time. It therefore is possible to imagine that a future constitutional complaint challenging the law might lead to a revision of the Constitutional Court's current position.

A much more lenient approach to lustration policies was adopted in Poland and Hungary, where the ostensible object of lustration was to verify and reveal the past of public officials (and candidates for public positions) without, however, banning those 'positively lustrated' (i.e. certified as connected in the past to the security services) from such offices. It is significant that both in Poland and Hungary the terms of transition were negotiated in round-table discussions between Communist Party officials and the opposition, and the loyalty of Communist Party activists (however renamed and reformed) to the negotiated rules was a central factor in a peaceful and eventually successful transition. The weak retribution meted out by lustration in the years after transition (as well as the relative lateness of

---

[109] Constitutional Court of the Czech and Slovak Federal Republic Decision No. 1/92 of 26 November 1992, see: http://www.concourt.cz/angl_ver/decisions/doc/p-1-92.html.
[110] Ibid, at 3.

any measures imposed) can therefore be seen as functionally linked to the role of ex-communists in transition itself and also to their influence upon legislation in the first post-transition period.

In Hungary, the legislature passed a fairly mild lustration law in 1994 providing for the creation of three-judge panels to examine whether *present* public office-holders (the President, ministers, high officials, members of parliament, judges, some journalists, and persons with high positions in state universities and public companies) had either collaborated with state security services or been members of the fascist Arrow Cross Party. Even if a person was found 'guilty', relevant information would only be made public if he or she refused to resign his or her post; and 'guilty' persons could hold onto their jobs even once such information was made public. The Constitutional Court found the 1994 law to be partly unconstitutional and offered some pointers and a time limit (July 1996) for the enactment of a new law.[111] Parliament sought to comply with these suggestions by enacting, in 1996, a new and greatly weakened lustration law.[112] This limited the category of people subject to the law to persons required to take an oath before Parliament or the President, and those elected by Parliament. Also narrowed was the concept of collaboration with the state security apparatus, now restricted to those belonging to a state security organization, who actually submitted reports or otherwise informed on others, or were paid by the organization.

The current Polish position is quite similar in that it applies only to collaboration with the secret police, and 'positive lustration' does not necessarily result in the loss of one's position or eligibility for such a position. However, the model adopted differs from Hungary's in that it requires various position-holders and candidates to declare publicly whether they had been collaborators. It is only in the case of a declaration established by a court as *false* (the so-called 'lustration lie') that a person loses the right to hold public office or run in elections (for a period of ten years). That penalty is, strictly speaking, for lying about one's past, and not for the fact of one's prior collaboration with the secret police. The range of positions addressed is relatively broad, including all elected state officials from the President downwards, including parliamentary candidates, ministers, state functionaries above the rank of deputy provincial governor, judges, prosecutors, barristers (on the basis of a 1998 amendment to the law), and leading figures in the public media. As a result of the 1997 law, about 22,000 public officials were obliged to disclose all forms of voluntary, secret collaboration with the security service between 1944 and 1990.

---

[111] Decision 60/1994 (X11.24) of 22 December 1994, reprinted in (1995) 2 *East European Case Reporter of Constitutional Law* 159–93; excerpts in Sólyom and Brunner, above, n. 20, at 306–15. The references below are to the excerpts in the latter volume.

[112] Law LXII/1996. For a discussion on the political background see G. Halmai and K. Lane Scheppele, 'Living Well Is the Best Revenge: The Hungarian Approach to Judging the Past,' in A. J. McAdams (ed.), *Transitional Justice and the Rule of Law in New Democracies* (Notre Dame, CT: University of Notre Dame Press, 1997), 155–84, at 176–77.

In the end, after the fall of communism, lustration and decommunization were undertaken on a reasonably wide scale only in the ex-GDR (where their success was facilitated by the special situation of the absorption of the whole defunct state into the new unified Germany, with its Western part playing the role of judge over its Eastern, communism-tainted brethren) and in the Czech Republic. In our view, the Czech lustration law has resulted in the retention of significant structural defects in the liberal democratic rule of law. Legal certainty has been compromised by the temporal extension of lustration, raising doubts about the quality of the political process in the Czech Republic. The 'normalization of lustrations' within the Czech political and legal context is one of the biggest failures of the transitional period.

In contrast, lustration practices adopted in Poland, Hungary, and other states of the region were more timid and limited. They can be seen principally as symbolic measures, emphasizing more the value of transparency than that of purge (although the scale of the actual purge occurring in the Czech Republic must not be exaggerated either).[113] In Hungary and Poland, in slightly differing ways, the aim was to elicit statements from public figures about their past rather than to remove from their current positions those implicated in discreditable activities, or to disqualify them from applying or running for such positions in the future. This was partly for self-serving reasons (stemming from the influence of ex-communists on the law-making process during the transition period) and partly a result of the non-revolutionary nature of the transition, which necessitated a degree of continuity, including at the level of personnel. The discourse of constitutional continuity, propounded vigorously by constitutional courts, made it very difficult to draw sharp distinctions between different candidates for public offices based on their previous activities.

5.7 CONCLUSION

Political rights played a central role in the democratization of CEE states after the fall of communism. They determined the post-1989 democratic political

---

[113] It is estimated that only a few hundred Czechs lost their jobs due to lustration after the law had been enforced and that around 5 per cent of the members of parliament were forced to resign, see Tucker, above, n. 99, at 84. The Ministry of Interior of the Czech Republic currently receives between 6,000 and 8,000 lustration requests per year and the total number of lustration certificates issued between 1991 and 2001 was 402,270. In 2001, the Ministry of Interior received 6,770 lustration requests (7,280 requests in 2002), out of which 2.5 per cent did not receive confirmation of a clear record. For details see US Department of State Report on Human Rights Practices in the Czech Republic, 2001, issued by the Bureau of Democracy, Human Rights, and Labor on March 4, 2002, available on: http://www.state.gov/g/drl/rls/hrrpt/2001/eur/8243.htm; for an update, see US Department of State Report on Human Rights Practices in the Czech Republic, 2002, issued by the Bureau of Democracy, Human Rights, and Labor on 31 March 2003, available on: http://www.state.gov/g/drl/rls/hrrpt/2002/18361pf.htm.

discourse and transformation, and comprised a central marker of the distinction between the authoritarian past and the democratic present and future. Political rights provided the basis for the institutional design of new political institutions, the benchmark for assessing the quality of institutions identified as indispensable in a democracy, and a new tool empowering the citizen against the emerging democratic state. They were also key at the level of the Europeanization process, as part of postcommunist 'return to Europe' policies, as a crucial point of reference for judging the distance which still separated countries in transition from their goal identified with the (real or perceived) model of liberal democracy in Western Europe, and as a technical criterion of the EU accession process.

Political rights had been the top priority of dissident groups and pro-democracy movements in the late 1980s. In contrast to socio-economic rights, they were seen, rightly, as the most fundamental vehicle for the transformation of the authoritarian, undemocratic states to the system of constitutional democracy. However, the change has been more difficult than many had expected. The legacy of an authoritarian mentality and habits, combined with the weakness of civil society, resulted in many failings and inconsistencies in the implementation of political rights, as evidenced earlier in this chapter. The political rights agenda was inseparable from democratic state-building and therefore significantly affected constitution-making and the emerging systems of the separation of powers in the post-1989 CEE states. Different policies of decommunization, including retrospective legislation and lustration laws, illustrate the dilemmas of the democratic rule of law after the fall of communism.

The European aspect of the postcommunist democratization processes in the CEE enhanced the institutional power of political rights and limited the danger of authoritarian policies emerging in the region in the 1990s. The European Union functioned as a centre of gravity, preventing the CEE postcommunist states from wandering from the path of 'return'. Slovakia, experiencing the most turbulent political developments after the split of the Czechoslovak federation in 1992, yet still managing to join the Union together with the other new Member States in 2004, probably offers the best example of EU 'gravitational pull'.

At the level of the organization of state institutions, standards achieved in the building of such institutions safeguarding political rights has been quite impressive in the CEE states overall. However, the robustness of political rights depends also on the institutions of civil society, such as associations, trade unions, professional organizations, local self-government, consumer groups, etc., with incentives, capacities, and the necessary resources to claim their political rights: the 'demand' side is at least as important as the 'supply' side as far as rights are concerned. Rights which are not aggressively claimed by non-state actors will be restricted or under-protected by the state and powerful private interests alike. Political rights signal the process of democratization and form the public sphere by providing legal protection for the citizen against the state. Nevertheless, their legal protection is meaningless unless it is fully exploited politically by a range of different actors.

6

The Political Rights of National Minorities: Lessons from Central and Eastern Europe

Gwendolyn Sasse

6.1 NATIONAL MINORITIES WITHIN THE CONTEXT OF RIGHTS[1]

Constitutionally enshrined rights are both a traditional safeguard against the arbitrary use of power and the foundation for participation in a polity. Rights that are enforceable reflect the values on which a political system is founded. As a defining marker of the polity, rights fulfil an integrating and legitimating function, and they embody an aspirational element.[2] The notion of rights has become more elaborate and differentiated over time. T. H. Marshall's classic study 'Citizenship and Social Class', which traced both the expanding catalogue of rights and the growing number of people to whom these rights apply, located the formative period of civil rights in the 18th century, that of political rights in the 19th century, and that of social rights in the 20th century. In Marshall's account, social rights were not necessarily tied to citizenship, a political and economic reality that still holds today.[3] Despite the widespread references to civil, political, social, and economic rights in legal, political, and public discourse, the distinctions between

---

[1] The research for this chapter was supported by a Leverhulme Research Fellowship.

[2] See also Damian Chalmer's definition of political rights as 'a form of reason grounding the justification for politics in popular authorship' in this volume.

[3] Marshall's main concern was the lack of a social dimension to traditional notions of citizenship. He defined civil rights as 'the rights necessary for individual freedom—liberty of the person, freedom of speech, thought and faith, the right to own property and to conclude valid contracts, and the right to justice' and linked them to the courts of justice. Political rights are defined to include 'the rights to participate in the exercise of political power, as a member of a body invested with political authority or as an elector of the members of such a body' and correspond to parliament and local councils. Social rights in this definition range from 'the right to a modicum of economic welfare and security to the right to share to the full in the social heritage and to live the life of a civilised being according to the standards prevailing in the society', all of which are most closely connected with the educational system and the social services'. See T. H. Marshall and T. Bottomore, *Citizenship and Social Class* (London: Pluto Press, 1992), at 8.

the different rights remain fuzzy.[4] In fact, the processes of globalization, migration, and supranational integration have further blurred the distinctions in the context of changing notions of sovereignty and territory. The increasing disassociation of civil, political, and social rights from state sovereignty 'give(s) rise to different spheres of belonging and spheres of political participation'[5] which can, but do not have to, overlap. This chapter is divided into two parts: first, it will place the issue of minority rights in the wider legal and theoretical context of rights and classify them as political rights; second, it will draw on the experience of Central and Eastern Europe to analyse the politics of minority rights.

There is a clear overlap between certain civil and political rights, in particular with regard to the right to freely assemble and form associations. The boundary between social and economic rights also remains blurry, as social and economic rights tend to target the same groups—for example migrants—and pursue the same overarching goals, such as poverty reduction or social inclusion. An economic right such as the freedom of movement has both a social and a political dimension. Apart from these linkages between different sets of rights there is the issue of an underlying hierarchy of rights.[6] Civil rights come closest to the notion of human rights, but any link to citizenship ties them to the idea of political rights. By comparison, the gap between civil and political rights, on the one hand, and social and economic rights, on the other, appears to be wider. Social and economic rights are more specific and targeted and by definition require positive state action. They do not depend on citizenship per se and may be cast as more limited or as a corrective and potentially temporary measure. By contrast, the principle of the 'indivisibility' of rights, which remains controversial in both the national and the EU context, posits an inclusive package of interdependent rights. In a recent study of the impact of European rights on the legal cultures of the Member States, Aziz has demonstrated that political and social rights are at times impossible to separate.[7] A meaningful implementation of political rights presupposes a notion of economic and social rights.[8] Moreover, the increasing 'multijurisdictionality may also disaggregate rights protection so that it becomes fragmented across a number of borders both within and without the nation-state in which scattered networks of both institutional and extra-institutional actors operate'.[9] The Council Directive 2003/109/EC on the status and rights of Third Country Nationals provides one of the best illustrations in this context.

---

[4] Marshall himself admitted the existence of overlap, especially between political and social rights.
[5] M. Aziz, *The Impact of European Rights on National Legal Cultures* (Oxford: Hart, 2004), at 79.
[6] One view holds that social and economic rights are superior to civil and political rights, the opposite view holds that social and economic rights do not constitute rights and threaten to undermine individual freedoms as enshrined by civil and political rights; see H. J. Steiner and P. Alston, *International Human Rights in Context: Law, Politics, Morals* (Oxford: Oxford University Press, 2000), at 237.   [7] Aziz, above, n. 5, at 7.
[8] For a similar argument, see the chapter by Michel Rosenfeld in this volume.
[9] Ibid, at 19.

The use of the term 'fundamental rights' allows for a wide definition of rights, including social and economic rights. The EU's Charter of Fundamental Rights, which has yet to become a legally binding document, provides a good example in this respect, as it breaks through the dichotomy of social and economic rights versus civil and political rights. The European Court of Justice (ECJ) case law does not make a principled distinction between social and other fundamental rights and the EU Charter of Fundamental Rights includes social rights, but overall the trajectory of social rights in EU law is still distinct from that of other fundamental rights (though not less prominent).[10] Evidence drawn from policy-making indicates a greater willingness on the part of politicians to engage with the concept of social and economic rights, for example in order to facilitate access to the labour market or equal opportunities. From a politician's point of view, the provision of social and economic rights to vulnerable groups, such as immigrants, is perceived of as a smaller political risk than the extension of political rights, such as the right to vote in local elections irrespective of citizenship. The impression created is one of social and economic rights being essentially apolitical and therefore less controversial or far-reaching than political rights. This logic is inherently flawed: if social and economic rights target specific, vulnerable groups of residents, they tend to go hand in hand with political judgments and perceptions. Ultimately, they are bound to define or reinforce the distinction between political insiders and outsiders.

Social rights are an intrinsic part of the welfare state, which, in turn, was tied to the concept of the nation-state. The notion of the homogenous nation-state has come under pressure by waves of migration, and the notion of welfare needs to be rethought if it is to incorporate anti-discrimination, minority rights, and supranational integration. In the EU context, social rights are prominent in a number of areas, such as social policy, labour, and anti-discrimination. The basic question of what constitutes a justiciable social right is wide open and ultimately forms part of a political or ideological judgment, thereby illustrating another overlap of the social and the political. Potentially, there is even more room for disagreement and controversy in the sphere of social rights than in the area of civil and political rights. Many post-communist constitutions still contain a reference to the right to work, one of the widest possible definitions of a social right extended to all citizens.

Political rights are inextricably linked to issues of identity and the demos. They define the scope for participation and are, first and foremost, tied to citizenship or, at least, a residency status. As such, they define the polity and legitimacy of the political system. Increasingly, however, 'political participation through judicial activism has rendered the distinction between political rights stricto sensu and rights of interests with a political dimension ambiguous'.[11] In the EU context, the traditional link between citizenship and political rights has become more tenuous,

---

[10] B. de Witte, 'The Trajectory of Social Rights in the European Union', Paper presented at the workshop 'Social Rights in Europe', European University Institute, Florence, 18–19 June 2004.

[11] Aziz, above, n. 5, at 70.

not least through the (limited) elaboration of EU citizenship and a wider range of forms of political participation, including recourse to the courts.[12]

Three instruments make up the so-called International Bill of Rights, which maps the range of different rights discussed so far: the Universal Declaration of Human Rights of 1948, the International Covenant on Civil and Political Rights (ICCPR), and the International Covenant on Economic, Social and Cultural Rights (ICESCR).[13] Individual rights form the core of these instruments, though the ICCPR asserts or hints at rights pertaining to and being exercised by a collectivity. Article 1 restates the provision from the UN Charter that 'all peoples have a right to "self-determination"', which allows them to 'freely determine their political status and freely pursue their economic, social and cultural development'; Article 27 stipulates that 'in states in which ethnic, religious or linguistic minorities exist, persons belonging to such minorities shall not be denied the right, in community with other members of their group, to enjoy their own culture, to profess and practice their own religion, or to use their own language'.[14] It is telling that the ICCPR groups civil and political rights together.

Steiner and Alston have distinguished five main categories of rights enshrined in the ICCPR which, however, exclude the more controversial Articles 1 and 27: the protection of an individual's integrity, procedural fairness when government deprives an individual of liberty, equal protection norms defined in racial, religious, gender and other terms, freedoms of belief, speech and association, and the right to political participation.[15] The overlap between civil and political rights could not be more obvious. Moreover, the existence of two covenants reflects the disagreement over the position of social and economic rights in particular, although the UN posits that the two covenants are 'interdependent' rather than hierarchical.[16]

As we have seen so far, the context of rights is already complex before minority rights enter the picture. There is as yet no agreed-upon international definition of what constitutes a national minority, thereby leaving the notion of minority rights in an international legal and political limbo. The evidence of 'rights protectionism',[17] which views a certain set of rights as the natural heritage is particularly relevant in the sensitive field of human and minority rights. Most definitions of a national minority describe a numerical, non-dominant minority that combines objective criteria, such as specific cultural characteristics distinct from the majority of the population, and subjective criteria, such as a collective sense of community.[18]

---

[12] Ibid, at 67.

[13] Both these Covenants became effective in 1976. For a systematic discussion on these three instruments, see Steiner and Alston, above, n. 6, at 136–320.

[14] ICCPR, reprinted in Steiner and Alston, above, n. 6, at 1381–94.

[15] Steiner and Alston, above, n. 6, at 145.   [16] Ibid, at 247.

[17] Aziz, above, n. 5, at 6.

[18] P. Thornberry, *International Law and the Rights of Minorities* (Oxford: Clarendon, 1990); J. Jackson-Preece, *National Minorities and the European Nation-States System* (Oxford: Clarendon Press, 1998).

The 1992 UN Declaration on the Rights of Persons Belonging to National or Ethnic, Religious or Linguistic Minorities follows up on Article 27 of the ICCPR, referring to the right to express one's culture in private and in public without discrimination, 'the right to participate effectively in cultural, religious, social, economic and public life', 'the right to participate effectively in decisions on the national and, where appropriate, regional level' (Article 2), and allows for persons belonging to minorities to 'exercise their rights . . . individually as well as in community with other members of their group' (Article 3).[19] The overall absence of clear-cut definitions and binding guidelines, however, makes it difficult to locate minority rights in the system of rights discussed above. The starting-point is twofold: first, the relationship between human rights, understood as individual rights, and minority rights, understood as group-specific or collective rights, has long been disputed, and the discussion tends to go round in circles. Secondly, minority rights could be defined as civil, political, social, and economic rights or, put differently, they could have a bearing on the whole catalogue of rights.

The concept of 'minority protection' hovers between the prohibition of discrimination on the basis of ethnic origin, race, or nationality (understood as citizenship) as the minimum standard, on the one hand, and the preservation and promotion of the separate identity of minority groups, on the other. The former is concerned with formal equality and is undisputed within the discourse on the principles of liberal democracy. It can be understood as the precondition for the preservation and promotion of minority identities, which in turn can also be conceptualized as contributing to the overarching goal of creating equality of access and opportunities. In the field of anti-discrimination legislation both in EU law and at the level of EU Member States, measures actively combating discrimination potentially create a channel for the promotion of minority identities.[20] In particular, immigrants—so-called 'new minorities'— have been given social and economic rights, while in the case of 'old minorities' a distinctive cultural identity and/or political representation tends to be of primary importance.[21]

It is suggested here that within the existing catalogue of rights, minority rights are best understood as political rights. A sufficiently flexible definition of political rights can usefully incorporate cultural rights. Governments may prefer

[19] See reprinted Declaration in Steiner and Alston, above, n. 6, at 1298.

[20] B. de Witte, 'The Constitutional Resources for an EU Minority Protection Policy', in G. N. Toggenburg (ed.), *Minority Protection and the Enlarged European Union: The Way Forward* (Budapest: OSI/LG, 2004), at 107–24.

[21] The increasingly widespread distinction between 'old' and 'new' minorities suggests rigid categories, clearly demarcated needs of certain groups and an inherent hierarchy of claims. Therefore, the distinction is better understood in terms of trends and emphasis rather than irreconcilable differences which would ignore the logical link between 'old' and 'new' minorities resulting from different waves of migration. See G. Sasse, 'Securitization or Securing Rights? Exploring the Conceptual Foundations of Policies towards Minorities and Migrants in Europe' (2005) 4 *Journal of Common Market Studies* 673–93.

to keep the two separate, and minority groups themselves may choose to restrict themselves to cultural issues. Despite these tactics, the inherent logic linking cultural and political claims should be recognized. Ultimately, the right to a distinct cultural identity and its active preservation and promotion embodies a political claim to difference and recognition, and it may be articulated in public, though not necessarily through political institutions.[22]

Minority rights as political rights cover three main domains: access to citizenship, political representation, and the institutionalised expression of a cultural identity. Minority rights are closely tied to the definition of citizenship and straddle the fuzzy borderline between civil and political rights. Citizenship can be a condition for an individual to be considered a member of a national minority. Thus, the criteria and process of becoming a citizen in the country of residence is a cornerstone of the political rights of minorities. Political representation guarantees individuals and groups a say in the political process. Voting rights at the national level result from citizenship, while voting rights at the local level may only depend on a residency status. Apart from the basic right to vote, electoral systems and political institutions can adopt minority-sensitive policies, such as lower electoral thresholds, national quotas, issue-based veto rights or a parallel vote of consultative national councils, or an upper chamber fully or partly defined along national lines. Thus, the political rights of national minorities are critically shaped by the minority-sensitive institutional features of the voting and decision-making processes. Cultural rights, defined as the right to learn about, preserve, and express one's cultural identity, are often centred on the minority's language. The right not only to learn but also to use one's own language in public—for example when dealing with administrations or courts—moves cultural rights beyond the private sphere and underpins their political relevance. Moreover, the cultural rights of national minorities are only worth the paper they are written on if there is the political will coupled with sufficient means to implement them. Thus, the formulation of cultural rights needs to be scrutinized with regard to their scope for implementation and use in the public sphere.

The International Covenant on Civil and Political Rights (ICCPR) makes the most explicit statement about the nature of minority rights (Article 27), but their content and implementation mechanisms have never been spelled out in any detail and, therefore, do not commit signatories to concrete actions. Recommendation 1201 of the Parliamentary Assembly of the Council of Europe, adopted in the mid 1990s, though never accepted as a common standard, marks another explicit reference to minority rights. According to its Article 6 'all persons belonging to a national minority shall have the right to set up their own

---

[22] This point echoes Szporluk's critique of Miroslav Hroch's distinction between a cultural and a political stage of nation-building. As Roman Szporluk pointed out convincingly, nation-building is political *ab initio*; see R. Szporluk, 'Ukraine: From an Imperial Periphery to a Sovereign State' (1997) 126:3 *Daedalus*, at 91.

organisations including political parties'. Article 11 refers to the 'right to have at their disposal appropriate local or autonomous authorities or to have a special status'.[23] It echoes the CSCE 1990 Copenhagen Document, which shifted the emphasis from non-discrimination of minorities to state responsibilities towards minorities, but it does not reflect a tangible international legal or policy consensus on minority autonomy.

The emphasis has remained firmly on the less controversial right to 'effective participation' which seems easier to square with the principle of non-discrimination. Article 15 of the Council of Europe's Framework Convention on the Protection of National Minorities (FCNM) of 1995 states that: 'The Parties shall create the conditions necessary for the effective participation of persons belonging to national minorities in cultural, social and economic life and in public affairs, in particular in those affecting them.' As of yet there is little guidance on how this goal is to be achieved. The FCNM cautiously sidesteps not only a definition of what constitutes a national minority—it leaves this definition to each individual signatory—but also the issue of rights more generally.[24]

6.2 DEMOCRATIC THEORY AND MINORITY RIGHTS

For theorists of liberalism and modernization ethnic diversity has been a marginal phenomenon with, at best, temporary resonance in democratizing and modernizing states. Liberal democracy is modelled on the idea of the homogenous nation-state, although in reality very few democracies fit this homogeneity standard. The freedom and equality of its individual citizens are the fundamental norms of a liberal democracy. They translate into a list of constitutionally guaranteed civil and political rights tied to citizenship. While proponents of a traditional view of liberal democracy posit that liberal democracies should be ethnoculturally neutral,[25] critics have advanced a wider definition of 'plural liberal democracy' that attempts to move beyond the dichotomy between universalism and particularism or individual rights versus group rights. Kymlicka has argued forcefully against the misperception that group-differentiated rights are per se inimical to individual rights as defined by liberal democracies. He defines minority rights as 'basic rights' and a means of protection against the political, social, or economic power of the majority. In fact, many co-called 'collective rights' are exercised by individuals (e.g. language rights), although they aim to rectify the unfavourable balance between

---

[23] See: http://assembly.coe.int/Documents/AdoptedText/TA93/erec1201.htm.

[24] In this context Deets pointed out that 'minority language, education, and culture have shifted from a question of rights to a matter of providing public goods'. See S. Deets, 'Liberal Pluralism: Does the West have anything to export?' (2004) 4:3 *Journal on Ethnopolitics and Minority Issues in Europe*.

[25] B. Barry, *Culture and Equality: An Egalitarian Critique of Multiculturalism* (Cambridge: Polity Press, 2000).

minorities and majorities in a multi-nation state (provided there is equality between groups and freedom and equality within groups). 'Liberal pluralism' postulates the need for a public recognition and the continuous accommodation of diversity within states.

Following Kymlicka's typology of minority rights or 'group-differentiated rights', one can distinguish between self-government rights for national minorities, 'polyethnic rights' for immigrant groups (defined as anti-discrimination measures and financial support or legal protection of certain practices associated with particular ethnic or religious groups) and special representation rights (e.g. guaranteed seats within central state institutions).[26] There can be an overlap between these types of rights, and as Kymlicka has pointed out, 'virtually every modern democracy employs one or more of these mechanisms'.[27] Loobuyck has tried to refine Kymlicka's argument by arguing against the notion of permanent minority rights and in favour of 'multicultural measures' as an exceptional, temporary means to rectify inequality of opportunity or resources and facilitate the enjoyment of universal individual rights.[28] Thereby, he aims to stay clearly within the parameters of liberal democratic theory. However, the distinction between temporary and permanent measures is as hard to establish as the benchmark of a minimum standard required for equalizing opportunities.[29] While the accommodation of national diversity within states generally poses a challenge to democracy, in states undergoing a fundamental regime change this issue adds to the simultaneity dilemma inherent in the multi-facetted transition process. The assumption that societal cleavages make for a 'stateness' problem that has to be resolved before democracy can become consolidated has informed much of the discussion about transitions, in particular postcommunist transitions.[30]

Democratic theory is characterized by the tension between the principles of the consensus and majority rule or between the participation of all citizens and majority rule. Lijphart summed up the dilemma: 'On the one hand, broad agreement among all citizens seems more democratic than simple majority rule, but, on the other hand, the only real alternative to majority rule is minority

---

[26] W. Kymlicka, *Multicultural Citizenship* (Oxford: Oxford University Press, 1995), at 6–7, 30–31.

[27] Ibid, at 33.

[28] P. Loobuyck, 'Liberal multiculturalism: A defence of liberal multicultural measures without minority rights' (2005) 5:1 *Ethnicities*, at 108–35.

[29] These and other criticisms were brought up in response to Lookuyck's article; see the debate following his article, at 123–35.

[30] J. Linz and A. Stepan, *Problems of Democratic Consolidation: Southern Europe, South America and Post-Communist Europe* (Baltimore, MD: John Hopkins University Press, 1996); D. Rustow, 'Transitions to Democracy: Toward a Dynamic Model' (1970) 2:3 *Comparative Politics*, at 337–63. Kymlicka suggested to test the applicability of the notion of 'liberal pluralism' in Eastern Europe but his—mostly East European—contributors proved sceptical and stressed the distinctiveness of East European states, societies, and legacies. See W. Kymlicka and M. Opalski (eds.), *Can Liberal Pluralism be Exported? Western Political Theory and Ethnic Relations in Eastern Europe* (Oxford: Oxford University Press, 2001).

rule—or at least a minority veto.'[31] Most democratic systems institutionalize majority rule for 'business as usual' and extraordinary majorities for the most fundamental decisions, such as constitutional amendments. The government-versus-opposition pattern is the norm. One assumption is that the political minority will be kept out of government; the other one is that over time minorities will become political majorities and vice versa. Majority rule works best 'when there is considerable consensus and the majority and minority are in fact not very far apart'.[32] Conversely, in a system with separate and hostile political segments, the perceived stakes of any decision are higher, and strict majority rule can put additional strain on the system. Lijphart pointed to the fact that plural societies have achieved political and democratic stability through institutional means, such as consociationalism.[33]

The political balance between majorities and minorities is of crucial importance for political stability and the consolidation of states and their respective democratic political and legal orders. Majority-minority relations and the way in which they are institutionalized, through minority rights or otherwise, provide a window on to a number of interrelated issues, such as political mobilization, social cohesion, state capacity, regime types, the dynamics of transition politics, and the leverage of external actors. Majority-minority relations denote a dynamic process of interaction rather than a fixed structure or a stable set of actors. A procedural understanding of democracy and democratic consolidation follows from this logic.

It is important to note that the phrase 'majority-minority relations', used by international organizations to avoid the definitional intricacies associated with the terms 'national minority' or 'minority rights', is problematic and highly political. The supposedly value-neutral term comes with a heavy baggage of norms and rules embedded in the theory of liberal democracy. The term 'majority', in particular, is implicitly and explicitly linked to specific ideas about the outlook of the polity and, therefore, speaks of power and legitimacy. Depending on the setting, the term 'minority' can also be a powerful political point of reference. The relationship between majorities and minorities denotes a balance that needs to be continuously implemented, monitored, and adjusted as part of a dynamic and ongoing process. As Pehe points out, 'the fair treatment of minorities . . . cannot be fully guaranteed only by a proper legal framework and institutions. It depends to a large extent on how majorities choose to act, and on how strongly let themselves be influenced by historical and other experiences.'[34] Ultimately, the implementation of rights—political or otherwise—is the crucial test of a regime type. The study of implementation has not been a natural strength of the discipline of law, as it requires attention to a particular political context.

---

[31] A. Lijphard, *Democracy in Plural Societies: A Comparative Exploration* (New Haven, CT: Yale University Press, 1977), at 28. [32] Ibid.
[33] Ibid, at 23.
[34] J. Pehe, 'Consolidating Free Government in the EU' (2004) 15:1 *Journal of Democracy*, at 46.

In an attempt to link legal and political analysis, the remainder of this chapter will explore minority rights in the context of postcommunist Central and Eastern Europe. The implementation through law and governance (or the lack thereof) of minority-sensitive rights and policies in Central and Eastern Europe provides a particularly instructive lens through which to assess the type of democracy that is emerging during or as a result of transition.

6.3 CENTRAL AND EASTERN EUROPE: A TEST CASE FOR MINORITY RIGHTS AND MOBILIZATION

Post-1989 Central and Eastern Europe (CEE) provides a fertile ground for analyzing political rights, including minority rights for two reasons: first, rights form an intrinsic part of state-building, and the ongoing processes of state- and nation-building in the CEE provide direct insights into this nexus.[35] The formulation and implementation of rights in the postcommunist context is a litmus test for the regime types that have emerged in the region. Secondly, the states of the CEE have been keen to 'return to Europe', a slogan that translated into EU accession. The simultaneous process of nation-state building and supranational integration through conditionality—alongside a political and economic reform process—captures an additional dimension within a condensed time frame. It sheds light on the international environment of rights as well as on the interaction between international and domestic factors in the formulation and implementation of rights.

The EU's definition of the conditions for membership, as set out by the Copenhagen Council of 1993, marked a significant disjuncture through the explicit mention of minority protection among the political norms associated with democracy. The EU's external relations provided the key momentum for the internalization of an explicit commitment to human rights and a greater awareness of minority issues. Human and minority rights map an area in which external relations have pushed for a (partial) rethinking of the EU's internal values, objectives, and policies. The nexus between human rights and conditionality had been an integral part of the EU's external relations since the Luxembourg European Council of 1991.[36] The EU's eastward enlargement extended this normative conditionality in an international context that highlighted the salience of minority issues and the potential for ethno-regional

---

[35] For a discussion of the wider context of political rights and postcommunism, see the chapter by Jiří Přibáň and Wojciech Sadurski in this volume.

[36] For a reminder of the limits of this human rights conditionality, see B. de Witte and G. N. Toggenburg, 'Human Rights and Membership of the European Union', in S. Peers and A. Ward, *The EU Charter of Fundamental Rights: Law Context and Policy* (Oxford: Hart, 2004), at 61–62. For a study of the inconsistencies of EU conditionality towards non-CEEC third countries see K. Smith, 'The EU: Human Rights and Relations with Third Countries', in K. Smith and M. Light (eds.), *Ethics and Foreign Policy* (Cambridge: Cambridge University Press, 2001), at 185–203.

conflict amidst multifaceted transition processes. A mixture of humanitarian, 'hard' and 'soft' security concerns informed the push for a greater internationalization of minority rights in the early 1990s.

Minority issues have a significant historical resonance in the CEE. The experience of genocide, expulsion, coercion, or accommodation is intrinsic to the emergence and development of many of the states in the region. After 1989, most of the postcommunist countries prioritized the strengthening of the central state capacity and the position of the titular nationality, thereby running the risk of discriminating against, alienating, and politicizing minority groups. The violent disintegration of the former Yugoslavia and a number of intractable post-Soviet conflicts as well as a perception of further conflict potential in view of sizeable minorities in many East European countries (in Latvia the titular nationality accounts for only 58.2 per cent of the population; while countries like Slovakia, Romania, and Bulgaria have to accommodate politically organized Hungarian and Turkish minorities of 7–10 per cent, and most CEE countries have to develop policies to overcome the social exclusion of the large Roma populations) informed the EU's approach.

The political Copenhagen criterion stipulates the need for 'stability of institutions guaranteeing democracy, the rule of law, human rights and respect for and protection of minorities'. The EU's political conditions for accession took shape against the background of a widening pan-European normative and institutional framework. The nexus between democracy and human rights had always been at the core of the Council of Europe's self-definition and membership criteria. The quick engagement of the Council of Europe in the CEE—Hungary became a member as early as 1990, followed by the Czech Republic and Poland in 1991—turned it effectively into an institutional stepping-stone towards the EU.[37] The EU's first Copenhagen criterion bears the imprint of the rather amorphous democratic conditionality of the Council of Europe. A country's democratic credentials had been a prominent point of reference, though not an explicitly formulated condition during the EU's southern enlargement in the 1970s. After the EU Copenhagen criteria were formulated, but before the accession negotiations began, the Council of Europe's Framework Convention for the Protection of National Minorities (FCNM) of 1995 put in place a complex and legally binding pan-European instrument for the continuous assessment of minority issues. Thus, the democracy criterion of the Council of Europe was extended to include minority rights. Members (and

---

[37] According to the Statute of the Council of Europe, any European state accepting the rule of law, human rights, and fundamental freedoms qualifies for membership. Institutionally, these two vague conditions translate into the ratification of the European Convention on Human Rights and Protocol 6, which requires members to abolish the death penalty. See also P. A. Jordan, 'Does Membership Have its Privileges? Entrance into the Council of Europe and Compliance with Human Rights Norms' (2000) 25 *Human Rights Quarterly* 662–63.

non-members) of the Council of Europe can choose, however, whether or not they want to ratify the FCNM.

The CSCE/OSCE process from 1990 onwards further enhanced this normative basis by making explicit the link between democracy, human rights, conflict-prevention, and minority protection.[38] The CSCE Paris Charter of 1990 stipulated that 'peace, justice, stability and democracy, require that the ethnic, cultural, linguistic and religious identity of national minorities be protected and conditions for the promotion of that identity be created'.[39] The OSCE General Recommendations of 1996, 1998, and 1999 subsequently attempted to refine a European standard of minority protection.[40] The EU explicitly adopted the CSCE norms in the context of the Badinter Arbitration Committee. Its emphasis on the rights of 'peoples and minorities' was affirmed by the EU Foreign Ministers' Declaration on the Guidelines on Recognition of New States in Eastern Europe and the Soviet Union and the Declaration on Yugoslavia of 16 December 1991 which made recognition conditional upon, among other things: 'guarantees for the rights of ethnic and national groups and minorities in accordance with the commitments subscribed to in the framework of the CSCE'.[41] While the EU borrowed the link between democracy and human (and later) minority rights from the Council of Europe, the CSCE/OSCE provided the EU with the security-based rationale for minority protection, a combination that resonated strongly with the Member States in the early 1990s.

The relationship between 'democracy' and 'the respect for and the protection of minorities' is an ambiguous one. The wording of the EU's political condition for membership is vague and avoids the stronger notion of 'minority rights'. Even without the explicit reference to 'rights', however, the minority criterion raises conceptual and empirical questions about the type of democracy the EU has promoted in the CEE. Some academics and policy-makers have perceived an explicit or implicit promotion of collective rights through the EU, the

---

[38] See Chapter 4 of the Document of the Copenhagen Meeting of the Conference on the Human Dimension of the CSCE, 5–29 June 1990: http://www.osce.org/docs/english/1990–1999/hd/cope90e.htm. The tension between advocates of a traditional concept of state sovereignty and those who favoured a reformulation of sovereignty to include an obligation of minority protection first surfaced at the CSCE Copenhagen meeting in 1990.

[39] The text cited is in the 'Human Dimension' section; see: http://www.osce.org/docs/english/1990–1999/summits/paris90e.htm#Anchor-Huma-3228.

[40] See the Hague Recommendations on the Education Rights of National Minorities (1996), the Oslo Recommendations on the Linguistic Rights of National Minorities (1998), and the Lund Recommendations on the Effective Participation of National Minorities in Public Life (1999): http://www.osce.org/hcnm/documents/recommendations/index.php3.

[41] In its first opinion, the Badinter Committee advised that the successor states to Yugoslavia must abide by 'the principles and rules of international law, with particular regard for human rights and the rights of peoples and minorities'. For the full text see A. Pellet, 'The Opinions of the Badinter Arbitration Committee: A Second Breadth for the Self-Determination of Peoples'; and ibid, 'Appendix: Opinions Nos 1, 2 and 3 of the Arbitration Committee of the International Conference on Yugoslavia' (1992) 3:1 *European Journal of International Law*, at 178–85.

Council of Europe and the OSCE of collective rights and positive discrimination. Riedel, for example, has pointed to an increasing ethnic segregation in society and the political instrumentalization of the norms of minority protection, resulting in a social and political conflict potential.[42] Scepticism has concentrated on the lack of genuine choice in the CEE with regard to the adoption of norms, including minority protection. Tesser has described tolerance as a 'geopolitical matter', suggesting that with regard to minority rights displays of tolerance rather than 'the real thing' result from an instrumental, elite-driven adoption of minority rights, which in turn can undermine liberal values and legitimate nationalist claims.[43] Moreover, minority nationalisms can be just as intolerant as majority nationalisms and might gain in legitimacy through the internationalization of this policy area.

The political Copenhagen criterion generally, and in particular the reference to minorities, defies the basic principles of conditionality, such as an inherent consensus on rules and their transmission within the EU and beyond, clear-cut benchmarks as well as clear enforcement and reward mechanisms. Through enlargement, the CFSP and Justice and Home Affairs minority-related issues have increasingly come onto the EU's agenda—more by default than by design. Article I-2 of the Draft Constitutional Treaty of June 2004 stipulates the Union's values and refers to 'the values of respect for human dignity, liberty, democracy, equality, the rule of law and respect for human rights, including the rights of persons belonging to minorities'. An even more explicit reference is contained in the Charter of Fundamental Rights, which formed the second part of the Draft Constitutional Treaty: Article II-21 lists 'membership of a national minority' as a ground of discrimination which shall be prohibited, while Article II-22 enshrines the Union's respect for 'cultural, religious and linguistic diversity'. Despite the uncertain future of the Draft Constitution and the fact that the Charter of Fundamental Rights is not legally binding, these references suggest that national minorities are gradually becoming a part of the EU's constitutional resources.[44] For the time being, the Race Equality Directive of 2000 and its (as yet incomplete) transposition into national legislation still provides the most concrete avenue for the protection of minorities across a range of different spheres.

The postcommunist transition states have focused on building the central state capacity in line with the classical definition of a liberal democracy based on the nation-state, individual rights, and majority rule. The EU's minority criterion, however, inserted an emphasis on the accommodation of minorities,

---

[42] S. Riedel, 'Minderheitenpolitik in der EU-Erweiterungsperspektive. Neue Konflikte durch Maßnahmen der positiven Diskriminierung' (2001) *SWP Studies* 24.

[43] L. M. Tesser, 'The Geopolitics of Tolerance: Minority Rights under EU Expansion in East-Central Europe' (2003) 17:3 *East European Politics and Societies*, at 489, 493, 532.

[44] See G. N. Toggenburg, 'A Remaining Share or a New Part? The Union's Role vis-à-vis Minorities after the Enlargement Decade' (2006) *EUI Law Working Papers* 15.

thereby confronting the candidate states with a not too specific but different conception of democracy, a potential opening towards 'plural liberal democracy' and an external stake in a sensitive internal sovereignty issue. Having formulated an entry criterion as wide as the first Copenhagen criterion, the EU faced the difficult task of unpacking and communicating it vis-à-vis the potential candidates for EU membership. The 'respect for and promotion of minorities' could either be interpreted as a negative right, namely the protection from discrimination, or as a positive right to enjoy one's culture and the right to effective participation.

The EU's minority 'condition' posed several compliance problems during the accession process: firstly, it lacked a firm foundation in EU law and concise benchmarks. The practices of the current Member States range from elaborate constitutional and legal means for minority protection and political participation to constitutional unitarism and the outright denial that national minorities exist. Secondly, minority rights have never been an internal EU political priority. Thirdly, the question of what constitutes a 'national minority' and the nature of minority rights are deeply disputed in international politics and law. These dilemmas were further compounded by the fact that the first Copenhagen criterion had to be 'fulfilled' by the time the accession negotiations got underway, thereby limiting the EU's subsequent leverage in the political sphere. Moreover, the minority criterion did not figure prominently in the EU's pre-accession funding. The paradox is that despite all of these caveats politicians and analysts have continuously emphasized the EU's success in promoting stability and minority protection in the CEE.

The Commission's annual Regular Reports, following on from the Opinions of 1997 and the Accession Partnerships, have been the EU's key instrument to monitor and evaluate the candidates' progress towards accession.[45] The political Copenhagen criterion rests on generic concepts, such as 'democracy', the 'rule of law' and 'the respect for and the protection of national minorities', and, therefore, leaves a wide scope for interpretation. Moreover, it was not based on the *acquis* as such. The Commission had to find a different way to operationalize the political criteria. In the case of the minority criterion it based its monitoring exercise on a set of values and non-EU documents, namely the European Convention on Human Rights (which by now has become part of the *acquis*), the major OSCE documents of the early 1990s, and the UN Declarations. Though not a source of inspiration and legitimacy at the outset of the accession process, over time the FCNM of 1995 became the Commission's primary instrument for translating the minority criterion into practice.[46]

---

[45] For a more detailed review of the monitoring exercise, see J. Hughes and G. Sasse, 'Monitoring the Monitors: EU Enlargement Conditionality and Minority Protection in the CEECs' (2003) 1 *Journal on Ethnopolitics and Minority Issues in Europe*, at 1–36.

[46] Author's interviews with officials from the Country Desks in DG Enlargement, the Horizontal Co-Ordination Unit and the Legal Service, Brussels, 12–13 January 2004. The manual,

Accordingly, the Regular Reports frequently reminded the candidate states to sign and ratify the FCNM—despite the fact that several EU Member States, such as Belgium, France, Greece, Luxembourg, and The Netherlands, had not done so.[47]

A closer analysis of the EU's monitoring exercise and the empirical evidence from the CEE suggest that international actors and a vaguely defined European norm have framed the debates and perceptions and affected the timing and nature of specific pieces of legislation (e.g. the gradual modification of restrictive laws in Estonia and Latvia), while the domestic political constellations and pressures ultimately had a more significant effect on the institutional and policy outcomes.[48] Some of these outcomes have remained ambiguous or failed to address the underlying issues at stake, most importantly the exceedingly high number of stateless residents in Estonia and Latvia. The cases of Slovakia and Romania confirm that the EU's political leverage is greatest in the early phase of the accession process in countries which are perceived as being undemocratic by outside actors. In the presence of organized minority interests, the EU can help to legitimize reformist actors—whether ethnically defined or not. EU conditionality has anchored minority rights in the political rhetoric of the candidate states, but the EU had little to offer in terms of substantive guidance, as the lack of benchmarks, inconsistencies, and the limited scope for follow-up on implementation in the Commission's Regular Reports demonstrate. The actual policy leverage of the EU in minority protection borrows from the instruments and recommendations of the Council of Europe and the OSCE, and a range of other actors, including NGOs, have translated them into the domestic political context. The overall impact of the EU's monitoring exercise is best understood as having a 'lock-in effect' and reinforcing domestic trends.

There is considerable variation across the CEE constitutions with regard to the balance between ethnic and civic conceptions of statehood, the generic recognition of minorities (or lack thereof), or an explicit list of national minorities, as well as the references to the rights of minorities (e.g. linguistic rights, the right to parliamentary representation, or consultative minority councils) and the state's responsibilities vis-à-vis its minorities (e.g. funding). In line with the definition of minority rights as political rights, the following section will discuss the constitutional commitment to national autonomy, the link between effective participation and citizenship, and the role of ethnopolitical parties in the CEE.

which was prepared each year by the Horizontal Co-Ordination Unit for the Country Desks in advance of the drafting of the Regular Reports, listed the FCNM as an explicit point of reference.

[47] The Netherlands ratified the FCNM in 2005.

[48] See G. Sasse, 'EU Conditionality and Minority Rights: Translating the Copenhagen Criterion into Policy', EUI Working Paper, Robert Schuman Centre for Advanced Studies, 16 (2005).

6.3.1 National Autonomy in Central and Eastern Europe

Several CEE countries legislated for minority protection, or were in the final stages of doing so, prior to the formulation of the EU's Copenhagen criteria. Some of these were inclusive measures, providing for autonomy arrangements and privileged quotas of representation in national parliaments. Through the incorporation of the norm of 'national' autonomy, Hungary, Slovenia, and Estonia come closest to the notion of collective rights, even though the implementation of this norm has proved problematic.

6.3.1.1 Hungary: Minority Rights as the State's National Interest

Hungary passed a law on 'The Rights of National and Ethnic Minorities' in 1993 that granted collective rights and cultural autonomy to thirteen recognized minorities.[49] This law built on discussions within Hungary's political institutions in the 1980s, a constitutional amendment of 1989, which had granted minorities the right to their culture, religion, and the use of their language, and, in particular the new Article 68 of the amended Hungarian constitution of 1990, which had anchored the protection of 'national and ethnic minorities' by defining them as a 'constituent part of the state' (Article 1), guaranteeing their political representation and collective participation in public life through local and national bodies of self-government (Article 1, Paragraphs 3–4) and the establishment of a minority ombudsperson in parliament (Article 32). While the 'Minorities Act' stipulated the procedure by which the bodies of minority self-government were to be set up, the principle of guaranteed parliamentary representation was left to separate legislation and remained a controversial issue throughout the 1990s.

Most of Hungary's minorities are quite small and not politically mobilized. According to the 2001 Hungarian census, about 3 per cent of the population (just over 300,000 people) identified with one of the thirteen recognized minorities.[50] On the whole, they had little impact on the 1993 Act. Instead, the historical resonance of the Treaty of Trianon (1920), which left large territorialized Hungarian minorities in neighbouring states (Slovakia, Romania, Serbia, Ukraine), has underpinned the political will in favour of minority protection both at home and abroad. The 1993 'Minorities Act' mentioned above clearly reflected Hungary's state interests in the preamble, which defined peaceful minority-majority relations as a principle of international security.[51] The Roma as Hungary's predominant minority group provided an additional incentive for

---

[49] http://www.riga.lv/minelres/NationalLegislation/Hungary/Hungary_Minorities_English.htm.

[50] These statistical figures, however, represent very modest estimates. The census result of just under 200,000 Roma, in particular, is an understatement.

[51] P. Vermeersch, 'EU Enlargement and Minority Rights Policies in Central Europe: Explaining Policy Shifts in the Czech Republic, Hungary and Poland' (2003)1 *Journal on Ethnopolitics and Minority Issues in Europe* 13.

progressive minority policies. Over time the Roma have been increasingly singled out as a social group whose problems require attention beyond the general legal and political framework for minority issues, thereby simultaneously making the Roma a more visible and separate policy and rights issue.

While the endogenous incentives for a far-reaching minority rights regime are easy to trace in the case of Hungary, the effects are more difficult to assess. In terms of intra-state relations, Hungary's policies have both encouraged bilateral agreements and provoked concern and angry responses from political groups in neighbouring countries. The implementation of the 1993 Act led to some peculiar outcomes: local governments received payments to offset the costs of minority education, thereby creating an incentive to inflate the number of children requiring education in their own language. According to Hungarian government statistics of 1998, almost 45,000 primary-school children were enrolled in German-minority programmes, although the last census recorded only about 8,000 Germans living in Hungary.[52] Local minority self-governments mushroomed as a result of the simple procedure by which they are set up.[53] By 1999, there were already more than 1,400 registered across the country, half of which are Roma councils, followed by German councils as the second most represented group.[54]

The local minority councils elect a national council. The councils are supposed to have extensive consent and consultation rights with regard to laws impacting on minority issues, such as culture, education, and the media. While there is evidence of such consultation between the national councils and the Hungarian parliament, the involvement of the local level appears to be minimal. The main function of the councils, therefore, is to promote minority culture, but the limited funding at the local level has curbed their potential. While the national minority governments received state funding according to the size of the minority, the local governments all received a small flat sum. There is also evidence of local governments trying to shift responsibility for minority issues to the minority councils, especially in the case of the Roma. The election of the minority self-government councils took place alongside the national elections in a two-ballot system. Anybody was allowed to vote for the members of self-governments irrespective of his/her nationality, which was not registered. The only restriction was that a vote could only be cast for one of the self-governments. It is hard to track voting patterns in these elections, but the emergence of a Serbian nationalist on a Croatian council or the popularity of German councils, which are associated with external funding and travel opportunities, suggested a range of voting motivations.[55] The minority groups,

[52] See S. Deets, 'Reconsidering East European Minority Policy: Liberal Theory and European Norms (2002) 16:1 *East European Politics and Societies* 39.
[53] Local self-governments are either set up by the local government or by the initiative of five minority members who gain the support of 100 people in the elections.
[54] Deets., above, n. 52, at 49.   [55] Ibid, at 50.

in turn, were interested in high voter turnouts to boost their national-level funding.

In June 2005, the parliament adopted amendments to the 1993 Act aiming to increase the transparency of the minority rights system, modifying the minority electoral procedure and enabling county-level minority representation.[56] According to the 2005 Act, only those Hungarian citizens are entitled to take part in the elections who register in the minority voters' register ahead of the elections by stating their minority affiliation. The register is not public, it is kept and later destroyed by the chief administrator in the mayor's office.[57] Minority candidates can now only be fielded by minority organizations that have existed for at least three years and list the representation of specific minority interests in their statute. Candidates are further obliged to publicly declare their knowledge of the language and culture of the minority they represent and whether they were a member of a different minority self-government in the past. These new provisions aim to counter some of the institutional abuses of the system discussed above. Local and medium-level minority self-governments will consist of five to nine members, at the national level the total number can vary from fifteen to fifty-three, depending on the number of local self-governments formed across the country.[58]

Most importantly, Hungary's progressive 1993 law represents only one of several elements of minority-relevant policy-making. The highly controversial Hungarian 'Status Law' of 2001, giving rights and entitlements to Hungarians living in other countries, brings the main rationale of the 1993 Act to a logical conclusion but can hardly be seen as a contribution to the consolidation of good, neighbourly relations and stability within neighbouring states.[59] Moreover, Hungary produced a draft anti-discrimination law in the second half of 2003, suggesting a slow uptake of minority-related issues inside the country.[60] Commission officials from DG Employment and DG Enlargement, however, emphasize that the anti-discrimination legislation represented a more comprehensive package than in some other candidate countries and was based on a wider process of consultation.[61] The Act on Equal Treatment and the

[56] Ibid. The Hungarian president referred the new act to the Constitutional Court to clarify the constitutionality of a preferential seat provided to a member of the minority self-government in the local council.   [57] Ibid.

[58] Ibid and Office for National and Ethnic Minorities, *Detailed Summary of New Minority Legislation in Hungary* (Budapest, June 2005).

[59] See B. Fowler, 'Fuzzing citizenship, nationalising political space: A framework for interpreting the Hungarian "status law" as a new form of kin-state policy in Central and Eastern Europe' *ESRC 'One Europe Or Several?' Programme, Working Paper* (2002) 40.

[60] G. Schwellnus, 'Conditionality and its Misfits: Non-Discrimination and Minority Protection in the EU Enlargement Process', Paper given at the Workshop 'The Europeanization of Eastern Europe: Evaluating the Conditionality Model', EUI, Florence, 4–5 July 2003.

[61] Author's interview with a Commission official, DG Enlargement, 20 February 2004 and with a Commission official from the Unit Anti-Discrimination, Fundamental Social Rights and Civil Society, DG Employment and Social Affairs, 20 February 2004.

Promotion of Equal Opportunities, adopted by the Hungarian parliament in December 2003, prohibits discrimination in line with the EU's Race and Employment Directives. The body monitoring the enforcement of this act under the government was set up at the beginning of 2005. Although Hungary has tried to market its progressive minority policy as part of its bid for EU membership, the EU's response has been very cautious.

The case of Hungary demonstrates the overarching significance of domestic incentives for minority protection, the ambiguity and practical difficulties attached to the implementation of collective rights and a certain corrective effect of EU conditionality (underpinned by the Council of Europe and the OSCE High Commissioner on National Minorities) on potentially destabilizing policies like the 'Status Law' and the referendum on Hungarian nationals 'abroad' ('referendum on dual nationality') on 5 December 2004. The government was forced to hold this referendum based on an initiative collecting the required number of signatures. As the government had changed by the time the referendum was held, Fidesz tried to turn it into a vote of no-confidence against the new socialist government. When in government, Fidesz had seen the issue of citizenship for Hungarians abroad as the first step towards increasing its share of votes. In return, the socialist government's referendum campaign tapped into a traditional right-wing rhetoric, kindling fears of unemployment and in-migration. In the end, just under 52 per cent voted in favour of the vaguely worded question about preferential naturalization for Hungarians abroad, but the referendum failed due to a low turnout (just over 37 per cent).

Minority representation has been anchored *de jure* in Hungarian politics (e.g. the Standing Committee for Human Rights, Minority Rights and Religious Affairs, a parliamentary ombudsman responsible specifically for national minorities, the Office for National and Ethnic Minorities and the Office of Hungarians Abroad in the state administration) and—since EU accession—de facto in EU institutions (for example through two Roma MEPs and Hungarians in leading positions in the Intergroup for Autochthonous National Minorities, Constitutional Regions and Lesser Used Languages and the Intergroup Anti-Racism and Diversity).

6.3.1.2 Slovenia: Different Rights for 'Old' and 'New' Minorities

Slovenia's 2002 census only listed Slovenian, Hungarian, and Italian as possible ethnic identities. Everybody else, including the Roma, was left with the option to tick the box 'other'.[62] The Slovenian constitution carried over the former Yugoslav constitutional commitments to the Hungarian and Italian minorities without, however, recognizing the considerably bigger Croatian, Serbian, or

---

[62] The 1991 census listed 8,000 Hungarians and 3,000 Italians; by the census of 2002 their numbers had decreased to about 6,200 Hungarians and 2,300 Italians.

Bosnian minorities, which count as recent immigrants. Constitutionally, the Hungarian and Italian minorities are recognized as 'autochthonous minorities' and are guaranteed one seat each in the national parliament. They are granted dual voting rights at the national and municipal level in their traditional areas of settlement. One of the two votes is cast for the autochthonous representative, the other one for another deputy or electoral list. Article 64 of the Constitution lays down the obligatory consent of the ethnic representatives on laws and legislative acts affecting the rights and status of the ethnic communities.

The Constitution (Article 64) and the Law on Local Government give national minorities the right to establish self-governing minority councils, which are recognized as legal entities and a form of national autonomy. They are meant to represent minority interests and facilitate and organize participation in public life. They can submit proposals and opinions on matters concerning their communities to state bodies. The minority councils are directly elected alongside the local self-governing bodies in municipal elections. The activities of the Hungarian and Italian councils benefit from guaranteed state funding. The Roma by now have the right to a local representative in areas where they are recognized as 'autochthonous' rather than a recent immigrant group. Amendments to the Law on Local Government in May 2002 introduced the right of the Roma minority to direct representation in twenty municipalities. The implementation of this right has been slow, and in 2002 the Roma still only had one local representative.[63] Many Roma have not been officially registered in the local registers, thereby not fulfilling the minimum legal requirement for the elections. Moreover, several councils objected to what they saw as 'positive discrimination' of the Roma to the detriment of the Slovene majority.[64]

Slovenia is one of only few CEE countries that ratified the European Charter for Regional and Minority Languages during the EU accession process.[65] However, the Charter is interpreted as referring only to the two autochthonous languages. Slovenia's state language is Slovenian, but the Constitution guarantees the right to use other languages and scripts in the areas inhabited by autochthonous minorities (Articles 11 and 62). In these localities street signs have to be bilingual, administrative officials have to be bilingual, and Hungarian or Italian can be used in court. Autochthonous minorities are guaranteed the publication of newspapers in their languages, but the state financially supports several newspapers in other minority languages. In areas of traditional settlement, members of the Italian and Hungarian minorities have the right to education in their own languages from pre-school education through to the completion of elementary education (Articles 11 and 64 of the Constitution). Provisions for bilingual instruction are in place in ethnically mixed areas. In the Italian-populated areas,

---

[63] Open Society Institute: Monitoring the EU Accession Process: Minority Protection, Budapest: OSI/EU Monitoring Accession Program, 2002, at 627.   [64] Ibid, at 628.
[65] Hungary and Slovakia were the other two accession countries ratifying the Council of Europe's Charter.

minority education tends to be provided in separate schools in either Slovenian or Italian. Areas populated by the Hungarian minority have generally offered bilingual instruction in kindergartens and schools for both Slovenians and members of the Hungarian minority. There is no apparent reason for the different implementation of minority-language education, and it has been the issue of constitutional complaints.[66] Roma-language education exists but its scope and effectiveness are limited, not least due to the fact that a disproportionately high number of Roma children attend 'special needs' classes.

Slovenia is an example of a rights distinction based on a definition of autochthonous versus 'other' minorities or 'old' versus 'new' minorities. Such a distinction establishes a hierarchy among the minorities irrespective of their size or other specific features. The case of the Roma illustrates the difficulties in defining autochthonous groups and guaranteeing their political rights. The political rights of the Hungarians and Italians, including their educational and cultural dimensions, have on the whole been implemented but the system of differentiated rights has left the issues of the more sizeable and vocal minorities, such as the Croats, Serbs, and Germans unresolved.

6.3.1.3 Estonia: National Autonomy in a Vacuum

During the interwar period, Estonia copied the Austro-Hungarian concept of minorities constituting a legal entity with the right to establish cultural, educational, and other institutions to preserve and promote their community. The provision survived in the post-1991 era, albeit as an empty shell. No minority has made use of it so far. The 1992 constitution revived the principle of non-territorial cultural autonomy from the interwar period, during which the ethnic balance of Estonia looked very different. The majority of Russian-speaking settlers are the result of Soviet migration. According to the constitutional provision, members of national minority groups numbering above 3,000 have the right to form public bodies and set up a cultural autonomy if at least half the group's members are registered nationally. They can hold elections to a Cultural Council and—based on a two-third majority vote—implement an administrative and cultural autonomy over minority schools and cultural institutions (Article 50). The non-territorial Cultural Council has the right to raise taxes to supplement official funding for minority schools and cultural institutions. In localities where half the residents belong to a minority, members of the group have a right to receive responses from state authorities in their native language. However, the thresholds for these rights are high, especially given that the term 'national minority' only refers to citizens with 'longstanding, firm and lasting ties with Estonia'. The Russian-speakers' initially difficult access to citizenship limited the applicability of national autonomy. The fact that none of these

[66] A. Petricusic, 'Slovenian Legislative System for Minority Protection: Different Rights for Old and New Minorities'; see: http://www6.gencat.net/llengcat/noves/hm04tardor/petricusic1_2.htm.

cultural autonomies have been set up so far indicates that these types of formal rights may never become a cultural or political reality. Moreover, Estonia's constitutional right to national autonomy conflicts with the reluctance to allow the use of minority languages even in localities in which the minority is a majority. In localities where the Russophones account for 50 per cent (rather than 20 per cent as in most countries with a similar provision) the local population has the right to request the use of Russian in public administrative matters in addition to Estonian. Local government decisions on language need the approval of the national government on a case-by-case basis, and in practice the right to minority-language use has rarely been approved.[67]

National autonomy for minorities has not been a prominent political right in the CEE, and its implementation has remained ambivalent. The examples discussed here demonstrate the difficulties attached to this principle both at a conceptual level and with regard to implementation. The constitutional provisions on autonomy were either a paper tiger (Estonia), gave rise to a hierarchy of minority groups (Slovenia), or revealed both implementation problems and an underlying foreign policy agenda (Hungary).

6.3.2 Citizenship and the Right to Effective Participation: Estonia and Latvia

In the CEE, Estonia and Latvia provide the best illustrations of the link between citizenship and the political rights of minorities, on the one hand, and the limits of international conditionality in the field of minority protection, on the other. The Russophone minorities in both countries (together with the Roma across the CEE) were also the group the EU emphasized most during the accession process. In the absence of organized minority interests, the domestic pull for a minority-sensitive policy in Estonia and Latvia was small. Restrictive laws and procedures have been amended gradually in the context of EU accession,[68] but the persistently high numbers of stateless residents (22.4 per cent and 12.5 per cent of Latvia's and Estonia's resident population, respectively[69]) highlight the fact that the overall effect of international pressure has been limited.

The Popular Fronts, spearheading the pro-independence movement in the Baltic states, thrived on inclusive membership, irrespective of national background. Similarly, the referenda on national independence were supported *en*

---

[67] J. Priit and C. Wellmann, *Minorities and Majorities in Estonia: Problems of Integration on the Threshold of the EU*, European Centre for Minority Issues, Meeting Report (1999) 2.

[68] For an overview see O. Norgaard (ed.), *The Baltic States after Independence* (Cheltenham: Edward Elgar, 1996); P. Kolsto, *National Integration and Violent Conflict in Post-Soviet Societies: The Cases of Estonia and Moldova* (Oxford: Rowman and Littlefield, 2002). For a critical analysis see J. Hughes, ' "Exit" in Deeply Divided Societies: Regimes of Discrimination in Estonia and Latvia and the Potential for Russophone Migration' (2005) 43:4 *Journal of Common Market Studies* 739–62.

[69] See the EU Commission's Regular Reports on the Accession Countries (2002).

masse by the Russian-speaking minorities. Only small pockets of Soviet-oriented opposition argued for the maintenance of close links with Russia and territorial autonomy in the north-east of Estonia.[70] Most importantly, the loose category of 'Russian-speakers' represents a diverse group, including Russians, Ukrainians, Belarusians, Jews, and some smaller minority groups. Not all the Russian-speakers are recent, Soviet-era migrants. Estonia and Latvia started their post-Soviet state-building project with 'nationalizing policies' restricting access to citizenship and, thereby, to political participation in the newly independent polities. Accordingly, the emerging political systems have been characterized as 'ethnic democracies'.[71] This concept is, in fact, a contradiction in terms, conflating democratic procedures with an ethnic control regime.

The principle of 'state continuity'—the historical-legal fact that Soviet rule over the Baltic states had never been recognized by the West—informed both state-building in Estonia and Latvia and the moderate responses from Western powers and international organizations.[72] The speedy establishment of an economic record in line with or superseding the expectations of the West strengthened the position of the Baltic states and distracted from the shortcomings of their political systems. Estonia and Latvia have compared their citizenship criteria to the policies on immigrants (or 'new' minorities) in numerous West European countries. They have done so despite several distinct features of the Russian-speakers, not least the context of their migration, the size and concentration of the group, and the potential for substantial political, social, and economic exclusion.

On the whole, Latvia pursued a more restrictive path throughout the transition and accession process than Estonia. In 1991 only 52 per cent of its residents were Latvians, compared to 37.2 per cent Russophones. The Latvian president repeatedly acted as a moderating force, whereas in parliament and government it proved impossible to generate a consensus on moderate policies in the early 1990s.[73] Delayed membership of the Council of Europe and the EU provided important catalysts for a partial rethinking of minority rights. Based on the notion of state continuity, Latvia reinstated its 1922 constitution and 1919 citizenship law (as amended in 1927) after gaining independence from the Soviet Union. Individuals who were Latvian citizens before 1940 automatically became citizens of the 'restored' Latvian state. Only citizens of inter-war Latvia

---

[70] D. J. Smith, 'Narva Region within the Estonian Republic: From Autonomism to Accommodation' (2002) 12:2 *Regional and Federal Studies*, at 89–110.

[71] See G. Smith (ed.), *The Baltic States: The National Self-Determination of Estonia, Latvia and Lithuania* (Basingstoke: Macmillan, 1994); V. Pettai and K. Hallik, 'Understanding processes of ethnic control: segmentation, dependency and co-optation in post-communist Estonia' (2002) 8:4 *Nations and Nationalism*, at 505–29.

[72] N. M. Gelazis, 'The European Union and the Statelessness Problem in the Baltic States' (2004) 6:3 *European Journal of Migration and Law*, at 225–42.

[73] H. M. Morris, 'EU Enlargement and Latvian Citizenship Policy' (2003)1 *Journal on Ethnopolitics and Minority Issues in Europe*, at 3–4.

and their descendants were granted the right to vote in post-Soviet Latvia's founding elections in 1993.

From 1993 the OSCE High Commissioner on National Minorities addressed first the issue of a peaceful withdrawal of the Russian troops and then increasingly the issue of the stateless residents, especially with reference to the citizenship law.[74] Van der Stoel strongly recommended a five-year residency requirement for the naturalization process. In the context of accession to the Council of Europe, Latvia's citizenship law was amended in a stop-and-go process.[75] In 1994, Latvian President Ulmanis sent the early amendments to the citizenship law back to parliament, urging it to include the Council of Europe recommendations. The new citizenship law of July 1994 not only defined the provisions for naturalization (five-year residency since May 1990; command of the Latvian language, anthem, history, and constitution; a legal source of income; the need to renounce another citizenship), it also granted citizenship to pre-1919 residents, to Soviet-era Estonian and Lithuanian residents, to non-Latvian residents who finished Latvian-language secondary schools, and to spouses of Latvians (after ten years) (Article 13) and excluded specific groups from the right to citizenship (especially those occupying official positions during the Soviet era) (Article 10).

The take-up rate remained low under the changed naturalization procedure, suggesting that the costs of naturalization, including administrative fees, learning Latvian or preparing for the citizenship test, were still too high or people felt too alienated already at this stage to be attracted by a new procedure. The 1994 law, the Citizenship Law, also marked the beginning of the so-called 'window-system' of naturalization, according to which a fixed number of residents, grouped according to age, were allowed to apply each year. Those born in Latvia and between 16 to 20 years of age could begin the naturalization procedure in 1996. The eighth and last group of applicants—those born outside Latvia and over 30 years of age—were only supposed to start the naturalization procedure in 2003. In April 1995, a special law on stateless citizens provided a guarantee of basic fundamental rights. It extended the law 'On Rights and Obligations of Persons and Citizens' to registered non-citizens who would qualify for citizenship (this rule excluded Soviet army personnel). The 1995 law permitted non-citizens to travel, to admit their spouses and dependents into Latvia, the right to preserve their language and culture, and have access to translation services in court proceedings.

The exclusion of Latvia from the first-wave accession countries in December 1997 acted as a further catalyst in the field of minority policy. The slow rate of naturalization, in particular, remained a persistent concern of the EU. In June 1998 the Latvian parliament passed amendments to the citizenship law, paving

---

[74] For a detailed overview of the OSCE High Commissioner's involvement in Latvia, see J. Dorodovna, 'Challenging Ethnic Democracy: Implementation of the Recommendations of the OSCE High Commissioner on National Minorities to Latvia 1993–2001', *CORE Working Paper*, 9, 2003.   [75] For details see Morris, above, n. 73, at 5–7.

the way for the 'window system' to be abolished. In line with the recommendations of the OSCE High Commissioners and the EU, a referendum in October 1998 abolished the 'window system' and confirmed the right of children of noncitizens to obtain citizenship.[76] The timing of these decisions was closely related to the annual reporting mechanism of the EU. Apart from citizenship, language remained the key issue during EU accession. The 1999 language law, for example, aimed to regulate the Latvian language use down to private-sector jobs and private meetings, thereby eroding the distinction between the public and private spheres.[77] Latvian President Vike-Freiberga returned the law to parliament, a move that had a positive impact on the EU's decision in December 1999 to start negotiations with Latvia. Of the countries that joined the EU in May 2004 Latvia remained the only one that had not yet ratified the FCNM.

Estonia also adhered to the principle of state continuity, but rather than reinvigorating its old constitution, a new post-Soviet constitution was drafted and adopted by referendum in 1992. This constitution provided both citizens and non-citizens with access to fundamental freedoms and social and economic rights. The non-citizens enjoy the freedom of association (excluding membership of political parties), the right to vote—though not to stand (see the 1993 electoral law)—in local elections, and local governments in localities with a majority of permanent residents belonging to a national minority have the right to use the minority language as an internal working language.[78] The Estonian parliament reinstated the 1938 citizenship law in 1992, including its restrictive amendments of 1940 but excluding its original rather liberal residency requirement. As a result, only those residents who had Estonian citizenship prior to June 1940 and their descendants were entitled to citizenship. A loophole allowed those who could prove that they had supported the national independence movement by means of their Congress of Estonia membership cards to obtain citizenship.[79] The regime enjoyed a small degree of discretion to speed up the citizenship procedure of a select few, but the majority of residents were subjected to a naturalization procedure that only gradually took shape. The initial citizenship provisions excluded a significant proportion of the resident population from the 1993 national election. The right-of-centre government and parliament subsequently proved reluctant to amend the citizenship and electoral laws.

---

[76] Ibid, p. 17.

[77] V. Poleshchuk, *Estonia, Latvia and the European Commission: Changes in Language Regulation in 1999–2001*; see: http://www.eumap.org/journal/features/2002/jan02/languagereg.

[78] D. J. Smith, 'Minority Rights, Mulitculturalism and EU Enlargement: The Case of Estonia' (2003)1 *Journal on Ethnopolitics and Minority Issues in Europe*, at 19; D. Laitin, 'The Russian-Speaking Nationality in Estonia: Two Quasi-Constitutional Elections' (1993/1994) 2–3:4–1 *East European Constitutional Review*, at 25.

[79] A. Semjonov, 'Citizenship Legislation, Minority Rights and Integration in Estonia', Paper presented at the ECMI Baltic Seminar 'Minorities and Majorities in Estonia: Problems of Integration at the Threshold of the EU' (1998), at 25.

The 1993 Law on Aliens envisaged declaring everybody an illegal immigrant who failed to apply for new residence and work permits within a year. A vaguely defined 'legal income' had to be proven, and in the first instance these permits were valid for five years, an only weakly disguised encouragement of out-migration to Russia. The 1993 Law on Education, prescribing a switch to Estonian in all Russian-language gymnasiums by 2000 proved unrealistic but was designed to have a similar psychological effect.[80] The two towns of Narva and Sillamäe began organizing local referenda on national-territorial autonomy, a standoff that was defused not least due to the involvement of the OSCE High Commissioner and the subsequent amendments to the Law on Aliens. International intervention facilitated an ongoing dialogue, for example through the 'Roundtable on Nationalities' under the auspices of the Estonian president.[81] Estonia's 1995 Law on Citizenship defined a naturalization procedure similar to that of Latvia. Instead of the 'window-system' in Lativa, however, naturalization in Estonia was opened to all permanent residents in 1995, making naturalization dependent on a five-year residency and new tests of the applicant's knowledge of the Estonian constitution and political system. The pace of naturalization has remained slow in both countries. Estonia's left-of-centre government of 1995 continued along the same path as its predecessor, partly amending restrictive provisions. The so-called 'Aliens-Passports' alleviated the situation of non-citizens somewhat; and the presence of a small number of Russian-speaking deputies in parliament from 1995 onwards as well as the position of local elites in the north-east provided a base for moderate domestic political pressure.

In 1993 Estonia became a member of the Council of Europe—two years ahead of Latvia—and in 1998 it became the first Baltic country to start accession negotiations with the EU. In 1997–98 the prospect of EU membership underpinned domestic political initiatives aimed at simplifying the naturalization procedure. In its assessment of Estonia's readiness for EU membership, the EU was cautious, combining a generally positive note on the fulfilment of the first Copenhagen criterion with the recommendation to ease the procedures for naturalization and integration. In 1996 President Meri vetoed a law that would have tied the right to stand in local or national elections to a knowledge of the Estonian language. New attempts from 1997 at reinforcing the language criteria for local and national-level politicians and private-sector employees and businesses were continuously toned down in the dual context of Russia's vociferous complaints and international criticism from the EU and the OSCE.[82] The 1999 Law on Local Elections allowed legal residents the rights to vote, though Estonian language proficiency remained a condition for candidates in national and local elections.

Overall, there appears to have been a slow shift in the public perception towards defining the Russians and Russian-speakers as a 'minority' and

80 Smith, above, n. 70, at 22–3.   81 Ibid, at 24.   82 Ibid, at 29–30.

'rights-based politics'.[83] The government programme 'Integration into Estonian Society 2000–2007' was the first comprehensive attempt at a strategy for
the integration of non-citizens, replacing, for example, the previous emphasis
on linguistic assimilation with more leeway for bilingualism.[84] Russia
has tried—by and large unsuccessfully—to internationalize the issue of the
Russian-speaking minority in Estonia and Latvia and to gain some leverage
vis-à-vis the EU. The controversial closure of the OSCE missions in Latvia
and Estonia in 2001 undermined Russia's commitment to the OSCE as a
whole.

Estonia and Latvia provide ample evidence for 'nationalizing' policies,
especially in the early transition period. Access to citizenship as the main
gateway to rights proved to be the main hurdle for the minorities. The absence
of an overarching ethnic identity among the Russophones and a tangible avenue
for political mobilization have hindered the formation of coherent minority
parties or organizations. Out-migration, primarily to Russia, was the preferred
option in the early to mid 1990s. International pressures and incentives contributed to the gradual toning down of the initial citizenship and language
policies, but the limitations in scope and effectiveness of international measures
are equally apparent. Estonia and Latvia have established a traditional 'liberal'
democracy in the name of the titular majority. Moreover, the new EU Member
States have brought with them a plethora of unresolved issues, such as an
unprecedented number of stateless residents whose political rights are limited
and whose socio-economic position has been affected during transition as a
result of their concentration in the bankrupt Soviet-era industries. Statistical
data allowing for an assessment of ethnic employment patterns and discrimination is rare and inconclusive. What is most striking is the lack of minority
representation in certain sectors and institutions (local government and
administration, most state institutions with the exception of the Ministry of the
Interior, prison administration, and the police) resulting from the Soviet-era
ethnic division of labour, the consequences of the citizenship and language
policies, and a degree of self-segregation on the part of both the majority and
the minorities (especially in educational institutions and small private companies).[85] Minorities were quite well represented in state-owned enterprises,
while the division of ethnic groups in large private enterprises mirrored the
overall ethnic segments in society.

A few trends and developments from post-accession Latvia suffice to
underline the continuing significance of minority issues. Latvia's take-up rate of
naturalization has remained low despite the gradual legal changes mentioned

[83] For this gradual shift in the domestic debates see ibid, at 31–32.
[84] For details of this state programme, see Smith, above, n. 70, at 26–27. The budget earmarked
for this programme amounted to about Euro 370,000.
[85] A. Pabriks, *Occupational Representation and Ethnic Discrimination in Lativa* (Soros
Foundation Latvia: Nordik Publishing House, 2002).

above.[86] It reflects a considerable lack of social and political cohesion, which may act as a catalyst for westward migration once the restrictions on free movement imposed on the new EU Member States are lifted and the Council Directive on Third Country Nationals applies.[87] In domestic politics, the ethnic divide has become more polarized over time, though this has not led to sustained societal mobilization on the part of the Russophones. As of September 2005, 25 out of a total of 100 deputies in parliament were considered to be in favour of minority-friendly policies (from three different parties).[88] Latvia's political scene illustrates that even sizeable political rep-resentation at the national level does not necessarily guarantee influence over policy-making, especially if the other factions in parliament stand united on minority-relevant legislation. Parliamentary representation of minority interests even seems to feed directly into a more extremist rhetoric among the main parties of the Right in the run-up to elections. Thus, in a political climate where the issue of minority integration is highly sensitive—to an extent that it precludes domestic and international debate—political minority representation can also deepen rather than bridge the gap in majority-minority relations.

The post-enlargement context further narrows the scope for international intervention. The Council of Europe, less visible during the EU accession process when the EU and the OSCE were the primary actors in the field of minority protection, has taken centre stage in the post-enlargement period, namely through the monitoring processes linked to its Parliamentary Assembly and the Framework Convention. Latvia provides the best example to date of a new EU Member State engaging with the Council of Europe. On 26 May 2005, the Latvian parliament ratified the Framework Convention, which entered into force in October 2005. During the EU accession process, the EU's calls for Latvia's ratification of the Framework Convention proved unsuccessful. Latvia's

---

[86] Between 1 February 1995 and 31 August 2005, 100,285 persons (of 117,072 persons applying) were granted Latvian citizenship (Naturalization Board, Information Centre, 31 August 2005). 4,419 applications as to the recognition of a stateless person's or non-citizen's child born after 21 August 1991—a new provision of 1999—had been received and 4,245 accepted (ibid). In 2002, only 9,844 persons were naturalized (in 2003 the number was 10,049, in 2004 16,064 persons, and by 31 August 2005 it was 14,933 (ibid). Applications have steadily increased from 4,543 in 1995 (1996 and 1997 saw a temporary drop in application numbers) to 21,297 in 2004 (with a notable hike to 15,183 in 1999). From 2000 to 2002 the number of cases in which citizenship was granted exceeded the number of new applications by 1,000–3,000. This trend resumed in the first eight months of 2005. Russians and Belarussians account for 68.1 per cent and 10.4 per cent of all applications since 1995. In recent years the most significant increase in the number of applications has occurred among the 18–30-year-olds (29.7 per cent of applications since 1995). Instrumental factors account in parts for this trend, for example the avoidance of Latvian military conscription, preference for visa-free travel to Russia, and the fee cost (though since 2001 about 40–50 per cent of applicants have paid a reduced fee).

[87] Council Directive 2003/109/EC has been interpreted to include all non-EU citizens irre-spective of their citizenship or statelessness. See also Hughes, above, n. 68.

[88] Author's interviews with members of the Latvian Parliament, Riga, September 2005.

post-accession ratification demonstrates the importance of domestic political considerations shaping the adoption of internationally binding documents, irrespective of EU deadlines. Latvia added three declarations to its ratification of the FCNM. The first one goes beyond those commonly attached by other signatories: in it the Republic of Latvia recognizes the diversity of cultures, religions, and languages in Europe as a constituent of a common European identity and a particular value; refers to the experience of the Council of Europe Member States and the wish to foster the preservation and development of national minority cultures and languages, while respecting the sovereignty and national-cultural identity of every state; affirms the positive role of an integrated society, including the command of the state language, to the life of a democratic state; and refers to the specific historical experience and traditions of Latvia.

The term 'national minority', which remains undefined in the Framework Convention, applies 'to citizens of Latvia who differ from Latvians in terms of their culture, religion or language, who have traditionally lived in Latvia for generations and consider themselves to belong to the state and society of Latvia, who wish to preserve and develop their culture, religion or language'. A fuzzy formulation was adopted that allows 'persons who are not citizens of Latvia or another state but who permanently and legally reside in the Republic of Latvia, who do not belong to a national minority within the meaning of the Framework Convention for the Protection of National Minorities as defined in this declaration, but who identify themselves with a national minority that meets the definition contained in this declaration, shall enjoy the rights prescribed in the Framework Convention, unless specific exceptions are prescribed by law'.[89] The other two declarations state that Latvia will apply Article 10, Paragraph 2 (the recognition of the right to use minority languages in relations between individuals and administrative authorities), and Article 11, Paragraph 2 of the Convention (an individual's right to display minority language signs, inscriptions, and other information of a private nature visible to the public) in line with the Latvian constitution and other legislative acts defining the use of the state language, thereby effectively limiting their scope.[90]

A critical report by the Council of Europe's Parliamentary Assembly rapporteur, Gyorgy Frunda, was overruled by the Assembly's Monitoring Committee in November 2005. This decision, taken by an unusual majority-vote, is noteworthy, as the Assembly tends to accept a rapporteur's recommendations. The fact that Frunda is also an active member of the Hungarian minority party in Romania documents another trend: the pro-active minority policies by Hungarian politicians, advisors, and officials at home and abroad. Frunda's criticism was interpreted as endorsing 'Moscow's agenda'. Frunda's

---

[89] See: http://conventions.coe.int/Treaty/Commun/ListeDeclarations.asp?NT = 157&CM = 8&DF = 4/19/2006&CL = ENG&VL = 1.
[90] http://www.mfa.gov.lv/en/news/press-releases/2005/May/27–3/?print = on.

recommendations included a call for Latvia to drop its declarations attached to the Framework Convention, to waive completely or partially the naturalization of Soviet-era immigrants, and to allow non-citizens to participate in elections.[91] Latvia had graduated from the Council of Europe's monitoring to a procedure called 'post-monitoring dialogue', involving biannual inspections to certify compliance with Council of Europe standards. The Monitoring Committee had recommended that the 'post-monitoring dialogue' be discontinued when Latvia ratifies the Framework Convention (which would start a different kind of monitoring process) and demonstrates a commitment to accelerate the natur-alization of non-citizens under Latvia's existing law on citizenship. The first condition was met in May 2005, and the second one allows for a flexible interpretation. OSCE High Commissioner on National Minorities Rolf Ekeus welcomed Latvia's ratification of the Framework Convention during a visit in June 2005 and spoke of significant progress on naturalization. Despite Latvia's various reservations, the ratification of the FCNM provides the Council of Europe with a legal basis for an elaborate monitoring process. This type of monitoring is the only official international influence on minority issues in the post-EU accession era.

6.3.3 Ethnopolitical Parties and the Right to Effective Participation: Romania, Slovakia, and Bulgaria

Romania's population totals 21.7 million people, and the official ethnic breakdown looks as follows: 89.4 per cent Romanians, 6.6 per cent Hungarians, 2.4 per cent Roma, plus some smaller minority groups.[92] Slovakia has a total of 5.4 million inhabitants; the Slovaks account for 85.8 per cent, the Hungarians, for 9.7 per cent, and the Roma for 1.7 per cent.[93] Roughly comparable in size, the Hungarian minorities in Slovakia and Romania are represented by eth-nically defined parties. Moreover, the Hungarians in both countries represent a territorially concentrated minority: in the Transylvanian region in the western part of Romania, Hungarians account for about 20 per cent of the population, in two counties (Harghita and Covasna) they are a majority. Slovakia's Hun-garian minority is primarily concentrated in the southern regions. In both countries the 'Hungarian' regions have distinct institutional features, such as a significant number of Hungarian mayors, Hungarian-language schools (plus a Hungarian-language university in Transylvania), and Hungarian cultural institutions and media. Historically, the Hungarian minority in Transylvania enjoyed a distinct status within the empire due to the size of the group and

---

[91] V. Socor, 'Council of Europe's Biased Rapporteur Overruled on Lativa', see: http://www. jamestown.org/edm/article.php?article_id = 2370534.

[92] See: http://europa.eu.int/comm/enlargement/romania/#Country%20profile.

[93] See: http://europa.eu.int/comm/enlargement/slovakia/#profile.

Transylvania's long tradition of multi-ethnicity. The socialist system tried to divide the Hungarians by splitting them into different sub-groups. Especially since the clampdown of the Hungarian revolution in 1956 the Hungarian minority in Romania emerged as an opposition group within the regime. The Hungarians in the regions now forming part of Slovakia enjoyed a similar tradition and status, although the Hungarian minority in Slovakia experienced greater disruptions due to the 'exchange' of Hungarians for Slovaks after 1945, a policy of 'Slovakization,' and encouraged migration to the Czech part of the state of Czechoslovakia.

The Hungarian minorities can be compared with territorially concentrated minorities in Western Europe. Their calls for autonomy have provided the biggest bone of contention. The engagement of Hungary as the kin-state, however, sets these cases apart from other cases of sub-state nationalism in Western Europe. The postcommunist Romanian constitution of 1991 does not single out ethnic Hungarians or other minorities, but it generally commits the Romanian state to the development of the ethnic identity of people belonging to national minorities. The Slovak constitution also restricts itself to the individual rights of people belonging to minorities when referring to the right to association, culture, eduction, and the use of minority languages.

Romania's Hungarian minority belongs to an educational elite, which enjoys (or is perceived of as enjoying) a higher standard of life based on a different occupational profile. According to 1994–95 data, the Hungarians accounted for 8.4 per cent of those in the overall pre-university education in Romania and 10.3 per cent in state-run higher education.[94] At some universities, notably the university in Cluj, many subjects, including natural sciences, are taught in Hungarian.[95] Nevertheless, the Democratic Alliance of Magyars in Romania criticized the educational act of 1995 on the basis of its numerical restrictions on establishing Hungarian minority classes, the integration of previously separate Hungarian schools into joint schools mostly run by Romanian principals, the compulsory teaching of the Romanian language and Romanian history in secondary schools, and the lack of measures to increase the low participation of Hungarians in vocational training.

By comparison, Slovakia's Hungarian minority has a somewhat lower educational track record. According to official 1994–95 data, the Hungarian minority was represented by 7.3 per cent of children in pre-school education, 7.1 per cent in primary education, 11.04 per cent in gymnasia, 10.42 per cent in secondary professional schools, and 9.79 per cent in professional schools. With a share of only 4.7 per cent in state higher education, the Hungarians are clearly underrepresented at this level.[96] As of 1994–95, 30.5 per cent of

---

[94] G. Szépe, 'The Position of Hungarians in Romania and Slovakia in 1996' (1999) 27:1 *Nationalities Papers*, at 72.
[95] A separate status for the Hungarian university in Cluj has made for a long-standing dispute.
[96] Szépe, above, n. 94, at 78.

Hungarian children were enrolled in Slovak-language schools, a figure influenced by the state's educational policy, for example the integration of separate Hungarian schools into joint schools under a Slovak director or the lack of young Hungarian-language teachers.[97] Romanian and Slovak are the only state languages in Romania and Slovakia, respectively. There have been fewer open conflicts over the lack of bilingual signs in Romania's Hungarian-populated areas. Up to the mid 1990s, the use of bilingual signs was not allowed in Slovakia, and the 1995 Law on Local Administration did not allow the use of the minority language in local councils. In Slovkia, by contrast, the post-communist Meciar regime targeted the Hungarian minorities in the southern regions with a repressive Language Law in 1995 and a redrawing of regional boundaries cutting across Hungarian settlements in 1996.

Romania adopted complex provisions guaranteeing the political representation of minorities in parliament. The 1992 election law enables minority organizations to field candidates in the elections and guarantees a seat in parliament for a minority failing to cross the 3 per cent threshold on the condition that they receive more than 5 per cent of the average vote needed to elect one representative.[98] This provision was not the result of active minority campaigning, but an early signal to the West and the EU—preceding the Copenhagen criteria—that the Romanian government protects its minorities. The law was also a goodwill gesture to smaller minorities, but it failed to address the most pressing minority issues concerning the Hungarians and the Roma. The fact that representatives of the state-funded minority organizations—the state funds one organization per minority—dominate among the minority deputies in parliament and that there are low rates of ethnic voting of medium-sized minorities compared with a proliferation of very small minorities demonstrate the pitfalls of a policy which looks progressive at first glance.[99]

In Romania a single Hungarian party, the Democratic Alliance of Magyars in Romania (UDMR), emerged as early as 1989. Within its own ranks it combined a range of different political and ideological viewpoints. Diverging views within the UDMR, most importantly on the most controversial issue of territorial autonomy, have counterbalanced and neutralized more extremist claims. The party has made the representation of different Hungarian constituencies a part of its electoral strategy, thereby accepting the need to avoid the taboo subject of territorial autonomy. Instead, the UDMR has supported local government reform, decentralization, regionalization, and regional development, hoping to address minority concerns more effectively at the sub-national level where legislation and policy have to be implemented, including provisions on language. In this context the EU discourse on regional policy and regionalization

[97] Ibid.
[98] In the 1996 election this number was as low as about 1,800 votes; see Deets, above, n. 52, at 46.
[99] Ibid, at 48.

has provided a point of reference. The UDMR has a stable track record in bringing out the ethnic Hungarian vote in national, regional, and local elections. At the local level Hungarians play a decisive role in some administrations, but there are also openly anti-Hungarian local and county administrations in Transylvania. The majority of the Romanian parties have been sceptical about the Hungarian party, especially with regard to any claim to autonomy.

Ion Iliescu's National Front initially proclaimed a commitment to collective minority rights in return for the Hungarian party's support, but Iliescu—like Vladimir Meciar in Slovakia—polarized ethnopolitical differences in their attempt to build nation-states. Iliescu's regime lasted from 1990 to 1996, while Meciar stayed in power from 1992 to 1998. In both cases Hungarian minority parties were represented in parliament, questioning their respective governments' policies, especially regarding institutional safeguards for minority representation, language, and regional administration. In Romania, the Hungarian party countered the increasing centralization and restrictive language legislation with calls for territorial autonomy. While national territorial autonomy did not emerge as the Hungarian parties' priority in Slovakia, they went on a collision course with Meciar's plan to redraw regional administrative boundaries so as to break up the relatively compact Hungarian settlements.

In Romania the 1996 elections marked a turning-point in majority-minority relations in national-level politics, as the Hungarian party joined the government for the first time and secured two ministerial posts.[100] The Democratic Alliance of Hungarians remained in government from 1996 to 2000 as a coalition partner of the Democratic Convention of Romania (CDR), surviving several government changes and nominating ministers, state secretaries, prefects, and deputy prefects, facilitating amendments to the education and self-government laws, and putting related minority issues forward for debate.[101] In 1997 a Department for the Protection of National Minorities was established and chaired by a UDMR minister. Originally, it was subordinated directly to the prime minister. During its time in government the UDMR affected legal changes, making Hungarian a language of instruction, paving the way for bilingual signs and allowing for the use of the minority language in public administration in municipalities with more than 20 per cent of minority residents.

From 2000 to 2004 the Hungarian party was not part of the government led by the Party of Social Democracy (PSD) and Ion Iliescu, although a range of agreements between the PSD and the UDMR contributed to the survival of the minority government after 2000. In return for a number of concessions, the UDMR refrained from taking part in the no-confidence votes in parliament and supported government-sponsored legislative projects. Among the concessions

---

[100] N. Medianu, 'Analysing Political Exchanges between Minority and Majority Leaders in Romania' (2002) 1:4 *The Global Review of Ethnopolitics*, at 29. [101] Ibid, at 32.

granted were consultation rights for the minorities on a range of political issues. The Department for the Protection of National Minorities was downgraded institutionally, however, and now forms part of the Ministry of Public Information. The UDMR's participation was institutionalized through an Inter-Ministerial Committee for National Minorities, and the social democratic government set up a consultative Council for National Minorities in 2001.

In accordance with the CDR–UDMR coalition government, the PDS-led government's Law on Local Public Administration of 2001 reinforced the possibility to use the minority language as an official language in municipalities with more than 20 per cent of minority-language speakers.[102] The government also committed itself to an increase in school and university education and broadcasting in Hungarian, the ratification of the European Charter of Regional and Minority Languages, the return of real estate confiscated under the socialist regime, and the recruitment of Hungarian police officers in municipalities with more than 20 per cent Hungarians. The latter policy builds on a 1999 law, which stipulates that in such municipalities some public service officials should have knowledge of the minority language. In 2004 the Hungarian party obtained 5.1 per cent of the votes and rejoined a centre-right governing coalition.

In Slovakia, four Hungarian parties emerged in the early transition phase, illustrating that the Hungarian minority did not represent a unified political force. The first—ethnically inclusive—government, involving a Hungarian party, collapsed quickly. The emergence of the sovereignty issue on the political agenda 'ethnicized' statehood and the political process as a whole. The Slovak majority and the Hungarian minority favoured a common state with the Czechs, but the distance between the Slovak political elite and the Hungarian minority grew, especially when the Movement for a Democratic Slovakia (HZDS) formed a coalition with the Slovak National Party in 1992.[103] The Hungarian coalition (SMK), made up of four Hungarian parties, formed part of the government from 1998 to 2002 and again since 2002, both times as part of a broad coalition government. The combined electoral support of about 9–10 per cent since the 1992 elections demonstrates the near-complete mobilization of the Hungarian minority electorate.

In 1992 a coalition of three parties secured 7.37 per cent of the votes and 13 seats in the 150-seat parliament. The Hungarian Civic Party abstained from the coalition and failed to gain entry into parliament. At the local level Hungarian representatives played a decisive role in administration from the beginning, but they were not represented in higher government offices. From 1998 to 2002 the

---

[102] M. Brusis, 'The European Union and Inter-Ethnic Power-Sharing Arrangements in Accession Countries' (2003) 1 *Journal on Ethnopolitics and Minority Issues in Europe*, at 9.

[103] Z. Csergö, 'Beyond Ethnic Division: Majority-Minority Debate about the Postcommunist State in Romania and Slovakia' (2002) 16:1 *East European Politics and Societies*, at 4–5.

SMK nominated the deputy prime minister, whose portfolio included minority issues, two ministers, and a state secretary in the Ministry of Education. In the new government of 2002 the SMK again secured the post of deputy prime minister (including a responsibility for minorities) and one further ministerial post as well as deputy chairmen of parliament and state secretaries in the Ministries of Economics, Finance, Regional Development, Education, Culture, and Foreign Affairs.[104]

The 1999 law easing the use of minority languages and the upgrading of the status of the consultative Government Council for National Minorities and Ethnic Groups marked the beginning of a new era in majority-minority relations in Slovakia. The government also ratified the European Charter of Regional and Minority Languages (neither Romania nor Bulgaria have done so) and established a degree of regional self-government in 2001.[105] In the context of decentralization in the summer of 2001, the SMK threatened to leave the government after the deputies from the governing coalition and the opposition had voted down a government proposal to divide the country into eight instead of twelve regional self-governments. This went against the SMK's perception of smaller regions being a better safeguard for minority interests. Verheugen, the Commissioner for Enlargement, immediately emphasized the importance of a stable government including representatives of the Hungarian minority, thereby enticing the SMK to stay in government, accept the law on regional self-government, and gain some concessions in other areas.[106]

The Hungarian minority elites formed part of the political opposition in both countries (including opposition to the break up of Czechoslovakia in 1992), but the majority-minority ethnic division did not become the only or predominant cleavage structure. Instead, three clusters of parties representing 'majority nationalist, majority moderate and minority pluralist perspectives' on state-building crystallized.[107] Gradually, the Hungarian parties increased their cooperation with the Slovak and Romanian opposition parties, although these attempts were initially overshadowed by frictions. In 1994 the Slovak-Hungarian opposition managed to topple the Meciar government in a vote of no-confidence, but already six months later the HZDS was re-elected and, under Meciar's leadership, managed to divide and suppress the opposition forces. Thus, the friendship treaty with Hungary, which clearly ruled out autonomy rights for minorities, was signed in 1995 and a number of laws was passed with the full or at least partial support of the Slovak opposition: the State Language Act of 1995, making Slovak the only official language, the act on the redrawing of the territorial administrative boundaries in 1996, trying to minimize the political strength

---

[104] Ibid, at 10.
[105] See J. Hughes, G. Sasse, and C. Gordon, *The Myth of Conditionality. Europeanization and Regionalization during the EU's Enlargement in Central and Eastern Europe* (Basingstoke: Palgrave, 2004). [106] Brusis, above, n. 102, at 12–13.
[107] Csergö, above, n. 103, at 13.

of the Hungarian minority in areas where it constituted a numerical majority, amendments to the act on school administration, limiting the authority of local communities over schools, and a law on the elevation of a national Slovak organization (Matica Slovenská) to the highest national cultural, social and scientific organization.[108] On the basis of the political Copenhagen criterion, Slovakia was excluded from the first wave of candidates at the Luxembourg Council in 1997 and was sharply criticized in the Report of 1998.[109]

The Hungarian parties' demands for regional self-government proved the biggest stumbling block for the cooperation between Hungarian and Slovak opposition parties. Over time the Hungarian parties switched to an emphasis on decentralization and local government, thus allowing for a narrowing of the political divide within the opposition. The electoral law of 1998 led to the consolidation of one moderate Slovak opposition party (Slovak Democratic Coalition) and the Hungarian Coalition, made up of three Hungarian parties. In Romania, the Hungarian party and the Romanian political opposition encountered similar differences in defining more coherent positions and reaching a compromise. Shared conceptions regarding the nature of the post-communist state and its relationship with other European democracies were at the heart of the political coalitions toppling Iliescu in 1996 and Meciar in 1998.

In Romania, the resulting coalition governments struggled for a political compromise on amending restrictive laws on language use, education, and administration and managed to forge a consensus in the end. The regime change in Slovakia marked the beginning of a new state policy on minorities, which quickly became an integral part of the attempt of Dzurinda's government to speed up economic reforms and integrate into Western security and political and economic structures. In a direct response to the earlier criticisms of the EU and the OSCE High Commissioner on National Minorities it prioritized the adoption of a new language law in advance of the Commission meeting of July 1999, which was scheduled to review Slovakia's accession prospects.[110] The new language law came to symbolize the regime change and placed Slovakia in the first wave of the candidate countries. The language law allows the use of minority languages in local public administration, subject to a minority population threshold of 20 per cent in a given area.[111] The Commission's 1999 Report declared that the requisite 'significant progress' in this policy area had been delivered, despite the fact that the final text of the law was adopted without the support of the governing Hungarian parties. Definitional ambiguities in the text and

[108] Ibid, at 17–18.
[109] By 1998 Romania was already seen to fulfil the political Copenhagen criteria; see EU Regular Report on Romania, 1998, at 12; see: http://europa.eu.int/comm/enlargement/report_11_98/.
[110] The coalition also agreed to sign the European Charter on Regional and Minority Languages and the FCNM.
[111] See Slovakia's Law on the Use of Minority Languages (11 July 1999), Article 2(1), 51; see: http://www.riga.lv/minelres/NationalLegislation/Slovakia/Slovakia_MinorLang_English.htm. The Romanian Law on Local Public Administration (23 April 2001) envisages the same threshold; see: http://www.riga.lv/minelres/NationalLegislation/Romania/Romania_LocAdm2001_excerpts_English.htm.

a problem of legal precedence with regard to the more restrictive provisions of the constitution of 1992 Council of Europe's Advisory Committee overshadowed the implementation of the law.[112] In its Opinion on Slovakia, adopted on 22 September 2000, the Advisory Committee on the FCNM noted, on the one hand, that the implementation of the 1995 State Language Law 'has not, to date, had a widespread negative impact on minority languages', while stressing, on the other hand, 'that the State Language Law is lacking in clarity' and could at the very least 'produce a "chilling effect" extending to legitimate activities of minorities'. Moreover, it asked for the relationship between the Law on the Use of National Minority Languages of 1999 and the State Language Law to be clarified.[113]

Ultimately, the bargaining power of the minority parties may be limited, and their biggest 'veto right' is the withdrawal from government (or the threat to do so). The November 2000 elections in Romania saw a surge of extreme nationalist rhetoric, which sidelined the minority leaders. Slovakia and Romania are instructive cases in several respects: firstly, they demonstrate how the incentive of EU membership, tied to a bundle of political criteria, can help to galvanize domestic political forces in favour of a democratic regime change. In both cases minority parties, which already existed as organized opposition forces, played a crucial and active role in this process. The minorities' de facto political participation was ahead of the *de jure* elaboration of minority rights. Furthermore, the EU's critique of the 1995 Slovak language law is a rare example of an explicit EU stance on a specific piece of minority-sensitive legislation. Secondly, in Slovakia and Romania the predominant political conflicts did not hinge on ethnic divisions despite the early ethnopolitical mobilization of the Hungarian minorities.

In the early transition period the main political majority embarked on centralized nation-state building. The Hungarian parties fairly consistently represented the ethnic and political minority in opposition to the ruling party. Over time they built a joint electoral platform with the moderate Slovak and Romanian forces, thereby cutting across ethnic divisions and forging a new political majority. These coalitions proved essential for state consolidation and democratization. Thirdly, the EU contributed to the creation of the domestic political space for minority participation, but it did not intervene in the internal disputes over the formulation of rights and the appropriate institutional responses to minority demands, as seen in the case of the new Slovak language law of 1999. Moreover, the democratization and Europeanization processes neither put an end to the domestic disputes over minority issues, nor did they guarantee a smooth political and economic reform process, as the case of Romania demonstrates.

---

[112] For a discussion on the interaction of Slovakia's laws and EU pressures, see F. Daftary and K. Gál, 'The New Slovak Language Law: Internal or External Politics', ECMI Working Paper No. 8 (2000). See: http://www.ecmi.de/doc/download/working_paper_8.pdf.
[113] GVT/COM/INF/OP/I(2001)001 E Slovakia; points 33–36.

Bulgaria is a case that contrasts the active participation of a minority-based party in domestic politics with the near-absence of formal minority rights and limited international involvement.[114] The Bulgarian constitution (Article 11) and the Law on Political Parties prohibit organizations threatening the country's territorial integrity or inciting ethnic, racial, or religious hatred, thereby effectively outlawing ethnically defined parties. This is one of the most explicit provisions of this kind in Eastern Europe. In line with these provisions the government has refused to register a Macedonian human rights group since 1990. However, there is a tension between Article 11 and Article 6(2) of the constitution, which reads: 'There shall be no privileges or restrictions of rights on the grounds of race, nationality, ethnic affiliation, personal or social status or property status.'[115] According to the 1992, census the breakdown of Bulgaria's population of 8 million looks as follows: 85.8 per cent Bulgarians, 9.7 per cent Turks (about 800,000), and 3.4 per cent Roma.

The Turkish minority in Bulgaria is comparable to the Hungarian minority in Slovakia and Romania in terms of its size, geographical concentration (over 80 per cent are concentrated in the north-eastern region, especially in the districts of Razgrad, Silistra, Turgovishte, and Shumen where they make up 30–40 per cent of the local population; and the south-eastern districts of Haskovo and Kurdzhali—in Kurdzhali district they account for the majority of the district population), its degree of political mobilization and visibility, and cohesion, as well as the interest of a kin-state (Turkey). Friendly Bulgarian–Turkish relations are a recent post-Cold War phenomenon.[116] Compared to Hungary, Turkey's position vis-à-vis Bulgaria has been weaker within the context of EU enlargement. Turkey has primarily encouraged politically negotiated solutions to address the needs of the Turkish minority and raised the issue of minority protection through international channels, such as the Council of Europe, the OSCE, and NATO.

The socialist era was dominated by assimilation and out-migration. The collectivization of the 1940s forced Turkish landowners in north-eastern Bulgaria into emigration. A steady flow of out-migration was encouraged both by a bilateral agreement between Turkey and Bulgaria to reunite separated families and an official assimilation policy by the Bulgarian government from the 1960s/70s which culminated in 1984–89 in the official denial of the existence of a Turkish minority in Bulgaria, the forced replacement of Turkish names and the encouragement of mass emigration under communist leader Todor Zhivkov.[117] As in Slovakia and Romania, the Turkish minority was in opposition to the socialist regime, in particular in the 1980s, and contributed to the overthrow of Zhivkov in 1989, not least through their mass emigration. Between June and

---

[114] The EU concentrated on the Roma issue rather than Bulgaria's Turkish minority.

[115] A. Eminov, 'The Turks in Bulgaria: Post-1989 Developments' (1999) 27:1 *Nationalities Papers*, at 36.

[116] L. Petkova, 'The Ethnic Turks in Bulgaria: Social Integration and Impact on Bulgarian-Turkish Relations 1947–2000' (2002) 1:4 *The Global Review of Ethnopolitics*, at 54–56.

[117] For a detailed account of these different periods, see ibid, at 42–59.

August 1989 alone some 350,000 Turks left. Eventually, the Turkish government responded by closing its borders in August.[118]

The political and societal distance between Turks and Bulgarians has been greater than that between Hungarians and Romanians or Hungarians and Slovaks. It is reflected in the political campaigns against Bulgaria's Turkish politicians, but also in sociological survey data on inter-ethnic perceptions and interactions.[119] In contrast to the Hungarians in Romania and Slovakia, the Turks in Bulgaria, especially those in the south-east of the country, have suffered disproportionately from the transition. The Soviet export market for Bulgarian tobacco has collapsed, and regional unemployment has soared to about 80 per cent.[120] The ethnic earnings differentials between Bulgarians and Turks have increased steadily from the mid 1980s, especially during the 1990s as a result of relative returns to skills and changes in the composition of demand for goods and services during market reforms.[121]

The Movement for Rights and Freedoms (MRF), which de facto represents the Turkish minority, is not officially registered as an ethnic party, although its rationale has been the representation of Turks and other minorities in the elections. The Supreme Court initially denied the registration of MRF, a decision that was overturned only two months before the elections in June 1990 where it immediately won 23 seats (out of 98). The system of proportional representation (including a 4 per cent threshold) enabled them to establish themselves on the Bulgarian political scene. The new parliament passed a resolution in support of the rights of ethnic minorities in Bulgaria, followed by a law allowing minorities to resume the names they were forced to give up in the 1980s.[122] The MRF was effectively the third biggest party after the Bulgarian Socialist Party (BSP) and Union of Democratic Forces (UDF). This position is an achievement given the concerted effort by the Bulgarian Socialist Party, the communist successor party, to ban or split it. The MRF remained politically isolated, although it ultimately proved an important anchor of support for the first and second government under the United Democratic Forces in 1991–92 and 1997. Moreover, in a period of political instability and paralysis within the two major parties, it fell upon the MRF to propose a compromise candidate as prime minister—the independent academic, Lyuben Berov—although it nevertheless failed to shape the policy agenda according to its priorities.[123]

---

[118] Of these last émigrés, about a third returned after 1989, a reflection of the misjudged opportunity structures in Turkey. See Eminov, above, n. 115, at 32.

[119] L. Giddings, 'Continued decline for ethnic minorities in the transition? Changes in ethnic earning differentials in Bulgaria, 1986, 1993 and 1997' (2003) 11:4 *Economics of Transition*, at 624.

[120] Eminov, above, n. 115, at 34.   [121] Giddings, above, n. 119, at 621–48.

[122] R. V. Vassilev, 'Post-Communist Bulgaria's Ethnopolitics' (2002) 1:2 *The Global Review of Ethnopolitics*, at 41.

[123] C. Johnson, 'Democratic Transition in the Balkans: Romania's Hungarian and Bulgaria's Turkish Minority (1989–99)' (2002) 8:1 *Nationalism and Ethnic Politics*, at 1–28; Vassilev, above, n. 122, at 37–53.

When in opposition, the UDF eventually formed a coalition with the MRF ahead of the regional and local elections in 1995. This cooperation resembles the Romanian and Slovak variant—the cooperation with the minority parties to form a new political majority against the joint 'enemy' in power. Despite its political significance in the Bulgarian party scene, the MRF with its astute political leadership has not managed to stop the economic downturn in the Turkish populated regions, mandatory Turkish classes in municipal schools in ethnically mixed areas have not been implemented, religious properties confiscated under socialism have not been fully returned, and the issue of Turkish-language broadcasting is ongoing. The constitution guarantees the rights of non-Bulgarian citizens to use their mother tongue and establish private schools at their own expense (Articles 36, 53, and 54), but these 'guarantees' are not easily implemented and put the financial burden on the minority groups themselves. In December 1991 the Ministry of Education announced that Turkish would become a required subject in schools with a majority of Turkish children and as an optional subject where they were a minority for the first eight years at school, but the implementation of these measures has been stalled politically on numerous occasions. In October 2000 Bulgarian National Television for the first time broadcast Turkish-language news.[124]

The year 1997 marked a change in Bulgarian politics: the socio-economic crisis led to organized street protests and strikes, forcing the BSP Prime Minister Zhan Videnov to resign and the BSP to call early elections in April 1997. The UDF dominated a four-party coalition that won 52 per cent of the vote (137 seats). The BSP won 22 per cent (58 seats), the Alliance for National Salvation—a coalition dominated by the MRF and including left-of-centre, centrist, and monarchist parties—8 per cent (19 seats), Euroleft—a defector party that emerged from within the BSP—6 per cent, and the BBB 5 per cent. The new government under Prime Minister Ivan Kostov embarked on a reform course in line with IMF recommendations, social and land reforms in view of NATO and EU membership. The new government made human rights and democracy a cornerstone of its rhetoric. Human rights organizations could make themselves heard, but the push for legislative change with a view to minority protection remained limited. In particular the Roma were still a prime target of violence and discrimination.[125] In December 1997 the government set up the National Council on Ethnic and Demographic Questions at the Council of Ministers, a consultative body meant to develop strategies on a wide range of issues, ranging from demographic policy, the promotion of tolerance between ethnic and religious groups, and support for Bulgarians abroad. Bulgaria signed the FCNM in 1997 and ratified it in 1999. Here the timing must have been

---

[124] Petkova, above, n. 116, at 52.
[125] See, for example, Human Rights Watch: World Report 1999, Bulgaria: Human Rights Developments, http://hrw.org/worldreport99/europe.bulgaria.html.

influenced by the prospect of EU accession. In December 1999 the EU decided to open negotiations with Bulgaria.

The MRF eventually became part of the government in 2001 when it gained 7.5 per cent of the vote and formed a rather paradoxical 'centrist' coalition with the National Movement Simeon II (NDST). Both parties had made ethnic issues part of their election programme and made explicit references to national minorities. The MRF was represented at ministerial level, and at the level of regional prefects, mayors, and executive agencies. The parliament also simplified the procedure for the reintroduction of Turkish names.[126] The constitutional non-recognition of national minorities underpinned several attempts to outlaw the MRF, but an informal arrangement has facilitated an equilibrium: the MRF has avoided radical ethnopolitical positions in return for the mainstream parties' tolerance. This informal compromise was helped by the MRF's emphasis on classical liberal values, such as individual rights and non-discrimination, decentralization, and rural development, the latter reflecting the fact that most Turks are located in the country's eastern rural areas. Ironically, both the MRF and NDST registered as members of the international organization of liberal parties. After the elections of 25 June 2005 the MRF remained in government with 12.7 per cent of the vote, this time in a 'colourful' and inherently unstable coalition with the BSP (31.1 per cent of the vote) and Simeon's Party (19.9 per cent) under Prime Minister Sergei Stanishev (BSP). The coalition demonstrates the malleability of Bulgaria's political parties.

The Bulgarian case is a clear example of a gradual democratization with a strong emphasis on individual rights. In Bulgaria—even more so than in Romania and Slovakia—the political rights of minorities are best understood as a process. The MRF has been represented in parliament since the fall of the socialist regime and repeatedly provided the swing vote, thereby illustrating the stabilizing effect of political representation. In turn, it has enshrined the salience of ethnic issues and inter-ethnic bargaining in daily politics. The MRF has called for rights to guarantee political representation and limited cultural autonomy, but it has refrained from demanding political or territorial autonomy. Thus, political representation of minorities, whether facilitated by the state or brought about by mobilization and stealth, can be politically stabilizing.

However, party representation has been insufficient for improving the socio-economic conditions of particular minority groups. The gap between the MRF political leadership and the grassroots population appears to be widening, although the MRF's hierarchical structure and internal discipline disguises this gap in elections. Moreover, the stabilizing role of an ethnopolitical party might be limited to a particular time period: in the case of Bulgaria the MRF played this role primarily in the early transition period. It is too early to judge the long-term effects of an ethnopolitical party like the MRF on political stability and

---

[126] Brusis, above, n. 102, at 7.

democratization. The 2005 elections demonstrated that its political prominence also provides a platform for the mobilization of extremist right-wing and xenophobic parties like Ataka, which emerged as the fourth-largest party in the 2005 elections, with 8.2 per cent of the national vote. This can either be interpreted as a temporary political phenomenon in a flattened political land-scape (to which EU accession has contributed) or as a medium-term effect of the presence of one prominent de facto minority party.

6.4 CONCLUSION

The postcommunist CEE provides useful insights into the nexus between political rights and national minorities. The dual process of transition and EU enlargement has underscored the difficulty to draw the line between the pro-tection of individual rights and minority-sensitive policies. Citizenship, polit-ical representation, and language have been the key rights-based issues of national minorities. As the cases presented here have shown, the salience of minority issues and political minority mobilization were determined domest-ically, but the subsequent context of EU accession bolstered their political salience. The EU has had an impact through the (re-)formulation of rights or support for an ongoing political process and inclusive governments, if its vague conditions in the field of minority protection fit the domestic agenda of the political majority. The three countries with minority parties (Romania, Slovakia, and Bulgaria) have gone furthest in making minority interests a regular item on the domestic political agenda and establishing a formal or informal majority-minority equilibrium. Interestingly, these arrangements are only partly anchored in a constitutional and legal catalogue of rights.

The conclusion is threefold: firstly, the general pattern of democratic development in the CEE has closely followed the traditional definitions of a liberal democracy, often with additional assurances for the titular majority and restricted political rights for the minorities. The emphasis of the international institutions has been on citizenship and language provisions. Overall, the EU lacked the competence, capacity, and political will to take a pro-active role in this policy area beyond acting as a corrective mechanism for issues related to security considerations (Russophones, Roma, and Hungary's Status Law). The formulation of rights of self-government marks an exception to the wider trend. In Hungary, it was linked to a wider definition of national interests abroad, in Slovenia it prioritized two minority groups over others, and in Estonia it has not become a political reality. Secondly, citizenship has been the main gateway to rights, including those of national minorities, although gradually post-communist legislation has created room for social and economic rights (and limited political rights) tied to residency criteria in line with EU-wide norms. Thirdly, political representation has been partly guaranteed through electoral and institutional quotas or separate minority councils. The most effective political say has been achieved by minority-party representation and inclusive governments—whether defined as ethnic parties, as in the case of Romania and Slovakia, or as a de facto minority party, as in Bulgaria.

Minority rights straddle the fuzzy distinctions between different sets of rights. The notion of 'effective participation' encapsulates the composite nature of minority rights, and firmly embeds minority rights in the political and public sphere. A meaningful definition of 'effective minority participation' in a democracy rests on the access to and an active demand for citizenship. The experience of the CEE demonstrates that institutions such as national autonomy and actors such as ethnopolitical parties can play an important role in the implementation of the political rights of minorities.

Index*

*   *Compiled by Mr Cormac Mac Amhlaigh, Researcher at the European University Institute, Florence.*